To Write the Africa World

Critical South

The publication of this series is supported by the International Consortium of Critical Theory Programs funded by the Andrew W. Mellon Foundation.

Series editors: Natalia Brizuela, Victoria Collis-Buthelezi, and Leticia Sabsay

Leonor Arfuch, *Memory and Autobiography*
Paula Biglieri and Luciana Cadahia, *Seven Essays on Populism*
Aimé Césaire, *Resolutely Black*
Bolívar Echeverría, *Modernity and "Whiteness"*
Diego Falconí Trávez, *From Ashes to Text*
Celso Furtado, *The Myth of Economic Development*
Eduardo Grüner, *The Haitian Revolution*
Premesh Lalu, *Undoing Apartheid*
Karima Lazali, *Colonial Trauma*
María Pia López, *Not One Less*
Achille Mbembe and Felwine Sarr, *The Politics of Time*
Achille Mbembe and Felwine Sarr, *To Write the Africa World*
Valentin Y. Mudimbe, *The Scent of the Father*
Pablo Oyarzun, *Doing Justice*
Néstor Perlongher, *Plebeian Prose*
Bento Prado Jr., *Error, Illusion, Madness*
Nelly Richard, *Eruptions of Memory*
Silvia Rivera Cusicanqui, *Ch'ixinakax utxiwa*
Tendayi Sithole, *The Black Register*
Maboula Soumahoro, *Black is the Journey, Africana the Name*
Dénètem Touam Bona, *Fugitive, Where Are You Running?*

To Write the Africa World

Edited by
Achille Mbembe and Felwine Sarr

Translated by Drew Burk

polity

Originally published in French as *Écrire l'Afrique-Monde* © 2017 Editions Jimsaan, Dakar, Sénégal

This English edition © Polity Press, 2023

Polity Press
65 Bridge Street
Cambridge CB2 1UR, UK

Polity Press
111 River Street
Hoboken, NJ 07030, USA

All rights reserved. Except for the quotation of short passages for the purpose of criticism and review, no part of this publication may be reproduced, stored in a retrieval system or transmitted, in any form or by any means, electronic, mechanical, photocopying, recording or otherwise, without the prior permission of the publisher.

ISBN-13: 978-1-5095-5106-4- hardback
ISBN-13: 978-1-5095-5107-1- paperback

A catalogue record for this book is available from the British Library.

Library of Congress Control Number: 2022936522

Typeset in 10.5 on 12pt Sabon
by Fakenham Prepress Solutions, Fakenham, Norfolk NR21 8NL
Printed and bound in Great Britain by TJ Books Ltd, Padstow, Cornwall

The publisher has used its best endeavours to ensure that the URLs for external websites referred to in this book are correct and active at the time of going to press. However, the publisher has no responsibility for the websites and can make no guarantee that a site will remain live or that the content is or will remain appropriate.

Every effort has been made to trace all copyright holders, but if any have been overlooked the publisher will be pleased to include any necessary credits in any subsequent reprint or edition.

For further information on Polity, visit our website: politybooks.com

Contents

Thinking for a New Century   1
Achille Mbembe and Felwine Sarr

I

(European?) Universalism Put to the Test by Indigenous Histories   9
Mamadou Diouf

Laetitia Africana: Philosophy, Decolonization, and Melancholy   31
Nadia Yala Kisukidi

For a Truly Universal Universal   44
Souleymane Bachir Diagne

Migrant Writers: Builders of a Balanced Globalization of Africa/Europe   50
Benaouda Lebdai

II

For What is Africa the Name?   65
Léonora Miano

Epistemological Impasses Concerning the Object Africa:
Imprudence and Impudence of a Subjugated Exoticism
and a Hyperbolic Narcissism   79
Maurice Soudieck Dione

Reinventing African Modernity   92
Blondin Cissé

What Is a Postcolonial Author?   106
Lydie Moudileno

III

How Can One Be *African/e*? From Self-Shame to the
Consciousness of the Oppressed: Philosophical Reflections
by Way of Steve Biko, Malcolm X, and Audre Lorde   121
Hourya Bentouhami

Rediscovering Meaning   136
Bonaventure Mve-Ondo

Esteem for Self: Creating One's Own Sense/Carving Out
One's Own Path   148
Séverine Kodjo-Grandvaux

Dictionary for Lovers of the African Continent: Two Entries   161
Alain Mabanckou and Abdourahman Waberi

Emancipatory Utopias   168
Françoise Vergès

IV

Martiality and Death in Sexual Relations in Cameroon:
Sociology for a Lexicon of Copulation   185
Parfait D. Akana

Demographic Challenges and Technological Mutations: Does
a Good-Paying Job Have a Future in Africa?   203
Ndongo Samba Sylla

Healing Commonality: Contribution to an Anthropology of Political Corruption in Senegal *Abdourahmane Seck*	216

V

Paths of the Universal *Sami Tchak*	243
Re-enchanting the World: Husserl in the Postcolony *Nado Ndoye*	250
Writing about the Humanities from the Vantage Point of Africa *Felwine Sarr*	260
Thinking about the World from the Vantage Point of Africa: Questions for Today and Tomorrow *Achille Mbembe*	266
Notes	277
Index	316

Thinking for a New Century

Achille Mbembe and Felwine Sarr

The new century that confronts us opens up to a horizon comprising two historical displacements. Europe is no longer understood or viewed as the center of the world even though it is still a vibrant and relatively important and decisive actor on the global stage. For its part, Africa – and the Global South in general – has seen its status continue to rise in importance as one of the principal theaters where, in some distant point in time, the future of the planet will more than likely play out.

For those who, for a long time, have grown accustomed to being snared in the conquering gaze of the other, the moment has come once again to launch a new project of critical thought that will not merely be content with just a series of lamentations and taunts. Confident in its own manner of speaking and at ease wading through the archives of all humanity, this thought is capable of anticipating, of truly creating, and, in so doing, of opening up new paths able to face up to the challenges of our current era. In order for such a project to run for the long term, it seemed to us appropriate to invent a new, open platform in favor of a form of speech and discussion that would necessarily be understood as plural, both confident in its own potentials and powers of speech, and allowing for the unpredictable if necessary – in any case, a platform open to the vast horizon in front of us.

And it's with such a platform of thought in mind that we held the inaugural event, the Ateliers de la pensée (Workshops of Thought), between October 28 and 31 in Dakar and Saint-Louis-du-Senegal.

About thirty intellectuals and artists were invited from across the African continent and the diasporas to reflect on the present and the possible future of an Africa that finds itself in the midst of contemporary global transformations. Not only was this workshop a way to get a better overall idea of the ongoing renewal of French-speaking Afro-diasporic critical thinking; it also served as an impetus for generating new perspectives concerning the contribution from Afro-diasporic discourse to debates on the contemporary world. For those intellectuals and artists who had the privilege of participating, this unique and unforgettable gathering was a momentous occasion for renewed reflection – Africa's time is inseparable from the time of the world, and the creative task that confronts us is seeking to enable Africa's future to come into being.

If there is a general optics to be found in the essays gathered together in this volume, it is certainly in the notion of "the event to come," and it is in this "call to creation" that one will be able to find it. The only Africa that exists is the one that will be created. And for us, then, the fundamental task before us is to make believable, or to believe in, this creation. In order to do this, we must take as our starting point the interconnection between the future fate of both Africa and the world and finally reflect on how to end the misconception that there is a vast separation between them, which has often been taken as a given between the sign that Africa constitutes and the time of the world. And it's precisely this conception and rather archaic notion, which we will also reflect upon, that, over several centuries, has attempted to claim and make a general population believe that Africa constituted a *world apart*, *un hors-monde* – an outside world.

At the dawn of this new century, in seeking to restore a kinship identity between Africa and the world, one recognizes that there exists a variety of ways of being-in-the-world, of being a world, of composing the world one wants to shed light on. How can we bring together all these diverse ways of being and composing, of deciphering and expressing, of articulating what such a call responds to? Such will be the object of our reflection. Each time we attempt to employ such a thought of a world, it will serve as a way of conceiving the possibility of a surprise. From such a perspective, then, this book is not so much a manifesto – in the sense that it would somehow serve to reveal or traverse a threshold into some newfound light of day, unearthing some hidden truths from the preceding generations – and yet it will nevertheless present several vital analyses.

First and foremost, this volume will deal with the notion of *urgency*. Given that, for Africa, time is now both of the essence and favorable, there is no reason to wait. We are our own witnesses. We must absolutely unite if we are to take back this essential task that we can't simply delegate to others – namely: reading, writing, deciphering, decrypting, sketching, and calling into question our age, creating a blockade around those languages (our own as well as others) in which we speak in phrases that no longer ring true, which have become mute. We must rehabilitate, in the very act of thought, a form of errancy, of wandering, which serves as a condition for surprise.

Second, thinking for oneself is an exercise that is inseparable from action, since, in Africa, as in the rest of the world, one doesn't act without thinking, in the same way that one doesn't think without acting, except when, in both cases, one wants simply to yield to a path of catastrophe. In the end, what we are seeking here is a way to create a new form of construction. To accomplish this, we must first begin by not only opening up all the borders, but also by inventing a way to render the archive – every archive – as legible as possible.

This book is therefore a general call, as pressing as it is intense, to take up the old battles that have never quite been completed and to engage in others that this new century calls on us to address, which inevitably calls for scrambling and erasing many demarcation lines so as to be able trace and sketch out new ones.

The workshops in Dakar, as well as the ones in Saint-Louis-du-Senegal, constitute our response to an amalgam of reconfigurations dealing with the overall conditions for the construction of contemporary thought. On the one hand, the hegemony exerted by Western discourse concerning almost every construct of human knowledge and culture – be it in literature, art, philosophy, or, more broadly, the humanities or social sciences – either is now in retreat or, at the very least, is being strongly contested. There is no doubt that academic institutions in the Global North continue to be powerful. But over the last quarter of the twentieth century, we began to bear witness to the emergence of new trends in many disciplines that called into question this Western-centric worldview of cultural production. And thanks to the arrival of such new interdisciplinary approaches, we are also furnished with new ways of interpreting world history.

This movement in favor of a decentering of thought and the humanities in general is nothing new. However, it is accelerating. Today, pretty much everywhere around the world, new territories of life are taking hold and seeing the light of day. Informal policy practices call into question and overthrow what had, up until now, been considered common sense. Democracy itself is in the throes of reinventing itself, starting in the most common areas of ordinary life. We are all now living with migrants and other peoples who, perhaps at first glance, don't seem to belong to our community; yet today, we recognize that we are, in fact, all in the same boat. Computational techniques not only transform knowledge into information; they have multiplied our ability to produce knowledge outside the current institutional models as we have come to understand them.

In spite of all the attempts to create enclosures, borders are increasingly becoming elastic, and all sorts of basic dichotomies have begun to collapse. Deterritorialization and reterritorialization go hand in hand. Far from being oppositional, subject and object now form one and the same foundational framework. The conceptions of *here* and *elsewhere* have become entangled. Nature is found in culture, and vice versa. Human beings and other living creatures have begun to partake in relations of co-constitution. There is no history that does not simultaneously encompass human persons; technological ensembles; objects; mineral, vegetal, and geoclimatic materials; and even spirits. Given these new conditions, *to decenter thought* is, above all, to return to a certain conception of the Whole, or *Tout*.[1] Or, to use Édouard Glissant's term, we must return to a conception of the *Tout-Monde*. And in this case, we must recall and understand the *Tout-Monde* not as something that is complete, but rather as something that forces us to reflect and think about how to make life habitable for all.

We therefore find ourselves at a propitious moment to relaunch a project of critical thought – what we call a practice of creation – that will draw its forces and originality through an encounter between the humanities, the disciplines of the imagination, and what we can refer to in a general manner as the arts of the living. For, as far as we are concerned, critical thought is not merely limited to the production of philosophical texts. Far from it. It comprises both a literary and a non-discursive corpus (be it graphic

---

[1] In English, *Tout* can refer both to the notion of the Whole, or the All, a conception of Totality, and also, simply, to the primordial All or wholeness, or, as in this case, to a reference in the work of Édouard Glissant and his conception of the *Tout-Monde*, whereby everything can be understood as resonating within a Whole or a conception of all. [T.N.]

or pictorial). It includes a multiplicity of gestures, fields, and styles, which include music and dance, architecture and photography, as well as cinema, among others. It gathers together all practices of writing, of creation, interpretation, and imagination. Such a thought comprises and makes use of all threads of the imagination. From time to time, both here and elsewhere, this thought is also of a purely performative nature.

The imperative to decentralize thought and the humanities is not a task confined simply to those regions that have, up until now, been found at the margins of the West. Such a project began to take shape in the very heart of the citadel itself, nourished as it is by feminist critique, race critique, a return to conceptions of deep history, and a number of other epistemological currents. On the African continent and in its diasporas, over the past decade, we have also started to notice an upswing in intellectual and artistic creativity, a rekindled vitality in the principal themes, and a fervent desire to renew the forms, the frameworks of thought, and the attempts to grasp the real in the process of being created.

So, we see here that there is something worth exploring and creatively playing with, a new toolbox that we can make use of in order to construct something else with our creative energies. We once again have at our disposal a new generation of critics, intellectuals, researchers, writers, and artists who are working on the African continent as well as in a great many establishments of higher learning throughout the rest of the world. For a number of years now, this generation has been proposing renewed approaches and innovative concepts that, today, serve as new cartographies for reading the world and for interpreting the time period in which we live, while at the same time recording the African and diasporic predicate in a larger framework, one that could truly be understood as global. From now on, it's clear that, in order to move forward, the world at large can no longer ignore the oeuvres from Africa or its diaspora, whether in the arts, critique, forms of knowledge, literature, or other domains of creativity and imagination.

To be more precise: there is no longer an African or diasporic question that is not at the same time a global question.

Or, to put it another way: the Africanization of the global question will perhaps constitute, at the level of the philosophical and the aesthetic, the event par excellence of the twenty-first century. If there is no African question that is not also a global one, and if, perhaps, the future of the planet largely plays itself out on the African continent, then there exists a variety of challenges that are truly and wholly new for African and diasporic thought, as well as for creativity, and writing. In order to accept the task of confronting these challenges, we can no longer afford not to think together, not to reflect and move forward on common ground. We must therefore compose a body – a body that is entirely open, flexible, and made up of a network, an impactful body whose multiplication of forces will generate and contribute to a much vaster conception of the world itself.

The principal task of these workshops was to take up a theoretical initiative and to focus our diverse gaze on the realities of the African continent and the futures to which it will give rise, starting from a conception of place: Africa. But equally, our task was also to propose renewed frameworks of analysis, of the production of significations and meaning, and the innovative and fertile dynamics at work across the entire continent.

The questions put forward were multiple, and the colleagues invited were first asked to come together to reflect in the workshops themselves, to debate, discuss, to test out their respective propositions, and attempt to open up, by thinking together, a reflection that would be enriched by the contributions of each and every one of them, in a space for debate whose sights were set on such an end goal. Subsequently, further engagements and gatherings with the general public were organized where an even more open dialogue allowed participants to not only truly identify their preoccupations or concerns, but also to give way to a larger demand for a social and collective intelligence emanating from the public itself.

The texts presented in this volume consist of the contributions written by participants in the Workshops of Thought. They are thus the fruit of the distinct perspective of each of the authors, enriched, without doubt, by the exchanges in both Dakar and Saint-Louis-du-Senegal. They deal with questions of decoloniality, the elaboration of social utopias, the global condition of the African question, the articulation of the universal and the singular, the reconstruction of self-esteem, and the practice of thinking-in-common. From these contributions, what can be seen posited is a constant concern for the production of new forms of intelligibility concerning the different realities and future of Africa. The authors, from a broad range of disciplines, have chosen to join forces in order to shed new light on the challenges faced by an Africa World in full mutation, and open to a universe of plurality and myriad horizons.

Dakar-Johannesburg, March 2017

Part I

(European?) Universalism Put to the Test by Indigenous Histories

Mamadou Diouf

Mamadou Diouf holds the Leitner Family Chair in African Studies and History at Columbia University in New York City, where he is also director of the Institute of African Studies. From 1982 to 1991, he taught in the history department at the Cheikh Anta Diop University of Dakar, where he also directed the Council for the Development of Social Science Research in Africa (CODESRIA). His large number of publications include Tolerance, Democracy, and the Sufis in Senegal *(Columbia University Press, 2013);* Les Arts de la citoyenneté au Sénégal. Espaces contestés et civilités urbaines *(Karthala, 2013);* The Arts of Citizenship in Africa. Spaces of Belonging *(co-edited with Rosalind Fredericks; Palgrave Macmillan, 2014);* Rhythms of the Afro-Atlantic: Rituals and Remembrances *(co-edited with Ifeoma Nwankwo; University of Michigan Press, 2010);* New Perspectives on Islam in Senegal: Conversion, Migration, Wealth, Power, and Femininity *(co-edited with Mara Leichtman; Palgrave Macmillan, 2009). He is on the editorial committees of several journals, including* African Studies Review, Social Dynamics, *and* Comparative Studies of South Asia, Africa, and the Middle East *(CSSAAME). He is president of the council of directors for the Social Science Research Council (SSRC) and the scientific council of the Réseau français des instituts d'études avancées (RFIEA).*

But education is something to make you fine!
    No, education is planned to make a sharp, snooty, rooting hog. A Negro getting it is an anachronism. We ought to get something new, we Negros. But we get our education – like our houses. When the Whites move out, we move in and take possession of the old dead stuff. Dead stuff that this age has no use for.

Claude McKay[1]

The following reflection focuses on a specific moment in the intellectual history of an African and Black community, whose history, pain, and suffering, and social, political, and religious interrogations are etched in the Atlantic space. A territory that is the product of a vast structure of networks connecting worlds, European, African, and American, under the impetus and drive of an expanding Europe. However, this essay does not fail, in its ambition, to incorporate the world-system of the Indian Ocean. Its ambition is to open up, rather than simply pursue, a discussion whose principal object is to appreciate the formulas put in circulation so as to determine one or more African modernities capable of taking charge, or reassessing, the various distinct non-European cultures, in order to reconsider what we understand as a universal history;[2] to recivilize a humanity that was decivilized by colonial barbarism,[3] and to contribute to the emergence of a civilization of the universal.[4]

The universal enterprises in question have their sights set on a dual objective: to dismantle the imperialist maneuver of expropriating non-Western societies from the field of history that has been defined as that of political affairs and to firmly establish a historicity set to other rhythms than that of "Western reason," namely, to establish something of an everyday history.[5]

To a certain extent, this process is one where philosophy (Plato's *Republic*), political economy (Karl Marx's *Capital*), and sociology (Max Weber's *The Protestant Ethic and the Spirit of Capitalism* as well as his *Economy and Society*)[6] will be replaced by poetry, the only practice capable of narrating, in a creative manner, the daily affairs under way in contrast to the history taught in academia, which is often focused exclusively on that of the nation-state and public affairs. What we are speaking of here is an invitation – already offered up to us by Rabindranath Tagore – vigorously taken up so poetically, and subsequently moved forward, by Guha.[7]

The experience of daily life in the imperialist metropolises, during the interwar years, laid bare the contradiction between universalist ideas and discriminatory practices, and also exposed the evil that still resided in certain Western "civilizing missions." It puts into context the questions of the first generations of Black intellectuals, from Africa as well as the diaspora, relating to modernity, modernization, and their meanings. Indeed, they constitute the very core of universalism. And it calls into question the event and arrival of modernity. Why did modernity occur? Is there some sort of meaning and significance that connects its diverse resources into a unique and intelligible narrative? What are the distinctive elements that make it so that modernity is such a singular event? Is it truly possible to account for modernity in a human history considered as a totality and not simply as a series of fragments? Is it possible to reconcile – *pace* Weber – magic and reason, the kingdom of childhood (Senghor), and world history (Hegel)? Should reason (perhaps) recoil, withdraw, and give way to faith and/or traditions? Is it possible and productive to negotiate the spirit of modernity (the sciences, arts, and politics) and the rules of the concept of a generation and the genre of the African tradition? Such questions are as important as they are urgent. Do they not affect the very debates concerning democratic traditions? In *Democracy in America*, Tocqueville refers to a twofold transition: that of authoritarian political systems toward democratic political systems and that of traditional societies to modern and open societies. In the case of the *Ancien Régime* in France, he refers to aristocratic rule.[8] What rules should we do away with in order to better promote open societies?

The context in which such a discussion is led is characterized by several propositions. Nativist propositions are interested in the exhumation of African traditions and reconnection with an African past. The Marxist theory of history in its diverse variants, of which the main ones – revisionist, Trotskyist, and Maoist – celebrate the heroic achievements of the bourgeoisie as the collective agent of global change, before the arrival of the proletariat and the realization of its historical mission, thanks to the modernization of the world by capitalism. This theory considers that the dissolution of the last vestiges of feudalism, the suppression of local customs and traditions, and the growth of industrial production, leading to a reduction of social categories into two antagonistic classes that engage in a fight to the death, announce the end of capitalism and history itself. An indigenous modernization/modernity in the Western margins and in the imperial peripheries of capitalism is, according to the Marxist schema, impossible. Marx himself, in *The Communist Manifesto*, asserts that all nations should submit, under penalty of extinction, to the bourgeois forces of modernity. As a result, the end of the precapitalist and precolonial era is the very *sine qua non* condition for the beginning of scientific, technical, and social progress in non-Western societies. This position is affirmed with force through the correlation it establishes between the introduction of the steam engine and the dissolution of the "village system."[9] Weber's ambition and that of his theory of modernity is to identify and analyze the forces that contributed to the arrival of modernity as the only rational civilization. His point of departure: the structure of authority from which he lists three forms – traditional, charismatic, and legal-rational. Weber notes that the legal-rational form is the most dominant in the Western world and constitutes the reason why "Western civilization" has a "universal meaning and validity." The ongoing progress of rational procedures serves as the very foundation for the production of the institutions of the ideals of Western modernity. The price to pay for the extraordinary gains produced by reason is the departure from religious territory. And some of the lasting effects of this departure are the following: a disconnection from cosmic and religious structures, the imposition of bureaucratic rules, the market economy, and the progress of science and forms of knowledge.

The highest price to be paid is disenchantment of the world, and its most unfortunate consequence is the arrival of "antihumanism."[10] Against this, theoreticians of negritude oppose a militant commitment whose primary preoccupation is the reconstruction of a humanism that has been led in the wrong direction by colonialism. The humanism found in negritude is a response to a certain "disenchantment" of the world. It is on a quest to uncover another kind of rationality that emerges out of a refusal to abandon intuition and spirituality. A spirituality that is expressed in a pagan grammar. This transactional commitment collides with and responds to another commitment of the proponent of negritude and African presence, Richard Wright. Wright's paradox can be summarized in the following way: an ardent defense of Enlightenment philosophers and the modernization of Asia and Africa; the celebration of secularism and reason – rationality and industrialization considered as antidotes to non-Western spiritual traditions and economies; the impossible capacity of African and Asian societies to imprint themselves in world time, threatened by the erasure of their traditions and the denial of their spiritual or religious beliefs and cultural aesthetics, as well as the economic and social practices of humanity. Wright asserts forcefully that the realities of the political order of the postwar period require the imposition of a modern subjectivity along with various institutions associated with it, secular democracy, the rule of law/nation-states, industrial and technological progress, bureaucratic order and rational organization of the public space – physical and institutional – and a rigorous defense of the "spirit of the Enlightenment, of the Reformation, which made Europe great, [and which] now has a chance to be extended to all mankind!"[11]

In contrast, Henry L. Gates considers that Wright's total adherence to the Enlightenment protocols leads him to concede the superiority of Western rationality. Let's quickly summarize Wright's argument: "Colonization was the best thing that could have happened to the African continent" and, in spite of its destructive rage, it was, in the end, beneficial to the non-Western world. Colonization led to the liberation of the masses in Asia and Africa, freeing them from the smothering tyranny of their old traditions and religious beliefs.[12] They should thank "the White man" for having freed them from their rotten traditions and customs marked with a seal of irrationality.[13] In contrast, Manthia Diawara maintains that Wright's approach is inscribed in a reinterpretation of the secularism of industrialization and the Enlightenment: two universal paradigms that were betrayed by the West, initially meant to serve as a means of granting true independence to third world nations. In light of this, Diawara considers that Wright is by no means an advocate of mimicry; on the contrary, he proposes postcolonial versions of modernity.[14]

Under these circumstances, how should we configure an African modernity that corresponds to a specific historicity in the more general historical landscape of modernity? Should we simply erase or reconfigure political formations, as well as the social, economic, and intellectual structures based on ethnicity, which has become the accursed part of African societies? How then, under these conditions, can they be reconstructed, taking into account the contradictory trajectories of geographies, sources, and resources of power, authority, and representation? So many questions that encourage us to look again and reflect on paganism with a critical eye, understanding it as a "tribal encyclopedia"[15] that nourishes the pluralism of African societies, to re-read Marc Augé's *Génie du paganisme*, and translate his conception of religious anthropology into a political anthropology. Augé's ambition is to restore to paganism its sociological and religious meaning, distinguishing it from Christianity. In the preface to his book, he affirms that paganism "can be radically distinguished, in its diverse modalities, from Christianity and its diverse versions," at least concerning three points:

> Paganism is never dualist and never attempts to contrast the body with the spirit (mind), nor faith with knowledge. It does not constitute some sort of morality that is, in principal, external to power relations and meaning [*rapports de force*] that are translated through the various currents of individual and social life. It postulates a continuity between the biological and the social orders that, on the one hand, relativizes the opposition between individual life and that of the collective in which it is situated. On the other hand, paganism also tends to make of every individual or social problem a question of reading: it postulates that all events comprise signs and that all signs make sense. Salvation, transcendence, and mystery are essentially foreign to paganism. As a result, paganism welcomes novelty with interest and in a spirit of tolerance, always ready to expand the list of deities in an ever-growing list, and always open to addition and change, but not to synthesis.[16] Such, doubtless, is the reason for the most profound misconceptions and conflations of paganism with Christian proselytism: for paganism has never included, as part of its practice, any form of missionary work.[17]

A world where everything is visible and where there is no reliance on any principle of exteriority to legitimize its order and history, opening itself up to constant negotiation and transactions that are likely to be called into question. Augé uncovers an indigenous anthropology that inserts the individual along a relational path in which everyone recognizes their dependence on each other, dramatizing and highlighting their differences in rites and rituals that are meticulously orchestrated.

The exercise at the heart of this examination of Augé's proposition is to test and attest to the consistency of African spiritual, communitarian, cultural, and economic boundaries and to establish the structural rules of the genre and generation so as to administer pluralism and diversity. Either, following Wright's reflections, we must resolve to bring Africa into the time of the world, burying its traditions as deeply as possible so as to be reborn in the history of others; or Africa should become accustomed to a permanent crisis caused by the impossible reconciliation between the two very different public spheres identified by Peter Ekeh: "the primordial public" and the "civic public."[18] This claim made by the Nigerian sociologist has been corroborated by historical studies. Catherine Coquery-Vidrovitch is well aware of such an issue when she proclaims:

Power, in sub-Saharan Africa, is the result of a long-term process that inextricably mixes elements inherited from successive and largely contradictory political systems, schematically speaking: precolonial, colonial, and postcolonial; hence the emergence, even dominance, of phenomena that it would be completely erroneous to analyze today in a static fashion, that is, without referring, in depth, to diachrony. But it is also necessary to escape the ethnographic temptation, which was often a tendency to insist on, beyond any sort of proper means of measure, a heritage derived exclusively from a precolonial past: the colonial episode, although brief in the wider history of the continent, was nevertheless profoundly traumatizing since it led to an indelible transformation of previous structures.[19]

She identifies, in a very precise manner, the dilemma in which African intellectuals find themselves trapped, since the very early days of nationalist struggles, a forced second-hand modernization (to use Al Schwartz's highly effective expression[20]), which yields to a rather outrageous form of "Westernization" – the condition of their claim to a messianic role – a façade of nativism, in order to mobilize the masses and, worse still, the rejection of ethnicity understood as a primitive principle of social organization. In this sense, African intellectuals are the true heirs of colonial ethnology and its civilizing mission. If ethnicities have a history,[21] this history is contemporary, not simply because of their resilience, but because of their ability, starting in the 1960s, to defeat, or resist, all forms of political construction.

Nascent Africanist political science shares the same preoccupations as history and sociology. It investigates the nature of political regimes in formation, the possible futures that they authorize, whether authoritarian, totalitarian, or democratic, and the resources at their disposal, as much in terms of infrastructures (political parties, unions, youth movements, women's movements ...) and ideologies as in the treatment of ethnicity and modes of organization of power and authority. Aristide R. Zolberg provides a hint of his investigations, taking into account the "drama of the human quest for a political regime that plays itself out across the new and strange environment" of Africa.[22] He elucidates this area of research by commenting on the "argument between the optimists and the pessimists." The first camp, represented by David Apter, maintains that the democratic future of Africa is based less on democratic constitutions than on the actions of leaders of nationalist movements and their effects on society as a whole. In the case of the Gold Coast, before independence, he assures us, there is an undeniable success in the transition from tribal dependence to parliamentary democracy, thanks to the leadership role played by Nkrumah and the Convention People's Party.[23] Apter ends with a powerful conclusion: "Ghana is, for all intents and purposes, a one-party democracy."[24] The second camp, represented by Henry Bretton, makes use of the same Ghanaian sources, analyzing the role of "Kwame Nkrumah, the structure of the party and the political thought of the new leaders in order to announce that the political trajectory will not conclude by way of the arrival of a parliamentary democracy." The only conclusion appears to be authoritarianism and totalitarianism.[25]

The urgent need to definitively put an end to questions of ethnicity and its manifestations, for the benefit of the citizen and his or her national symbols – of political modernity – becomes the *sine qua non* condition of the establishment of democracy and the stability and organization of the nation-state. Such imperatives certainly explain how the struggles of the first independent "evolved" states in the British and French empires were directed against the early leaders introduced into the inner workings of the colonial administrations. In the case of Senegal, we can trace this suspicion vis-à-vis ethnicity and the science that produced it, along with the ethnology and colonial governance that supported it. When Mamadou Dia became president of the Council of Senegal after the creation of *Loi-Cadre* in 1957,[26] he enlisted the help of Père Lebret, who established a series of in-depth investigations throughout all Senegalese regions in order to produce a knowledge whose principal function was to support a new administrative geography of a territory in the process of decolonization. A territorialization that would wipe the slate clean of a colonial architecture that had been encumbered by circles and cantons, without, however, returning to the traditional precolonial provinces. Abdou Diouf, for instance, would redesign, on several occasions, the foundational framework of the administrative cartography under pressure from the International Monetary Fund, the World Bank, and the crisis in the Casamance. In 2001, claiming to be attentive to the social and political imaginary of Senegal's populations, Abdoulaye Wade, newly elected president of Senegal in 2000, proposed a return to the historic provinces and ethnic territories, in contrast to the colonial, nationalist (Senghor, Mamadou Dia), and technocratic (Abdou Diouf) geographies. Following the disgruntled responses of intellectuals, Wade had eventually to forgo and withdraw his project.

Returning to the inscription of Africa in the time of the world requires setting out on an indispensable detour in order to rethink the twists and turns of the production of African modernity and its variants, in multiple temporalities and spaces that are constantly reconfigured. It makes it possible to trace the contours of the territory in which the questions identified in the introductory section must be shaped.

The first moment established the West, its territorial expansion, its discovery (or – to use the concept proposed by Edward Said, Terence Ranger, and Valentin-Yves Mudimbe[27] – its invention) of other peoples and their identification, their classification, their place in the history and geography of Europe. Europe becomes the only reference point and metric for the human condition and civilization, along with its religious, cultural, scientific, moral, and philosophical typologies. Europe confiscates, for its benefit alone, the historic initiative. It combines an imaginary cartography of the universe and a universalist philosophy that conjointly set up the scaffolding for new imperial and conceptions of political domination and a modernity that grants itself the right to impose cultural and religious formulas on others, in a permanent tension that has ensured fluidity and flexibility toward colonial domination in its different incarnations.

After the First World War, concomitantly with the consolidation of colonial rule, the intellectual, religious, economic, and military elites maneuvered between the colonial administration and its privileged interlocutors – traditional tribal leaders, guardians of centuries-old tribal traditions – so as to stake a claim on the world stage. An "African presence" outside tribal cages, soliciting a plurality of resources as much African as European or Asian in order to celebrate humankind and universal values and reclaim a reconditioning of the history of humanity – seeking to render to ancient Egypt and Ethiopia its roots of Black Africa and the queen of Sheba. These African elites begin to incorporate African contributions into the civilization of the universal (Léopold Sédar Senghor), into Western modernity (C. L. R. James), as well as into ongoing struggles for emancipation, freedom, and citizenship (Aimé Césaire, C. L. R. James, and E. Glissant). The flash point: the most radical revolution of the eighteenth century of the slaves of Santo-Domingo and the establishment of the Haitian Republic. They proclaimed the universality of freedom, dissociating race and humanity, thereby reclaiming – with insistence, violence, and supporting arguments – a place at the world table. In taking

Haiti as the founding moment and space for the erasure of the colonial condition, the Afro-Atlantic, African, and Afro-American community (in a broad sense) inscribed its action in a perspective of inclusion, refusing to grant any sense of centrality to the notion of race. On the contrary, this community attempted to submit the concept to intense questioning concerning its narrative construction relating to progress, culture, and civilization.

The debate on race, modernity, and the necessary inclusion of "dark races" – black, yellow, and red (W. E. B. Du Bois and Bernard Dadié) – into a humanity that had finally become truly human, was once again reopened during this time period. It was the start of the negritude movement, which Sartre qualified as "antiracist racism." The same period came to a close with the ascent, during the 1950s and 1960s, of the former European African colonies toward international sovereignty. The Gold Coast became independent, and took the name of Ghana, in 1957. It was followed, just as quickly, by the independence of almost all the French, Belgian, and English colonies. Their independence was quickly followed by the Portuguese colonies in 1974, Southern Rhodesia in 1980, and, finally, South Africa, where apartheid came to an end in 1994.

The debates and controversies surrounding the consequences of European expansion concerning the Indian Ocean world system have not lost their intensity. Historians, novelists, poets, and other experts in the social sciences continue to partake in the most sophisticated arguments. In contrast with the Atlantic world in formation, the precolonial Indian Ocean was characterized by a non-stop traffic of capital, work, ideas, and forms of knowledge and cultural formulations that largely participated in the configuration of modernity and universalism, whose commercial and financial pillars were solidly established in a territory understood to reside somewhere between Zanzibar on the African coast, and Singapore and the China Sea. For some, this commercial, cultural, and financial space – principally energized by Chinese and Indian merchants – would have constituted its own "specific international system."[28] For others, the territory was engulfed by European political and economic domination throughout the second half of the eighteenth century, eventually leading to destruction of the zone's organic unity. The latter thesis was rejected by those who continued to affirm that the Indian Ocean "never lost its identity in a world largely dominated by the West."[29]

The singular trajectory of the region would be achieved around three unifying nodes: a racial node constructed of continuous migratory flows, a cultural node whose rhythms and forces are Indian, and, finally, a religious node configured by the expansion of Islam, a universalist religion whose unity, in a constant state of renewal, would accommodate itself to the regional and cultural variations.[30] One should nevertheless note that disagreements remain among historians in relation to the geography and history of the Indian Ocean.[31] Kirti Chaudhuri, for example, identifies four different but comparable civilizations in this space: an Islamic civilization, an Indian/Sanskrit civilization, a Chinese civilization, and a Southeast Asian civilization. The Indian Ocean side of Africa is excluded from the circles of convergences and divergences drawn by their interactions because of a difference in historical logic and the autonomy of African communities in relation to the rest of the Indian Ocean.[32] These circles constitute historical logics opening up to multiple modes of universalization whose principal characteristics are contingency and instability. It's perhaps Sheldon Pollock who provides the best illustration of this in his reflection on the ancient history of precolonial India, making a comparison between the Indian and European "imagination of empire."[33] The former rests on what he refers to as a "finite universalism," which eventually conforms to universal political formulas while simultaneously recognizing the cultural and religious pluralism of communities (multiple Indias in the same region). In contrast to this, Pollock posits the conception of the Roman empire – a reference to the European colonial empires – that, on the contrary, is characterized by centralization, ethnicization, racialization, and a universalist cultural and religious aggression.

The imagination of empire therefore deploys, if we are to follow Pollock's logic, the Roman *imperium* and its unique *urbs* at the heart of an undeniable *orbis terrarum*, so as to found its civilizing mission. While proposing these contrasting trajectories between India and Europe, Pollock does not neglect pointing out the controversies related to the interpretation of modern European political thought. Several sequences can be unpacked from the proposed interpretations.[34]

In this context, taking account of the identical, parallel, and divergent developments between Europe and non-European societies helps to better situate the specific history of the deployment of the universal, by identifying with a certain precision the moment when their cultural and artistic narratives, their moral and political orders, slowly became divergent. Sheldon Pollock, in my eyes, proposes the most productive approach to understanding these differences of the universal by raising several questions that merit our attention when he writes:

> Although the histories and processes of vernacularization in the domain of expressive literature were remarkably similar in India and Europe, why did only the latter proceed to vernacularize in the domains of science and scholarship more generally? Why did Dinkara's quest to "uproot the thoughts of the outmoded authorities" fail, whereas that of Descartes, "to start anew from first principles," succeeded? Why, when both India and Europe witnessed a strikingly similar Quarrel of the Ancients and the Moderns, was the one case settled in favor of the Ancients and the other in favor of the Moderns? Why did both experience a kind of neoclassicism at the political and cultural level, yet only Europe witnessed the correlative development (if it was correlative) of true absolutism, revolution, and intellectual upheaval?
>
> These are hard questions to answer, but even harder is my last, which concerns the interpretation of comparative data. Would India have remained premodern so long as it remained precolonial? Was there another modernity – or if we have no need for the self-constituting value of this import, another sufficiency – lying hidden in what colonialism and capitalism came to define as premodernity?[35]

Here, we see the dual perspective, which forces us to take into account, and reflect upon, the significance as well as the places and moments of contact between Europe and other peoples. Contact spaces are sites for the production of knowledge, which, by inventing or (re)imagining the other, encloses it in an epistemological construction that establishes a large place for its living area, its customs and daily habits, so as to inscribe it – and no longer enclose it – in a stage setting [*mise en scène*] that is, at the same time, a setting of meaning [*mise en sens*], reducing the world to that of the explorer/director [*réalisateur*]. Certainly, the *mise en scène* and setting of meaning have undergone, and will continue to undergo, revisions since the very founding moments of the long colonial period that began with the discovery of America by Christopher Columbus.

Several figures take into account the universality that accompanies European expansion and the implementation of its political, economic, and social hegemony. Such expansion bestows upon Europe a monopoly over historical initiative and the civilizing mission in order to incorporate non-European populations into a history that has ceased to be geographically determined. This civilizing mission rests on the promise of reason and the emancipation of universals that, carried by the philosophies of the Enlightenment, associate modernity with progress and powerful capacities for the destruction of irrational and unreasoned practices, in a struggle between science and rationality, on the one hand, and faith and religion on the other. Understood in this manner, the universal is a singular moment in Western history whose principal signs are the following: secularism, humanism, and, above all, modernity – technical and scientific progress whose crowning achievement can be seen in the industrial revolution and its rhythms.

As a result, Western universalism is the product of a vast and unstable history. It established its referentiality in Europe at the end of the seventeenth century.[36] A historian of China, Bernard Schwartz, highlights the fact that universalism, just like its attributes, does not refer to a simple geographical entity – Europe/the West – nor even to a combination and homogeneous series of manifestations or practices, or modes of thought, nor even to its place of origin (European countries that often maintained very different traditions), nor even to its non-European space of deployment. And yet, taking all this into account, such a universalism should not be considered a complete and synthetic whole. Rather, it is fraught with tensions and conflicts.[37] In order to decipher the ambiguous nature of this universalism, Schwartz, for example, draws attention to the need to take into consideration the shared experience of crises, traumas, and convulsions that shook Western society during and after the First World War. They clearly had a strong influence and led to a restructuring of Western modernity, as much at the level of its infrastructural contents and identity as in the way it tested various nations.[38] In this same vein, in focusing on the Indian trajectory, Sheldon Pollock is adamant that we must focus on the contemporary situation and context in order both to interpret this history (the intellectual history of non-European worlds) and to test the very definition of history – two operations that are constitutive of the "historiographical adventure."[39] The contemporary context to which he makes reference is that which associates the triumph of capitalism in India with the end of the indigenous intellectual history. Such an association makes it very difficult to gather a full picture and understanding of the history of India that is only revealed – that only takes on its signification – via the country's contact with Europe.[40] Sheldon Pollock presents us then with a challenge: "how to chart a path between an Occidentalist narrative of the inevitability of the triumph of capitalist modernity and an indigenist belief in the perfected world of India before that modernity destroyed it."[41]

In the end, what should we retain from discussions concerning the universal? As regards the African situation, Ivorian writer Bernard Dadié interprets the encounter with European presence in terms of an introduction of noise: "A new sound had added itself to those ancient sounds – the noise of air conditioners. Now, when the European travels, not only does he bring his habits and customs with him, but also his climate."[42] In contrast to Dadié's proud indigenous irony is the unbridled celebration of the philosophy of the Enlightenment, and its universalism, which reorganizes the world and its specific histories in order to inscribe them in a unique narrative: that of the deployment of emancipatory reason. Contained in, and expressed by, the West, such reason imposes its most significant norms on other non-European societies in such a manner that they have no way of ridding themselves of them. On the contrary, they must conform to them, submit to them, since these non-European cultures have no choice but to aspire to them. Concerning this question, Bernard Dadié, once again, provides us with a striking aphoristic shortcut when he writes: "Intelligence and genius are not the privilege of one race, or one color. And yet, the White man outside of his continent would like for everything to revolve around him, subordinating everything to his color."[43]

The erasure of geographical place, which completes the passage from a mapped territoriality to the constitution of one fixed reference point, is accompanied by a logic that creates an impassable boundary between the general – European sources and resources – and the particular of indigenous cultures. The general (the universal) in this way ensures the subordination of the particular and, in case of any resistance by the latter, organizes its definitive eradication. In the first instance, indigenous populations are relegated to territories exclusively reserved for private and domestic affairs. Such an inscription, while completely stripping them of any political or historical momentum, reconfigures the indigenous as objects of knowledge and as primary materials subject to the operations of transformation and recuperation. Colonial modernity functions, it is true, by disqualifying both indigenous forms of knowledge and their philosophical foundations.[44] It simply substitutes its own colonial forms for indigenous forms, or reinvents them, using and abusing their syntax.[45] The dissymmetry that colonialism establishes as constitutive is what, to refer once again to the situations meticulously studied by Sheldon Pollock, leads to the impasse concerning the parallel development of European and Indian traditions.[46] Following the trace of the logics of convergence and divergence between them, he forcefully affirms the symmetry between European and Indian traditions up to the eighteenth century and the divergence of political trajectories in the seventeenth century, after a parallel development that had endured for almost a thousand years.[47] In this way, he is capable of demonstrating how the politics of distinction and difference, indispensable to the colonial project, was established through so-called imperial and colonial sciences: orientalism, religious and biblical sciences, but also history, anthropology, and linguistics in their different figures and variations.

In other words, two principles seem to have guided the deployment of Western universalism: an expression of scientific rationality and the insistence on forms and formulations of democracy. The particular emphasis on secularism and human values excludes religion from the public domain.

The enthusiastic promotion of a Western universalist narrative and its attributes carefully distracts one's gaze from its entanglement with a history of colonization, coinciding with a violence that stages and practices the repressive formulations of governance. Colonization is just as much physical as it is moral and rhetorical. Born out of the violence of its very site of production, modernity deploys itself via a violence that is itself beyond borders. "How ironic then," Pollock writes, "that the very project of modern discourse, albeit so deeply rooted in its specific contextual determinants, was to believe itself capable of rising above context so as to produce universalist theory."[48] Despite such proclamations, modernity will not recognize the existence of a universal domain of political rights, or admit racial or national differences as identitarian referents.[49] Indeed, the construction of universalism is realized through exclusion and inclusion, subsequently establishing a strong complicity between modern forms of knowledge and regimes of power.[50] In the colonial space, universalism encloses peoples in a dialectic of inclusion and/or separation, by way of a grammar that configures or reconfigures them in order to reinvent them, in one and the same movement. The only choice left to them is that of a complete refusal, reformulation/subversion, or total submission.

This contradiction between universalism, with its civilizing mission, and its actual colonial practices was clearly brought to light and largely exploited by the colonial subject. One of the best illustrations of this is offered by Dadié's literary oeuvre. The ironic gaze and incomparable acuity he makes use of to depict colonial practices meticulously identify the barriers erected to keep the colonized outside the territory of the universal, in spite of all the claims that colonization was a civilizing endeavor. First, he shows us that, in the cohabitation between the library and the school, on the one hand – the spaces where knowledge is safeguarded and distributed – and the commercial establishments where colonial exploitation is realized, on the other, the scale tilts toward the latter.[51] Associated with the numerous works hidden from the insight of the African, the gaze focused on him keeps him at an inaccessible distance from the territory of the universal. He can only partake in it as its external face, the incomplete project that modernity sets as its task, thereby giving it the right to describe and maintain the African on the periphery, and imposing a special gaze on the colonized world – for example, on Africa and its peoples. This imperial choice details the originality of the African, "the naked man; his brilliance … his wife on a pedestal [*femme à plateau*]. What are the intentions for popularizing such a schematic view of Black Africa? Is it up to us to say that we must return to our own source, to not let ourselves be uprooted, or de-rooted, so we can thereby hold on steadfast to our traditions?"[52]

Dadié's narrative subverts Western universalism by revealing its instruments and procedures, and, above all, its repressive technology (prison and order), its networks of economic exploitation (tax and other requisitions of goods and labor force). Two symbols, the *chéchia* and the *chicotte*, are testament to this.[53] In a certain way, the very defense of civilization, of order, law, and liberty, by way of cannon balls and bombs, constantly reclaiming a systematic recourse to force, without being truly preoccupied with justice.[54] "'What would White folk be without their guns?' Africans wonder. Their civilization is so fragile and so precarious that they must protect it, defend it."[55] In contrast to colonial barbarism and its essentialist production of the colonized, Dadié evokes a process of assimilation in a universalist project: "the right to read great amounts, perhaps more than any other people in the world, because we are at the crossroads of numerous paths."[56]

He reflects on this possible difference in contrast to "our ancestors who fought over water sources, or a piece of land, goods and wealth."[57] Dadié's method follows the position of Aimé Césaire and distances itself from the anguished and tragic questioning found in the *Ambiguous Adventure* [*L'Aventure ambiguë*] by Cheikh Hamidou Kane. Oscillating between a condemnation of the brutality of colonial domination and the quest for inclusion in the political economy of a universalist Republicanism, these Black intellectuals all express, each in their own brilliant way, an "ambiguity of dependence."[58] Césaire expresses this dilemma with disarming clarity in his *Lettre à Maurice Thorez*,[59] by identifying two ways of losing oneself: a segregation that would either enclose itself in an absolute indigeneity (the particular) or become enclosed in the unrestrained celebration of the universal. By claiming an "African presence" in the universal conceived as the "rendezvous of giving and receiving,"[60] the *sine qua non* condition (to borrow an expression so dear to Léopold Sédar Senghor) of the edification of a "civilization of the universal" and a "humanism of the twentieth century,"[61] Césaire provides a dual signification for his departure from the French Communist Party.

> Not only was [it] a protest against the Party's alignment with the Soviet Union but also an affirmation of the reality of a particularity whose fate is not to be dissolved in universality, but rather to find itself there, in all senses of the term. In this letter, Césaire begins with the grievances one can have against a party that has not managed to assert its independence from Russia before arriving at what he describes as "considerations related to [his] position as a person of color." These considerations involve the exaltation of singularity: the singularity of a "situation in the world that cannot be confused with any other ... of problems that cannot be reduced to any other problem ... [and] of a history constructed out of terrible misadventures that belong to no other.[62]

Aimé Césaire, like C. L. R. James, Richard Wright, and James Baldwin, therefore fits into a long tradition opened up by the Haitian Revolution. This tradition grants an Atlantic dimension to the internal debates within the Black community around race and its different figures in the construction of identity and Black modernity. It is tradition that continues to this day around contradictory themes of Afrocentrism and proclamations such as "race matters," and "against race."[63] The Haitian Revolution opened up one of the most explosive indigenous frontiers of universality, repelling the modernity of the Enlightenment that neither the American Revolution (against colonial domination) nor the French Revolution (for social justice) had wanted to resolve. A revolution for human rights, beyond questions of race or territory, the Haitian Revolution sketched out the contours for universalism and cosmopolitanism, defying the prejudices and pre-judgments that had accompanied the establishment of the Atlantic world economy and calling into question the social and economic order established by the slave plantation.[64] Following a similar optics – prior to his work on *Toussaint Louverture and the Colonial Problem*,[65] where negritude stands on its own two legs for the first time – Césaire, in his *Notebook of a Return to My Native Land*, proposes an admirable reading of the Caribbean imagination in terms of a "radical universalism."[66] In order to reinforce Césaire's reading, Frantz Fanon focuses his interest on those who took down Toussaint Louverture and maintained slavery and its scientific essentialism and morality so as to denounce "the great mirage of the colonialist discourse," which constituted imperialist France as the sole bearer of universalist values, and which made Victor Schoelcher its most striking symbol. Fanon thus rubbed salt in the wound of an ethnocentric appropriation of universalism by an imperial Europe.[67] In this same register, it is tempting to note that the only study undertaken in order to meticulously counter *De l'Inégalité des races*, by Count Gobineau, is by a Haitian, Firmin Anténor: *De l'Égalité des races humaines* (1885). In his book, Anténor proposes a non-essentialist conception of the universal, refusing to explain cultural difference in any sort of innate or genetic manner, and serves as an advocate of a hybrid modernity that would render racial difference obsolete.[68]

As far as Africa is concerned, the work of the Senegalese writer Ousmane Socé Diop bears witness to the same attempts at inclusion of the African in the universalist narrative. In his novel, *Karim*, he narrates, with sumptuous delectation, the metamorphoses of the main protagonist, Karim, who dons multiple identities – from being an accountant educated in French schools, to being a Muslim from Saint-Louis du Senegal educated in the traditions of Islam and the aristocratic values of the Wolof culture, to being a dancer and a charmer sensitive to urban opportunities and colonial events. With each identity, there seems to be some sort of corresponding clothing, dance moves, ways of being and acting that all become superimposed, with careful attention, on lessons and equations regarding French, African, and Muslim aesthetics, fashion, rhythms, love, and eroticism. *Karim* is a celebration of hybridity, refusing the draconian choice of the mortal consequences of *Ambiguous Adventure*.[69]

The method deployed by Socé Diop is shared by other "translators of colonial modernity" analyzed by Simon Gikandi.[70] His elegant method of perspicacity reveals their obsession consisting "of installing themselves in a political and cultural economy of Englishness so as to make of colonization a source of moral, cultural, and political authority."[71] He then magnificently describes, on the one hand, the dilemma of the construction of an indigenous culture that is simultaneously inscribed within and without a colonial political economy, and he questions, on the other hand, the production of colonial modernity in the permanent negotiation that exists in the desire to maintain the integrity and autonomy of colonized societies faced with the desire, will, and/or imperious need to cope with the European presence and its political economy.[72] Relying heavily on the case of the Buganda, he shows, following Donald Low,[73] how the adoption of Islam, its writing, instruction, and forms of knowledge, was an instrument of adaptation of the elite of the kingdom to the emerging economy of the Indian Ocean and East Africa in which they wanted to participate and benefit. This same elite adjusted itself and took a similar approach to Christianity, which is, according to Gikandi, a central element in their elaboration of a certain modernity, conceived as an inscription in colonial culture. The same characteristics that are deciphered and analyzed by Gikandi, taken from the narrative of the voyage of Ham Mukasa, are also found in the ethnographic and religious work of Father David Boilat. The title of Boilat's book, *Esquisses sénégalaises*,[74] reveals the direction of the gaze of the first mixed-race and multicultural priest, the formation of his multiracial identity under the dictates of the Christian church in the four communes of Senegal.[75] A bit closer to home, another Senegalese priest, Father Augustin Diamacoune Senghor,[76] the late leader of the separatist movement in the Casamance region (in southern Senegal), proceeds in the same way – using colonial culture as something like a chemical-developing agent in the photographic sense of the term – thereby revealing something of indigenous religious beliefs and moral values.

In the case of these two individuals, the actors in question are interested in how to reorient modes of expression and the satisfaction of their desires toward indigenous ends. They are attempting in some way to transform the very nature of "colonial library" and its universalism through the introduction of their voices, passions, and disquietude so as to be present, no longer as objects of European invention, but as subjects of their own cultural destiny.[77] Their presence at the intersection of colonial and indigenous societies legitimizes their claims to be the most efficient agents of the propagation of the colonial culture of modernity, which is expressed in civility, order, law, justice, and access to social, cultural, and economic infrastructures, most notably healthcare and education. In the case of Cheikh Hamidou Kane,[78] the ambiguous character in *Adventure*[79] is the central theme of the novel. The Most Royal Lady who pleads for the education of the youth of the kingdom of the Diallobés, contesting her brother, the chief, and going against the religious guidance of the community, puts forward two reasons for doing so: in order to understand why the colonizers were able to come out victorious over the Diallobés even though it was done incorrectly, and second, in order to acquire from them the skill of "joining wood to wood," that is, acquiring technical competence. In Kane's reading, neither morals nor authentic values are enough to preserve the autonomy of the community. The academic and scholarly adventure of Samba Diallo, the main character of the novel, his frequent reading of the Koran along with his discovery of European philosophers – most notably, those of the Enlightenment – merely open up a solitude and death that in their own manner authorize failure, assimilation, and hybridization. Cheikh Hamidou Kane is even more explicit in his contribution at a conference organized for the French journal *Esprit* in 1960. According to him, "the obvious internal feeling that we have of our cultures will not resist entering into the cycle of technical progress; before putting on the blue attire of the mechanic, we should first make sure to place our souls in a safe place."[80] By considering "that an oral culture [that] cannot be taken seriously in a world where neither time nor distance are any longer obstacles to communication [constitutes] a serious handicap in our attempts at an apprehension of the world," Kane shuts the door on any possibility of conversion defended by the advocates of inclusion in the universal, either by assimilation, or by hybridization – and he shuts it with a key: writing.[81]

The multiple engagements of non-European societies with Europe, during its phase of conquest of the earth and the establishment of its cultural and economic hegemony, have, it would seem, produced narratives that are more or less structured in opposition to Europe's universalism and its various attributes. And, in some cases, in spite of European hegemony, the profound imprints of a precolonial or premodern universalism have somehow managed to be retained. Which lends itself to an intuition held by Senghor: "Each civilization has thought at the scale of universalism."[82] An intuition largely confirmed by the more historical, literary, and philosophical works from the Indian School of Subaltern Studies, by Sheldon Pollock, Sugata Bose, and the novelistic verve of Bernard Dadié. Dadié rejects two eminent historians: the Nigerian Jacob Festus Adeniyi Aiayi[83] and the Burkinabe Joseph Ki-Zerbo,[84] who affirm that the colonial enterprise has failed in its desire to erase Africa's past. It succeeded in changing neither the historical continuity of Africa[85] nor the strength or prevalence of the African initiative.[86]

Bernard Dadié recounts the colonial theater, its dispositions, and the state of mind of its actors, identifying with lyrical precision the struggles, opportunities, and constraints of colonial domination, and reducing the civilizing mission to nothing but a vain rhetoric of defensive practices.

> I have finally understood that every action of a European, in this country, is a self-defense reflex: self-defense against the climate, first, then against other peoples, maneuvers, the intellectual, the child who leaves for school, and even against the tam-tam drums ... But the tam-tam. Looking deep into our hearts, our spirit, our soul, so as to achieve total assimilation, the European asks himself, "How can I dominate this continent, these peoples, when the tam-tam grants them their ancestral language every evening, connecting them to the past?" Round tam-tams, twinned tam-tams, tam-tams of all shapes and sizes and sounds, which each evening ring out the rallying call through the transmission of messages faster than any telegraph, news sent by the villages concerning the dead, or news sent concerning the children. The youth, no doubt, don't understand your language. By instinct, they respond "Present!" You are part of the community. And your notes will vibrate along more than one chord. Tam-tams for funerals and tam-tams for festivals. You played well on the July 14, and on November 11, you did well in repeating the linked refrains of French words, you were good to remain specifically African and capable of holding the people at bay, in suspense, on the edge of the bottomless abyss of depersonalization.[87]

Two questions nevertheless persist. They should help to fuel the reopening of the debate around "African" thinking and African presence in the world. Should we content ourselves with simply rearranging the genealogy of rationality arising from Enlightenment philosophy and its modernity, even though it's not complete,[88] and its multiple philosophical challenges, in order vigorously to reinsert Africa within it and to claim its paternity/maternity (Cheikh Anta Diop and his pharaonic disciples), or in order to reorient the production flows of various forms of contemporary knowledge in the humanities and social sciences so as to propose new epistemological resources (Jean and John Comaroff[89]) – a spectacular turnaround for Africans who have been excluded from the human condition and whose exclusion has made it possible to think about the human – or should we exhume an "African rationality" producing scientific and technical forms of knowledge outside European dictates (Clapperton Mavhunga[90])? Should we not understand, in this perspective, Senghor's invitation proclaiming that "emotion [intuitive reason] is African in the same way [discursive] reason is Hellenic",[91] the celebration of a cosmic fusion of beings (whether human, animal, plant, or mineral) all sung and chanted in the kingdom of childhood[92] and the poetry of Birago Diop?[93] Here, we find already a profound concern for the Anthropocene before it became the official slogan of our current times.

Laetitia Africana: Philosophy, Decolonization, and Melancholy

Nadia Yala Kisukidi

Nadia Yala Kisukidi *is an associate professor in philosophy at Université Paris 8 Vincennes-Saint-Denis and a member of the Laboratoire d'études et de recherches sur les logiques contemporaines de la philosophie (LLCP). She served as vice-president of the Collège international de philosophie (2014–16), where she used to lead a seminar on* Africana *philosophy. She is editor of the collection "Négritude et philosophie" for the journal* Rue Descartes *(2014), "Eboussi Boulaga. Défaites et utopies," for the journal* Politique africaine *(2021), and author of* Bergson ou l'humanité créatrice *(CNRS, 2013) and* Dialogues transatlantiques, *with the Brazilian philosopher Djamila Ribeiro (Anacaona, 2021). Her first novel,* La Dissociation, *launched in August 2022 (Éditions du Seuil).*

> … solar gaze of conviviality
> exchanged by dancers
> Suzanne Césaire

The names of philosophy

The thing is known. Why must we recall or remember it yet again?
Philosophy possesses a body, a color, a place.[1] It manifests a desire: to abstract itself from its faces, skins, and places. This movement of abstraction bears a name: the movement of the

universal. Not that which is produced out of place, but which, being written from within a place, appears valid across all places, without exception. Terrestrial conditions, the materials for the production of the universal, do not, in this manner, appear to determine this movement.

As such, the places, faces, and bodies that shape philosophy are accidents. Contents and forms of discourse are, by right, capable of being appropriated by everyone and comprise a signal to everyone. After all, mythology continues to survive. The question of the "proper" forms the heart of the utopia that the name of philosophy bears:[2] that which is proper to humankind, the sign attesting to the excellence of a thinking humanity. Where the body and its wildness are nothing more than mere accidents. Astonishingly, such a conception of the "proper" seems to play with and against the administrative logic that bestows upon it its very signification: that of titles, heritages, testaments, property rights assuring the owner their most complete enjoyment of their resources.

This mythology that bears the name "philosophy" is desirable. It upholds a real, minimal, vital emancipation. The subjects of philosophy are indifferent bodies. Or better, they are dead to their own bodies. To partake in such a mythological discourse bearing the name "philosophy" is to enter into a kingdom – into genuine equality. Nothing the body endures or suffers – through histories, stigmata, marks of domination – can affect the life of the mind. This philosophy, or mythology, truly begins to blossom once it has traversed that which, in the world, has encumbered it, thereby introducing violence and distinction.

To exclaim this is certainly to recall to mind an old saying. A wise old saying that has crumbled under the weight of so many contemporary critical theories (poststructuralism, feminisms, critical race theory, postcolonial/decolonial studies, etc.). The body of philosophy – however spiritualized it might be – is not an indifferent body. To get straight to the point: it is white, masculine, bourgeois, European, and inhabits the center ground.[3] It's the dominating body.

Criticism has done a good job at unmasking this lie and false conception of the universal. But in so doing, it might sometimes have left intact the desire for philosophy. A desire that nevertheless arises in a philosophical library that remains divided. The split reveals a first library that is not shameful, and which even recalls a utopian surplus that runs through the name "philosophy": that of a sovereign, heroic reason, which never becomes unreasonable,[4] and which supports, against powers and theologies, the political and intellectual emancipation of the human species. The second library consists of a series of torn pages – pages furiously torn out by those who, as they read, find themselves being targeted. At which point, the readers finally learn that they are without a history or a civilization, without rationality, without a foundation. Simultaneously Black, woman, and child, and much more besides.

In the economics of the humanities or human sciences, philosophy is certainly no exception. And yet, it certainly seems to keep its utopia intact, whether it has to be reconfigured by adapting it to the current circumstances, to those voices of protest that remind us that its discourse is based on gestures of exclusion and territorial markings. In contrast to the dominating body of philosophy, we must lay claim to "a right to philosophy," to use Derrida's expression[5] – or better, take to practicing philosophy in the "margins." To finally take into account those properties that are lacking, as well as the excluded subjectivities so as to provide them with a place; to explode the geographies of philosophical reason; to pluralize its meanings without renouncing the unique desire that philosophy's name recovers and incites – to participate in a larger community of forms of knowledge, minds, and spirits.

As Fabien Eboussi Boulaga has shown us, this desire of philosophy and the assertion of one's rights to philosophy have been at the heart of arguments in African philosophy since the middle of the twentieth century. However, it appears somewhat transformed today: we must take seriously the complaints of those who have found themselves at times the target of philosophy and on whom philosophy's discourse has exerted symbolic violence. The critical work that is now beiong formed is no longer concerned with the becoming *in itself* of philosophy. Quite the contrary, we must seriously raise the question of whether or not the practice of philosophy still has any merit, once we have sapped it of the mystifications and fabulations that it has produced. Above all, the challenge is to give content to a specific imperative: the decolonialization of philosophy.

What remains of philosophy if it is no longer the exclusive property of the dominant bodies that practice it? Will philosophy's contents and very project be affected? Will its utopia be turned into nothing more than a site of ruins?

Beyond philosophy, the demand for an "epistemic decolonialization" has, for more than fifty years, run through many *africana* writings, as bell hooks reminds us in her work *Teaching Critical*

Theory.[6] Sometimes they are directly derived from practices of struggle or the result of critical theoretical operations that call into question the very modes of knowledge production. Since the 1960s, this demand has been at the heart of an entire tradition of *africana* critique, implicating both African and diasporic writing, and it has extended across all academic and creative disciplines. This imperative for "decolonialization" was, first, directly tied to the singular history of bodies seeking to evade forms of knowledge in which they found themselves constrained, so as to think for themselves and reflect on the forms of knowledge they were made up of and which still perhaps presented them with problems. According to bell hooks, the practice of "decolonialization" is specifically tied to one's personal reading and teaching. It becomes more complicated through a close literary analysis of the work of writers such as Twain and Faulkner.[7] It yields a body of incisive, clear, and situated questioning: what are we to do with a racist, misogynistic library – when it also constitutes its own readership and turns them into banished objects? What are we to do with writers whose works are as deceptive and disappointing as they are profoundly loved?[8]

The demand for "epistemic decolonialization" takes an entirely singular form when it relates to philosophy. If "there is, however, perhaps no greater controversy in philosophy than its definition,"[9] this controversy gets played out, perhaps indefinitely, under the injunction to decolonialize. This powerful injunction resignifies the critique of axiological neutrality in the concept of "colonial difference." This analytical concept resides at the heart of the work of Walter Mignolo. It denotes the systematic forms of disqualification of all expressions of the existence of the colonized (their forms of knowledge, their cultures, and their very being) through a "colonial matrix of power" – a "colonial model of power."[10] Colonial difference describes a hierarchy that sanctions the inferiority of peoples belonging to so-called "discovered" territories. It relies on a practice of power, operates an invalidation of the symbolic productions of the colonized, and fabricates the negation of their very being. This threefold dimension of colonial difference ("power, knowledge, being") is also analyzed, starting in the middle of the twentieth century, in the diasporic writings of the negritude movement.[11]

Epistemic decolonialization would therefore have two specific tasks: to develop alternative epistemologies that do not renew either norms of knowledge that are preconstituted and imposed in or by colonial violence, or their models of institutionalization and registration in universities that are not subject to principles of unconditionality.[12] To decolonize knowledge is to invent other forms of life and knowledge that do not proliferate based on the notion of *colonial difference* and thereby put an end to it. Such is the sense of how to understand Walter Mignolo's conception of epistemic disobedience found in his writings.[13] It is perhaps not so much a fixed method as a critical operation that remains unspecified at the normative level and which is constantly to be repeated.

The commitment involved in keeping such a practice going invites us to question the forms that can serve to refashion effective decolonializations of philosophy in a more specific manner. If it is a question of confronting an ensemble of epistemic arrogances, the decolonialization of philosophy is not indifferent to these sites of effectuation.

What could be the object of such a decolonialization in European worlds and in the West more broadly? What sort of theoretical practice of decolonialization needs to be promoted in the academic institutions of the Global North? Are certain subjects excluded in principle from such critical practices and reflections? What practices of decolonialization can be implemented, more specifically, by *African* consciousness and its diasporas, in all their plurality and heterogeneity?

African worlds have become deprovincialized. And yet, in the Global North, the call for a decolonialization of thought traverses myriad voices in the diaspora that are often, but not always, called to reflect on and relive a certain connection to a traumatic history that, in a variety of ways, took hold of the African continent. Transatlantic deportations/the slave trade, colonization, neocolonializations. These three moments do not appear as "phobic objects";[14] rather, they allow for the formulation of hypotheses from which a rational analysis and structural forms of violence are redirected toward certain populations of the Global North, which bear with them various signifiers (language, skin, cultures ...), recalling rightly or wrongly memories of the Global South. On an epistemic level, they help us to understand how certain forms of knowledge historically developed from within coded axiological disciplines. The historicization of philosophy as a discipline[15] – particularly in France – operates on a difference between the Beautiful, the Good, and the True, which is supported by way of a precise cartography with regard to reason.

What could certain effective forms of a project concerning the "decolonialization of philosophy" comprise that are carried out in the Global North and underpinned by writings from the Global South? Better: what would such a project look like if it took place in France – where philosophy, since the end of the nineteenth century and still today, appears as an intellectual passion[16] constitutive of a dimension of the republican narrative?[17]

Before even attempting to bestow positive content on the imperative for a decolonialization of philosophy, we should first recall the pitfalls that are likely to be encountered in universities of the Global North: that of being an empty or hollow injunction, or of simply replaying, with some nostalgia, past forms of heroic materialist struggles that have not truly been lived and can only be mimed on some sort of symbolic theatrical stage.

Nevertheless, the enterprise for a decolonialization of philosophy must, above all, confront the very ruses themselves of coloniality. In decolonial language, coloniality denotes an apparatus of power born in historical colonialism, but whose form is perpetuated beyond colonial politics. This apparatus of power rests on colonial difference and continues to nourish it. The ruses of coloniality describe the ways in which structural expressions of colonial difference can re-emerge in the heart of critical practices targeting its very abolition. They assail, in spite of themselves, the bodies and hearts of their desires. They traverse the production of knowledge that wants to identify itself as being emancipatory in the context of universities on a global scale.

In the optics of a decolonialization of philosophy, such ruses essentially take on two forms.

From the perspective of dominated bodies – that is, excluded bodies – the decolonization of philosophy becomes a battle for the property of the name, often supported by a tacit desire for vertical recognition. It produces what Fabien Eboussi Boulaga already called, when there were disagreements in African philosophy, "the syntheses for the poor and alienated people."[18] In targeting ethnocentric writings and those of negritude (of Leopold Sédar Senghor), Boulaga returns to the arguments concerning "dosage," "blends," "hybridizations," and *"métissages"* – creolizations[19] – through which subaltern subjects, the *Muntu*, justify their practices of philosophy. For Boulaga, such practices are what enable what he refers to as the universal *rendezvous*,[20] where each person effectively shows that they have contributed to the enrichment of a paradigm that appears fundamentally truncated if it is only understood from their European point of view. Beneath the rhetoric of contribution is replayed, in a subterranean way, a rhetoric of defeat and lack:

contributions were made to discourses that the subalterns did not have the initiative to create and in front of which they still bow down. In such a framework, there is nothing decolonial about the disruption or disturbance of the typical norms of philosophical discourse in diasporic writings. All they do, yet again, is point toward a rhetoric of deprivation, of impoverishment – that of those, as the prose of the colonist reminds us, who invented nothing.[21]

In the neoliberal context of the commodification of knowledge that universities have become accustomed to creating, the project of decolonialization must also confront the ruses of coloniality. The defense of projects of decolonialization in the university system itself can lead to all sorts of suspicion. Such projects are forced to confront all kinds of cultural and economic forms of anthropophagy: absorbing, assimilating new flesh to renew theoretical paradigms that have already been judged as outdated.[22] The recognition and legitimization of subaltern forms of knowledge respond to a frenetic injunction for creation to be commodified. What's at stake here is to save a name – the name of "philosophy" – to render it once again attractive, profitable, capable of being appropriated into the market of knowledge. The principle of the margins, of the inside/outside, facilitates such an enterprise: it demarcates a line between that which is assimilable and that which is inassimilable. The inassimilable comprises a reserve – the possibility of ensuring the endless reoccurrence of new events, of new theoretical excitement, of desirable and competitive conceptual constructions. The margins serve as a philosophical trust fund for the future.

This second ruse displaces the meaning of the colonial relationship. It is not simply reduced to a relationship between self and the other. Rather, in a much more metaphorical manner perhaps, it describes forms of predatory material appropriation that are as much neutralizations as they are dispossessions.

What becomes the imperative of "the decolonialization of philosophy" when it doesn't surreptitiously nourish an endless and vertical desire for recognition? When it is no longer snared in a trap of a knowledge economy that undermines its critical radicalities?

Futures, defeat, and melancholy

Attempts to decolonize philosophy shine a light on the difficulties and contradictions that afro-diasporic subjectivities encounter in the dismantling of axiological coded forms of knowledge. Above all, it reminds us the defeat was total – in that, on the strict level of knowledge, we must constantly dismantle the ruses of coloniality and recognize the multiple faces of its metamorphoses.

Once such a proclamation is established, is not every attempt at a decolonialization of knowledge and philosophy nothing more than an identification with a commemorative practice – that of a constant reminder of the depth of the wound inflicted? A form of commemorative practice that would seek to unravel, endlessly, the mystifications of the "grand European narrative of modernity"?

The work of the decolonialization of philosophy also contains a healing dimension. At both the politico-institutional and the symbolic levels, it aims to undo the forms of epistemic injustice[23] that underpin a cultural axiology and the institutional practices that are fundamentally gendered, classist, and racialized. At the clinical level, it underpins and supports affirmative practices of subjectivities confronted with the multiple forms that serve to erase their memories and obliterate their suffering.

The critical project dedicated to the imperative of decolonialization derives from the very experience of the violence that has been inflicted.[24] It describes the colonial wound that the subjectivities have been affected by, via a mode of separation, splintering, and loss.[25] A separation that marks the impossibility of expressing oneself in any other way than in a major language that exerts its dominance. A splintering that marks the impossibility for a subject to coincide with themself – the memorial and symbolic universe in which, from now on, the subject will evolve constantly, serving as the signification of their very inadequateness, their strangeness.[26] Loss – that which has been destroyed by way of colonial violence – has definitively disappeared.[27]

These figures of the subject indicate that a practice of epistemic decolonialization necessarily must confront what we can refer to as the "un-decolonizable." On a subjective level, the un-decolonizable describes an experience of irremediable loss – namely, that which has disappeared under the blows of a total colonial violence and toward which it is impossible to return.[28] At an epistemic level, the un-decolonizable denotes that which can't be sifted through the decolonizing framework precisely because it forms the very conditions of possibility for decolonialization as a critical operation. It constitutes the limit of every epistemic project of decolonization as soon as it is carried out on the institutional site of the university, while retaining solidarity with the norms of knowledge that are created therein.[29] These norms, whose history is connected to the modern development of a certain idea of critique and emancipation, become metamorphosized and reconfigured in a clandestine manner in the interior of theoretical projects that place them in constant tension by calling them into question. And yet, in spite of this, the declaration and discernment of this limit should not merely provide us with the elements for sketching out a "politics of despair";[30] it doesn't simply lead to an idea of an intrinsic impossibility of every epistemic project of decolonialization. It nevertheless recalls and reminds us through its utterance and expression from the very sites that condition and constrain it – sometimes even serving to restrict the theoretical satisfactions that we can, in a visionary mode, expect from it.

The mutilations that have taken place are definitive and tap into the depths of our subjectivity. They comprise the narrative thread of a large part of what Achille Mbembe calls "the African writings of self"[31] of the second half of the twentieth century. The afro-diasporic subjectivities closely relate to each other by way of languages that appear desirable thanks to the utopias they nourish, but which, in the end, prove to be just as appropriate in that they partake in the very othering of the subject – that is, as their very constitution as "other" – other than of humanity and civilization. The decolonialization of philosophy is situated in this stress point.

In the end, when all is said and done, we understand that the decolonialization of philosophy has as its unique task nothing to do with philosophy. Whether it remains – purged once and for all of the demons engendered by the diurnal activity of reason[32] – or whether it succumbs to the blows of critique, the task of the decolonialization of philosophy only concerns the name of "philosophy" in a secondary way. And, more specifically, once we question its aims and objectives, without falling away from the subjective perspective of damaged lives, the imperative of epistemic decolonialization, to the extent that it can circulate, in the twenty-first century, at the heart of *africana* diasporic writings, has a singular meaning.

Beyond mere separation, splintering, or loss, the practice of the decolonization of knowledge reveals above all a double experience of subjectivity. First, it refers to the life of the subject to the extent that the subject's life is fully constituted by way of the relationship. Second, it describes the irremediable material and political violence that concretely affect the subject. These two experiences comprise two forms of "dispossession." Athanassiou and Butler have invited us to think of this in terms of "dispossession" of a philosophy of the subject and the myriad forms of brutalization – material and social – that have their grip on the subject's life.

The subject is not self-sufficient and impermeable because of a certain "dependence and violent relationality that is nevertheless incapacitating,"[33] in which the subject is ensnared. More generally, the subject thinks of himself in terms of a double loss, a double dispossession. Such a dispossession defines a subjectivity that is essentially constituted as availability. What inaugurates the constitution of the subject is exposure to the outside: the thick and layered depths of our existence do not come from us.

We cannot avoid discussing another experience of material and political dispossession. It has to do with counts, "police arrests," "inflicted violence" (Athanassiou). This experience of economic, social, material, and symbolic dispossession stifles the possibility of a relationship, in its multiple personal and political dimensions.[34] Black skin, queer bodies, those of veiled and unveiled women, the nakedness of lives subjected to neoliberal/colonial violence, to imposed exiles ...

To think of decolonialization as a critical operation is to think at the heart of this very tension that connects two experiences of "dispossession" (Butler/Athanassiou). Subjective life is relational, always already reconfigured by whatever is exterior to it. It is sometimes subjected to forms of diminishing or deleterious structural violence: *we arrive as available subjects into a world that does not support us.*

The critical operation of decolonialization is clearly specified: it's about constructing, producing, and imagining at a theoretical level the subterranean structures of a world that can serve as foundational support. Whatever the practical forms of these theoretical practices (be they literary, anthropological, sociological, philosophical, theological ...), whatever the inherent traditions of thought from which they construct their lexicon and grammar, it's about taking up again the question of the unity of the world, by breaking with concern (dubious) for the universal.[35] A unity of the world where the double experiences of exposition to the exteriority and violence, always heterogeneous and localized, are potentially shareable and are often shared.

This comprehension of subjectivity as availability opens up a type of critical practice that dismantles national and identitarian narratives that nourish the idea of substantial and authentic cultural life, produced according to distinct political strategies (domination or healing) by varying political subjects/bodies (nation-states, parties, associations) within European and African worlds. The substantialization of identities under the idea of one's own, of an authentic national life, belongs to a history of a brutalization of the social world. And yet, acts of violent dispossession lead to the reconstruction of collectives, at the political level, that are opposed to the privations and systematic injustices to which they are subjected.

In this light, the critical operation of epistemic decolonialization tends to break from a type of theoretical production, centered around a certain affect: namely melancholy. Antiracist and anticolonial struggles, decolonizations led in the African diaspora, have produced a memory of struggles that is also a long memory of defeat. This memory of defeat points to a larger series of traumatic experiences of lack and disappearance. The subjective interiorization of rhetorics of deficiency that become lodged in a conception of racial insults. The erasure of cultures and the brutalization of bodies. The end of the great revolutionary struggles that didn't know how to create true and viable futures or produce the imaginaries or horizons of the future.

In her book *Melancholia Africana*, Nathalie Etoke describes these writings of melancholy in a dialectical mode; they "reflect the essential vulnerability of a crumbling humanity that reconstructs itself again upon the very site of its initial collapse."[36] Melancholy does not have a pathological dimension; it refers more to a disposition of the spirit, a state of one's soul that remains connected in the same way that pain serves as the connective tissue or social fabric of diasporic consciousness.[37] Namely, the way in which lives tend to seek to escape the constant threat of possible death and the way in which they are capable of enduring in spite of this constant threat.

It is therefore the past that we see in the diasporic consciousness, as a fantasized and nostalgic longing for a lost paradise, but also as a memory of the cruelties and history of the failures of the struggle. Memory is dispersed in these multiple relationships to loss, but is also expressed as the inability to overcome loss, precisely because the present appears as "a heritage of suffering and always open wounds."[38] The melancholic disposition signals to the subject that it is still alive, but the defeats and privations that have shaped the subject have rendered it incapable of reintegrating itself into a long view of the future. The affective investment in the future is surrounded by suspicion – in that it systematically reactivates a memory of fragments and broken enthusiasms. The requisite memory for actively embarking on new affirmative plans of construction and projects of liberation remains flabbergasted when faced with these hecatombs, these tombs, and the dead.[39]

The melancholic disposition remains attached to such practices of decolonization – in that these practices convoke the memorial and memory work of multiple, heterogeneous, and localized histories, all connected through a sense of loss. The risk of such memory work is to surreptitiously transform such histories of defeat into ontology. They give way to the reification of the critical gesture within repetitive and undefined practices of the dismantling of the "grand narrative of modernity" that has fabricated beings predicated on lack and deficiency, and non-humanities.

And yet, the challenge is to initiate and perform an affective conversion of these theoretical practices. Not to repress a past characterized by violence so as to produce some sort of vigorous philosophy of forgetting that would alone allow for the subject to reconstruct itself. What is at stake is rather more a question of "forcing" a kind of opening up for other affective and fertile dispositions. If *africana* theoretical practices rightly focus their attention on healing wounded subjectivities, then the gesture of healing – whether material or symbolic – incubates a utopia that has yet to take into account the question of the various becomings of the world.

To decolonize is to produce a version of the world that, in spite of the ruses of coloniality, does not rest on colonial difference. And if one must think of a more flexible method, it would consist in performing a strategic reading of the past starting from the future, which would be eminently desirable. The contours of this future politics remain necessarily fluid: they designate the interior of a world where projects for societal change and the struggle against domination have often failed. These failures are not the sign of the ruin of all utopian consciousness; rather, they indicate that one must consent to taking up the task of formulating it – if only temporarily – via a negative mode.

If we question the objectives of epistemic decolonialization, it would appear that we can redirect their signifying chain around such a utopian consciousness. We could place such theoretical attempts under the term *Laetitia africana*, at the heart of diasporas, in an attempt to produce decolonized versions of the world. An attempt to shake ourselves free from neocolonial evenings. By distancing ourselves from melancholic fixations, the term *Laetitia* would affirm creative activities whose affective manifestations are joyful. Not the obscenity of the big laugh that a racist and colonial literature plastered on Black jaws. But rather, that which accompanies, as

Bergson reminds us, every creative gesture emerging forth as soon as a vital interest is at stake.[40]

Laetitia africana defines epistemic decolonization as an affirmative critical operation that diasporic writings seek to oversee and take responsibility for. There is nothing of Nietzsche's gay or joyous science within this practice, in the sense that it would somehow not renounce being accusatory, nor does it succumb to the seduction of some *amor fati*. The refusal to forget the past does not necessarily nourish a conservative aspiration for a return to origins or for some sort of pathology for attempting to dwell on reactive affects. More, more, more ... *future*, chants the choreographer Faustin Linyekula, who carries on her back, onto the stage, in a dance, the very youth of Kinshasa confronted with an endless colonial devastation and a universe of ruins from neocolonial violence.

To create an opening that blooms in the night. Such will be, metaphorically, the meaning and direction of a practice of decolonialization at the theoretical level. If it begins by questioning the disciplines upon which it has in its very interior inscribed its own routines (am I not part of philosophy?), its results remain indifferent to their becoming. Its end goal is to open a politics. Whatever its textual and theoretical form may be, whatever its liberatory intensity of material and social effects – its aspirations are crystal clear: put an end to a politics of *jouissance* (socioeconomical, institutional, aesthetic, scientific, etc.) that feeds off a brutalization and repeated erasure of bodies and mutilated memories.

For a Truly Universal Universal

Souleymane Bachir Diagne

Souleymane Bachir Diagne is Professor of Philosophy and Francophone Studies at Columbia University in New York City. His most recent publications include Le Fagot de ma mémoire *(REY, 2021),* Postcolonial Bergson *(Fordham University Press, 2019),* The Ink of the Scholars: Reflections on Philosophy in Africa *(CODESRIA, 2016),* Open to Reason: Muslim Philosophers in Conversation with the Western Tradition *(Columbia University Press, 2018), and, with Philippe Cappelle-Dumont,* Philosopher en islam et en christianisme *(Éditions de Cerf, 2016).*

We will never be able to celebrate the Bandung conference enough. The sixtieth anniversary celebration of the conference, held in 2015, should have incited celebrations the world over at all the "Bandung Squares." These sorts of celebrations should serve to teach younger generations the meaning of such an important historical occasion so as to recall that, in a tiny village in the middle of Indonesia, nothing less than an affirmative and radical condemnation took place against any form of colonization whatsoever, for whatever reason that may be. In his time, Aimé Césaire admirably referred to the event at Bandung as a *gesture of culture*. Indeed, the occasion merited such a phrase. For in 1955, in the presence of around 2,000 delegates from more than twenty-nine African and Asian countries that served as representatives for more than 1.5 billion people, an entire colonized people were able to speak directly (without imperial powers being present to put themselves in a central position that would thereby serve as the official interlocutor) and thereby set about establishing the construction site for a new universalism, a truly universal universal, following Immanuel Wallerstein's conception of a "universal universalism."

In the July 1955 edition of the journal *Esprit*, Jean Rous expressed what he felt was so significant about the conference:

> The unified action proposed by the continent that had only just been liberated [Asia] to the continent two-thirds of which still remained colonized [Africa] will have long-term repercussions. If Europe wants to continue to be obstinate in its colonialist rut and only conceive of Euro-Africa via a form of exploitation, Asia will end up lending a hand to help free Africa. In the years to come, such an attraction and fervor for an Afro-Asian nationalism will only gain significant traction.

The first thing worth noting here, as if it were a natural topological slope, is the paternalistic undertones present in Rous's remarks, explaining that Africa would be taken under the wing by some other power and would therefore be protected from Europe, which would subsequently learn to no longer behave as an exploiting force. We could easily draw a parallel with what's going on today with regard to the presence of China in Africa, which, in turn, serves as a reminder to both Europe and America that there are still parts of the global market not yet under their control and which are still contested by other state actors (India, Turkey, Brazil, as well as other African countries) across a continent that today is no longer looking for more institutional tutors but, rather, simply for economic partners.

We also note the reference to a new Afro-Asian culture (that Jean Rous quickly attempts to erase by instead referring to the establishment of a Euro-Africa) by returning to the important fact that, at the Bandung conference, those who no longer saw themselves as colonized subjects (an independent Liberia was present, but so was a country that would become sovereign two years later under the name of Ghana) spoke among themselves about imperialisms without having to address the imperialist powers. The fact that a gathering could take place in which Europe could be the object of discourse, but not at its center, was a way of starting to project a world that would quite simply no longer have a center. This provincialism of Europe that we often hear discussed at length through an unending litany of citations referring back to the work of Dipesh Chakrabarty was a result of the Bandung conference. For it was this conference that granted these non-Western countries the capacity to express themselves: "We are not a periphery because there is no center."

Let us pause and reflect on the philosophical consequences of the symbolic birth of a postcolonial world that took place at Bandung: a world where Europe will no longer have to be preoccupied with the universal, where such a weight will be lifted from its shoulders, and where the universal will no longer serve as its destiny or mission.

Two diametrically opposed epistemological affirmative perspectives can be taken from Bandung's assertion of a postcolonial world, both of which are drawn from the premise that Europe is no longer at the center, therefore the universal no longer has a place and no longer is a place.

The first position can be identified, as I've often said before, with Emmanuel Levinas's work, *L'Humanisme de l'autre homme*. In this, he denounces the world created at Bandung as a world that (in confronting the end of Europe's dominance and what he considers, elsewhere, as an irruption within history of "Afro-Asian masses") will have lost its true north and will have become a "disoriented" world due to its "de-Westernization." This denunciation is expressed in the name of a universalism that, for Levinas, can only be vertical, imposing itself as a *logos* from on high and requiring that all cultures and languages – certainly, arising from a pluralist world – align themselves under this European *logos* on the understanding that Babel can only be overcome through Europeanization. Since Europe, with its cultures and its languages, and its civilization, is the very incarnation of the *logos*, Levinas's conclusion is that, from now on, one must separate culture and colonization. No longer a question of colonization? So be it. But Levinas will go on to proclaim that there is no greater or more urgent time for Europe to recognize its ongoing mission toward the universal and toward "cultivating" the world.

The second position is one that identifies the universal with domination and cultivates relativism as a way of always undoing one from the other. This second position maintains one should take the diversity of the world as the very principle of universalism. And here, where Levinas refuses a world of fragments, "each fragment can only justify itself within its own given context," let us ask: "Why not?" Let us cultivate: but each in their own garden. Which really means: let's set to work on the "project of the decolonization of forms of knowledge" so as to invent different epistemologies.

We are all in agreement: the world for which Levinas expresses nostalgia, the Europeanization of the world in the name of the universal, was a given that Bandung erased. We should be clear here: it's not that the world is no longer becoming Europeanized. Rather, it's that the world is also becoming Indianized, Sinified, and Africanized – in other words, a Creolization of the world is under way: "the Afro-Asian masses," which are presented as the "philosophy of the other," spoke condescendingly about Europe, thereby making their presence felt.

We are also in agreement: we must continue the project of decolonization, and therefore continue with the decolonization of forms of knowledge. But we must also carefully examine and be attentive to what this truly implies. And whether or not this means simply renouncing the concept of the universal. My position is exactly this: no. We shouldn't renounce the universal. It's precisely within the world after Bandung – when the question is no longer decided by a Europe that can still define itself, among the rest of the provinces the world over, as the lone exclusive rights-holder or bearer of the universal and its embodiment – that the universal can finally come into existence. When the very question of striving toward the universal can be shared equally by all. When it finally becomes a question of granting, to borrow Wallerstein's expression again, a truly "universal universalism." But what does this mean?

So as to begin to answer this question in full, one must carefully take into account two warnings spelled out to us by Aimé Césaire and Édouard Glissant. In a letter sent to Maurice Thorez in 1956, Césaire warns us to be suspicious of any universalism in which we don't find our own identity, even if it's a universalism declaring that the "world has changed its very foundations"; nor should we, he continues, close ourselves off in our own particularity, that is, we shouldn't have a carceral conception of our identity. Césaire as much as Senghor foresaw that "thinking for ourselves and by ourselves" is not some kind of separatism, but, rather, something that is effectuated with an aim toward "a civilization of the universal." The other warning, which we received from Glissant, is to always keep open the notion of plurality, to not be in a hurry to create one, so as to fully take into account the "opacity" of what one is charged with thinking about in any relationship without dissolving it in an impatience to leap into the universal.

In conclusion, in attempting to respond to this question, "What is to be done?," I would like to consider two points.

The first point concerns the notion of an episteme that would properly be called African. When we see that, in the name of a necessary "decolonization of forms of knowledge," students from the prestigious School of Oriental and African Studies (SOAS) in London proclaim that philosophers such as Plato, Descartes, or Emmanuel Kant should no longer be included in their curriculum and request that the majority of the philosophers they study in their programs hail from Africa or Asia, we see the extent to which expressions such as "decolonization" can lead to strange impasses whereby they become slogans more than actual practices that one has reflected upon. Obviously, one should seek to reflect upon and rethink the history of philosophy in face of the simplification that began in the nineteenth century, and in particular with Hegel, whereby the history of philosophy became in some manner the history of Europe. We should certainly advise that Asian and African philosophers be part of the core curriculum and that the famous phrase *translatio studiorum* be taught, reminding us that the transfer-translation of Greek philosophy and science was not merely a road that led from Athens to Rome, and then on into the Christian world of the West; the philosophy also traveled from Athens to Baghdad, to Cordoba, to Fez, and Timbuktu … By *translatio studiorum*, one must understand the practice of "complicating the universal,"[1] which has nothing do with preventing one from thinking with (that is, also perhaps thinking "against") Plato, with Descartes, or with Kant.[2]

Generally speaking, thinking for ourselves and thinking by ourselves was never a question of forbidding certain forms of knowledge or certain authors in the name of the "proper." In terms of knowledge, there is no *proper*.[3] Should we think about the African question starting from Africa? Certainly. But one must first know how to start taking these questions into our own hands while also reflecting on the need for specific methods and conceptualizations that are coextensive to them without exhausting the preconditions of a definition of the "proper" that is impossible to locate. And to take into one's own hands, as our encounter here has indicated well, that African questions are also planetary questions.

Complicating the universal leads us back to the question: what could in fact be considered as a "truly universal universalism"? Let's return to Levinas, for whom the universal can only be conceived of in a "verticality," where Europe looms over the rest of the world. And he mocked an expression used by Merleau-Ponty concerning the exploration of a "lateral universal."[4] For the author of *L'Humanisme de l'autre homme*, this is nothing but an empty oxymoron. And yet, what Merleau-Ponty implies by such a phrase opens the horizon and affords a way to think of a new universal as being required by and for the world according to Bandung. According to Merleau-Ponty, in a postcolonial world, we can no longer remain attached to some universal that would "loom over us." Rather, we must set about building a universal of the encounter that would be inscribed in a plurality of languages by knowing how to understand other languages starting with the language we refer to as "maternal." And now we can see it: the lateral universal can be understood as the horizon of this open negotiation that is translation. Is the world of Bandung the world of Babel? It is no use lamenting the loss of the adamic language that descended from heaven. It's through starting from the plurality of languages that one can begin to glimpse the language of languages. In understanding that, as Ngugi wa Thiong'o states: translation is this language of languages. Granting life to the universal of the encounter, a universal of translation, seems to me to be one of the projects that our Workshops of Thought laid the groundwork for.

Migrant Writers: Builders of a Balanced Globalization of Africa/Europe

Benaouda Lebdai

Benaouda Lebdai is a professor at Le Mans University and a literary critic. He specializes in colonial and postcolonial African literature. He has published a number of books and more than fifty articles on writers from both sides of the Sahara. His area of research focuses on the relationships between literature and history, literature and memory, on questions of migrations, exile, and gender, as well as autobiography. He has organized a number of international conferences in France, the United States, Tunisia, Morocco, and Algeria.

The principal focus of the African Workshops of Thought held in Dakar and Saint-Louis was on the presence of Africa presence and the role it will play at the beginning of the twenty-first century. In this framework, I would like to analyze the role that African migrants play in the balance of globalization in the world. "Displacements from one place to another, deportations, exiles"[1] – this is how Jacques Lacarrière defined the various migrations and, more specifically, the African migrations, for, at a historical level, one can distinguish between Africa's own internal nomadism, the slave trade, and postcolonial exile. Moreover, Gilles Deleuze referred to the displacement of migrants as a "sacred exile,"[2] which lends itself to the possibility of a poetics of exile, present in postcolonial literatures – that, for example, of "the poetics of exile, the grim prose of political and economic refugees"[3] – and which I would like to propose to analyze in this chapter. Migrations are the result of the colonial fact, on the one hand, and, on the other, of postcolonial waste. There is no doubt that the political stakes that migrants pose are significant, and I will seek to emphasize the literatures of migration for the positive presence of Africa in the world today. As such, I will begin by discussing the determining role that memory plays within postcolonial texts before engaging with an initial question: that of borders, which at once implies a world of the global, but simultaneously implies a certain notion of enclosure. *In fine*, my main objective is to show to what extent writers of the African diaspora both north and south of the Sahara are the harbingers, even perhaps the precursors, of a new world that would place Africa at the center of new political power struggles. The second question will concern the writings of migrants, challenges that would mark the end of the postcolonial era and announce the beginning of a new era in Africa–Europe relations.

Reconstructive memory

African migrations contain a tragic dimension, such as the deportation of millions of Africans to the Americas – the slave trade is a trauma that remains forever present on both sides of the Atlantic. The colonial event forced a number of those opposing it into exile. One example is that of Abdelkader in 1847, the first historical African figure known to have been exiled,[4] or the king of Behanzin, exiled to Dahomey in 1892, to Martinique, then to Bilda in Algeria, where he eventually died in 1906. For a multitude of Africans, the post-independence years were years of exile largely due to economic and political reasons. Several writers have created artistic works focusing on the pains endured by these tragic and undesired departures. Powerful works reveal the interior weight, the psychological wounds, even the profound traumas expressed through a variety of themes. It is memory that precisely reveals this unease, while simultaneously playing the role of a catharsis, a role that can serve as a palliative as it can also allow for memories of one's home country and family to rise to the surface. For a migrant worker, ancestral sources and childhood memory can return like a boomerang during specific key moments. All the literary texts by migrants show that the role of the memory of origins is fundamental in the structure of fictional and autobiographical narratives, such as those written by freed slaves like Olaudah Equiano, author of *The Interesting Narrative and Other Writings*, published in 1789.

In slave narratives and those of migrants, ancestry and memory make use of the "I" that helps in the reconstruction of the self and one's own self-worth. A happy childhood, being torn away from a peaceful childhood, are examples of such leitmotifs. Olaudah Equiano recollects that he was like a "deer or wild buck,"[5] hunted by slave merchants, and his troubled memory resuscitates this image of innocence and evil. So as not to lose their reason, adult migrants make use of memories from their childhood that play a comforting and restorative role of integration that slavery had all but ruined. Slave narratives – *Roots* by Alex Haley, *Two Thousand Seasons* by Ayi Kwei Armah, *The Color Purple* by Alice Walker, *Esclaves* by Kangni Alem, or *Season of the Shadow* by Léonora Miano – all demonstrate that amnesia does not serve as a good remedy and that the reconstruction of one's self takes place by way of an emotional memory, as the psychoanalyst Cathy Caruth affirms in her work, when she maintains that trauma becomes significant when it serves as a "response, sometimes differed, to a calamitous event." Such a traumatic response increases "the memory stimuli of the event."[6] And this is exactly what happens with regard to slave narratives and other literary works written by exiled writers. It is what we see in the work of Helen Cooper when she tells the tale of her exile in her autobiography *The House at Sugar Beach*, in which she demonstrates that her reconciliation with her "ego" is only done thanks to the reconstruction of her childhood in Monrovia, which she brilliantly narrates "through walking along the path of her memory."[7] This memory spurns mute anger that provoked a number of difficulties undergone in her new host country. We can see an almost identical process at work in the writings of postcolonial migrants. The memory of some sort of lost paradise is therapeutic, as the writer Jamal Maljoub demonstrates in his work, where he revisits his childhood at Khartoum in order to fully assume his existential duality of being both a migrant and of mixed African and European descent. He confided this to me during an interview that was held between us in Djanet, Algeria:

> I feel the need to rise up to the dual challenge of both these national identities. I know that if I don't recognize the part of me that is half English, then I will simply ignore a large part of my history, which is that of being born to an English mother and a Sudanese father; that is, I would ignore part of my history tied to a colonial past. I'm a child of a very specific moment of history that tells me who I am, and

which explains the context of the writing that I've chosen to dedicate myself to.[8]

In this way, the postcolonial writer claims his country of origin so as to integrate his status of being double and to find a certain serenity in his plurality of identities. The same can be seen in the work of novelists such as Calixthe Beyala, Malika Mokeddem, Léonora Miano, and Nina Bouraouri. Migration transforms being. What is at stake is a claim for a new cosmopolitanism and a new relationship between the place of departure and that of arrival. Concerning this important theme, the Haitian writer Henri Lopes for a long time attempted to erase his white heritage, thereby provoking a trauma that he could only overcome by assuming both sides of his memory: his white memory and his black memory. His black Haitian familial memory helped him to accept his duality arising from his migration to Canada. In this way, the assumed memory serves as a way to heal wounds. Accepting his duality re-established ties between the two countries, bringing together the being of the two countries and conferring a positive sense regarding cultural hybridity.

One of the realities of the postcolonial twenty-first century is the perception of a new geography where the country of departure and the country of arrival become one and the same in the spirit or mind of the migrant and the migrant writer. This new perception of time and space both in the mind and in writings brings another political dimension into the state of the world. Novelists such as Nurrudin Farah, who claimed loudly and proudly that he carried "Somalia in his heart wherever he traveled,"[9] or Abdourahman Waberi, who affirms that "Africa will always inhabit him"[10] wherever he may reside, in Paris, Washington, or Berlin, are becoming more and more numerous, and demonstrate it through their writing and through multiple displacements. The strength of engagement of all these African novelists is that they each carry within themselves several worlds. Alain Mabanckou has a brilliant way of expressing this with significant pertinence in his novel *Le Monde est mon langage*.[11] As for Helen Cooper, she is able to integrate her new multicultural identity in her book *The House at Sugar Beach*[12] by establishing bridges between Africa and America, since the airplane that has crossed over the borders "has engulfed us in its foreignness,"[13] a deliverance in relation to the war, but also a ripping away from the soil of her birth. In a similar fashion, in the work of the Zimbabwean writer J. Nazipo Maraire, memory plays a significant role in the acceptance of this "elsewhere": she expresses it in *Zenzele*, a testament work in which an African mother reminds her daughter not to forget her childhood memories and, therefore, the memories from her native country. In these instances, markers of identity are reclaimed so as to construct an Afropolitan identity. The source culture is reborn, producing a recuperation of self in exile, an escape from the gray zone that consists of being neither from "a black culture, nor really from a white culture"[14] so as to become part of both. African origins remain present in the memories, palliating traumas and allowing for the creation of a new cosmopolitan being. Migrant narratives preserve sensual [*charnel*] connections with the places they left. For Fatou Diome, such a place is Senegal. For Éric Essono Tsimi or Victor Bouadjio, it is Cameroon. For Alain Mabanckou, it is the Congo. Algeria for Assia Dejbar. Senegal for Ken Bugul. South Africa for Zoë Wicomb. Cameroon for Calixthe Beyla or Léonora Miano. Writers in exile reclaim their dual identity, their double vision of the world: the Algerian Nina Bouraoui has decided to be a Franco-Algerian novelist – neither French nor Algerian, but both one and the other. Maïssa Bey makes this same reclamation.[15] This desired mixture of cultures is far from being an assimilationist stance and it is precisely in this light that Homi Bhabha affirms that, more and more, exile expresses "an articulation of cultural hybridity"[16] through a memory of redemption that heals the wounds of departure and allows for the reconstruction of a "self" in a global world, toward a new human geography.

The deconstruction of borders

Physical geography is at the heart of this question to the extent that borders are a postcolonial problematic, and literary critics such as Homi Bhabha affirm this: "The demography of the new internationalism is the history of postcolonial migration," and therefore of border crossings.[17] This new configuration disturbs those in the West since it deconstructs in a subversive manner the postcolonial being: writings from the postcolonial African diaspora assume this change by describing how official borders are denied, erased, transgressed, attained through administrative or physical traversing. If Europe closes its borders through the use of an impressive juridical arsenal, through the construction of walls and barbed-wire fences, migrants from the Global South attempt to overcome such obstacles, often to the detriment of their own lives. So it is that the world map is redrawn according to their own reading, thereby deconstructing physical and psychological borders. Postcolonial narratives open up, in a striking way, multiple interstices of interpretations in the world map, revealing side roads and the capacity for human adaptation. Migrant writers give birth to paths of freedom for their characters in search of the absolute, refusing enclosures and rejecting any fatalism where there would be no hope. Migrants become "active subjects," "courageous subjects" that blur lines and shift boundaries, such as the Nigerian writer Chimamanda Ngozi Adichie in *Americanah*, Zoë Wicomb in *The One That Got Away*, or Alain Mabanckou in *Black Bazar* or *Le Monde est mon langage*. Voluntary departures transform borders into openings onto the world and those exiled can reclaim an open geographical cartography, unfettered by demarcation lines. In Michael Ondaatje's *The English Patient*, the main character declares: "We are the real countries, not those traced lines on a map bearing the names of powerful men ... All I desired was to walk upon such an earth that had no maps."[18] Departures linked to despair and anger proclaim the rejection of wars, poverty, and the closing of borders for the formerly colonized. The desire for exile is an acerbic criticism of fratricidal wars, of African governance, of nepotism, and an unequivocal rejection in the rise in fundamentalism and iniquity in our current times. The desire for exile is tied to a survival instinct that defies all fear. It's a rejection of unjust confinement. The "boat people" haunt the spirits; they occupy literary texts like those of Boualem Sansal, who shows that such an influx of "people without a land, the 'harragas,' these burners of the road" only continues to increase, and he describes the improbable routes that defy the borders as "the circuits of contraband that weave their way through Saharan and sub-Saharan Africa ... zig-zagging through no man's land, through Algeria and Morocco, at night rather than in the day and far from routinely traveled roads always toward the northwest."[19] Other narratives relate this deconstruction of borders through irony, as in the following excerpt from Éric Essono Tsimi, who makes a "harraga" say: "When we ask Chinese Smartphones ... Google Maps humbly recognizes and admits that it is impossible to calculate the path between Cameroon and Paris."[20] Migrants cross deserts and seas at their own peril, which only increases their despair, but also their courage, described by Malika Mokaddem in *La Désirante*, Yasmina Khadra in *L'Équation africaine*, Victor

Bouadjio in *Les Lucioles noirs*, and Hakan Günday in *Encore*. Novelists speak of trafficking of illegal immigrants and denounce those people smugglers who take no notice of either faith or law.[21] Fatou Diome expresses the attraction of exile by accentuating the negation of borders, and denounces these new slave routes:

> Passports, certificates of lodging, visas
> And everything else they don't tell us
> Are the new chains of slavery
> Bank IDs
> Address and origins
> Criteria of modern apartheid
> Africa, rhizocarped sea, gives us her breast
> The West spoils our desires
> And ignores hunger pangs.
> African generation of globalization
> Attracted, then filtered, parked, rejected, desolated
> We are the in-spite-of-us of the voyage.[22]

In spite of strict border rules, the "harragas" derange and disrupt postcolonial time, which remains frozen within borders decided by officials of the colonial event in 1885 in Berlin. Migrants cry out their existence and make their way toward wealth, hoping for a dignified life,[23] denouncing, in their own way, the failure of the independence of nations for significant portions of forgotten populations. Works such as Salim Jay's *Tu ne traversera pas le détroit*, Youssouf Amine Elalamy's *Les Clandestins*, or Sadek Aïssat's *Je fais comme fait dans la mer le nageur*[24] recount the tales of hopes and despair of those left-behind outcasts. Éric Essono Tsimi narrates with humor that, in Africa, "even the bananas are leaving,"[25] which confirms the deconstruction of borders. The novelist Hamid Skif writes about the solitude of exile in his *Géographie du danger*, where he explores the psychology of the migrant who lacks proper papers and is therefore beyond borders, by imagining his fantasies and his desires, his misery and his sexual frustrations. Skif pits the humanity of the character against the administrative term *"sans-papier,"* which makes of the migrant a pariah, a terrorized and nonexistent person, since he didn't pass through the proper border channels. The risk of being arrested or even killed is omnipresent. Politically, Skif accuses wealthy countries of ignoring the new postcolonial human realities and, above all, of not moving past colonial history. Such migratory voyages dismiss borders that are supposed to be unpassable, as

Fatou Diome notes in *Celles qui attendent*: "We made use of desire [*volonté*] like it was a fence post, to plant it firmly in the ground, as if firmly securing our desire to live. And even if life was nothing more than endlessly flowing sand, the kamikazes confronting poverty held onto it nonetheless."[26] Migrations transform the image of the ex-colonized who proclaim their own conception of the geography of a new global world. The exiled individual becomes human again under the pen of Mahi Binebine in the novel *Cannibales*,[27] and Hicham Tahir's *Jaabouk*, with its stunning short story "Mama Africa," whose main character proclaims: "I realized that it had become more than a choice or a desire. It was an obligation, life had obliged me, imposed upon me, demanded of me. To leave my family, my village, my country, my continent, my life. My life? My life no longer had any reasons to remain here."[28] The tragedy of such exiles is striking, as is detailed in Aminata Traoré's *L'Afrique humiliée*, through the words of an exile who deconstructs the borders but who nevertheless remains critical of the situation: "I wish nobody to know the fear that I experienced in confronting the ocean waves on departure out into the vast open sea, when at night in the cold waters, we continued to have no idea where we were drifting. Currently, in the hell of Eldorado, we suffer all sorts of humiliations."[29] The exiles are in effect described as "zombies."[30] These texts absorb the tensions and frustrations of the postcolonial exile with his or her somber zones and dreams, striving toward a new global world where wealth and culture should be shared and where Africa would finally be at the center of the world and no longer in its margins.

The innovative role of African migrant writers

Migrant novelists write from a dual anchoring and it's within this dual role that their convincing force resides. They develop the idea of the freedom of being in the world, simultaneously in the West and in Africa, without holding on to any sort of antagonism or domination of one country or continent over the other. While they don't escape the disillusion born out of being rejected in their new host country, it's through this rejection that their writing and perspective become a saving grace. The stories of Rachid Boudjedra (*Topographie idéale pour une aggression caracterisée*), Michael Ondaatje (*The Cat's Table*), and Amma Darko (*Not Without Flowers*) all integrate trauma, while simultaneously claiming a new transculturality that shatters the notion of binary borders imposed by colonial ideology and that still persists in the "postcolony," to reference the title of a work by Achille Mbembe.[31] These texts shift the center in a direct manner, as in the work of the Kenyan Ngugi wa Thiong'o,[32] and find their balance in a deconstruction of the ideological and psychological lines drawn through a cultural creolization or *"métissage"* professed by Henri Lopes – "Being of a creole mixed cultural background is an opportunity. The marriage of cultures is nourishing [*fécondant*]"[33] – or in the work of Zoë Wicomb, who expresses it with finesse (in her short story "A Clearing in the Bush"[34]). Cultural mixing blurs the lines of real borders as well as racial borders. The call for hybridity and cultural diversity leads to an innovative proposition: the central role of Africa in the world. In this mindset, migrant writers encourage the comprehension of the other, plead for tolerance in the two continents where they have anchored themselves, demonstrated by the cultural voyages – both real and imaginary – back and forth between Europe and Africa, such as those written about by Alain Mabanckou, who claims his state of being both a "writer and a migratory bird,"[35] but always haunted by the village of his birth in the Congo.[36] The critic Derek Wright says – of both texts of exile and texts by migrant writers – that they are written within "transit zones and spaces between two worlds."[37] Migrant writers are presented as multiple according to Danny Laferrière, who affirms his belonging to the world in the following way: "I want to listen to the song of the world and I refuse the ghettos."[38] These writers reject any kind of house arrest, refuse communitarianism, denounce any form of ghettoization, and call to move beyond disenchantment to an enchantment that rests on multiple identities in order to uncover a new universalism. Plural identity along with territorial transgression sheds light on the psychology of "Afropolitans": citizens of a world without borders who make a claim for re-establishing a new relationship between Africa and the West.

Cultural hybridity, the evolution toward a new and different world, can be read in these powerful aforementioned writings, marked as they are by the traumas of colonialism, postcolonialism, and exile. Migrant writers seek to interconnect cultures, and to place Africa at the center. Born out of the memory of origins and the desire to be inscribed in a more balanced global world, new transnational identities and new geographies become installed. The writers of the diaspora belong to a new generation, a new order, and their works seek to change mentalities both in Africa and in Europe. Receptive to literary creation and to new possibilities for change, Europeans will be inspired to aid in the larger dissemination of their work, since the vast political and optimistic vision contained within them outweighs any wounds. If a number of the narratives seek to recount memories of a lost country, it's only so as to integrate a more permanent present in an uninterrupted relationship with Africa. "Migrants/those who have remained" seek to negotiate new spaces – between exile and kingdom, between disenchantment and enchantment, through the strength of a discourse and vision of positive change in Africa, constructing and building new bridges. Edward Said, Paul Gilroy, Achille Mbembe, Homi Bhabha, Boualem Sansal, Assia Dejbar, and Felwine Sarr[39] all nourish their critical studies by way of new visions of Africa and the world, all of them emphasizing in an explicit or implicit manner that the notion of "long-term residence" opens up national borders so as to create "kaleidoscopic" spaces,[40] to borrow the expression of the critic and migrant Julia Kristeva. All these thinkers express their hope of seeing the emergence of a solid, unfragmented Africa at peace with itself, since the potential for such peace and solidity is there. They plead for a Europe with open borders that finally rids itself of its colonial complex. The *tout-monde*, according to Édouard Glissant, comprises multiple identities that are resolutely affirmed, since "literature has nothing to do with the personal address of the writer,"[41] who integrates all his or her addresses so as not to be in exile anywhere. Such is the project for universalism undertaken by these African intellectuals, wherever they might be, and such should also be the task of European intellectuals, as has been expressed by J. M. G. Le Clézio. I have no doubt that African migrant writers largely contribute to a visibility and constructive presence of Africa in this global world.

Bibliography

Chinua Achebe, *Home and Exile* (New York: Anchor Books, 2000).
Sadek Aïssat, *Je fais comme fait dans la mer le nageur* (Alger: Barzakh, 1999).
Amnesty International, *Refugiés, un scandale planetaire* (Paris: Autrement, 2012).
Emilie Apter, *Against World Literature: On the Politics of Untranslatability* (London: Verso, 2013).
Maïssa Bey, *L'Une et l'autre* (La Tour-d'Aigues: Éditions de l'Aube, 2009).

Homi Bhabha, *The Location of Culture* (London: Routledge, 1994).
Mahi Binebine, *Cannibales* (Paris: Fayard, 1999).
Victor Bouadjio, *Les lucioles noires* (Avin: Luce Wilquin, 2011).
Rachid Boudjedra, *Topographie idéale pour une aggression caractérisée* (Paris: Gallimard, 1986.)
Cathy Caruth, *Trauma: Exploration in Memory* (Baltimore, MD: Johns Hopkins University Press, 1995).
Amma Darko, *Not without Flowers* (Ghana: Subsaharan publishers, 2007).
Fatou Diome, *Celles qui attendent* (Paris: Flammarion, 2010).
Olaudah Equiano, *The Interesting Narrative and Other Writings* (London: Penguin Books, 1995.)
Éric Essono Tsimi, *Migrants Diaries* (Paris: Éditions Acoria, 2014).
Youssouf Amine Elalamy, *Les Clandestins*, (Paris: Au diable vauvert, 2001).
Paul Gilroy, *Against Race: Imagining Political Culture beyond the Color Line* (Cambridge, MA: Harvard University Press, 2000).
Hakan Günday, *Encore* (Paris: Galaade, 2015).
Salim Jay, *Tu ne traverseras pas le détroit* (Paris: Mille et une nuits, 2000).
Yasmina Khadra, *L'Équation africaine* (Paris: Julliard, 2011).
Julia Kristeva, Étrangers à nous-mêmes (Paris: Gallimard, 1988).
Jacques Lacarrière, "Le Bernard-l'hermite ou le treizième voyage," in *Pour une littérature voyageuse* (Paris: Éditions Complexes, 1999).
Benaouda Lebdai, *Écrivains africains, entretiens* (Beaucouzé: Éditions Ebena, 2015).
Henri Lopez, interview with Pascale Haubruge: "L'Afrique intérieure d'Henri Lopez. Retour à la case départ," *Le Soir*, February 27, 2002.
Alain Mabanckou, *Black Bazar* (Paris: Le Seuil, 2009).
Alain Mabanckou, *Petit piment* (Paris: Le Seuil, 2015).
Alain Mabanckou, *Le monde est mon langage* (Paris: Grasset, 2016).
Achille Mbembe, *De la postcolonie. Essai sur l'imagination politique dans l'Afrique contemporaine* (Paris: Karthala, 2000).
Léonora Miano, *Habiter la frontière* (Paris: L'Arche Éditeur, 2012).
Malika Mokeddem, *La Désirante* (Paris: Grasset, 2011)
Chimamanda Ngozi Adichie, *Americanah* (Paris: Gallimard, 2015)
Carrie Noland and Barret Watten, *Diasporic avant-gardes, Experimental Poetics and Cultural Displacements* (New York: Palgrave Macmillan, 2009).

J. Nozipo Maraire, *Zenzele* (New York: Delta, 1996).
Michael Ondaatje, *The English Patient* (Toronto, ONT: McClelland & Stewart, 1992).
Michael Ondaatje, *The Cats' Table* (Toronto, ONT: McClelland & Stewart, 2011).
Christophe Pradeau and Tiphaine Samoyault, *Où est la literature mondiale?* (Paris: Presses Universitaires de Vincennes, 2005).
Salman Rushdie, *Joseph Anton* (New York: Random House, 2012).
Edward Said, *Réflexions sur l'exil et autres essais* (Arles: Actes Sud, 2008)
Boualem Sansal, *Harraga*, (Paris: Gallimard, 2005).
Felwine Sarr, *Afrotopia* (Paris: Philippe Rey, 2016).
Hamid Skiff, *La Géographie du danger* (Paris: Naïve, 2006).
Hicham Tahir, *Jaabouq* (Casablanca: Casa Express Editions, 2012).
Aminata Traoré, *L'Afrique humiliée* (Alger: Cabash Editions, 2008).
Ngugi wa Thiong'o, *Moving the Centre* (London: James Curry, 1993).
Zoë Wicomb, *The One That Got Away* (New York: New Press, 2008).
Zoë Wicomb, "A Clearing in the Bush," in *You Can't Get Lost in Cape Town* (New York: The Feminist Press, 2000).
Catherine Withol de Wenden, *La Question migratoire au XXIe siècle. Migrants, refugiés, et relations internationals* (Paris: Presses de Sciences Po, 2010).

Part II

For What is Africa the Name?

Léonora Miano

Léonora Miano *was born in Doula (Cameroon) in 1973 and has lived in France since 1991. Beginning with her first novel,* L'Intérieur de la nuit, *published in 2005, she has won a number of literary awards. Today, her collection of works includes more than fifteen novels, plays, and essays. Her writings focus on understanding the sub-Saharan experiences of Afro-descendants in order to inscribe them on the consciousness of the world. In 2006, she received the prix Goncourt des lycéens for* Contours du jour qui vient, *the prix Seligmann contre le racisme in 2012 for* Écrits pour la parole, *and, in 2013, the prix Femina for* Season of the Shadow.

The question of knowing what the name of our continent conceals no longer seems to be a question that one reflects upon. And while the answer seems quite obvious, if it was in fact not the case, we could take to examining the historical dimensions of how its naming came about. We could then take to analyzing maps, pointing our fingers directly at the specific spaces concerned; we could debate around the topic, and perhaps the trustworthiness of the elements presented. But this is not what I want to embark on today. Rather, the question is twofold. It concerns Africa both as symbolic content and as a project. The populations of our vast continent have assimilated more than they have appropriated the name chosen by others to designate them. From the barges on the Senegal River all the way to the banks of the Mississippi, we are therefore *Africans*, and, whatever this might actually mean, the ordeal is nevertheless well understood. And yet, a wide gap still remains that separates assimilation and appropriation. The former term implies an unwanted, or involuntary, ingestion, and does not contain the value found in the latter, which implies, in its turn, an actualization of a force or power.

In the case of assimilation, the ingested element is of course metabolized by the organism that has swallowed it, but what such an element provides to the individual depends on its initial natural quality and on the element's compatibility with the needs of the body subjected to its action. Whereas, conversely, appropriation is something one masters so as to nourish the project of the one who not only has chosen to appropriate it, but who is also then free to decide how they will make use of it. To illustrate this idea more clearly, we could say something to the following effect: the colonized assimilate elements arising from imperialist cultures without appropriating them. Because they did not choose these colonies, or the practices that the colonies and colonists imposed on them. Because, in large part, the practices and contributions brought by the colonists were mostly incompatible with local systems of thought. Conversely, one can see instances of practices of appropriation where cultural elements belonging to minority cultures [*cultures minorés*] are used for entertainment or as a disguise [*travestissement*] in environments of cultural hegemony where their actual meaning is unknown or misunderstood, mocked or distorted.[1] Appropriated cultural elements are often only appropriated for a short time and in a playful fashion. They normally don't lead whoever is in the process of appropriating and enjoying themselves to question the very foundations of their culture. They are often appropriated just to add a bit of color to the monotony of their daily ordinary existence. Whereas, in complete contrast, assimilated elements profoundly affect the societies concerned and can potentially lead to devitalizing effects. Such dissymmetry certainly deserves to be pointed out and reflected upon.

Assimilation, the practice of validating or ratifying the position of those who have been dominated, is therefore also fraught with questions. However, a variety of diverse elements would seem to plead in favor of the name *Africa*. First, there is the simple practical element of the name. Quite simply, such a name is, by now, quite old. It appears in a variety of works and books of all kinds across a vast landscape. The name has forged both militant factions, including the most radical, from pan-Africanism to Afrocentricity, and although no one uses the term "blanco-African," another equally curious term, negro-African, has nevertheless found itself firmly rooted in our spaces. To reflect back on this whole history of the name seems almost impossible or unimaginable. But we should perhaps remind ourselves that the name that has been bestowed upon our soil has its origins in the Berber tribe, so it's clearly continental. Not to mention the fact that most North Africans reserve the name *African* to describe the populations found in the sub-Saharan part of the continent.[2] In conclusion – although this is not a trifling detail – mutations have been produced in our countries since the fifteenth century to such an extent that our identities have for quite some time now been created in such a way as to recall not only the initial encounter with a conquering and predatory Europe, but also the continent's very impressions on our lived experience, yesterday as much as today. Since, in part, this is also what the name *Africa* bears – a name unknown to our precolonial ancestors, which has nevertheless become our own.

Our ancestors are a testament to their capacity of resilience, to their incredible adaptability and aptitude for integrating exogenous cultural elements [*apports*], even if some of them were poorly metabolized. They survived and overcame a great many upheavals and, whereas Europe, perverted by its own greed, eradicated entire peoples across the face of the earth, we are the very site of the initial creation of peoples. Right here, in our region of the world, was the very birthplace of humanity. Where humanity first saw the light of day. And our final hour has not yet arrived. There is no doubt in our minds that our ancestors, whatever name our continent might bear, will recognize us when our time has come to leave this life and join them in the next. Moreover, it just so happens that sometimes they even pay us a visit. Those among us who are artists and creators understand this very well: our ancestors are to be found wherever we reside. They are not impressed or distracted by concepts such as the boundaries of space and time. Since they populated this world, it belongs to them. The territories where their sweat and blood flowed belong to us by right, in spite of what some may say.

And yet, as I mentioned earlier, there's still something troubling, there's still a subject worth discussing. Given that the assimilation I highlighted earlier was not a practice of appropriation, we can still feel something unsettling within us, perhaps even something like a rejection. The need for finding their name, and with it some sort of trace of their destiny, has preoccupied many peoples both on the continent and in the diasporas. As such, the ancestral land for some bears the following names: Alkebu-Lan, Katiopa, Farafina, Afuraka, TaMery, or even Kama – which we know is derived from Kemet – and I'm forgetting others. Rediscovered, revisited, or invented, these other names grant a connection to some kind of ancestral soil, and the very fact that they are being commonly used today by various peoples and groups that cherish them has certainly garnered some attention. These myriad denominations reveal that, in an intuitive as well as a carefully and maturely reflected-upon manner, a great many people have understood what Toni Morrison made the voice of the narrator in her book, *Beloved*, express: "definitions belong to the definers – not the defined."[3]

No doubt this whole obsession and attention around naming is perhaps something shared by novelists and writers. The quotation from *Beloved* can be interpreted in two ways that are useful for our reflections. First, that definitions belong to those who express them, and not those who are designated by them. The latter would therefore have the greatest of interest in preserving within themselves what they feel is profoundly their own, in knowing themselves without having recourse to some other name imposed from the outside: the discourse of the other concerning self. This is precisely what old Baby Suggs, one of the more powerful characters from *Beloved*, invites one to do in the profane preaching she shares with her community, inciting both a self-care and self-love. It's also this very autonomous self-apprehension that the Afro-descendants in the French Antilles sought by instituting the practice of a secret or hidden name that was whispered from the midwife to the mother when the priest announced the child's baptismal name. Sacred, the secret anthroponym had to contain the very truth of being, in those islands where the name served to reduce individuals and families. Regarding this subject, Philippe Chanson argues that "the secret name was definitely one of the ancient practices of resistance to colonial depersonalization ... it's in such a name, in all its mystery, that one thought that the most impenetrable and substantial force of any individual truly resided."[4]

We know very well that, here in the sub-Saharan regions, individuals can have a number of names, some of which can only be revealed as a shared common name. One's name will change according to the spiritual or social evolution of a person. However, for a subject as well as for the group, it would appear to be fairly difficult to project, around oneself, the power of a name whose proliferation is already largely proscribed. Having a name for oneself that isn't the one communicated to others has a certain validity only to the extent that one is navigating between various spaces, whereby there exists at least one space in which it is permissible to inhabit fully the most meaningful idea of oneself. To transcend their conditions in a place where the practice of secret names was not known, slaves in the USA dissociated the body from the soul so as to create "an inner domain wherein the authority of subjectivity in discord with their so-called condition can be expressed."[5] Throughout sub-Saharan Africa we find eminent territories of the legitimate name. It's in these communities that we are Bandjoun, Duala, Sérère, or Muluba. There, being is inscribed in a filiation allowing for the reflection of belonging that is forced upon oneself by History. And such practices relativize bearing the name of *African*. Inoperative when it is merely a question of defining oneself for oneself, it becomes a name for another, a mask.

Outside intellectual circles, far from militant milieux, for a vast portion of sub-Saharan peoples, *African*, in spite of the transformations implied by such a term, is a secondary appellation. Nationality, which was once often ignored by those designated by it, has only recently become a more hospitable and user-friendly identifier. It's only when one leaves one's own people behind that such names granted during the colonial era seem to acquire a certain pertinence. Far away from the continent, all of a sudden, the term *African* serves as a saving grace, one's last hope for a support structure. Isolated among people whose phenotypes and codes largely differ from those to which we are accustomed, the eventual meanings of the term slowly begin to flourish. Faced with myriad adversities, these meanings become consolidated. Suddenly, *Africa* becomes the name both of that which endures and of the resources pitted against hostilities. It also becomes the name for new fraternities among inhabitants from the sub-Saharan region, opening onto unknown proximities and arts of living that are often better shared elsewhere than on the continent itself. Such a context gives way to a spontaneous movement that is also keenly sensitive and is not yet of the order of appropriation, but which nevertheless sketches out such a possibility. It is also the confluence where the identity of the Afropean is formed by weaving together the diversity of interlinking cultures.

Morrison's reflections can also be understood in the following way: definitions belong to those who utter them but not those toward whom such definitions are aimed. In this way, those who have been defined remain their own possessions. They are not the goods or resources of the one who utters the definition, since the performative power of the word finds itself annihilated by that which is borne by the groups, whereby a definition would merely have wanted to limit its vast horizon. This latter reading is of interest, given that there is not much chance that the term *Africa* will be the object of modification any time soon. In delving more deeply into this question, we are not seeking out some sort of counterfactual version of History of those possible events that didn't happen, by evoking names that the continent could have borne if its historical trajectory had been different. Nor is our discussion here merely a way of soothing our pains, of establishing the wound as the singular characteristic of experience. However, we should recall that language, words, labels, and names are not neutral. Languages, which are systems of thought, have also been instruments of submission, tools of a penetration serving as a kind of breaking and entering into the heart of other worldviews that language itself has contributed to scrambling. The very words that comprise the myriad of languages have also served to fracture the unity between human beings. Here, throughout our continent, nations have deemed it necessary to do away with certain names or designations that have not conformed to their aspirations, as they sought to take back control of their destiny. In these instances, such a practice was a necessity.

My objective here is not to call for a modification of the name *Africa*, even though such a name remains, for the most part, absent from my literary oeuvre. Rather, what I'm suggesting is that it's up to us to question for ourselves the very meanings of words themselves. To carefully look onto the horizon, and by way of the use of catachresis, to seek out new metaphors for how we can inhabit the continent and by which the practice of appropriation will not simply be one of an upheaval of stigmas attached to a certain name or relation but rather would serve as the foundation for an original autonomous project of civilization. Those who study literary texts know that beyond what a written text exposes at the level of narrative, it just as much conceals, in the vast depths of its catalysis, another semantic layer or level of meaning which can only be uncovered by way of a methodical analysis. Every text is irrigated by the theoretical discourse that produced it. And such additional discourse always exists whether the author is truly aware of it, or not. The same goes for any discourse regarding the name *Africa*. Such a designation cannot simply be understood as a mere place name. *Africa* is a narrative, and also a multisecular history that today deserves a broader meaning in order to fully take ownership of it. Every pan-African tradition rests on the content bestowed on the name *Africa* by those who seek to actualize it.

And yet, every one of the pan-African projects can either palliate or exacerbate the current situation on the continent, when for example they seek to dethrone the hegemony of foreign powers. The *Africa* text refers to a metalepsis whose meanings can be seen in the treatment, across all domains, reserved for the continent and its peoples. What the name *Africa* assumes for the rest of the world is not a mystery – we shouldn't get hung up on it. What is of much more vital import for us is what the name signifies for us. Since the name appears to have become acclimatized to our latitudes, we should perhaps say a few words about what such a name indicates, not so much with regard to our identities that are always in perpetual movement and incomplete, but in terms of our situation and perhaps even our very condition. Since to call oneself *African* – in sub-Saharan *Africa* – is to express a very complex being in the world that makes of our various peoples human groups almost without any homologues.

Sub-Saharan *Africans* are not merely the inhabitants of geographical and political spaces that are specifically named and subsequently limited by others. They walk along a long intimate rift that one could describe as being at once the trace of an always evanescent past whose diverse echoes they perceive within themselves, as well as a future whose contours remain fuzzy and inexact. Sub-Saharan *Africans* are in an uncomfortable zone, often the site of both yesterday's and today's aggressions, which will then become the very site of a rehabilitation, a healing, and a blossoming. More than overcoming the challenge of having to recover at the very site of a fall, the greater difficulty resides in the feeling of having to do so using the tools – languages, technosciences, economic systems, political structures, etc. – that once served its very destruction. There is nothing easy about recognizing that one is the child of both a colonial rapist and the colonizer's victim, of having to serve as the arbiter of such a trauma within oneself, of not being able to reject one of them without inflicting some form of self-harm. Not to mention that – in stark contrast to those descendants of sub-Saharan Africans deported to the Americas – one must confront such past violent conflicts on one's own ancestral soil and learn to bear the scars gracefully.

Since that's how it is, and because examples of such instances are rare on this scale, two powerful but contradictory temptations tend to operate in sub-Saharan societies. One proposes looking to the past for a self-image that would be sovereign, appreciated, and that had not been violated. The other envisions the future as an ongoing Westernization project heading in a better direction, the latter being for many synonymous with modernity and the triumph of rationality. It should be understood, of course, that such a presentation of the current situation is nothing more than a sketch. In reality, these two trends are not parallel but are in fact intertwined, permanently tied together, which nourishes an inner tension. It doesn't seem possible that one can truly speak of a transversality with regard to the definition of self in sub-Saharan *Africa*. Transversality is not a negotiation with the aforementioned tension; rather, it would be its resolution, the full acceptance and embrace of living with such a mutation. So as to render such an acceptance effective, one must doubtless recognize – *for one's self* – that to refer to oneself as *African*, in our sub-Saharan countries, is to recognize and understand that one is the result of, and carries within oneself, a number of deep wounds.

If the transatlantic deportation of sub-Saharan *Africans* and European colonization do not in and of themselves comprise the very signature of the birth certificate of our peoples, they are nevertheless quite clearly the matrices of our *Africanity*. I'm careful to refer to this term in the singular, as *Africanity* can be defined as what is held in common among diverse populations. And what this entails, at first sight, has more to do with historical experience than with culture, more to do with political conditions and the assorted turmoil of a postcolonial era that we still expect will finally fade away so as finally to leave us facing up to a new fully sovereign era. In his work *Afrotopia*, which we have all read with great enthusiasm, Felwine Sarr suggests, in particular, that we "provide a place for traditional and customary forms that have already been tested which have demonstrated their value and continue to do so in areas as diverse as conflict resolution, restorative justice, and forms of representation and legitimization."[6]

Related to our cultural differences, such a discussion raises the question of an attempt at an eventual harmonization of things in the fields mentioned by Sarr. The example of restorative justice in the way it was practiced in Rwanda more than likely can't be transposed elsewhere if we understand that such justice was a result of a very precise categorization with regard to the crime and the specific sanctions called for. The tradition that gave birth to such a practice is articulated in the very intimate experience of a people, and the specific acts concerned would more than likely be considered unresolvable in other regions on the continent. If we refer to the foundations of some of the other sub-Saharan cultures,[7] blood crimes were sanctioned by way of the banishment, pure and simple, of peoples, and led to a kind of unbridled nationalism prior to its more recent forms. The other example Sarr mentions regarding the commonly held notion of a "larger extended family of cousins" is perhaps viewed as exotic for those cultures where this isn't practiced.

What I'm attempting to clarify here is not so much the impossibility of finding in the common traditions of the continent modes of functioning that would allow *Africanity* to transcend the experience of colonial domination and the misguided paths of the postcolonial era, so that it could finally establish itself as an original model of civilization. It's simply the fact that a number of the cultures in question are sometimes rather divergent, and that the path toward an *Africanity* cured of its murderous bloodshed must, without a doubt, privilege creativity and the mixing of our cultures without necessarily influencing each other. On the continent, we hardly know each other, and we are rarely in the habit of partaking in practices from each other's cultures. What we share, what seems to align us, are first and foremost exogenous influences. And yet, the most important thing is to establish a future based no longer on a common bedrock tainted by a stigma – which is currently still the case – but, rather, on decisions taken together and in good conscience.

And it's this common vision that we will seek to apply to our spaces, as a means of achieving sovereignty. Given that sub-Saharan *Africa* is neither a vast Sahel nor some kind of large Rwanda, but, rather, an even greater expanse in which both these entities are nothing more than two elements, we must first and foremost begin by reflecting on the universals. What are they? Responses to this question will serve as prolegomena to a renewed thought concerning *Africa*. Sub-Saharan universals that one must shed light on have to do with sensibilities and the arts of living, philosophies, and spiritualities, which will serve as the foundations for the project of civilization. In order for the transposition of social practices to be accepted, so as to establish the possibility of elaborating a collective project, we must first uncover that which we already hold in common, reveal the cultural ties that existed prior to historical shocks, the persistent familial traits, the non-recessive characteristics. Once we've identified them, we will carefully examine them so as to retain only those whose value and utility have been proven.

Such proven traits may even need to be transformed when their expression, on the cusp of becoming obsolete, has to seek out an improved form for the sake of preservation. Such traits will also only be useful to the extent that they serve as reference points for establishing and inventing something entirely new.

And it shouldn't take long for us to realize that creativity will be an imperative for renewing this *Africanity*, guiding it beyond and away from the postcolonial phase in which it is currently still mired. We must be able to freely choose without abolishing cultural differences, since we are accustomed to a multicultural milieu – which is also characteristic of *Africanity*. It's therefore up to us to plumb the depths of our myriad and diverse cultural heritages and experiences so as to carefully select those we want to protect on the continent. And in those creative moments when we are not drawing from our concrete lived experience, such constitutive elements will emanate from dialogues and discussions during which our aspirations will have been expressed and shared. Of course, such a practice will require institutions, transnational organisms that have been formed for such tasks. This will also even imply that we will have to learn how to extract ourselves from various injunctions, mismanagements, or intrusions, or even striking and stumbling attempts at redirecting the project in hand. Such latter cases will certainly happen. What's more important here, in any case, is to select the initial receivers of a thought destined to nourish a liberatory action. The organization of non-mixed[8] events seems clearly necessary. Not in order to renew this taste for secrecy that may once have made our societies fragile, but because the transmission of knowledge is often reserved for restricted circles, which eventually hastened the disappearance of certain forms of knowledge. And yet, given that some of the difficulties in the sub-Saharan region are of a psycho-affective nature, we should not forget to take this into account. Outside these aforementioned instances, alliances and comradery with diverse partners should have a role to play, insofar as it is certainly true that the struggle we are engaged in also concerns elevating the human from wherever they might be, thereby freeing each of us from a given model that weighs us down and rejects fraternity.

In that light, it's not a question of denying Western influence, but of repudiating its hegemony so as to invent another model. Whenever the postcolonial vision sets its sights on a counter-discourse – an attitude that confirms the centrality of what we are attempting to oppose – what will be required is simply to remove ourselves from such a confrontation so as to express ourselves on our own terms, and first and foremost to ourselves. And this is what we have yet to attend to. We need to analyze our experience in a way that makes sense to ourselves. As long as this task hasn't been undertaken, *Africa* will remain the name of this deficiency, an emptiness disposed to welcoming the projections of those who provided it with a name. Prior to the upheavals that constituted the transatlantic deportation of sub-Saharan peoples and West European colonization – and I will insist on this point – nobody in this part of the world defined themselves as *African*. And it is indeed because of this that our people, both those on the continent and those who had undergone deportation or immigration, seek out other names, thereby exhuming or reinventing that of the ancestral land.

At first, the transatlantic deportation of sub-Saharan populations did not intervene in the trajectory of the *African* population that it mourns and mutilates; it's this that created these populations, that gave birth to them. As such, we are certainly the descendants of our ancestors, but we are first and foremost the fruits of the violence that was inflicted upon them. And if we must mention all our ancestors, honesty leads us to take into consideration all those whom we will never name, those whom we refuse to perceive as such since they were as much the operators as they were the beneficiaries of violence. And yet, in the current state of things, each time we refer to ourselves as *African*, we lay claim to both these lineages of belonging. They are inscribed in the very naming of the continent which is a mixture of a Berber and Roman origin, both of which have been reinterpreted from a European viewpoint.

Once all these elements have been posited, perhaps some of us will be ready to consider the notion of assimilation of the names *Africa* and *Africans* by sub-Saharan peoples as somewhat problematic. To reiterate: we are not seeking to advocate the banishment of the term, but rather to point out its profound significations, to express in what manner we are still tied, for the moment, to these terms. Each time we apply these labels to our ancestors whose daily life had yet to be influenced by the arrival of Europeans in the fifteenth century, we find ourselves making an egregious error and are even applying a falsification. Because of a lack of rigor, and perhaps also due to laziness, we have not bestowed a name on our ancestors – who were not *Africans* – and we end up hastily, by using *one word*, abolishing the distance that separates us from them. And yet it's quite clear that most contemporary sub-Saharan Africans attend to their daily life and reside in spaces where any remaining impression of the achievements or constructions of their elders is physically absent. Either such works have been destroyed – to the extent that the erasure of memory is one of the first gestures of domination. Or, because populations of a certain bygone era afforded little importance to the creation of an enduring material inscription of their presence in the material world, their only concern was generally to transmit oral narratives. Since then, the Westernized descendants of sub-Saharan peoples have felt the need to construct and retain archives, to visit and experience the relics and remnants of the past, as is the case elsewhere around the world.

If our ancestors reside within us, if they accompany us wherever we might be, they are nevertheless rarely surrounding us. The imagination alone allows us to represent them to ourselves in a world that was all their own. Neither the Chinese, nor the peoples of India, nor even those of Khmer, while also being inhabitants of a continent baptized by the West – none of them have had to confront such an incredible erasure of their cultural heritage. Outside gatherings and assemblies for political and economic aims, none of these cultures defines themselves as Asian. Nor, to my knowledge, have they ever sought out some ideal notion of what it means to be Asian, as has been attempted in the case of pan-Africanism, for example. And even this latter attempt is based on a fractured colonial past, on the ruptures that preceded it, and on a necessity due to this very interrupted history, so as to set in place a collective, transversal work that reinforces and allows African peoples to occupy an honorable place in a broader environment that now appears to be made up of large groups.

Africa could very well be the name of an original and sovereign project of civilization. It could be the name of a space whose populations are no longer principally federated by exogenous elements, but by the will to walk together toward a horizon that such populations will have given themselves. The obstacles in place are rather well known. The most frequent among them is the oft-cited pitiful quality of *leadership* on the continent. What is almost never mentioned is that contemporary sub-Saharan rulers are not some group of extra-terrestrials having arrived from some far-off galaxy. They are not just from amongst us; they are us. Before truly finding ourselves in a situation where we could validate replacing them, it is important to understand what part of *Africa* is incarnated within them. And that's not the least of the problems that we must elucidate. Every society produces both its shadows and the light that will dissipate such darkness. But the light is powerless faced with shadows whose source it cannot truly identify and can therefore only provisionally chase away. In truth, those who govern us, and the environment in which they attend to the life of citizens for whom they are responsible, constitute the figure of *Africa* as we currently conceive of it. All around us, the world is a projection of what we think of ourselves; it reflects the state of a consciousness that has been led astray. The forces of annihilation are often those to which we have delegated our power, due either to simply being accustomed to a misfortune that can no longer be endured, or to an utter exhaustion in face of innumerable shocks: for well over fifty years now, *Africa* has been the name of endless conflicts. The resilience demonstrated by sub-Saharan peoples in no way erases the experiences they have endured. Resilience alone does not lead toward any proper destination. Resilience is something that one carves out and carries within oneself. It's only by connecting it with other tools that one can then begin to recreate oneself. In other words, resilience only helps one to survive. As such, a thought based on a sovereign *Africa* cannot satisfy itself with resilience. The challenge of sovereignty, in the way it imposes itself, requires audacity. The first thing one must do is recognize to what extent we are made up of multiple forms of loss while also resisting any determinism of victimhood. To mourn that which is no longer is also to recognize that one is still alive – that is, one is an agent of possibles. In a now quite famous proclamation, Maya Angelou tells us: "You may encounter defeat but you must not be defeated. In fact, it may be necessary to encounter the defeats so you can know who you are, what you can rise from, and how you can still come out of it."

Such is the state of mind it's perhaps preferable to adopt. Not so much as a posture, but because it seems correct to do so given the experience of sub-Saharan Africa, marked as it is by this *melancholia africana* that Nathalie Etoke presents as a way of "resisting decline, of retaining a reverence for life counter to everything that attempts to render it profane."[9] As an essential resource, this *melancholia africana* that I consider as a creative and bright melancholy not only knows how to survive but it can also continue creative work in the very midst of troubled times. Such a melancholy knows how to set itself to work by relying on a joy that is not foreign to it (however surprising this might be to some) but is in fact one of its most well-known attributes. There is no doubt: *melancholia africana* emanates in the spiritual forces of sub-Saharan peoples and serves as one of the vital elements of the universal both of sub-Saharan Africa and of the diaspora, allowing itself to rise above suffering. At present, it must serve as an extension to the daily struggles and enrich itself with the cultural and social competences anchored in our communities, seek out the sources external to it that it may want to drink from in the future. It is incumbent on us to dare to define ourselves not only in terms of our needs and conceptions. The path cannot be dictated by others. Nor is the path lost and forgotten in some bygone era. It's up to us to invent a discourse that comprises our own language. To inhabit a space of the imagination that is still not frequented that often and from which we can give life to a new and fertile reality.

Epistemological Impasses Concerning the Object Africa

Imprudence and Impudence of a Subjugated Exoticism and a Hyperbolic Narcissism

Maurice Soudieck Dione

Maurice Soudieck Dione is a research instructor at the Université du Gaston-Berger de Saint-Louis. He received his doctorate in political science from the Institut d'études politiques in Bordeaux and also holds two Master's degrees, in philosophy (with an emphasis on religion and politics) and in information sciences and communication, from the Michel de Montaigne University, Bordeaux 3. He also holds a Master's in public law and international relations from the University of Cheikh Anta Diop in Dakar. From 2001 to 2004, he served as a research engineer at the CNRS at the Centre d'étude d'Afrique noire (CEAN) in Bordeaux.

Often considered as an exotic scientific object that authorizes all sorts of excessive caricatures, containing – at the epistemological level – a vast array of virtues and sparkling splendors, artifice and artifacts of scientificity, there are a significant number of difficulties involved in projecting a thought concerning Africa or in apprehending Africa by way of thought. For there still exist reflexive and expressive biases induced by the existence and persistence of asymmetrical relations of domination and exploitation with the West, and whose crucial games [*jeux*] and stakes [*enjeux*] are prolonged, declined, and perpetuated on the scientific and intellectual terrain.

The dominant thought of intellectuals seems to have hit a wall and finds itself unable to grasp the intrinsic and dynamic logic of an evolution specific to the African continent; it appears to continue willfully to nourish and perpetuate power relations founded on an ongoing devaluation of otherness.

A hyperbolic narcissism and a subjugated exoticism seem therefore to be engaged in a circular and dialectical relation. For the overvaluation of the political, economic, cultural, and social model of the West – to the point of making it the very exclusive and excluding measuring stick by which other human societies or foreign cultures take to appreciating their own evolving qualities and capacities, thereby subjugating these other cultures and placing upon them a sense of inferiority – is still sustained by an impetuous élan of restoration-reinvigoration of self-esteem, an upward replicating movement, consisting of constructing some sort of exalting form of thought for Africa in a dithyrambic manner.

Attempts at a synthesis by means of a cosmopolitanism and a universal and liberatory fraternity, based on dignity and equality, more philosophical, poetic, and aesthetic than political or sociological, seem often to have ignored the reality of things and the complexity and concrete contradictions of various powers and interests.

Throughout the course of these preliminary precisions, and in light of all that has come before, the uncontrollable traps of a universalist thought still merit reflection, as do the uncomfortable origins of a relativistic thought.

The uncontrollable traps of a universalist thought

The hegemonic ruses concerning developmentalism

Serving as a scaffold in the context of the Cold War, as regards the newly independent states (and more specifically in this case, those in Africa), developmentalist theories seem to have obeyed an ideological posture and positioning of harvest and capture, in the sphere of American influence, in order that they do not fall into the lap of the Soviets.

Through the academic institution called the Social Science Research Council, the United States launched a vast research program concerning the issue of development, based on a concept of modernization and resting on an ensemble of simultaneous transformations: from a subsistence economy to a market economy, from a political culture of subjugation to a political culture of participation, from the extended family to the nuclear family, from a system marked by the primacy of the religious to a secularized system. The emblematic figures of this movement were, among others, Gabriel Almond, Sydney Verba, David Apter, James Coleman, Lucian Pye, Edward Shils, Daniel Lerner, Samuel Huntington, and Seymour Martin Lipset.[1]

Throughout this complex project, the US development model is presented as the *nec plus ultra*, the pinnacle of a unidirectional and unilinear evolution of all human societies, politically and economically, culturally and socially.

Economics is generally set up as an essential matrix, for example in the Rostow model,[2] or the correlation established by Lipset: the higher the overall standard of living of a nation, the greater the chances of establishing a democracy.[3]

Basically, in the eyes of the developmentalists, there is no difference between Western countries and non-Western countries; rather, all that remains is nothing more than a difference of degree as regards economic development, a differentiation and complexity of political structures – the development thereby being inscribed in the genetic and genealogical code of each society.

Developmentalism places the accent on the universality of concepts and practices, and relegates to the background the local dynamics of the evolution of human societies, in time and space. For, even if they are carefully scrutinized and located, the specificities and nuances of each country – in Africa as much as elsewhere – have been called upon, during the process of modernization, to forgo part of their cultural uniqueness. And yet, universalism cannot even stand up to comparison between European countries, which, in spite of convergences and common characteristics in their sociopolitical trajectories, also possess their own irreducible particularities.[4]

In Africa, developmentalist theories are received and quickly instrumentalized by the many authoritarian, nepotistic, and neo-patrimonialist regimes that seek to negate and transgress human rights and liberties in the name of some kind of mythic or mystical ends of national construction and development;[5] they are also often used to mobilize endogenous doctrines such as the authenticity of Zaire or Togo[6] in order to assuage and self-legitimize politically and ideologically oppressive and corrupt delirium. At an institutional level, one can find at work, in a reckless and frenetic decalcomania, various mixtures of colonial governmental structures and infrastructures.[7]

The disavowed and unavowable foundations of developmentalism are laid bare by the school of dependency, which equally understood how to play its part in the power struggles and precedence in the international system, crossed as it was, moreover, by logics of recuperation, most notably via the socialist ideology that underpinned it.

The hegemonic ruses concerning dependentism

Taking its inspiration from Marxism, the dependentist paradigm was born at the beginning of the 1960s and expresses a continuation of the Cold War at a scientific level. Africa therefore found itself as a crucial political stake regarding questions of intellectual production. Developmentalism is understood to be an imperialist ideology, since the largely unequal, structural, and functional political and economic relations between the Global North, the Center, and the Global South, the periphery, underpin the development of the North, the corollary of which is the underdevelopment of the South. Reduced in the international division of labor to the production of commercialized raw materials in a disproportionate exchange system, the industrialization efforts in the third world increase its dependency on the so-called first world, via an unrestricted economy.

The moderate dependentists, notably the economists of ECLAC (Economic Commission of the United Nations for Latin America) under the direction of Raúl Prebisch between 1948 and 1962,[8] and featuring the work of the likes of authors such as Enzo Faletto and Fernando Henrique Cardoso,[9] estimate that, since the gains in productivity are actually higher in the Global South than in the Global North, the restrictions in the South on the export of more raw materials lead to an ongoing deterioration in terms of exchange that must constantly be corrected, most notably through an "industrialization by way a substitution of importations," actively organized and coordinated by the state, in the framework of a regional integration.

For André Gunder Franck, Samir Amin, and Immanuel Wallerstein,[10] the gears of the state are controlled by a peripheral bourgeoisie, in collusion with the dominant central bourgeoisie, to which it is bound by capitalist interests. As a result of the meager compensation that the dominant class receives from this dependence, the peripheral state bourgeoisie maintains the status quo through authoritarianism, if necessary, and with the purported aim of modernizing society.

Franck calls for a socialist revolution, while Amin calls for a disconnection from the global capitalist system requiring the installation of a self-reproducing economic system along with the articulation of goods and consumption as well as the requisite equipment for state planning, all in a framework of large collectivities.

In this manner, the dependentist school appears to be reactive in relation to the developmentalist paradigm and, as such, is nothing more than a continuation of the economic and social contradictions of an industrialized Europe projected onto Africa, which nevertheless contains other realities, as well as other social and cultural realities. By sticking with an anti-imperialist, anti-capitalist ideological explanation of politico-economic problems of the countries in the Global South, the school of dependence presents the major disadvantage of focusing exclusively on the "dynamics of the outside" to the detriment of the "dynamics of the inside,"[11] thereby creating the illusion of a transformation analogous with that of societies. As if it were enough, as soon as the capitalist ties of dependence are broken, for the desired internal changes to take place by themselves, as if by magic. The explanation for the dynamics of human societies can only be established through an economicist and mechanistic, transhistorical, transcultural, and universal overdetermination. For the economic act is first and foremost a social relationship,[12] and the economy is not conceived of in the same manner in every culture and its interconnectedness with the political and the social are therefore also not universally of the same nature.[13]

Furthermore, the referential matrix of the dependency theorists – scientific socialism – has been appropriated by African elites, with various intellectual efforts of tropicalization,[14] so as to construct an African or Africanized socialism.[15] In this sense, Senghorian socialism was purged of class struggle and atheism, and bestowed value on spiritual activities through the practice of religion and creative and artistic activities.[16] Established through the coupling of the development of administration and administrative development, it is doomed to failure because of a systematic and systemic clientelism, organized around politicians, spiritual leaders [*marabouts*], and businesspeople,[17] and leading to the bankruptcy of the state and placing it under eventual economic and financial supervision by the institutions of the Bretton Wood Accords.[18]

Beyond developmentalism and dependency and their reinterpretations and reappropriations for hegemonic, imperialist, or domestic ends,[19] African nation-states, invigorated by the Afro-Asianism of the Bandung conference, attempt a third way by means of a non-aligned movement. In most instances, such a realignment is done expressively or tacitly through an attachment to superpowers – through a diplomacy of upheaval: announced effects followed by the called-for effects, or sometimes not, with regard to the modification of political alliances and economic interests.[20] Moreover, the mega-powers, by balancing terror born of reciprocal nuclear deterrence, shelter their territories, and, through intermediary clients,[21] transfer their rivalries across the third world and in Africa in particular, through a controlled escalation of violence so as to avoid direct confrontation between the Titans.

In order to overcome these contradictions, a universalist thought proposes solutions arising out of a philosophical, ethical, and poetic order whose feasibility is problematic since it is situated outside relations of force, power, and specific interests that are often the determining and decisive factors in relations between state actors. Hence the lack of success for reclamations in the framework of the United Nations with regard to a new international economic order (NIEO),[22] of a new world information and communication order (NWIO),[23] and a new cultural and international order (NCIO). Hence the equally difficult attempts at building a universality rich in all the particularities of humanity, such as Léopold Sédar Senghor's civilization of the universal, also referred to as a rendezvous of giving and receiving,[24] which should be distinguished from a universal civilization resulting from a hegemonic and impoverishing universalization of culture; the construction of Senghor's civilization of the universal requires an opening that rests on an integration and recognition of cultural roots [enracinement], which thus implies some sort of thought that is culturally relativistic but which also suffers from certain idiosyncrasies or peculiarities.

The uncomfortable seats at the table of relativistic thought

Devaluing relativistic thought

Influenced by anthropology, as a reaction against dependency and developmentalist determinism, and the formalism of the juridico-institutional analysis,[25] the paradigm of politics from below in sub-Saharan Africa is initiated by way of a diverse number of specialists in the social sciences: historians, anthropologists, geographers, sociologists, linguists, political scientists – gathered around such figures as Jean-François Bayart, Christian Coulon, Comi Toulabour, and Achille Mbembe, inspired by thinkers such as Michel Foucault, Michel de Certeau, Georges Balandier, and Antonio Gramsci.

In the context of the 1980s, marked by a generalization of authoritarian regimes,[26] capacities for innovation, for a resistance and contestation of the order established by the dominant powers,[27] are privileged through modes of "popular political action"[28] or via UPOs (unidentified political objects),[29] such as music, dance, theater, violence, parallel economic networks, religion, sorcery, sport, ruse, silence, escapism, games, and jokes.[30]

Nevertheless, in spite of its attraction, this paradigm, in distancing itself from aristocratic sites of political science,[31] even without wanting to do so intentionally, produces the pernicious effect of stamping a seal of exoticism and subjugation on African studies, besides substantially jeopardizing the transition to the political arena,[32] due to the overinterpretation of facts or activities; hence the risk of substituting the subjectivity of the researcher with that of the actors, by conflating registers of behavior and action:[33] behaviors that are politically tolerable in an authoritarian situation[34] and subversive political actions requiring the planification of a counter-elite,[35] which cannot emerge without arousing the suspicions of power or, as a consequence, inducing repression.

And yet, today, very real dynamics of democratization are under way on the African continent, with elections leading to political change in Senegal, Mali, Benin, Ghana, and Kenya, as well as the additional exercises and practices of certain democratic freedoms. Why, then, should we remain exclusively in a reflexive posture from "below" for studying certain political phenomena that arise first and foremost from "above"? All the more so considering that a politics from below can be considered as "a politics of elsewhere"[36] in Western democracies, which doesn't exclude, for all that, the ongoing analysis of democratic institutions and canonical objects of political science, and even though the distinction between a politics from above and from below seems artificial, since the two levels partake in dialectical interactions.[37] They can be seen to complement each other in a fruitful manner if we consider, for example, the role played by rap music in social movements, such as *Y'en a marre* or M23 (Movement of June 23) for reinforcing democratic practices in Senegal in order to curb the abuses of the political regime under President Wade,[38] serving as a filter for "popular modes of political action," to provide just two artistic examples whose creative expressions and intentions were clearly focused on a certain political aim.

And yet, a certain paradigm or metaphor in Africa still remains, what Jean-François Bayart refers to as "a gut politics"[39] that doesn't take into account such ongoing evolutions in democratic practices.

Returning to the Braudelian idea of the continuity of civilizations,[40] Bayart shows, beyond the specific forms, how Africa manipulates Western domination within its borders, from which it continues to draw its dividends tied to the perpetuation of external regimes of income along with internal underdevelopment: "Today, as yesterday, Africa continues to export its factors of production – labor force, capital and raw materials – and the actors that manage this unequal relationship with the international economic system acquire resources from their own domestic domination."[41] They reject in the wake of this process a "paradigmatic yoke": the positioning of a yoke of Western countries on African countries and indigenous despots on their own people; a yoke imposed by an inclement nature and an obtuse tradition on a continent in decline.[42]

The state in Africa is not merely an exogenous structure, it's a rhizome state: "a protean multiplicity of networks whose subterranean stems connect a multitude of spread-out points across society."[43] The baroque character of cultural and political hybridization becomes conflated with the governability of manducation: so-called "gut politics" as a demonstration of the attributes of wealth and power through political and symbolic accumulation, through a magnificence and munificence expressed by way of a corpulence of valuable alloys and smooth talking – a game of many mistresses; furthermore, such a practice is maintained and perpetuated via a mastery of invisible forces, a form of sorcery.[44] The historicity of the state in Africa becomes a history of extraversion,[45] confined to the constraints of an unequal exchange with the exterior:[46] it becomes nothing less than the ongoing historical growth of the West.

As such, Bayart, it would seem, sees all politics exclusively in terms of sexual and material consideration that prevents us from truly envisioning any other possibility for a true economic evolution in terms of hybridization, beyond a mere "gut politics": "I graze, therefore I am," which precisely limits the very contours and perimeters of "the field of possible politics"[47] in postcolonial African societies.

In this light, it doesn't take much for one to collapse under the weight of the theses of cultural violence sometimes containing very pessimistic undertones,[48] often deterministic, as can be seen in the work of Patrick Chabal and Jean-Pascal Daloz, who, by way of the paradigm of the "instrumentalization of disorder,"[49] carefully reference the benefits that can be drawn from sowing disorder, uncertainty, and even from the chaos that reigns in most African political systems,[50] as a specific form of modernity,[51] where we see, in the grand finale, cohabitation of the informal and the infralegal, the noncodified and the nonpoliced.

The informalization of the political is characterized by a structural weakness of the state, the nonexistence of a civil society, and the recycling in a closed system of political personnel, and the re-traditionalization of society, through a communitarization of relationships, ethnicity, and sorcery, the Africanization of Islam and Christianity, leading Africans to act almost simultaneously in registers that are as contemporary as they are traditional. An increase in wealth by way of illegal but not illegitimate criminal activities, corruption properly understood, nourished by the fruits of economic failure and the interest of dependence, explain the insignificance of development.

In the end, five decisive points will help us to decipher the politics of sub-Saharan Africa: (1) the subordination of the individual to the group; (2) the imperative of reciprocity in the exchange; (3) a strongly personalized relation of inequality; (4) a conception of success involving generosity through a targeted redistribution rather than a productive form of savings; (5) primacy of the short term over the long term: a prevalence concerning immediate, factional, and concrete interests to the detriment of superior macropolitical perspectives.[52]

The deconstruction of this thesis, first in relation to violence, leads us back to the difficulty of upholding the thesis that for many countries – not including those at war – the overarching reasoning or elemental logic behind political decision-making[53] is to be understood in terms of a globalization of criminal activities. Because the criminalization of the political is more a sign of a collapse of the political or its delinquency rather than a properly organized form of the political. Furthermore, ethnic conflicts are not unique to Africa: in Eastern Europe, after the fall of the communist bloc, we saw a significant number of violent identarian confrontations, most notably in ex-Yugoslavia.[54]

The argument that there is a re-traditionalization under way throughout the world, resulting from an entanglement of the repertoires of the rational and the irrational, is erroneous since there has always been a permanent osmosis between tradition and modernity, including in the Global North where African *marabouts* prosper all the more from their European clientele,[55] not to mention the ongoing unbridled growth of the most whimsical and fantasy-laden sects whose gurus have generated vast numbers of victims in their wake. Lest we forget, as well, the increase in para-psychology: horoscope, fortune-telling, astrology, etc.

In the same manner, politics cannot be exclusively understood via its informal aspects, since its roles, official attributes, and formal rules, as support for domination, fill a symbolic role for the legitimization of power,[56] in the same way that corruption can't be simply understood as a purely African particularity, since its aspects can be found in most political systems the world over, most notably in Europe.[57]

In reality, by positing the criteria for specifying the political in Africa, Daloz and Chabal seem to have crystalized their findings – often generalized for the entire continent starting from a single country – in considering cultural elements that will forever be static and fossilized, whereas culture is a dynamically social product. And first and foremost, it is always in a state of movement and chance, being endlessly nourished by fruitful outside influences.

In other words, history is always an eternal new beginning, to the extent that this could take place under these conditions. For in the current system, there is no room for free movement, for freedom, for individuals that would grant them the space to cultivate their own unique creative capacities; they are understood merely as robots programmed once and for all in a singular cultural logic, viewed as nothing more than passive objects rather than as active and inventive subjects of their own becoming, in a process of continuing transformation comprising constraints that serve as inventive opportunities, which is the principal matrix at work in the evolution of every human society.

Understood in this way, individuals would be nothing more than agents that have been crushed under the weight of the cultural and communitarian structure, since the monetarization of the economy, urbanization, scholarization, the demonstrative effects of imitation drawn from wealthy countries in the realm of consumption, the economic crisis, the development of medias, etc., end up seeking to conquer the very impulse of the process of individuation.[58]

From this ensemble of ideas, it would seem that a certain relativistic thought, starting from a presupposed conception of African culture, has a tendency to continuously reproduce nothing more than clichés that are supposed in fact to fight, when the particular is not itself a justification for establishing a debased intellect. Hence the necessity and actuality for a thought that would seek to restore harmony and balance, but which in and of itself could be understood as biased or skewed in its own élan, based on a variety of often passionate identarian issues that underpin such restorative attempts.

An enthusiastic relativistic thought

This is the perspective one should keep in mind and inscribe in seeking to understand the literary and cultural movement of negritude that came to life in France during the 1930s, in order to respond to, as Amadou Kane put it, "the insolence of Europe that claimed to have colonized Africa, a barbaric soil, and who filled a cultural void thanks to their European civilization and its faith in democratic and humanitarian ideas."[59] In such a militant optic, what was at stake was an attempt to reclaim, defend, establish, and illustrate the values of a Black civilization, and to thereby allow Africans to regain a sense of their dignity and pride that had been kicked to the ground by a Western culture that had become full of itself, in order to establish the foundations whereby Africans themselves could take responsibility for their own destiny.

With this in mind, Aimé Césaire gives the example of the genius of African civilization from the twelfth to the fifteenth century: in Ghana, Mali, and Sonrhai,[60] where the Senegalese historian Cheikh Anta Diop traced it all the way back to the Egyptian pharaohs, to the Black civilizations of Egypt that civilized the world, and whose materiality of existence is incontestable – as the mummies, pyramids, columns, steles, and sculptures all attest to. From these historical facts alone, we can suddenly recognize that scientific and technological forms of knowledge do not merely belong to or derive from European cultures and were therefore diffused into other cultures through colonization. They existed much earlier already in Egypt – the cradle of civilization, where Greek thinkers, Thales of Miletus, Pythagoras of Samos, Archimedes of Sicily, Plato, Sabon, all traveled in order to discover knowledge from Egyptian high priests.[61]

To support his thesis of a Black Egypt, Cheikh Anta Diop provides some striking similarities, at both a linguistic and a cultural level, between ancient Egypt and African societies: totemism, circumcision, a vitalist conception of royalty, a kinship between the Egyptian language and African languages at both grammatical and lexical levels, etc.[62] He also has unanimous support from the ancients: Herodotus, Diodorus, Strabo, Pliny, Tacitus, who all taught, each in their time, that the Egyptians had black skin and frizzy hair.[63] And yet, Champollion de Figeac declared that these characteristics were not enough evidence to classify a Black person. But if that was the case, would we have not already come across some other people with black skin and frizzy hair that were not Black? In reality, for Cheikh Anta Diop, imperialism was the explanatory infrastructure for this larger ideological superstructure that led to the falsification of history, for hegemonic means, produced by "scientists" with a rather suspicious intellectual integrity.[64]

From then on, for the Senegalese Egyptologist, the liberation of Africa would only come about by way of a work involving the rewriting of history:

> The Black African is unaware that his ancestors, who adapted to the material conditions of the valley of the Nile, were in fact humanity's oldest guides on the path to civilization; that it was they who created the arts, religion (in particular monotheism), literature, the first philosophical systems, the invention of writing, the exact sciences (physics, mathematics, mechanics, astronomy, the calendar, etc.), medicine, architecture, agriculture, etc., during an era when the rest of the earth (Asia, Europe: Greece and Rome ...) were plunged into barbarism.[65]

The inculcation of this historical truth should put an end to "the floating of the personality of the African"[66] in order to allow him or her to "rediscover the continuity of their history and the consistency of their culture, while simultaneously acquiring the means for adapting their history and culture to modern demands";[67] so as to regain confidence and a fully integrated interiority – different than that of a mere sufficiency – and without which every human effort is hypothetical.[68] It thus becomes a question of "cadaverizing the old negritude"[69] as some sort of form of cultural domestication and retaining a partial inferiority complex, in a lived experience of self that is nothing more than a dead end, so as to resolutely engage in the conquest of the world, where there is a place for everyone, for "no race possesses a monopoly over beauty, intelligence, and force."[70] The only weapon that has any merit is the strong and unwavering will, drawn from the inexhaustible depths of an ego [*moi*] that has been rediscovered and which is reconciled with itself. And in so doing, according to the Martiniquan poet, Africa and Africans should be the most rigorous and demanding with regard to themselves, due to the continent's numerous difficulties, and the unspeakable suffering endured throughout the course of its history.[71]

In conclusion, the deconstruction of scientific and intellectual production, in the ideological and hegemonic foundational undercurrents, is a categorical imperative, for its insidious reappropriation stifles and confines Africa in a subjugated relationship with the West, at once bestowing upon Africa a sense of inferiority as well as a lesser sense of self-worth.

In the end, such a situation creates, by way of thought, an inverse excess overvaluation of the continent that is likely to be founded on denials of reality that are inherently linked to an enthusiastically proud conception of an identity of regeneration and revitalization of self-esteem, which has, for a long time now, continually wreaked havoc across the continent. Hence the analytical construction of competing and expanding ideals of thinking subjects, tending to distance themselves and seeking their autonomy in relation to a profound intelligibility of the object of thought: Africa.

The vastness, the enormity, and the acuity of the continent's ailments seem to exert a certain coercion on words and thought, to the point that sometimes such thought falls into a missionary catechism of civilization founded on solidarity and fraternity, of a bygone "civilizing mission" whose bearers we have never truly believed, today as much as yesterday.

In order to overcome this dead end, what is required is an African thought – not an African way of thinking. If that were the case, we would simply find ourselves succumbing to the same old traps and clichés. Rather, what is required is a thought formed by Africans concerned with Africa, emancipated from ideological postures, illuminating as much as programmatic and pragmatic, taking as its point of departure a lucid and realist analysis regarding all the problems on the continent, and, in order to resolve the impasses, they must elaborate strategies of the infusion and distribution of this thought at both the more elite levels and the popular levels, so as to mobilize the diverse political, social, cultural, and intellectual actors concerned, regarding its effectuation.

Reinventing African Modernity

Blondin Cissé

Blondin Cissé *holds degrees from the Paris Diderot University (Paris 7) in philosophy and political science. From 2008 to 2012, he was a researcher in the Laboratory of Political and Social Change (LCSP) of Paris 7, where he taught political philosophy. Currently, he is a lecturer at the Université Gaston-Berger de Saint-Louis-du-Sénégal, at the Centre d'étude des religions (UFR Crac), where he coordinates the Observatory for Civil African Societies in the Laboratory of the Societies and Powers of Africa and the Diaspora (Laspad).*

> Set thyself free from such a jagged, narrow space
> Escaping any ties with all dimensions
> Spread out, like the heavens, in all directions.
> The scent of a rose, in leaving it be,
> Will flee and spread itself throughout the rest of the garden.
> Thou, paralyzed in a nook of the prairie,
> Like a nightingale, you merely are content with one rose.
>   Mohammad Iqbal[1]

Ousseynou Kane, former chair of the University of Cheikh Anta Diop's (UCAD) philosophy department from 1990 to 2000, once opened a lecture by recalling, in front of a group of politicians and intellectuals, the claims of an eminent African intellectual whose diagnosis, in the course of his presentation, was that the ailments the continent was suffering from consisted of something he called "colloquium-itis, panel-presentation-itis, and conference-itis," before ending with, in a rather ironic manner, the following remark: "Asians don't engage in many conferences or colloquiums, but they sure do work a lot."

There must surely be something in such remarks that has influenced the politics of emergence in Africa, placing more of an emphasis on the economy than on the fundamental element of development: culture. As a result, it would perhaps be important to recall that the first utterance of the concept of culture, as conceived by the philosophers of ancient Greece, was through the notion of *paideia*, denoting both the teaching of human qualities as well as the ensemble of forms of knowledge that an individual must possess to rise to the level of a Greek citizen. Cicero used the term "culture" for the first time in his essay *Cultura animi philosophia*,[2] in order to signify any activity that would serve for the mental development by which humans would be able to access philosophical, scientific, ethical, and artistic knowledge. Such a humanist perspective of culture is all the more amplified, even perhaps surpassed, by the Cameroonian philosopher Fabien Eboussi Boulaga, who inscribes culture in a dynamic process of self-emergence, of the becoming-person, who actualizes the infinite potentialities of the individual in permanent tension toward the search for ideals and the total expression of freedom. Hence his comments in *Christanisme sans fétiche*: "The concept of culture is that by which man apprehends himself as genesis, as the auto-production of self, starting from the fact that he is no longer in search of that which he is not yet."[3]

And in that light, our method here today is to reconnect with our shattered heritages, our lost treasures, and therefore to reconstruct our relation to memory, since historiography is derived from the art of war above all in the context of a defragmentation and disintegration of human cultures in the name of the phenomenon of globalization, whose hegemonic pretensions are deployed under the pretext of development, the logic of progress, the growth of humanity, and the well-being of peoples. What is at stake in this operation is less the displacement of peoples, instruments, and forms of knowledge, and more the very deterritorialization of memory and the delocalization of mental structures.[4]

If it is fundamental to differentiate ourselves from a Eurocentric and imperialist vision of development in order to find an African path that is original and capable of integrating all the dimensions of being-in-the-world-of-the-*homo-africanus*, in a political, economic, and sociocultural logic of progress – in a way similar to that proposed by African socialism – our integral development also supposes, like Marcien Towa, the "firm decision to submit our cultural heritage to a critique without complaisance."[5]

On this perspective, would African modernity not end up letting itself be captured by a process of exiting the cloisters of a traditional Africa reliant on the supernatural or the fantastic – thereby yielding to a process of emergence of a "subject defined by its participation in opposites,"[6] that is, an identity that could be described as a *disidentifying identity* to the extent that it manifests an *I* tearing itself away from identitary inscription so as to expose itself to the outside?

Should we therefore sound the funeral prayer for African tradition, that is, refuse this moment of petrification in which it has been enclosed, sometimes unwillingly, by a certain intelligentsia in order to elaborate yet another management of memory at once faithful to the fundamentals of tradition yet also open to the future?

In this case, will African tradition end up positioning itself as the African modernity of tomorrow, above all if the modernity to which it has been accustomed until now continues to position itself as an exogenous memory, thereby imposing its political, economic, and cultural schemas thanks to a techno-scientific infrastructure that defines its own modernity?[7]

How, then, can we not think of Cheikh Anta Diop, who, in *Civilization or Barbarism*,[8] places an emphasis on the need for Africa to (re)connect with its more ancient past – since modernity has made out of the continent the very enterprise for a practice of disconnection: "The essential thing, for people, is to rediscover the thread that connects them to their most remote ancestral past. In the face of cultural aggressions of all sorts, in the face of a myriad of disintegrating factors from the outside world, the most efficient cultural weapon with which a people can arm itself is this feeling of historical continuity."[9]

From this perspective, if the condition of the African-being-there-in-the-current-world is dependent on our capacity to bear and hold onto the flame of tradition, the true question is knowing how to view this tradition with fresh eyes so as not merely to be content with the warmth still procured by its ashes, but rather to take these remaining glowing embers so as to light other flames. This is precisely the meaning of Jaurés's claim that tradition "does not consist in a conservation of ashes but in attending to keeping the fire burning."

In this chapter, my objective is, on the one hand, to revisit briefly several trajectories that allow us to think "a reinvention of African modernity," *hic et nunc*, starting from resources specific to African literature and philosophy through the thought of the Senegalese theoretician of negritude Léopold Sédar Senghor, of the Ghanaian philosopher Kwame Nkrumah, and the Cameroonian philosopher Marcien Towa, all of whom inscribed themselves in Black African ideologies, essentially produced by the Black African intelligentsia of Western descent, and centered around the postulate of a specific cultural identity and the social singularity of Black Africa.

Senghor and the philosophy of complementarity

Senghor's (1906–2001) idea is deployed through an African re-reading of Marxism and its model: socialism. Established around the concept of negritude, which he defines as "the sum of the cultural values of the Black world,"[10] Senghor's socialism is a critical adaptation of an experience of European politics to the conditions in Africa. But, if Senghor's socialism finds its foundation in an affirmation of the Black man and the liberation of his continent, his thought is conceived as a *philosophy of complementarity* functioning according to the dual demand of rooting in *Us*, that is, Black African traditions, while also maintaining an openness to modernity that is the *Other*. In *Nation et voie africaine du socialisme*, Senghor outlines his project: "It's about inserting our nation not only into the Africa of today, but also into the civilization of the Universal still to be edified. This will be a symbiosis of the most fertile elements of all civilizations."[11]

According to Senghor, it becomes a question of self-development, while also encouraging a dialogue among nations in order, finally, to constitute a panhuman civilization whose pertinence would be conferred by way of the plurality of the elements composing it. In other words, if this cosmopolitical vision can only be expressed by way of an adaptation of the Black African realities to the demands of the modern world, the necessary integration of the European political, social, and economic contributions remains, according to Senghor, an epistemological demand for African socialism. Thus, for Senghor, the "African rediscovery of Marxism" presupposes an endogenous reappropriation of his model, socialism – in other words, a road toward socialism conceived by Africans that would be rooted in African cultural values. Senghor demonstrates that such a point of view is not at odds with Marxism, and he backs up his claims by citing Marx's own reflections made in his *Eighteenth Brumaire of Louis Bonaparte*: "Man makes their own history, but he does not make it out of the whole cloth; he does not make it out of conditions chosen by himself, but out of such as he finds close at hand. The tradition of all past generations weighs like an alp upon the brain of the living."[12]

It's quite clear: Senghor's socialism is at once thought and action, a thought that has taken into account African reality, and an action that aims for the development of the African and his continent; hence his deployment of a veritable social praxis conceived in light of the concrete realities specific to Africa. In this light, Senghor writes: "A revolution remains ideological, and inefficient, as long as it is not practiced in a concrete action that, in transforming the structures, elevates the quality of life and culture of its citizens."[13]

Nkrumah or philosophical synthesis

Considered as one the most important moments of African socialism, the political thought of Kwame Nkrumah (1909–72), like that of Senghor, proposed to undertake a critical analysis of Marxism by having it confront African realities. In contrast to Senghor's critical analysis advocating an *African re-reading of Marxism*, Nkrumah's critique will lead to a new ideological thought predicated on the new situation in which Africa now found itself, consciencism, since the implementation of this ideology, he thought, could be explained at once by way of a profound mutation that Africa was in the midst of experiencing along with external elements arriving from outside African society. And it's for this reason that Nkrumah divides African society into three classes:

1. A class that is very well anchored in African values, faithful to the African traditional way of life.
2. A class that represents the presence of the Muslim tradition in Africa.
3. And finally, a class that represents the "Christian tradition and that of Western European civilization."

As a result of this, consciencism will have, as one of its foundational tasks, to synthesize the history of traditional African experience with the Muslim and European Christian experience. In other words, it is a question of merging these three classes into one during the process of transformation of African society. This point is essential in the Ghanaian's thinking, since, according to him, the separation and opposition of these three classes inevitably lead to a *social schizophrenia* at the antipodes of the liberation and development of Africa. And it's in this way that he defines his philosophy as "a new harmony that needs to be forged, a harmony that will allow for the combined presence of traditional Africa, Islamic Africa and Euro-Christian Africa, so that this presence is in tune with the original humanist principles underlying African society."[14] In other words, Nkrumah's doctrine can be understood as a philosophy of social praxis allowing Africans to become aware of their situation and to integrate traditional, Islamic, and Christian elements adapted to the *African personality*. Once assimilated, these different elements should be used with an eye toward helping with the harmonious development of African society on the basis of an ideology capable of accounting for the new metaphors of this society, hence Nkrumah's following comments in his work *Consciencism*: "Such a philosophical statement I propose to name *philosophical consciencism*, for it will give the theoretical basis for an ideology whose aim shall be to contain African experience of Islamic and Euro-Christian presence as well as the experience of traditional African society, and, by gestation, employ them for harmonious growth and development of that society."[15]

And so the function of consciencism becomes apparent, consisting not only in furnishing Africans with a doctrine capable of affirming them and recognizing their situation, but also in organizing their society by integrating external inputs for the betterment of their social, economic, and cultural development – hence Nkrumah's conception of consciencism as at once materialist and dialectical. Nevertheless, this philosophy, which presents itself as an extension of Marxism, is, in reality, a contextualization of this doctrine with regard to the already existing ideological superstructure and new African overdeterminations. In other words, if philosophical consciencism anchors itself in dialectical materialism, this in no way prevents it from embracing the contours of African society. But contrary to Marxism, while Nkrumah's materialism certainly recognizes the primacy of matter over idea, it remains profoundly rooted in the universe of the spiritual and religious values of the African, as can be seen when he writes, "Philosophical consciencism, even though deeply rooted in materialism, is not necessarily atheistic."[16]

Towa and the theory of alienation

Amplifying Nkrumah's perspective, which serves as an expression or way to reconcile contradictory terms (us/other, tradition/modernity ...) *in a manner that that allows for assumptions*, Towa (1931–2014) reflects on the situation of the African man in the modern world and discerns his lack of freedom. But in contrast to those who blame others for this, he asserts that the servitude of the African should be posited in the very relationship that he has with himself and not with the other. Placing himself at the antipodes of a differentialism, Towa posits the theory of *resemblance*, whose realization supposes that the African exits his particularity by elevating himself to the level of the *universal*. If overcoming this dilemma is resolved by way of *overcoming* and *alteration*, the challenge of this resemblance to the other is inscribed in a logic of "appropriation of a miraculous weapon of the West" – in other words, it is a question of overcoming our *differentialism* in order to snatch the secrets of the Other and his victory, even to resemble him in order to appropriate the scientific and technical thought that has allowed the West to subjugate us. Towa remains well aware of the fact that this logic of appropriation of "the miraculous weapons of the other" must begin by way of a philosophical renaissance that is the thought of our thought, not restricted to our own cultural schema. The challenge of this resemblance to the other is therefore, according to Towa, to derive a positive political and economic fate for Africa, so as to transform the Black continent into a superpower – knowing that power is the very foundation of philosophical grandeur. Developing this idea, Towa notes that Greece itself, which gave the world many philosophers, eventually became sterile as a result of losing its self-confidence.[17] We should nevertheless clearly specify that, for Towa, power is the initial necessary condition, however insufficient, for philosophy. Apart from the critiques that his points of view may elicit, many of which, moreover, have been furthered by ethnophilosophers, this position is, in a number of ways, similar to that held by African Marxists. In effect, they reproach the theoreticians of African socialism[18] for having rejected Marxism–Leninism in the name of their difference and under the pretext that it arose out of society at a certain moment in its evolution.

Should we distance ourselves, they wonder, from any foreign ideology whose universalism materialized through the multidimensional transformations that such an ideology gathered through its encounter in various societies. For them, the only question that merits being posed is not so much about the path one should take for development as about the development of Africa, which is first and foremost an epistemological and ontological question, as can be seen in the following remarks by Stanislas Adotevi:

> For Africa, there is no other way out other than development ... the choice is not between socialism and capitalism, the choice is between life and death, and between life and death there are only false dilemmas: either one decides to live, or one decides to die. The form that life ends up taking is another side of the problem.[19]

These brief African readings ranging from a theory of complementarity to self-alienation are more or less inscribed into a program of a philosophy of action and perspective, as can be understood in Nkrumah's *Consciencism*, where the enterprise of reappropriation, far from harping on about Black African values, and therefore enclosing in a cultural particularism, is, on the contrary (as the Ghanaian states), effectuated through a philosophy of intellectual synthesis by accepting the contributions made by each system of thought in an elaboration of human reflection.

But to reappropriate oneself, is that not also a way of thinking about Black African ideology in terms of a culture whose efficiency depends on its capacity to construct itself, to reinvent itself, and to deploy itself?

Within this framework, the Marxist Remo Cautoni noted: "A culture that does not want to change the world or its relations to the outside, or its living conditions, is a culture residing in a museum, which fears the fresh air of action."[20]

Consequently, the question is not so much about becoming closed off in the dilemma between the self and the other, of joining together or not the contours of a conquering and alienating Western modernity,[21] but of deploying an emancipatory strategy susceptible not only to allowing us a dynamic appropriation of tradition, but to confronting here and now the urgent tasks that our development throws up, namely, through adhering to a philosophy of actuality that is prospective and forward-looking, thereby freeing ourselves from the struggles of the past.

Such a formulation is precisely what we see revealed by the Cameroonian philosopher Marcien Towa in his *Essai sur la problématique philosophique en Afrique*:

The questioning of our profound destiny, of the direction our existence should take, must be the great task of our intellectual and philosophical effort; such a question should supersede and override any other question, whether it be that of our essence, our originality, or our past along with the question as to where we should situate ourselves with regard to European thought.[22]

Such a postulate is founded on a refusal to accept any backward-looking discourse by instead identifying with a *living discourse* that is nevertheless not a disqualifying discourse of the past but its actualization in the present as it appears in the concept of a living tradition proclaimed by the French-Senegalese philosopher Gaston Berger, in the following terms: "A living tradition is in no way a sterile evocation of dead things, but the rediscovery of a creative force or élan that is transmitted across generations at once serving as a source of warmth and light."[23]

Reinventing African modernity is therefore an activity of inscribing oneself into a philosophy concerned with actuality and the future in order, to borrow Marcien Towa's expression, to be capable of arriving at grasping an insight and expression of the *African-being-in-the-contemporary-world*.

But fundamentally, it's also about having the courage to think that exiting our political, cultural, and economic dependence, redeployed by a West that always props itself up by the universality of its civilization by virtue of which it imposes its paradigms, depends on our capacity to envision our alienation as self-alienation.

This is what the South African novelist Peter Abrahams observed in 1958, through the mouth of his fictional character Udomo – a Black agitator who, after struggling for independence, went into exile in London before eventually returning to South Africa, his homeland, where he ended up being assassinated by a member of his own political party due to his political compromises.

These are our three enemies:

When I first came back, I only recognized one of the three: the White man. But the moment I defeated him, I saw others and they were more dangerous than the White man. Besides these two, the White man was easy, almost an ally. Well, I turned him into an ally fighting against poverty ... Why do you think I spent so much money sending them abroad? I'll tell you. Because I need them as allies to fight our third enemy, the worst enemy we have: the past ... And you, Selina, and you, Ade, whom I once loved as a brother: you are the past. I'm going to defeat you! You are the ones who now stand in the way of Africa's greatness.[24]

In conclusion: Black African ideology – a doctrine in crisis

To ask questions about a Black African ideology in terms of a crisis can only have meaning if we consider it from its point of departure and follow it along the rest of its journey. From its constitution as a differentialist discourse founded on the vivification of the culture of a traditional Africa, to its formulation of a political, social, and economic liberation of the continent, the true question posed by a Black African ideology has always been about the endogeneity of philosophical reflection in Africa. In this context, philosophy becomes a certain discourse of a specific type of intelligibility, in the conditions of its production, and in the way it is practiced by those who elaborate it. However, it would seem that every philosophical production, and every practice of philosophy, is a function of the places occupied by those who formulate it in the given conditions of their own specific history. As a result, the centrality of such an attempt that exists in the interior of a Black African ideology can only be read starting from a situational determination – which is also simultaneously grasped in its very trajectory – of *the-African-being-there-in-the-concrete-world*. And yet, how are we supposed to take into account such preoccupations in an already established universalism understood as some indispensable horizon for the realization of any human culture whatsoever?

Just as quickly then, the universality in question becomes a perspective that is unique only to the extent that it has been postulated or imposed as such.[25] The question that then arises in all its relevance and acuteness concerns the affirmation of the African as an active subject who seeks to partake in his own self-development as an active creator and no longer as a mere beneficiary. It's precisely from such a perspective that Alioune Diop, in his last message to Africa and to the world, affirmed: "Resuscitate and animate the force and intellectual initiative of the African (inserted in his natural and sociocultural environment), so as to place him in a position to exercise his or her responsibility to directly judge both national and international realities. This is the first condition that must be filled so as to ensure the correct efficiency of our integral development."[26]

But it still remains to be seen whether the resumption of intellectual and practical initiative – whose effectiveness, let's be very clear here, deploys itself in light of a philosophy of responsibility and foresight – cannot be assumed within what, up until now, has been considered a Black African ideology. And yet, if there is an observation to be made today about any kind of objective approach to this doctrine, it can only be understood through a symptomatic reading that would shine a light on its failures as a philosophical, political, social, and cultural system. As soon as the problem is put in these terms, it no longer remains a question for us of returning to the same old criticisms and endless critiques that have been made against it, but rather to finally have the courage to declare a systematic rejection of this ideological stand. Such radicalism is what we can see defended in the work of Eboussi Boulaga in his book *Muntu in Crisis: African Authenticity and Philosophy*: "Indeed, it holds that a culture that has failed woefully should be rejected, that it would be immoral and, for that matter, vain to preserve and salvage it. ... Moreover, in the shock of cultures, certain combinations prove less stable and more fragile than others. They fall apart or crumble under the impact of the more resilient and fittest for collision or conflict."[27]

But let us note that such a proclamation, far from signifying capitulation or afro-pessimism, poses an urgency for a revival in the discourse involving a paradigmatic change – which, moreover, is only possible through a form of awareness based on a premise of accomplishing a real intellectual and affective catharsis. The awareness in this case is therefore "that the suppression of alienation is possible, that alienation is a self-alienation and not a simple or brute fact, a curse."[28] And therefore, at the end of this awareness, which is perceptible only in a trajectory that goes from "an alienation of oneself by the other to an alienation of self by oneself," the only existential and epistemological imperative that is sketched out is that posed by Frantz Fanon in terms that we can't state any more clearly than in the conclusion of *The Wretched of the Earth*: "Now, comrades, now is the time to decide to change sides. We must shake off the great mantle of night which has enveloped us and reach for the light. The new day which is dawning must find us determined, enlightened, and resolute."[29]

Bibliography

Peter Abrahams, *Anthologie africaine et malagache* (Paris: Seghers, 1966).

Stansislas Spero Adotevi, *Négritude et négroloques* (Yaoundé: Union Générale d'édition, 1972).
Louis Althusser, *Pour Marx* (Paris: La Découverte, 1986).
Samir Amin, *Impérialisme et développement inégal* (Paris: Minuit, 1976).
Gaston Berger, *L'Homme moderne et son education* (Paris: PUF, 1962).
Fabien Eboussi Boulaga, *Muntu in Crisis: African Authenticity and Philosophy* (Trenton, NJ: African World Press, 2014 [1977]).
Fabien Eboussi Boulaga, *Christianisme sans fétiche. Révélation et domination* (Paris: Présence africaine, 1981).
Fabien Eboussi Boulaga, *L'Affaire de la philosophie africaine* (Paris: Éditions Terroirs-Karthala, 2011).
Jean Buchmann, *L'Afrique noire indépendante* (Paris: Pichon et Durand-Auzias, 1962).
Mamadou Dia, *Réflexions sur l'économie de l'Afrique noire* (Dakar: NEA, 1961.
Mamadou Dia, *Émancipation des économies captives* (Paris: Anthropos, 1976).
Pathé Diagne, *L'Europhilosophie face à la pensée du négro-africain* (Dakar: Sankoré, 1981).
Souleymane Bachir Diagne et al., *Gaston Berger, introduction à une philosophie de l'avenir* (Paris: NEA, 1997).
Amdy Aly Dieng, *Hegel, Marx, Engels et l'Afrique noire* (Dakar: Sankoré, 1978).
Abdoulaye Dieng, *Crises d'identité et idéologies dans l'Afrique noire contemporaine*, thèse de philosophie, Paris I (1977).
Abdoulaye Dieng, *Économie: les règles du jeu* (Paris: Economica, 1984).
Cheikh Anta Diop, *Antériorité des civilisations nègres: mythe ou vérité historique?* (Paris: Présence africaine, 1967).
Cheikh Anta Diop, *Civilisation ou barbarie* (Paris: Présence africaine, 1981).
Frantz Fanon, *The Wretched of the Earth*, trans. Richard Philcox (New York: Grove Press, 2005).
Pierre Fougeyrollas, *Le Destin historique des idéologies sociales en Afrique* (Kampala: NEA, 1966).
Paulin Hountondji, *Sur la philosophie africaine* (Paris: Maspero, 1977).
Paulin Hountondji, *Les Savoirs endogènes* (Paris: Karthala, 1994).
Mohamed Iqbal, *Les Secrets du soi. Les mystères du non-moi*, trans. Djamchid Mortazavi and Eva de Vitray-Meyerovitch (Paris: Albin Michel, 1989).

Joseph Ki Zerbo et al., *La Natte des autres* (Dakar: Codesria, 1992).
Gérard Leclerc, *La Mondialisation culturelle* (Paris: PUF, 2000).
Lucien Lévy-Bruhl, *La Mentalité primitive* (Paris: Félix Alcan, 1922).
Claude Liauzu, *L'Enjeu tiers-mondiste* (Paris: L'Harmattan, 1987).
Karl Marx and Friederich Engels, *The German Ideology, including Theses on Feuerbach* (Buffalo, NY: Prometheus Books, 1998).
Achille Mbembe, *De la postcolonie* (Paris: Karthala, 2000).
Achille Mbembe, *Sortir de la grande nuit* (Paris: La Découverte, 2013).
Albert Meister, *L'Afrique peut-elle partir?* (Paris: Le Seuil, 1966).
Alassane N'daw, *La Pensée africaine* (Paris: Présence africaine, 1976).
Kwame Nkrumah, *L'Afrique doit s'unir* (Paris: Présence africaine, 1964).
Kwame Nkrumah, *Consciencism: Philosophy and Ideology for De-Colonization* (New York: Monthly Review Press, 2009 [1972]).
Kwame Nkrumah, *La Lutte des classes en Afrique* (Paris: Présence africaine, 1972).
Kwame Nkrumah, *Le Néo-Colonialisme: dernier stade de l'impérialisme* (Paris: Présence africaine, 2009).
Jean-Pierre N'diaye, *Monde noir et destin politique* (Paris: Présence africaine, 1976).
Julius Nyerere, *Socialisme, démocratie et unité africaine* (Paris: Présence africaine, 1970).
Jacques Rancière, *Aux Bords du politique* (Paris: Gallimard/La Fabrique, 1998).
Charles Saint-Prot, *La Tradition islamique de la réforme* (Paris: Éditions CNRS, 2010).
Felwine Sarr, *Dahij* (Paris: L'Arpenteur, 2009).
Felwine Sarr, *Afrotopia*, trans. Drew S. Burk and Sarah Jones-Boardman (Minneapolis: University of Minnesota Press, 2019).
Babacar Sine, *Impérialisme et théories sociologiques du développement* (Paris: Anthropos, 1972).
Léopold Sédar Senghor, *Liberté I. Négritude et humanisme* (Paris: Le Seuil, 1964); *Liberté II. Nation et voie africaine du socialisme* (Paris: Le Seuil, 1971); *Liberté III. Négritude et civilisation de l'universel* (Paris: Le Seuil, 1977); *Liberté IV. Socialisme et planification* (Paris: Le Seuil, 1982).
Babacar Sine, *Le Marxisme devant les sociétés africaines contemporaines* (Paris: Présence africaine, 1983).

Louis Vincent Thomas, *Les Idéologies négro-africaines d'aujourd'hui* (Dakar: FLSH, 1970).
Louis Vincent Thomas, *Le Socialisme et l'Afrique*, vols. 1 and 2 (Paris: Présence africaine, 1966).
Marcien Towa, *Essai sur la problématique philosophique en Afrique* (Paris: Éditions Clé, 1979).
Jean Ziegler, *La Victoire des vaincus* (Paris: Le Seuil, 1988).

What Is a Postcolonial Author?

Lydie Moudileno

Lydie Moudileno *is the author of* Postcolonial Realms of Memory *(with Étienne Achille and Charles Dorsdick) (Liverpool University Press, 2020),* L'Écrivain antillais au miroir de sa littérature *(Karthala, 1997),* Littératures africaines, 1980–1990 *(Codesria, 2003),* Parades postcoloniales *(Karthala, 2007), as well as a number of articles on authors and postcolonial cultural production during the twentieth and twenty-first centuries. She is Marion Frances Chevalier Professor of French and Professor of French and American Studies and Ethnicity at the University of Southern California (USC Dornsife).*

> It matters little whom the work was made for; what we should learn from is the imagination that produced it.
>
> Anthony Appiah[1]

The overflowing library

The first decades of the twenty-first century have led to significant visibility of African literature in France. The ongoing work of the elders, combined with an abundance of new authors whose cultural backgrounds continue to be all the more varied and diverse, has confirmed, over a number of decades, the important and essential place African literature holds in the production of knowledge in

Africa alongside other arts such as the visual and graphic arts. To this day, African fiction continues to assert itself as a major genre of representation, attaining similar proportions to that achieved in the 1950s during the "era of the African novel." But things have obviously changed since the early emergence of those first authors who contributed to establishing the field of African literature: first, the early pioneers have yielded their place to singularities that are becoming all the more assertive, no longer having to contend with and systematically respond to an unveiling of ethnography, the urgency of decolonization, reculturation, national responsibility, or the excesses of postcolonialism. In other words, the contemporary author has broken free from the injunctions that had once encumbered earlier generations, as were debated, for example, in 1956 in the pages of the *Congrés des écrivains et artistes noirs*, and in the journal *Présence africaine*.

Second, the current profusion of these writers (both men and women) means that the presence of African writers from now on is part of a larger national, continental, and planetary cultural landscape. Following the demographic evolution of the society at large, the "African presence" in literature has been rendered ubiquitous, to the point where the numerous examples of Black writers being published, especially on the Francophone cultural scene, is no longer seen as an anomaly. On the contrary, this vast publication output has led to growing numbers of original writers, presenting unique individuals, histories, and aesthetic projects that are distinguished as much by their originality as by their similarities.

Finally, the visibility of these authors (or in any case some of them) owes a great deal to the support of the publishing world, literary critics, and French cultural institutions that were already in existence at the beginning of the century. This phenomenon has also attracted the attention of sociologists of literature, such as Claire Ducournau, who notes "a more marked and more systematic interest for authors heralding from Africa" among editors, readers, and critics, beginning in the late 1990s.[2] For her part, Sylvie Ducas situates the early 2000s as "a full-on period of explosion of an editorial demand for African literature":

> We can really begin to start speaking about a new tendency toward African literature once we begin to take into account that, between 1997 and 2000, 1,250 new titles of Black African literature were published in France, namely a production of African literature that doubled in just ten years. Specialist publishers such as L'Harmattan, Le Serpent

à plumes, les Éditions Karthala and Dapper, as well as many general publishers, all launched their own collections.[3]

The publication of all these works merely emphasized the essential role that honors and awards played in a process of recognition for a variety of authors heralding from former colonies. For instance, we could look at how the election of Léopold Senghor into the ranks of the prestigious Académie française in 1983 (a rather isolated instance of recognition) eventually led to a wave of African selections to the Académie beginning with Assia Djebar in 2005. At the same time, we also begin to see the most prestigious literary awards bestowed on African writers – such as the Prix Renaudot given to Ahmadou Kourouma in 2000 and then, successively, to Alain Mabanckou (2006), Tierno Monenembo (2008), and Scholastique Mukasonga (2012) within just a few years of each other.

The vastness and diversity of the postcolonial library cannot be understood without taking into account the sites and mechanisms of visibilization and, in a more general manner, the processes of book promotion on the global book market. In this regard, Gisèle Sapiro recalls the crucial function of the practice of translation in the global circulation of literary works: translation into English, for example, not only increases the prestige of an author from the French-speaking peripheries, but also, in deterritorializing the work, inscribes it into a global economy that denationalizes its relationship with a Parisian center, while at the same time opening the works themselves up to a larger reading public.[4] It goes without saying that translation contributes to an expansion of forms of knowledge concerning Africa that characterize our sense of a global contemporary. We can also ask ourselves to what extent the growing number of book fairs and festivals, as well as conferences, has served as new spaces of visibility. This year [2016] coincides with the fiftieth anniversary of the first "Festival mondial des arts nègres," first held in Dakar in 1966. And with its arrival, the question of what we today refer to as "the biennialization" of culture arises with particular acuity concerning the modes of the representation of Africa throughout the rest of the world.

There is certainly reason to rejoice as one discerns the ongoing expansion of the postcolonial library.[5] One can also rejoice in the increased presence of authors of African origin who benefit from a legitimacy that is, if not already acquired, at least already growing. Thanks to them, Africa gains a cultural visibility and confirms its relevance as a continent that produces its own forms of knowledge [*savoirs*] and is engaged in the global exchange of ways of knowing [*connaissances*]. The phenomenon should therefore be interpreted positively with regard to a sense of innovations and distinctions that it would be wrong to understand simply as editorial choices or practices of the *postcolonial exotic*.[6] And yet, in spite of such a success, what is of import here is not "to naively rejoice in the fact that the Francophone writer has, for a number of years now, thanks to literary prizes, found another outlet or readership by way of such public success."[7] We should remember that this was the euphoric position of the manifesto "Pour une littérature-monde en français," published in the pages of the French newspaper *Le Monde* in 2006, whose forty-four signatories had wanted to believe in the advent of a veritable "Copernican revolution" for French-speaking literature.[8] At a time when it is undeniable that contemporary African cultures are working extensively on opening up a global presence for African culture, we should certainly recognize this event without having to take a critical or demanding look at the paradigms that have helped shaped this presence. As Felwine Sarr has noted, it's quite possible that, following the enthusiasm with regard to African literature, the winds have changed and "a spirit of optimism and euphoria has begun to radiate in the light of day" in terms of the discourse concerning the arts as much as the economy. But Sarr also draws attention to the fact that a "blissful optimism" concerning the African twenty-first century would be nothing more than "its inverted double" of an afro-pessimism of the preceding century.[9]

This moment of exceptional visibility that bodes well for African literature over the coming decades should also be an opportunity to look back at the way in which we receive such works, as critics, professors, and commentators on the cultural production of Africa. How are these texts finding their way into our midst? To what extent is their reception determined by a specific reading public awaiting their arrival and the accomplishment of a certain conception of African writing that should subsequently be realized? Are our hermeneutic tools and our methodologies adequate enough to make sense of this increasingly heterogeneous body of work? In our desire to promote the accumulation of forms of knowledge about Africa and to demonstrate its cultural presence in the world, in what regimes of truth do we situate them? And of course, the ultimate concern that we should bear in mind can be posed in terms of exclusion: in a variety of ways, the postcolonial library is overflowing, and that's great. But at the same time, we should also rcognize that, in our efforts to assert the legitimacy of non-Western canons so as to destabilize the hegemonic center through the voices of a so-called periphery, we have created other marginalities and established new centers. We know, for example, that certain books from the Global South circulate less than others and that a great number of books never find their way into the bookshops of the vast North Atlantic metropolises, by which means a certain consecration can be bestowed on them. We should obviously not lose sight of the exclusions and "losses" that result from this process and from our own arbitrariness. It's with such questions in mind that it seems important for me to submit for analysis the notion of "author" in the manner in which it circulates today as an essential element of culture. And to do this not simply in order to help in assigning them identities or establishing taxonomies of origin, but as a discursive category that allows us to rethink the production of imaginaries about/concerning Africa, taking into account who or what is gathering them together and who will continue to determine the modes of circulation in the world of the twenty-first century.

What is a postcolonial author?

The way in which it is often asked, and in complete contrast to what we would like to believe, the aforementioned question is not an attempt to come up with a definition that would, in this case, be "postcolonial." It is not about delving into the nuances of a precise definition so as to seek out an answer to what is postcolonial and what isn't, or what is more or less postcolonial, or what has falsely taken on the guise of the postcolonial, or has yet to become postcolonial. Rather, it's time to end the debate around questions concerning the functionality or inadequacy of the term "postcolonial," at the least as far as literature is concerned, and, rather, make use of the heuristic significance of the term. However, we've not paid enough attention to the notion of "author," although it is probably there – much more so than in adjectives such as "African," "postcolonial," etc. – that essential questions are raised about the way in which literature from Africa circulates and is conceived around the world. Let us then reformulate our title: "What is an author, in the context of postcolonial/African Francophone literature?" It would principally be a question of modes of presence and my remarks will focus on authors the majority of whom publish in French with Parisian publishers, regardless of their own origins, citizenship, or place of residence.

Epistemological considerations concerning the object "Africa" have been at the center of debate for a very long time in the social sciences and humanities. In political science, economics, and philosophy, questions are regularly asked concerning the pertinence of Western paradigms to the apprehension of African cultures. But have we systematically asked the same questions concerning literature? To what extent and to what degree has the framework of literary theory, which has served as a form of analysis in the French domain, been transposed, or is transposable, to a critique of the African literary field?

As Edward Said reminds us, the movement of ideas and the circulation of theories are indispensable for a universal intellectual activity. They must nevertheless be accompanied by conditions of acceptance and its terms of appropriation when migrating toward a period, situation, or culture other than those of its origin.[10]

How, for instance, does the notion of author travel (or not) from the French context to the African context? We would like to note, following Catherine Mazauric, that it is the modern figure of the author-*auctor* (the one who generates and guarantees meaning) who has, in a way, become "naturalized" in Africa, notably through traditional pedagogy.

> In Africa, the Western conception of the author, along with a certain form of written literature, was the first to be imported. By way of its correlation with the teaching of literary history, such a conception became "naturalized" in a certain way. Nevertheless, it also entered into contact and coalescence with many other contexts and specific phenomena that could only but contribute to its conception and subsequently redefine its scope.[11]

The end of the 1960s marked an important turn in both French literary theory and Francophone African literature. Such a turn is translated by way of a radical divergence between the postulates of the French avant-garde, determined to call into question the paradigms of preceding generations, and the claims of a literature that has only been alive for its first quarter-century, and which obeys, at the hour of decolonization, political-cultural imperatives that are vastly different. The consequences of such a divergence remain decisive both for the conception of the African literary field, and for the very idea of the function of the writer in postcolonial societies (in this case, France).

We should call to mind the French context at the end of the 1960s: the question of the role of the author is revisited in two decisive texts considered as foundational for postmodernist critics: "The death of the author" by Roland Barthes in 1968, and Michel Foucault's "What is an author?" published in 1969, which this present essay aims to echo. As we know, 1968 was a moment of protest against the authorities, when power structures were challenged and free speech was being advocated. In the wake of this, the old notion of the author is subjected to a similar regime of protest: the author should no longer be conceived as the exclusive interpreter of meaning or as the only holder of the key to a text. On the contrary, the author should be deprived of this privilege: "To give a text an author," writes Barthes, "is to impose a limit on that text, to furnish it with a signified, to close the writing."[12] And so it was that the symbolic death (distancing, absence) of the author imposed itself as the fundamental condition for the birth of a veritable writing whose semantic openness is returned to the reader(s).

For his part, Michel Foucault makes use of this epistemic rupture and calls into question in "What is an author?" the conception of a text as pure expression of its author, whereby, in a critical gesture at the conclusion we would arrive at some sort of revelatory message, intention, or biographical background. "What matter who's speaking?," Foucault (quoting Samuel Beckett) declared in 1969, rejecting the anteriority of the author to the text.

> In an indifference such as this we must recognize one of the fundamental ethical principles of contemporary writing ... Thus, the essential basis of this writing is not the exalted emotions related to the act of composition or the insertion of a subject into language. Rather, it is primarily concerned with creating an opening where the writing subject endlessly disappears.[13]

And yet, what we see taking place in African literature presents a completely different situation, and it is true that the "contemporary writing" Foucault refers to in his essay does not include writings from the French colonial empire that was in the process of crumbling. Indeed, after the "great negro cry" expressed by Césaire thirty years earlier, a literature starts to emerge from out of Africa, written in French, that finally makes itself heard, and, for these authors on the margins of France, it most certainly matters "who is speaking." "My mouth will be the mouth of those griefs which have no mouth," Césaire writes in his *Notebook of a Return to My Native Land*.[14]

In the literary history of Africa, 1968 is the year of the publication of Ahmadou Kourouma's *Soleils des indépendances* and Yambo Ouloguem's *Devoir de violence*, which won the Prix Renaudot. These are the first two important postcolonial works in the chronological sense of the term. Contemporaries of the postmodern theories posited by Barthes and Foucault concerning the author, these works signal a turning point of a completely different order: if, as we've already noted, 1968 marks an epistemological rupture for African letters,[15] this rupture resides in the fact that a New African writing is in the throes of taking shape, and, with it, a new conception of the author.

As Souleymane Bachir Diagne states: "The crisis in African letters [in 1968] marked by *Le Devoir de violence*, and *Les Soleils des indépendances*, must be characterized as a shift from the paradigm of transcription to that of writing."[16] In a way, this first decade of independence sees the birth of two *French-speaking postcolonial writers*, in the sense that their texts are recognized as the fruit of an invention generated by individual inspirations, trajectories, and aesthetic projects. Thus, we begin to see a gap that is widening dramatically between, on the one hand, a certain disavowal of the author by Western literary criticism and, on the other, the emergence of writer-subjects immersed in the realities of decolonization who summon Western readers to listen to the voices coming from spaces beyond those of mainland France. Kourouma, Ouloguem, and others provide works worth reading, in French – complex narratives – that in these instances require abandoning another privilege: the Western privilege of speculating (about) the other. These authors request that we receive their "message" and that we take the subject projected in them "seriously." Basically, that we recognize them as (postcolonial) writers. In other words, the authors symbolically reclaim their presence among the living.

At the end of the twentieth century, literary Africa is in search of writers, in the same way that it's in search of a grand narrative, heroic figures, rediscovered myths, and a national conscience – quite simply, it is living through its literary modernity.[17] The conception and definition of "Black writers" will be viewed through the lens of these terms for a long time, as much in the injunctions that will continuously be imposed on him or her so as to "represent" his or her people – and this will continue well beyond the post-independence years – as in how the authors' work is received by the critics. As such, the postcolonial authors will constantly find themselves reinvesting in their role as *auctor*: as writers who have something to say about the world in which they reside and through a criticism that expects the African narrative to be a reflection of this world. This dual "desire of authors," from my perspective, still seems to be a large determining factor in the conception of contemporary African literature.

The manifesto "Pour une littérature-monde en français," which led to much ink being spilled in 2006, was not entirely unfounded in proclaiming the return of referentiality in French-language writings at the beginning of the twenty-first century, nor to attribute its disappearance to a new criticism coming from France. "The world is returning, and it's the best news we could have," they write. "Has this world, for quite some time now, not been absent from French literature? The world, the subject, meaning, history, the referent; for several decades, they had all been placed in parentheses by the master-thinkers, inventors of a literature with no other object than itself, and simply creating, as one was accustomed to saying, its own criticism in the very movement of its utterance."

On closer examination, we must admit that African literature and its critique never really left the world of French literature and, consequently, it is clear that the postcolonial author was never subjected to the same regime of symbolic disappearance. But if production from the Francophone margins largely escaped the axioms of postmodern criticism, it also became crystallized in other types of reading, where the status of the author is subject to all sorts of tensions.

The desire of the author, denial of fiction, and literature in person

In 1983, Locha Mateso deplored the persistence of what he referred to as the "theory of reflection" in the criticism of the African text:

> The focus on writers rather than their works is a common practice in African literary criticism. What seems rather obvious is that the quality of the Black African writer counts much more than the mere literary production of the writers. One of the characteristics of the critical discourse dedicated to African literature is the search for external

phenomena for which the literary oeuvre would be the reflection. Such work would seek out the conventional signs affirming with some sort of certainty that the work in question referred to the outside world.[18]

Since that time, Lansonnian presentations of "the person and the work" have opened up a space for more subtle commentaries, but we will maintain that the "theory of reflection" still holds sway and can be seen in use in other forms. To begin with, the increase in the celebration and the reception of the works: if it is obvious that they respond in part to a voyeuristic demand, then testimonials and other genres of writing that draw on autobiographical material (notably narratives around the trauma of postcolonial violence as can be seen in the work of genocide survivors, child soldiers, or victims of sexual mutilation) continue to be written and still retain a significant place in contemporary literature. The desire of the author (that is, the legitimate desire to gain access to the truth of those who relate a singular experience) in this case renders impossible what Michel Foucault called an "indifference" to these texts wherein it would be a question either of approaching the alterity of a contemporary, or, by way of a realist bias, seeking the foundations for an elucidation of the postcolonial world.

However, this desire for the author constitutes a shackle on the freedom of the writer when it comes to African literature.[19] I'm thinking in this case of the relatively recent instance when the work of Léonora Miano was translated into English and had its title changed in translation. The work I'm referring to is *L'Intérieur de la nuit*, published in France in 2005 by Plon. The work in question is a fiction that takes place in Africa. On the basis of the work's success (the novel received critical acclaim), it was published in translation by the University of Nebraska Press.[20] The novel appeared under a different title in English translation, which made the author very angry: *The Dark Heart of the Night*. The resonance with Joseph Conrad's *Heart of Darkness* was not something that pleased the author at all, since it would steer the reader in "completely the wrong direction." The preface seemed so erroneous that Miano lodged a complaint against the English-language publisher and demanded its withdrawal. A seven-point corrigendum concerning the relationship between the work and the author's home country, the presence or not of autobiographical elements, the pan-African discourse of the novel or the choice of France as the country of residence, etc., accompanied the author's point-by-point corrections that circulated on the internet.

The incident and the way in which the author managed it revealed at least two things: first, that the theory of reflection had spread beyond the borders of France and had made its way onto the global book market, confirming the Western desire to uncover in the text a trace of the empirical person of the author. Such a desire was done at the cost of a denial of the fictional quality of the work, which also serves as reference to the status of African literature that is not granted literary space, as if African novels could only have value (economic, symbolic, or literary) in a referential relation with the real: it's this non-recognition of the capacity of the postcolonial author to produce fiction that in this case provoked the anger of the author in question. Second, the mediatized intervention (notably on the internet) of Léonora Miano concerning the translation of her work signals the *agency* an author possesses in the twenty-first century regarding the circulation of their image and that of their work. The incident reveals, paradoxically, the return of the author as a physical individual, determined to reclaim "in person" the right to fiction, by taking back from Western commentators the authority over what their work is about. The postcolonial author is alive, they have the capacity to respond, and they participate not only in the production of meaning, but also in the construction of their literary identity. The time when the preface writer was the sole authority concerning the narrative of the colonized has definitively come to an end.

The impossibility of the disappearance of the author in such a context leads us back to Foucault. In the same text in which he proclaims the death of the author, Foucault proposes reflecting on the persistence of what he calls "the author-function," which no longer refers to the empirical reality of the individual person, but to the discursive construction inscribed in a specific era, and is, in such instances, characteristic of a specific episteme. The author-function, Foucault writes,

> results from a complex operation whose purpose is to construct the rational entity we call an author ... [but that] which we designate as an author (or which comprise an individual as an author), are projections, in terms always more or less psychological, of our way of handling texts: in the comparisons we make, the traits we extract as pertinent, the continuities we assign, or the exclusions we practice. In addition, all these practices vary according to the period and form of discourse concerned. A "philosopher" and a "poet" are not constructed in the same manner; and the author of an eighteenth-century novel was formed differently from the modern novelist.[21]

Today, we could say that there is indeed something we could refer to as the "postcolonial author-function." It is the product of centuries of discourse on Africa and writing heralding as much from the West as from the pan-African world. Supported by texts as diverse and varied as *De la littérature des Nègres, ou Recherches sur leurs facultés intellectuelles, leurs qualités morales et leur littérature, suivies de notices sur la vie et les ouvrages des Nègres qui sont distingués dans les sciences, les lettres et les arts*, published by the bishop Henri Grégoire in 1808, *Les Trois Volontés de Malik* by Ahmadou Mapate Diagne (1920), *L'Enfant noir* by Camara Laye (1956), *Le Docker noir* by Sembene Ousmane (1956), *Le Devoir de violence* by Yambo Ouloguem (1968), *Trop de soleil tue l'amour* by Mongo Beti (1999), and *Black Bazar* by Alain Mabanckou (2009), this archive is full of recurring auctorial issues – intertextuality, plagiarism, notoriety, engagement, and the freedom of the writer.[22] To privilege the analysis of the "author-function" rather than the author in their own individual dimensions does not mean the individual is assigned to the outside nor that the subject becomes dissolved in some kind of postmodern difference wherein, as a consequence, no truth really emerges. On the contrary, the *agency* of the postcolonial author becomes reaffirmed as participating in the various modalities of the author's presence and notoriety in the world.

It would seem that this century equates to the return of a "literature in person" where the body of the author participates more and more in the media life of the book, and where authors "embody their writings" in performances of self [*mise-en-scène-de-soi*] – or "auctorial scenographies" – that are increasingly well publicized. The question of the writer's posture, or *ethos*, defined as the manner in which the author occupies a place in one or more given cultural fields, has become a principal preoccupation of French criticism in the past several years.[23] The way in which African literature circulates in a global network, ensuring its visibility, is no exception to this rule and postcolonial postures have become more and more sophisticated.[24] In this context, how is the definition of writer impacted by the notion of fame or celebrity?[25] How does a writer manage his or her capital of visibility and furthermore what are the political responsibilities that accompany their so-called rise to glory?[26]

The postcolonial author cannot help but be situated in their world, since he or she is of the world and this state of affairs necessarily orients our hermeneutics of texts and bodies.[27] The postcolonial library is overflowing and the vitality of its contemporary productions urges us to take seriously these innovations and the excesses they imply. Excess comes in all forms: aesthetic, epistemological, temporal, and spatial. It is quite clear that the more mobile the author is – that is, the more their text circulates and the more they present themselves in different spheres – the more their forms of auctoriality will be varied. This also means that our critical practice should always be exerted with more curiosity and vigilance when confronted with such diversity. If indeed the contemporary author is defined as a "moving kaleidoscope,"[28] then new issues are also presented for all these agents of the visibility of Afro-diasporic cultures from this new millennium, of which we are: writers, critics, journalists, professors, and readers with the task of considering all the facets of the author's work and revealing the infinite game.

Part III

How Can One Be *African/e*?
From Self-Shame to the Consciousness of the Oppressed: Philosophical Reflections by Way of Steve Biko, Malcolm X, and Audre Lorde

Hourya Bentouhami

Hourya Bentouhami is a lecturer in political philosophy at the University of Toulouse-Jean Jaurés. Her works bear on the relation between postcolonial theories and political theory (concerning notions of identity, culture, recognition, the memory of slavery, and most notably reparative justice) as well as their contribution to a re-elaboration of feminism. Her publications include Le Déport des armes. Non-violence et désobéissance civile *(PUF, 2015), and* Race, cultures, identités. Une approche féministe et postcoloniale *(PUF, 2015).*

How can one be *African/e*?[1] Or how can one be Black, or a Black woman? To use a slightly modified expression already found in Montesquieu's *Lettres persanes* in the following expression: "How can one be Persian?" We can interpret such an expression in the following manner. How can one love or even want to be African or, even, Black, or Arab? How can one not want to take flight from one's Africanness or negritude when everything speaks against these identities? So many questions seem to condemn Africa to the impossibility of finding in itself a universal future, a past, and a horizon around which all the members of its vast community can proudly seek out some sense of belonging and identity. The conditions of self-shame are explicitly explained as being at the core of Africa and its so-called powerlessness, whether we understand this identity crisis through a geographical or a continental collective or through its historical diasporas (more specifically that of slavery, which saw the constitution of African identities undergo a creolization outside the African continent). It's the very consciousness of Africans themselves – understood in the broader sense of the expression, therefore – that finds itself tied to the impossibility of self-love,[2] of what Steve Biko, the South African student leader during apartheid, understood when he promoted the Black consciousness movement, which sought to eradicate any form of self-shame among Black men and women: "At the heart of this kind of thinking [Black consciousness] is the realization by blacks that the most potent weapon in the hands of the oppressor is the mind of the oppressed. If one is free at heart, no man-made chains can bind one to servitude."[3] This attention paid to the consciousness of the oppressed, to the colonization of the unconscious and the very desires themselves of the oppressed in systemic situations of racism such as during the era of apartheid in which Steve Biko grew up between 1948 until his death in 1977, provide us with a glimpse of the philosophical dimension of a consciousness that can no longer be reduced to the monolingualism of the mind, talking to itself so as to know what it is right to do, or so as to seek out an agreement with oneself. Or rather, the Socratic demand of knowing oneself, or of a dialogue of the soul with itself, as we see it discussed in Plato's Protagoras (339c) or in the Sophist (263e), must think of its condition for the historical possibilities of realization: and one of these conditions is precisely the relationship that this consciousness maintains with the world, in the sense that, thrown into the world, I am also an object for the other, *I appear* in conditions that are not always those of novelty.

In colonial, apartheid, or racist situations, racialized beings – reduced to labor-power – who provide cheap labor in shantytowns and townships, become phobogenic objects by which any contact with them implies some kind of epidemiological racial contamination. The crucial question here, then, is what is the consciousness of such an infamous being, in the literal sense of a being who sees his or her entire being constituted by the *mala fama*, by a bad reputation, before having any possibility to express themselves in their own words. Audre Lorde (1934–92), an Afro-American lesbian feminist, has raised a similar point, namely that what has made life impossible for Afro-American women is precisely the fact that they are not authorized to "make a world" in a racial system that deprives them even of the possibility of being recognized as women in the same way as white women. One must therefore be able to "make a world" and change the definition of consciousness. For this, Arendt becomes a precious resource to the extent that she sheds doubt on the idea that we can reduce consciousness to merely an interior state, to purely internal memory, from the very fact that one never recalls something by oneself, but rather because "living beings have 'made so many worlds' that there is no subject that is not also an object and only appears as such to the other who guarantees them of their 'objective' reality. What we usually call 'consciousness,' the fact that I am aware of myself, that I can therefore in a certain sense appear to myself, would never suffice to guarantee reality."[4] Thought must appear in the eyes of others in order for it to express meaning or be resonant [*faire sens*]. It's therefore outside and behind the zone of non-being, in leaving behind the zone of all existential negation that the oppressed must set themselves to work in order to truly free themselves from the chains of servitude, which implies the activity of reappropriating a sense of one's value, of one's interiority, and to expulse anything in it that is hostile or resists the autonomization of consciousness. It's not simply a question of evoking the *sapere aude* of the philosophers, but rather to grasp that which is oppressed in one's very consciousness itself, that which within it has been co-opted by ideology to such an extent that one ends up considering self-love through the very rejection of others and all those who can connect us back to our community.

We find this idea in the writings and speeches of Malcom X (1925–65), as well as in the work of Steve Biko and Audre Lorde, the latter two having read the pamphlets and work about Paulo Freire's *Pedagogy of the Oppressed*.[5] This alienated way of expressing oneself, or elevating humanity, also takes the form of a cruel disavowal, and, according to Fanon, is the source of quite a few neuroses – read carefully by Steve Biko, Audre Lorde, and Malcom X attentively in *The Wretched of the Earth*: a disavowal from which one seeks to escape in the literal sense of wanting to shed one's skin, of becoming White, of grabbing hold of the very values of those who dominate. Hence the path formulated by all three of these historical figures: self-love, which takes on a particularly interesting form in the work of Audre Lorde, namely that of care. For her, the essential question becomes to know: who will take care of those who take care of others, the nonwhite women? The choice leading to the study of these three figures was precisely the fact that all three of them turn the question of self-love into a political question that was at once the horizon and condition of emancipation: self-love being politically what makes it possible to restore exteriority to the enemy. The question then arises regarding violence as a revolutionary strategy, since a self-love that expels the enemy must not – according to similar ideas held by Biko, Malcom X, and Lorde – personalize the enemy and become overly fascinated by a form of symmetrical violence, which would in turn only shame those who already made us feel ashamed of ourselves.

Epistemology and phenomenology of the oppressed consciousness

Why all of this political attention to consciousness in an epistemology of liberation (which, moreover, is also steeped in a *materialist* epistemology of liberation)? One can only begin to understand it by moving beyond the simple apprehension of consciousness as simple interiority, and as something that one could be capable of grasping, of appropriating: power is something exerted not only *on* bodies, but also *in* bodies. The other aspect that justifies such attention can be found in what Freudian psychoanalysis has put forward – and which is even more central in the work of Wilhelm Reich and, later, Frantz Fanon: the repression of desire, of the libido, is nothing more than an invested repression of the libido. This leads then to the following question: if consciousness aspires to be the way in which one accompanies oneself, whereby one is a friend to oneself, how is it possible that one can end up being an enemy to oneself? How is it then that nonwhites and, more specifically, those who are said to be African, end up participating in their own negation?

First of all, one must understand the consciousness of the oppressed through what W. E. B. Du Bois called "double consciousness." It has often been stated that the privileged sensorial organ – sight – is that from which we apprehend consciousness so as to denote reflexivity properly speaking, in the sense that consciousness sees itself think (it comes back to its own operations); the other sensorial expression – the voice – refers back more specifically to the modality of language by which consciousness, in speaking to itself, takes itself as an object of reflection in the form of a dialogue in which I become a friend to myself. And yet, what Du Bois shows us is that it's precisely such a process that, for Black individuals – and for our purposes we can extend his ideas to include nonwhites – functions in their minds as a strange and painful cognitive disjunction: in the framework of a post-slave society, following Du Bois's reflections, Blacks have continued to endure and suffer the brutality of racism and have subsequently been socially constituted as neurotic beings whose consciousness is always double or split [*dédoublé*], in the sense that, in the dialogue of the soul with itself, in the way in which the soul sees itself and grasps itself as an object of judgment, a third figure is introduced: a third voice that historically has been called the Master – namely, the one who has constituted *me* as an object for *his* consciousness, as a being-for-the-other. Since, as Sartre was known to say, including in the way oppression proceeds by reification – and all the more so in the case of slavery – "one does not oppress a stone ... what is aimed at in oppression is the Freedom of the Other, his suppression."[6] What is at work in oppression is of course to make bodies comply, but also to incite the surrender of minds so as to obtain consent to one's own servitude without this taking the explicit form of violence: one of the most subtle ways for this to take place was to inhabit the mind itself of the person who is enslaved by embracing the contours of his consciousness to such an extent that when the slave thought for himself it was actually the master who thought in his place.[7] In this sense, the Black cogito, the Black "I think," is troubled in its reflexivity in the very same way that consciousness turns toward itself and ends up being *a turning against itself*, in that it works at its own servitude. Audre Lorde, in asking why women turn against each other, comes to the conclusion that it's self-hate that has been inculcated in women and is the very source of such violence:

> We have been steeped in hatred – for our color, for our sex, for our effrontery in daring to presume we had any right to live. As children, we absorbed that hatred, passed it through ourselves, and for the most part, we still live our lives outside the recognition of what hatred really is and how it functions. Echoes of it return as cruelty and anger in our dealings with each other. For each of us bears the face that hatred seeks, and we have learned to be at home with cruelty because we have survived so much of it in our lives.[8]

Moreover, what happens in the functioning of racism itself is the way in which some bodies are always already labeled in advance, racism proceeding by the reification of individual characteristics that are then applied to a group habitus from which the individual cannot escape (whether it's due to biological genetic heredity or because of cultural ties). And this way of being labeled in advance, of being socially preceded by a narrative of our ineptitude, of our inadequacy, our incompetence, or by way of the very inverse of our supposed talent in a specific domain, deprives us of the possibility of appearing to the world in an oblique form, deprives us of a non-correspondence with self, in other words, in the form of a strangeness or novelty that would therefore not be seized in advance. In *Black Skin, White Masks*, Fanon uses the example of such an antecedence of a self-narrative that escapes us and opens itself up against us: he recounts how, in going to the cinema, or choosing a place to sit in a train, he is already expected, as if the seat is already awaiting him, in the sense that other people watch him arrive and get out of his way. The collapse of his being that follows turns him into a snake, a slithering and crawling being whose second skin is shame directed at himself, self-shame – to such an extent that in the relationship between self and self that will be undertaken by consciousness, shame, in the way in which I see others seeing me as a patchwork being [*être rapicié*], will end up becoming the very modality of self-identity. This is precisely what Stuart Hall calls "this self-as-Othered,"[9] by reinvesting Paul Ricoeur's notion by which he defines identity starting from the staging of events of his consciousness, taking as his model St. Augustine's *Confessions*. Moreover, it's in order to renew the very possibility of a biographical density of Black women who have been rendered invisible that Audre Lorde considers poetry as a veritable means for survival, the only means accessible to disadvantaged classes and far from the cliché of poetry as a luxury.[10] As such, as concerns this negative dialectics of the Black cogito, what we are also implying is the way we have of speaking with ourselves, of confessing to ourselves by way of a disavowal: this is typical of alienated behavior, to the extent that the assumption of my being that is supposed to register the awaking of my consciousness takes the form of my own imprisonment, to such a degree that, as Foucault states, "the soul is the prison of the body,"[11] thereby inverting the Platonic notion of the body as tomb of the soul.

This idea that the soul has become a prisoner of the body is, however, not immediately visible to an alienated consciousness that precisely thinks, as far as it is concerned, that its body is the enemy in the framework of a conception of identity that has internalized the idea that being only resides in appearance. This approach to alienation as an inner colonization is useful for understanding what the consciousness of the oppressed entails in the sense of the negative dialectics described below, and which takes self-shame as a form of self-love: the only way of loving oneself is to hate everything within us that was hated by the master or, at the very least, everything that placed us at a distance from him. And this was precisely the way in which Audre Lorde shows how one of the ways for Black women to love themselves was precisely to hate each other[12] and to consider Black men solely responsible for the sexist violence that they suffered.

We find two symmetrical examples of this negative dialectics in the writings of Steve Biko and the speeches of Malcom X; the way in which Africanity "comprises a body" is at the heart of this negative dialectics:

> We have been a people who hated our African characteristics. We hated our hair, we hated the shape of our nose – we wanted one of those long, dog-like noses, you know. Yeah. We hated the color of our skin, hated the blood of Africa that was in our veins. And in hating our features and our skin and our blood, why, we had to end up hating ourselves. And we hated ourselves. Our color became to us like a prison, which we felt was keeping us confined, not letting us go this way or that way. ... And the psychological reaction to that would have to be that as long as we felt imprisoned or chained or trapped by Black skin, Black features, and Black blood, that skin and those features and that blood that was holding us back automatically had to become hateful to us.[13]

Moreover, the Afro-American poetess Audre Lorde recalls how what was in fact the most intimate part of being a woman – namely, their sexuality – was used against them: "The erotic has been used against us, even the word itself, so often, that we have been taught to suspect what is deepest in ourselves, and that is the way we learn to testify against ourselves, against our feelings."[14]

We can see here that the objection that consists in claiming that consciousness or sexuality are secondary in emancipatory thought is quickly swept aside by an understanding of oppression that is also at work psychically, even at the level of the body itself, starting from a dialectics of freedom that turns against itself. So it is that, if oppression is never ideal, in the sense that it never simply resides at the level of ideas and that it always is exerted on bodies, it is nevertheless the case that oppression functions by turning freedom against itself.[15] To better understand what this implies, I think we can reflect on this notion either in Foucauldian terms or in Sartrean terms. In Foucauldian terms it implies something like the following: power first appears as external, imposed on the subject, restricting it to subordination, and assumes a psychic form that then constitutes the subject's self-identity. The form that this power takes can only be understood in terms of a figure that returns, understood at once as return toward self and then as a turning *against* self. In other words, there is no such thing as power without a relation to power.[16] In Sartrean terms, "oppression is an internalization of the movement of my freedom": what it is important to retain from this is that oppression is not a suppression of my freedom, but rather the transformation of my interiority as being the site of the expression of what comprises my very humanity, namely my freedom. The question then becomes knowing how, in the material dispossession of my resources, of my ancestral lands, of my very eroticism, something at the core of my very sense or meaning of life, and of any possibility of granting meaning, becomes somehow laid bare. Therefore, what's important here is understanding what this ontological expropriation refers to that deprives me not only of the meaning of my world, but also of my capacity to comprise a world. And here, Sartre's analyses seem pertinent:

> There is oppression when freedom turns against itself; that is, there has to be a duality at the heart of freedom. ... This turning against itself implies that freedom can be circumscribed by another freedom that steals its universe, the meaning of its acts, and the unity of its life from it. ... Ontologically, every look of a passerby at my universe steals the part looked at from me. But I grab back this fleeing something by looking at the passerby. However, if the passerby also possesses *knowledge*, there is something that I will never be able to grab back. He disarms my view of the object by reducing it to appearance. And, himself, sees the substance behind it. Without him, the distinction between substance and existence would have no meaning.[17]

The turning of freedom against itself then passes from a disappropriation of everything that had previously for me bestowed meaning and had existential depth. Audre Lorde's work echoes such an analysis when she says that the oppressed often see their knowledge as stolen:

> Whenever the need for some pretense for communication arises, those who profit from our oppression call upon us to share our knowledge with them. In other words, it is the responsibility of the oppressed to teach the oppressors their mistakes. I am responsible for educating teachers who dismiss my children's culture in school. ... The oppressors maintain their position and evade responsibility for their own actions.[18]

As for Steve Biko, he speaks of this misappropriation of African societies, of their spirit, namely of their culture, as if this latter was something to be destroyed or at least to be reduced to a simple folkloric expression as soon as the people found a possible body of resistance capable of expressing a human dignity that was no longer mediated by the master.[19]

But if the way in which consciousness speaks with itself is to adopt a language that misappropriates it and takes it as an enemy, how does one escape such a vicious circle? How can one finally escape from this oppression of consciousness? How can one resist in this framework of a consciousness that turns freedom against itself?

A politics of liberation: a becoming-negro

This question is crucial in that we can see very clearly that informing people, making a grand disclosure, bringing the truth is not simply a process of political awareness. Biko seeks to reflect on this problematic: "What makes the Black man fail to tick? Is he convinced of his own accord of his inabilities? Does he lack in his genetic make-up that rare quality that makes a man willing to die for the realization of his aspirations?"[20] Here it's interesting to examine the difference between the two responses to the questions posed (an affirmative response in the case of the first, and a negative one in the second) reflected along with the historical consequences of the "choice" made by the oppressed in order to liberate themselves: the answer that Biko arrives at, following both Malcolm X and Audre Lorde, is precisely that which consists of taking into account the fact that the oppressed have chosen as the elevation of their being to dissociate themselves from their own, to be no longer Black, to "de-negro" themselves, to use the term adopted by Fanon, and subsequently to constitute themselves, in the eyes of the master, as an "exception," that is to say, as the "good Black man," what Malcolm X referred to as "the house negro" in contrast to the "field negros" on the slave plantations. It's by dissociating oneself from one's own people and working to no longer resemble them that the domesticated or "house negro" elevates their humanity: today, the "house negro" wants to live alongside his master. He pays three times the price for a house he lives in, just to be closer to his master, and so that he can subsequently go and boast about being "the only negro in the neighborhood." "I'm the only one in my party," "I'm the only one in this school," etc.[21]

So we see here that there's a twofold problem with regard to political awareness: it resides first of all in what makes the desire of the master the master-desire in us, which prevents any form of revolt. Fanon showed in this way the inherent failure of the master–slave dialectics through the very fact that, in Hegel, the slave turns toward the object, whereas, in post-slavery and apartheid systems, he turns toward the master whose recognition he seeks out at the cost of his very own self disavowal.[22] And the other constitutive part of the problem is, above all, the way in which the very same enemy takes on the form of an *intimate* friend. This domestication of the desire for freedom can be explained through the phenomenon of the eroticization of domination, the real obstacle to political awareness to the extent that servitude becomes without a relation to the outside. How can we fight against something within us that takes the very form itself of our eroticism, and to which we "unconsciously consent," as paradoxical as that may seem?

It is at this crucial point in the epistemology of the oppressed consciousness that the question of how to escape from this negative dialectics of freedom comes into play. Should one turn one's own shame and self-hatred against White people in a deadly mimicry that would make White folk feel "their" sense of shame in return? Should one counteract the violence of this oppression with another form of violence that could inevitably only demonstrate the error of such a position as soon as the idea becomes clear to itself? And it's here that we begin to see that a discussion can take place between Biko, Lorde, and Malcolm X, all of them being readers of Fanon, who, in *The Wretched of the Earth*, recalls the need to resort to violence in colonial situations. One must read the insistence that Fanon places on violence in *The Wretched of the Earth* alongside what he exposes in *Black Skin, White Masks* regarding the eroticization of domination. The problem is the following: what new modality of desire and consciousness as self-enjoyment [*jouissance*] is possible? How can we exit from the deadly circularity of desire as suppression of self? In response to the question of how one can once again become a friend to oneself, Fanon's response seems to be that the only solution is to expel the enemy outside ourselves, and this can only be done by giving back our hostility to the enemy, who had become an intimate friend: so here again it is a question of a detoxifying violence within ourselves that speaks in the place of the master, so as to finally authentically think for ourselves.

My interpretation of Fanon is that what's at stake here concerns our actions – including our actions of thought – of making oneself a negro (and not Black).[23] Negro and not Black, to the extent that it's no longer a question, in *The Wretched of the Earth*, of losing oneself in the great dark night of negritude, of simply valuing what had for a long time been devalued – or at the very least it's no longer a question of simply turning back the stigma by positively reinvesting it, but rather of reconsidering what has emerged in the light of day from the experience of the negro, that is, from the being-made-negro, or of the Black-made-negro: namely the universal experience of oppression and resistance. And, I'm of the opinion that we can in this way understand or read the notion of becoming-negro in two different ways: either as Achille Mbembe defines it, as the universalization of the constitution of capitalism of the labor-body, of the body-waste [*corps-déchet*];[24] or in a Deleuzian formulation that I propose, like becoming a minority in the sense of an exposition of the contradictions of the universal. It has already been shown how the universal, in its historical institution, proceeded by way of a form of violence that consisted doubly in asserting itself as the only possible universal (and therefore of particularizing and disqualifying other forms of the expression of consciousness, that is, of other cultures) and as an injunction for individuals to loosen their particular affiliations (first and foremost for nonwhites, but not just them).[25] These contradictions of a universal that functions starting from categories of the constitution of equality and liberty are resolved in what Marx calls ideology, in the sense not only of an erasure of interests, of a chosen position, of the situation such a position expresses, but also in the sense of a denial of the universal's own centered position, which leads to a situation, as Étienne Balibar has noted, where "the language of the universal has no exterior."[26] I would therefore like to return to the fact that a *becoming-negro* is a way to propose another narrative for the universal starting from an interiority that produces a fissure in the very tautological logic of the universal.

We can, of course, understand the declaration in the Haitian constitution of 1805, which states that Haitians are now considered as Black,[27] as a way of putting an end to the arithmetic of racial categorization during the period of slavery that sought to index the shades of the darkness of one's skin as a means of discerning one's morality, all the way to the unmixed blood of the Black man who is the most unworthy of them all. But we could also take into account in this generic naming of Haitians, starting from the most denigrating or devalued term on the ontological scale, how this can be read more as a universal resignification not of a stigma, or of a victim's condition, but as what in the consciousness of the oppressed constitutes an irrepressible minimum: namely, a love the oppressed holds for his freedom and the way in which he works so as to refuse being denied this last dignity. And in this sense, the *becoming-negro* is to identify with another universal – that of fighting for one's own liberation, or at the very least, a resistance against its negation. A vast history of acts of resistance by slaves that has largely been undocumented, but whose traces we can uncover as soon as we traverse the Middle Passage.[28]

Consequently, if the becoming-negro proceeds by identification, then it also signifies a *de-ethnicization of what being Black means* (as we see in the Haitian constitution, since all Haitians, including Whites, will be considered as Black). Malcolm X, Steve Biko, and Audre Lorde also, in their own ways, semantically and historically redeploy what being Black and White means by freeing the terms from the sole logic of epidermal identification. In this epistemology of the oppressed consciousness, Black and White become floating signifiers following a historical social relationship in which individuals are inserted. In such an epistemology, considered as Black will be, at the same time, both the oppressed to the extent that their being is constituted by structural experiences or repetitive injustices, and the oppressed to the extent that they refuse to renounce themselves and or become accomplice to their own servitude or the servitude of their own. Being Black is therefore the one who suffers and fights to respect his dignity. This is what makes Malcolm X state that "the Black revolution is sweeping Asia, is sweeping Africa, is rearing its head in Latin America." And "When I say 'Black' what I mean is 'nonwhite' – Black, Brown, Red, Yellow."[29] At a certain point in his reflections, he even differentiates between a "negro revolution," which is the authentic revolution, and simply the Black revolution,[30] which is still seemingly stuck in a logic of alienation, since it thinks of the categories of the revolution in terms that dispossess Blacks: moreover, for Malcolm X, the Black Revolution is that of Martin Luther King, Jr., who strives, through means of nonviolence, to obtain civil rights, equal rights for all citizens. And yet, for Malcolm X, what is of vital import for a negro revolution are universal human rights.[31] And by this he understands two things: that what concerns Black Americans during the period of segregation is a problem that concerns not only Americans, but humanity the world over. And so he is seeking to globalize the question of civil rights for Black people. But he also understands by such a question that a democratic system founded on segregation cannot be reformed to such an extent that it's the very nation-state itself that has some sort of gangrene, and such a problem is one that concerns not only Blacks, but Whites as well. And, moreover, it's regarding this very problematic that Malcolm X sees a possible political alliance: according to him, what Whites must do is say, precisely, "not in our name" and bring their own nation-state to justice before the United Nations.[32] This is, for him, the becoming-revolutionary that makes someone nonwhite, which presumes that Whites will refuse that their freedom and their material comfort, as minimal as it might be, be produced not only to the detriment of or leaving aside Blacks, but even as a result of the subjection and exclusion of Blacks: from this perspective, we can easily begin to understand how a White person can become Black if he embraces this becoming-negro, that is, if he makes the revolutionary project of Blacks a project of his own liberation and not merely one of saving Blacks, as if he himself were absolved from this reversal of freedom against itself. And it is also a question of exiting from the notion of good conscience, from the white liberal *bona fides*, whereby it was thought that by preaching emancipation they were saving others and not themselves.

We find this same argumentative logic at work in Steve Biko, who was actually strongly influenced by a book by Stokely Carmichael,[33] who himself realigned his engagement in a logic that was more influenced by Malcolm X: for Biko, a Black man who worked for the police during the apartheid years, repressing anti-apartheid demonstrations, lost his right to be Black and simply became a nonwhite.[34] And furthermore, what Whites had to work at, according to Biko, was more specifically to enact civil disobedience – to refuse to practice that which is done in their name and to their detriment: "The liberal (white) must fight on his own and for himself. If they are true liberals they must realize that they themselves are oppressed, and they must fight for their own freedom."[35] For Audre Lorde, the possibility of a political sisterhood will come from the fact that each person can learn to understand the specificity of their own oppressions – what Lorde refers to as "differences" – and their articulation with other oppressions so as to comprise a people, which supposes putting an end to the general belief that heterosexuality in minority groups implies any sort of security against sexist violence, and to cease this "self-hatred, learned in childhood … to fight against those things in myself."[36]

And we can begin to see it: hatred of Whites not only serves no purpose, it is dangerous. We will never be capable of getting people to love themselves by cultivating hatred of the other. The reason for this theoretical and practical refusal of hatred as a strategy of the liberation of consciousness is threefold. First, hatred is always invested with envy, with a desire for what the White person is supposed to represent: namely, the master. Second, violence is first and foremost destructive to the one who inflicts it. Third, violence personalizes the relation of oppression even though the goal is to depersonalize violence, to stop women from tearing themselves apart, to stop Blacks from destroying each other, and to stop the oppressed from turning against each other, or against the simple White grocer, for example: what is required, according to Audre Lorde, is to direct one's anger, attacking the system at its roots.[37] According to her, one should take aim at capitalist violence whereby Black men only retain their virility by turning their feelings of humiliation against Black women, and more specifically, against lesbians.[38] This is also what Biko understood in preaching nonviolence, but so did Malcolm X, who ended up siding more in his ideas with Martin Luther King, whose ideas regarding nonviolence had also evolved.[39] This at least is the reading that Audre Lorde makes of it, and that I in turn take up.[40]

For Biko, Malcolm X, and Lorde, it is therefore a question of making a revolution in oneself, while simultaneously combatting structures that produce systemic violence. To restore a sense of self-confidence, to love oneself, constitutes such a revolution: it's via this perspective that we should understand separatist logic in the sense of a non-mixing of organizations or meetings in the way in which racism functions, which always proceeds through a threefold process of criminalization, pathologization, and infantilization. As a result, the Black consciousness movement undertaken by Steve Biko had intended to demonstrate, in contrast to an infantilization, that Blacks can do things for themselves, think for themselves, without having to convince others of their experiences. It's also about starting from a shared common experience of being rendered invisible, of being stigmatized, and of discrimination, in order to reflect on the best way to organize. Audre Lorde also liked to cite Malcolm X, who said that if we are not responsible for our oppression we are nevertheless responsible for our liberation: no one either can or should liberate us from our situation. The goal in any case is not to simply live separately. Biko as well as Malcom X – after returning from his third trip to Mecca[41] – and Lorde all understand that the need and the desire to live alongside Whites must be disalienated, but not suppressed. In a striking manner, Malcolm X recounts how the White Muslims in Mecca were not the same as the racist Whites he encountered in America: there was thus another way of being White, which did not necessarily mean being an oppressor.[42]

I will end this analysis by breaking down the initial question into a number of component parts: "How can one be a woman, homosexual, and poor?" Audre Lorde rightfully asserts that in any political movement where the survival of the oppressed is at stake, what is always first and foremost a priority is simply that of ordinary survival. And in order to survive, one must escape from the spirit of sacrifice that has wreaked so much havoc on women, especially nonwhite women, to the point that their affects, the way in which they loved, was turned against them:

> In this country, Black women traditionally have had compassion for everybody else except ourselves. We cared for whites because we had to for pay or survival; we have cared for our children and our fathers and our brothers and our lovers. History and popular culture, as well as our personal lives, are full of tales of Black women who "had compassion for misguided Black men." Our scarred, broken, battered, and dead daughters and sisters are a mute testament to that reality. We need to learn to have care and compassion for ourselves, too.[43]

Self-love is thus a fundamental part of escaping violence. And one of the essential aspects of escaping a violence that arises from an anger that one unfairly addresses to oneself is to give back to the oppressed a language that is *his*, one that literally speaks to him and honors what is most human in him: namely, dignity. But Malcolm X, Steve Biko, and Audre Lorde like to remind us that dignity can only be rediscovered through a revolution that must move from a transformation of our conditions of existence and most notably those that allow us to take care of ourselves: whether such a care takes the form of a revolution of the earth or a revolution in caring for our bodies following Audre Lorde. In the end, one thing alone is important with regard to any revolution: acquiring power. And in this light, one must want for oneself so as to consider oneself worthy of it.

Rediscovering Meaning

Bonaventure Mve-Ondo

Bonaventure Mve-Ondo *is a Professor of Philosophy. Former Rector of the University of Omar-Bongo of Libreville, he has also served as Vice-rector for the Agence universitaire de la francophonie. His works include* Un Homme debout. Jean-Marc Ekoh *(Alfabarre éditions, 2017),* Wisdom and Initiation in Gabon: A Philosophical Analysis of Fang Tales, Myths, and Legends *(Lexington Books, 2013),* À Chacun sa raison. Raison occidentale et pensée africaine *(L'Harmattan, 2013), and* Afrique, la fracture scientifique *(Futuribles, 2005).*

I would like to begin by way of a general impression – a general impression confirmed by our current actuality. For more than ten years now, African societies seem to have become swept up in a vertiginous quest for their identity, and the more they search, the less they are capable of finding themselves. The impression that one begins to see revealed here is that they are experiencing a difficult time, what could even be described as a sense of heading down the wrong path without ever finding their center of gravity. Or rather, the history of the past fifty years is, in essence, one of profound despair. A period during which, from one generation to the next, they've gone from certainty to brief moments of hope, followed by devastating disappointments. Disappointments first in the form of an inability to find meaning in their existence, and disappointments also in feeling constantly excluded from the rest of the world, a devastating situation that betrays the revolt of those who run around in circles without ever finding their way or discovering what makes sense.[1]

Attempting to understand today the immense need for a sense of identity, for a sense of re-establishing foundations claimed by African societies, requires reflecting initially on how the usual conceptual tools through which these societies were thought, or thought of themselves until recently, were very limited, even imprecise; above all, they must be clarified and questioned.

But to clarify something is also to question the sociocultural and political context, most notably the ongoing crisis that has lasted since the 1990s. What are we bearing witness to? Claims to identity that exploit the context, the process of democratization, and whose objective is to safeguard or acquire certain interests (often against all odds), or to assure basic rights that have been scoffed at or completely ignored. A number of internal conflicts of a political, social, economic, and cultural order; important sociological and economic mutations that mean we have moved from societies where ethnicity is the primary focus to societies based on peaceful interethnic notions of living together. Societies established around income economies and government workers have become more and more liberal and focused on the self-employed. In other words, we are witnessing an implosion of the traditional mechanisms that served as shock absorbers and which bore names such as culture, ethics, morality, a sense of sharing, family, clan, and a desire for living together. Faced with these conflicts and transformations, we finally arrive at our principal question: how can one find a sign that gives us back a certain notion of meaning in our lives, the requisite compass with which to orient ourselves and truly participate in the task of our current times: namely, the reconstruction of Africa?

This important question can be broken down into three fundamental sub-questions. What constitutes the creative core of Africa in its spatial and temporal diversity, on which the continent can rely so as to support these transformations? What are the requisite conditions needed so Africa can invent itself and continue to invent itself? And finally, in encounters with other countries, how does Africa reinvent itself today?

I will make use of these three questions in an attempt to engage in deconstructing, clarifying, and re-establishing meaning.

First question: What constitutes the creative core of Africa?

Despite the vast weight of colonization and in our journey through it, how can we uncover what remains of Africa's Islamization, Christianization, postcolonial independence, and, more generally, globalization? How can we once again uncover a universe of meaning that organizes the schemas of thought and attitudes of Africans today? Or, better still, how have African societies been able, throughout time and space, and in spite of reconstitutions, falsifications, and other mixtures, in spite of colonial restrictions, submissions, and conversions, in spite of a politics that has been more or less forced upon them with regard to an integration into the global and national economic markets since the early days of its independence, in spite of the shock of its Westernization and globalization, how have these societies been able to continue proposing a common vision of the world or a common relationship to the world?

The answer to this first question cannot be found in any great principles or ideological postures, but in the ontological, ethical, and mythological core that organizes the concrete attitudes of life and that we most often find in our traditions, in the transformations, and in our behavior toward our fellow citizens and foreigners. But also, we can find an answer through the available conceptual tools that come from elsewhere. A creative core, in our estimation, that will help us better orient ourselves in the future. It is then a question of carefully delving into the implicit categories that organize the sayings [le dire] and the habits of thought.

The analyses that Mamoussé Diagne and I have proposed concerning oral reason have shed some light on the social mechanisms and ways of thinking, that is, the socioculture and tools that have allowed African cultures to maintain this cultural continuity and even help to explain it. In traditional Africa, oral transmission is subject to mechanisms of a completely different nature than in the civilizations of written culture. The objective of such practices is never to arrive at a quantified result but, rather, to reflect on objects of thought that conceal kernels of meaning and that function in a sort of half-light. Under an apparent conversion, a prudent submission to the message of others, and a reformulating of their conceptual instruments, many African peoples have never thought of the world in terms other than those of their ancestors, and all their representations find themselves literally "encased" in symbolic images that allow them to plunge into the most profound psychic and affabulatory activity of the subject, conscious or unconscious.

The general conclusion at which we arrive is quite clear: there exists a language that is translated through gestures, stories, myths, ways of life, attitudes, and daily practices that reveal a strong and vibrant culture, a cognitive system, and a particular relation to the world. Such is the creative core of African cultures, which continues to animate attitudes and conducts, or, better still, the five implicit categories of space, time, causality, object, and person.

And in effect, in the larger collection of examined traditional texts (myths, legends, fairytales, proverbs, etc.) from yesterday to today, what remains is a particular apprehension of these categories that often help us to understand the conceptual impasses at work today. So it's important, if we want to seek out the origin of such traditions, to carefully account for the external centrality of the concepts and categories in terms of which this continent is thought and thinks. Concepts and categories that reduce the continent to nothing more than a simple object of thought for itself, and in so doing conflate a kind of fast-food thought for a more profound reflection and way of thinking.

To take one example, let's consider one of the categories in question: time. What the African myths we have examined reveal is not only that there is a place for distinguishing between sacred time (originary) and secular time (of degradation), but also that time should be considered as neither objective nor available, since it is entirely tied to invisible forces. This is a domain that is forbidden to man and to which he is obliged to submit. And since nothing happens that shouldn't happen, time is subject to general planning and refers to the notion of destiny, which is an intercultural constant and dominates existence. Since time is forbidden and predetermined, it's the technicians and specialists of the future – seers and sorcerers – who have the responsibility of taking care of it and revealing to men their future, of operating a partial reorganization, since we cannot contradict or cancel what is predetermined and, at best, we can transpose, divert, or compensate it.

We can begin to understand why such a conception of time and predestination implies that the notion of a project must be formulated with the utmost circumspection, since the declaration of intention and a calculation of the future are dangerous attitudes. To anticipate a happy event runs the risk of preventing its realization, whereas to anticipate a misfortunate event runs the risk of provoking it. In the contemporary world of the politics of development, it is quite clear that such conceptions constitute, and will continue to constitute, an obstacle, because the initiative must be suppressed and because any project by its very nature is dangerous in that it implies an incursion into a reserved domain.

As a result, we can note in a number of traditional and non-traditional societies that, on the one hand, the verbal mode of the future does not yet exist, or rather it functions in a metaphorical manner; and, on the other hand, the terminology of the future is relatively recent. And this isn't only the case for Africa! Even in the industrial societies of Western Europe, for example, we know that the terms *predictable* [*prévisionnel*] and *foreseeable* [*prévisible*] date, respectively, from 1848 and 1865, the term *program* – understood as the exposition of the intentions of a person or a group – from 1789, and the term *programming* [*programmation*] only goes as far back as 1960. *Prospective*, which signifies "optics" in the sixteenth century, takes on a different meaning, most notably with Gaston Berger in 1920. And finally, whereas the term *future* itself, meaning that which indicates an action to come, dates back to 1671, the terms *futurible*, and *futurology* date from 1966 and 1968 respectively. We can discern from this that, if these terms expressing a certain influence of time on man, such as predestination whose origin dates back to 1190, are all very old, those that denote man's action or influence on time are very recent.[2]

Such a distinction explains the need to rethink categories and concepts so as to better understand the difficulties experienced by a continent torn between "its traditions" and Western modernity. As far as time is concerned, traditional societies operate in a frozen temporal dimension that is inscribed in a perfectly coherent social logic, namely: things don't change, the world is how it has always been since the beginning of time. If change must be undergone, then it can only be done in a manner that is slow, unconscious, and involuntary – three terms that demonstrate the contrast between traditional societies and contemporary ones. The consequence of such difference, found in a dedication to obeying one's ancestors, is the following: the unwavering connection between the ancestors and the living, everything else being nothing more than mere accidents.

And now we can see it: one can't understand the erring of today's contemporary African societies and the uncertainty that bears on their future without taking into account this primordial epistemological foundation that, as a system, has not truly been deconstructed or called into question. And we could safely say that this deconstruction has not truly taken place, so it is often difficult for the ordinary person to fully enter into modernity and, above all, to think about the future.

We should recall that in *Tristes tropiques*,[3] Lévi-Strauss studied the behavior of an ethnic group that was brutally placed in a confrontation with "Western" machinery: they found themselves utterly incapable of assimilating, not for lack of ability in the proper sense of the term, but because their conception of time, of space, and of relations between people did not allow them to recognize the slightest value in performance [*rendement*], well-being, and the capitalization of means. And here is where we can uncover an unconscious resistance at work. As a result of this, we can see quite clearly that one of the causes of underdevelopment is not simply a technical one, but rather proceeds from a static conception of time and history. This was also magnificently shown by Pierre-Maxime Schuhl in his book *Essai sur la formation de la pensée grecque*.[4] For Schuhl, the reason why Greek technics or technology couldn't evolve is that, in having a limited conception of time and history, there was no positive conception of progress itself. In other words, it's not because the Greeks had a significant number of slaves at their disposal that they felt the need to replace human labor with that of machine labor, but rather because they had not yet conceptualized that the corresponding value of their technics was inherently linked to alleviating the suffering of humans in order for their technology to evolve.

And yet, if a conceptual tool can only operate through a process of valorization, it is still vitally important to understand the limits of such a value, to define the different levels at which this value resides. I spoke a bit earlier of "creative core" as an allusion to this phenomenon, as an allusion to this multitude of wrappings that one must pierce in order to attain it. We can imagine several distinct levels: the superficial level where the values of traditional African society are expressed through morals, in social practices, in the morality of one's actions. Such a level is not yet that of the creative phenomenon, it's merely that of reproduction – of a mimetics and adherence to "cultural habits" that one has yet to deconstruct. Whoever has not learned to decode cannot penetrate this mystery. This level constitutes a "foundation of habits" that doesn't allow one to express the essential. What matters here is knowing how to dissect it so as to grasp the hidden message.

From this foundational level, we move on to a less superficial level where the values are made manifest through traditional institutions, but these latter are nothing more than a reflection of a specific state of thought, of the will of a human group at a certain moment in history. This is why these very institutions themselves ask to be deciphered. It seems to me that if we want to reach the creative core, we must dig deep all the way to the layer of images and symbols that constitute the foundational representations of a people. As with psychoanalysis, the discovery of this core is not the result of a simple description, but of a veritable deconstruction and a methodical interpretation. This is what Mamoussé Diagne and I have attempted to do, starting from a corpus of texts belonging to the peoples of Senegal and Gabon, so as to display not only their brilliance but also their originality – namely, the foundation of each of these peoples' styles.

But this collection of images and symbols is still not the most radical phenomenon of creativity in African societies, it merely comprises the final wrapping. In contrast to the instrument or tool that can be conserved or become sedimented, or increase in capital value, a cultural tradition can only remain alive as long as it is endlessly recreated. How have African societies resolved such a problem? By contrasting the axis of temporality to that of sedimentation. We should recall that for humanity there are two ways to traverse time: civilization develops a certain sense of time, which is the foundation of accumulation and progress, whereas the way a people develops a specific culture rests on some sort of law of fidelity and creation. In other words, a culture begins to die as soon it is no longer renewed, recreated; in these instances, a thinker, or writer, a sage, or a spiritual individual must rise up and relaunch the culture and risk taking it on a completely new adventure. Such a creation escapes all planning and predictions, and any kind of decision from a specific party or nation-state. The tragic logic of the creation of any culture is not founded on a tranquil accumulation of tools that define it as a civilization, but in the very essential primary questioning, which is education in critical thinking. It is all the more urgent to get away from what Fabien Eboussi Boulaga called the position of the exotic intellectual: the one who is settled in the absence of thought.[5]

Second question: Under what conditions can Africa invent itself and continue to invent itself?

We must now attempt to respond to the second question: under what conditions can the creation of a people endure? A formidable question, posed by the development of a universal scientific, technological, juridical, economic civilization, in other words: the civilization of globalization. For, while it is true that all traditional cultures suffer under the same pressure and erosion of this global civilization, they do not all have the same capacity for resistance or, especially, the same capacity for absorption. What we can understand through the political struggles of African peoples today is that every "culture" is not necessarily compatible with global civilization. The following question then arises: what are the necessary conditions for achieving a successful integration into globalization?

First condition: only a culture capable of scientific rationality can be reborn and survive. What sort of politics is required so that a proper education can be set in place to ensure such an appropriation?

Second condition, which is just as important: only a faith that appeals to the comprehension of intelligence can "embrace" its time. Such a faith rests as much in a desacralization of nature and beings as it does in a desacralization and valorization of time. Only then would mankind have the capacity to survive and endure. In order for its fidelity to be more than simply a folkoric decoration, each culture must renounce just repeating the past and learn to grasp its limits so as to constantly invent itself. And it's through this process alone that culture will be capable of freeing up the paths toward its future or utopia. It is worth returning here to what is often skillfully presented as the fight against religious and identarian fundamentalism, developed as a phenomenon of resistance by Boko Haram. The objective of this terrorist group, whose name literally means "Forbidden Book," is a refusal of the Western form of schooling considered as a vector of modernity, of individual freedom, and therefore of democracy. Boko Haram's project is the return of the old established order by way of Islamic colonization: no school allowed for girls; man commands and is the owner of women (harem) – he even is required to marry young teenage virgin girls. No one will ever forget the kidnapping of several hundred high school girls in 2014 and the wave of protest that rippled throughout the rest of the world.

What is referred to in this instance as a "return" to traditions is in reality founded on "a concerted manipulation of memory and what has been forgotten" by this group that proposes a "fragmented" history of Africa and its traditions.[6] What is presented here as "traditions" is nothing more than the acknowledged acquisition and appropriation of a certain moment in the history of the continent: Arab colonization in the aftermath of European colonization. For Africa to truly be capable of fully inventing a future for itself, it is important that the continent is capable of letting go of pre-established or circumstantial certainties and for it to shed light on its non-history or on its forgotten "histories." And this is a task of great urgency.

The current silence of the media as well as African states regarding the struggle against the "Forbidden Book" is due to the fear of what such a reflection could trigger regarding the colonial traumas of the slave trade. And yet, now more than ever, we must refuse to submit instinctively to the persisting traumas that lead to non-history and violence. We must overcome and denounce such a reductive form of written African history, in a process not only of liberation but also of projective exploration. As Frantz Fanon used to say, the slave is first of all the one who doesn't know, and the slave of the slave is the one who doesn't want to know.

In reality, the contemporary crisis of African societies on which fundamentalist groups, such as the "Forbidden Book" group, have been trying to surf now for several years flows more from the post-World War II model of development that has begun to run out of steam, and which was imposed on Africa. This model, that of catching up not only economically, was also essentially founded on a theory of psychoanalytic transference, a cut-and-paste model that goes from a logic of investment to a logic of rent and a consumption of thoughts and lifestyles – elaborated without any true appropriation.

The response to this crisis of meaning, as well as to the fundamentalisms, resides in establishing a critical mind for decolonizing and for decolonizing minds, behaviors, and imaginations in order to rethink traditions, since there is no tradition that is superior to man: it's man who, as Valentin-Yves Mudimbe has demonstrated,[7] is the inventor of his traditions.

Third question: In its encounter with other cultures, how is Africa reinventing itself today?

How is it possible to allow for an encounter between diverse cultures – and by encounter, do we mean one that is not fatal for African cultures? Such an encounter that is not fatal supposes the acceptance of other cultures. Such an encounter is of extreme importance, since it is constitutive of every society. In order to accept in front of oneself someone other than oneself, one must have a self. Moreover, no society whatsoever lives alone and for itself. Every society is always in dialogue and maintains a connection with others. What must be refused are low-level syncretisms, pseudo-pop philosophies that are nothing more than historical precipitations. In contrast to them, we must propose communication, real communication, that is, a dramatic relationship in which, step by step, I slowly assert myself in my own culture while also acquainting myself with others according to their civilization, in other words through cultural creolization, *métissage*, hybridity.

The world to come will be an ensemble of peoples and the nations of the world will have decided to build the world together. Such a world can only be constructed through essential principles such as dialogue, solidarity, and co-responsibility.

Like the mixture of music proposed by Pierre Akendengue and Hugues de Courson in their album *Lambarena: Bach to Africa*,[8] a homage to Dr. Albert Schweitzer, the challenge is not about forging a synthesis between two universes (here musical and cultural), but about working and living together (here by means of musical expression), whereby each musician responds to the other through subtle exchanges without losing anything of their own identity or culture.

This encounter of peoples and civilizations disrupts our typical ways of thinking, since it marks the end of absolute certainty and opens up a horizon of thought: the creole world. The conditions for such a dialogue are well known. The first is that Africa must finally progress out of its infantilization in order to regain its maturity. The second condition is that it must recreate itself while keeping one ear open to the rest of the world. Africa has no one it needs to catch up with; all it needs to do is be itself and live its internal transformations, whether they concern sociology, economy, culture, or political model. The third and final condition is that all the nations throughout the world finally agree to move beyond the childish era of competition and begin to build a world together where humanity learns to live and work together.

The history of a humanity to come will not be that of a war of civilizations, but rather that of their encounter, not in the form of a shock or domination, but through real dialogue. Today, we find ourselves in a tunnel, in an interregnum, at the twilight of dogmas and extremisms, but perhaps this will lead us toward a threshold of true dialogues. But what is still no doubt lacking is that we don't yet know how to reflect on and think about the coexistence of these multiple styles, we don't have a philosophy of history capable of solving the problems of coexistence and of living together on a global scale. And from now on, the real question is how to make our way out of these vague and inconsistent syncretisms, to detect an Africa that has truly regained its footing in the world, without complexes, and which can enter into real communication with the other. This assumes that we are capable of posing the question of a dialogue between civilizations in another manner than simply that of conquest and power.

To rediscover meaning or that which grants meaning would be to dare to move beyond those who believe in an intangible identity for Africa and who hope for its salvation through a perpetuation of this identity, and those who have chosen to deny it and think only of Africa's identity in relation to others, in a sort of process of creolization. As Édouard Glissant remarked, true creolization "requires the heterogenous elements put into relation to 'intervalorize themselves,' that is to say, there must be no degradation or diminution of the being, either from outside or from within, in this contact or intermixing." It is "unpredictable."[9] Like in a loving relationship, it's the independence of the protagonists that is the primary constitutive element, even if it is made manifest in a paradoxical manner by bringing together two antinomies: the first is the mysterious genesis of love, the second is more implicit and rests on the principle that Octavio Paz recalls for us: "But we are not transparent, either, for others or for ourselves." Hence his wonderful formula for the romantic condition.[10] As such, what I am and what belongs to me, what I own, is, in the end, first and foremost that which comes from the other. Rediscovering meaning is to build an epistemology of epistemologies capable of a heterotopia, that is, capable of linking a plurality of utopias and having them engage in a plurivalent epistemology that would finally comprise what we could refer to as an "us" so as to be proud of our heritages as much here as there. It is what I refer to as an epistemology of encounter established on a truly assumed syncretism. A Chinese philosopher at the beginning of the twentieth century, Liang Shuming, defined Westernization as "essentially the desire to move forward."[11] But today, such a desire is not merely Western, it is also African to the extent that Africa is capable of reconnecting with its cultural heritages and projects. This is a major change since, as the Quebecois philosopher Jean-François Malherbe has emphasized:

Any relation with temporality that is not articulated together, in the density of the present instant, and the heritage of a past and the project of a future, is extremely reductive. There is no lack of pseudo-spiritualities today that appear as nothing more than banal nostalgias or trivial flights forward. Authentic spiritualities are those that deploy the uncertainty of the subject and propose that he or she inhabit it in a just relation to time, whereas pseudo-spiritualties reduce the relation to time to a nostalgia of origins or to a utopia of the ideal.[12]

Rediscovering meaning is therefore to escape from an epistemological nihilism that consists in thinking that there is nothing left to do and that refuses to evolve. And yet, Africa has for a long time now adopted the notion of linear time and has, in its own manner, already been inscribed in a *métisse*, hybrid, creole modernity that allows the continent to reinvent itself from now on beyond mere appearances and resistances. A modernity that is not a finishing line, but a starting line, a sort of open road or path, and, above all, an act of free will.

Esteem for Self
Creating One's Own Sense/Carving Out One's Own Path[1]

Séverine Kodjo-Grandvaux

Séverine Kodjo-Grandvaux is a journalist, philosopher, and associate researcher at Université Paris 8. She is the author of Philosophies africaines *(Éditions Présence africaine, 2013), awarded the Louis Marin Overseas Sciences Prize.*

Decolonizing forms of knowledge, breaking away from epistemologies that were generated by an ever-present coloniality. Decentering oneself so as to produce a new critical thought that would allow for each and every one of us to participate in the movement of the world. To be simultaneously an actor and producer of meaning. Under what conditions is all this possible? How can a subject be led into daring to partake in the uncertain paths of intellectual transgression and to invoke a kind of undisciplined posture so as to construct themselves? How can we allow for an "I can" to arrive in asymmetrical situations where recognition, at the height of what I am, is not given in advance?

We have lost sight of the fact that the history of ideas is also a history of emotions. Enclosed as we are in a conception of knowledge and the production of knowledge inherited from the European Enlightenment, where the Cartesian mind takes hold of reality as affirmed by way of *cogito ergo sum*, we have forgotten that philosophers are not simply their minds but are made up of flesh and blood, that is, they have bodies and that affect often plays an essential role in conceptual creation. Paradoxically, whereas the *ego cogito* imposed itself, the "I" became effaced by the well-known falsely modest impersonal "we" of academic writing. To affirm a subject engaged in an individual history and a personal sense of feeling [*ressenti*] engaged in an act of thought implies the impossibility of producing an objective thought whose scope is universal. And yet, only individuals exist, inscribed in singular, personal, and collective memories, in a specific era and culture, whose utterances emanate from a particular place.

To propose a decolonial gaze on philosophy is not merely to question the modalities of conceptual decolonization. It could also be to question the very feelings at work in intellectual production, in particular those that can help us to confront a dominant hegemonic system of thought. In the quest for a dignified life, one that is just and good, it would seem to me that appreciation of one's own worth is necessary for the elaboration of new epistemologies, for self-realization, and for the creation of spaces of individuation with one's sights set on a fully actualized citizenship. These are the three complementary dimensions of the constitutive functioning of an individuality, of a subject. Being for self. Being in the heart of the city, for and with others. Being the producer of knowledge. Self-esteem is the primary driving force of decolonization in that having esteem for oneself is also to make sense – to produce sensation and create one's own meaning. Such a feeling, which feeds itself and is also nourished from the outside, is what allows me to be at the height of my abilities to take action and be the author of my own existence.

The paths that I will take are not carved out in advance. My inscription in this world has a meaning that I alone must seek to define, actualize, and make others recognize. This is how one creates meaning for oneself as well as for others. To have self-esteem is to be aware of one's value, of one's capabilities and one's capacity to be oneself: to actualize oneself as a project, to reside in a possibility of oneself, and to become an autonomous subject. But in order to have self-esteem, to be capable of gaging one's own abilities, I owe it to myself to retain a certain fidelity to what I am. Traitors often have a rather poor opinion of themselves. Such fidelity must be experienced and proven by way of movement, in the very construction and actualization of my being. From this will emanate a certain respect from the other who will recognize what they owe me. Indeed, how does one expect that anyone else will grant me respect and recognize me for who I am if I myself am not capable of doing so? I must endow myself with the courage to affirm my identity in confronting such adversity. Whole and complete. Retaining my humanity, when it is denied to me and I am undervalued. When I've been reduced to a mere female body in a male environment, to a young person's voice in a gerontocratic society, to a Black body in a world where political, economic, epistemic, and cultural forces are in the hands of those with fair skin ... The situations in which one is a minority are multiple and often overlap, always accompanied by a symbolic and psychic violence that is more or less significant, even at times by extreme physical brutality that results in death. In such a context, more than ever, one needs the love of one's loved ones. This is the first recognition that one must retain in order to construct oneself. "To regain self-esteem, what's most important is to be – or feel – loved, more than simply being – or believing oneself to be – dominant," Christophe André, doctor of psychiatry at Sainte-Anne hospital (in Paris) explains. He is also quick to point out:

> Authors who have worked on the acquisition of self-esteem have all emphasized the importance, for the good development of such self-esteem, of the unconditional love of parents for their children that is not dependent on their performance or achievements. In this way, the child interiorizes that their value is not dependent on how they perform, but represents a stable given that is relatively independent, at least in the short term, from notions of success and failure.

We arrive into the world in a situation of total dependence. Without care or love, a newborn baby cannot survive. It's due to the fact that we have received a sufficient amount of maternal (parental) love that we are able to leave behind the loving embrace that nourished and cradled us in order to set out on our own and open ourselves up to others. Our initial sociability is anchored in the recognition of what this maternal (parental) love has given us. The child slowly but surely becomes cognizant that he or she is an individual separate from the mother. And that he or she must confront their own environment. It's only in being properly armed with confidence that the individual will dare to turn outward toward others, and then eventually present themselves to the world. But she can only do this if her mother (the parents) allow her to do so and encourage her. That is, if the mother recognizes her child as a being distinct from herself and helps the child to become autonomous. Self-confidence and self-esteem, nourished by the love of those who raised me, requires the other to recognize and accept that which distinguishes me from him. It's this sort of confidence in oneself along with a knowledge of my potentialities that will allow me to want to affirm my ipseity – to construct and assume a solid self that will allow me to set out to meet the other and, in doing so, not renounce self. This originary need for love is insatiable and we must sustain it throughout our lives. How can we continue to make our way when our neighbors – those with whom we share our human experience – hate us to the point of treating us like animals or things? Of placing us in a "colonial difference" (Walter Mignolo), a fantasmized identity during the imperial conquest, as they put us in chains and sent us to hell? During a time when those who were stronger forced us to renounce self in order to take on their own culture? Dispossessing us from our power of naming ourselves, depriving us from what "within each human is possibility, a promise of the accomplishment of humanity" (Jean Amrouche)?

> The most important field in which [colonialism] sunk its claws was the mental universe of the colonized: the colonizers were able, through culture, to control the perception that the colonized had of himself and his relation with the world. Social and economic control cannot be total without also controlling the mind or spirit. Controlling the culture of a people is to also control the representation that the people have of themselves and their relations with others. In the case of colonialism, the establishment of this control takes on two forms: the destruction or the systematic devaluing of the culture of the colonized, of their artforms, their dance, their forms of religion, their history, their geography, their education, their written and oral literature – and, conversely, the endless glorification of the language of the colonizer. (Ngugi wa Thiong'o)

Colonization's perversity resided in the fact that it proposed its model to those whom it wanted to exploit, making them want to take on the values of others. And such a practice was achieved through a horrific self-dispossession and mental alienation, though not, of course, without some form of resistance. In such a paradoxical movement, it's precisely because we have sufficient self-esteem in the first place that we refuse to let that self-esteem become diminished. Our dignity. Fanon's work had at least one saving grace in that it restored dignity to those who had been "racialized" by European colonial power by showing that they were not inferior, but simply "wretched," or, to be more precise with the French, "damned." Rejected by a precise political, economic, and ideological system.

When my dignity, my very being itself, is attacked, how can I find a way to begin again? How can one in fact escape from this *melancholia africana* (Nathalie Etoke) so as to transform it into a force of resilience that does not exhaust me? That does not reduce me to nothingness? At certain times throughout life we can lose confidence in ourselves and not be sure of how we're going to overcome obstacles that obstruct our view of the horizon. But it's precisely because we believe that we are still capable of plumbing the depths of our energetic reservoir to find the necessary energy to be successful in whatever our undertaking might be. Self-esteem is something bigger than self-confidence. It's also the way in which I judge myself and, therefore, how I evaluate myself. Which leads me to question the norms by which I think myself and construct myself. To regain one's self-esteem once it has been lost or broken by relations of domination and violence is at once a movement of self-affirmation and a critique of institutions and norms (be they colonial, imperial, masculine ...) that the power in place considers as the standard. Not living in a completely isolated manner, we think in terms of values that are culturally, socially, and historically determined. Hence the importance of changing one's perspective, or decentering one's gaze and valuing creative gaps that we must respond to in daily life as well as the other obligations and social norms that are imposed in a vertical relationship.

What should be the basis for criticizing such norms and obligations when one is part of a minority, or underrated, culture? For example, is the work of conceptual decolonization located in the interior or the exterior of a Western episteme from which it is attempting to break free?

> The struggles that we are leading are not simply struggles for recognition, but also of recognition: they get at the heart of the rules by which members of a community recognize each other as such. If esteem is accorded based on values in which I don't see a reflection of myself, to be esteemed amounts to being integrated into a culture that I don't want to belong to. (Davide Sparti)

And when we belong to a so-called majority culture, how do we not confuse that culture with universality? How can we shift our gaze when we are in a dominant position so as to recognize that our propositions are not valid for everyone? And that there is not one center, but a plurality of centers of knowledge production, many of which have been undermined by a university system (a Western model) imposed on Africa.

The colonial discourse sought "to bring science to peoples who are not aware of it" (Congrès national de la ligue des droits de l'homme), so as to reduce to nothing local symbolic and mythical forces. The result of such tactics: the university system, a colonial creation, gave birth to an alienated elite that "fosters a tacit self-hatred masked by – on the visible plane – an empty anticolonial rhetoric that was never emancipated from the consumption of colonial (symbolic and real) goods" (Jean Godefroy Bidima). Self-actualization therefore requires an epistemic rupture with the colonial order of knowledge. But often what happens is that this rupture is caused by those who were actually born into this very colonial system and structure of knowledge. The authors of the negritude movement had the courage to formulate a virulent critique of the colonialism in which they found themselves because they were convinced that Africa and its diaspora, given the richness of their diverse cultures, had something novel to share with the rest of the world and that, in so doing, they could help save the world from ruin. But they also found themselves in a privileged position because they embodied what the "masters" of the era considered as having value. At Louis-Le-Grand, the Sorbonne, they reached the pinnacle of knowledge reserved for the white elite, and could therefore lay claim to a certain social esteem.

The founders of the negritude movement therefore bore the values of the dominant society that they sought to deconstruct and contest from within. "The experience of being socially esteemed is accompanied by a felt confidence that one's achievements or abilities will be recognized as 'valuable' by other members of society" (Axel Honneth). It can, but not always, reinforce the self-esteem necessary for setting in motion the denunciation of "epistemic injustice" engendered by colonialism "when the concepts and categories by which a people understands itself and its universe are replaced or affected by the concepts and categories of the colonizers" (Rajeev Bhargava). Social esteem also allows us to dare to challenge institutional forms of knowledge and gives us the audacity to be undisciplined, to question the models of knowledge transmission as codified by Western systems of education, to participate in the development of critical thought outside the paths laid down in academia, for instance in literature, in the arts, and in the streets – and to seek out a relation with other cultures that have hitherto been underappreciated in terms of how we should think of the world of tomorrow, our world. By studying African languages, in the area of philosophy, for example, we can find, contrary to what Western philosophy will tell us, that every language is philosophical. And we can invest in African concepts such as ubuntu, bisoïté, terranga, and mbokk – questioning them, testing their validity, enriching them, and seeing in what manner they can enable us to think about our contemporary world, and how they can best serve to express African realities, but also how they can enrich non-African ways of understanding justice, intersubjectivity, recognition, self-care, care for others, etc.

Interest in this decolonial slogan, which we find being deployed in the twenty-first century by many African academics (philosophers, historians, sociologists, literary critics, etc.) is shared by other thinkers on the continent and in the diaspora, who express themselves through other mediums than academic texts: novels, painting, sculpture, video installations, photography, choreography, dance, performance, etc. Fruitful and sincere exchanges between these two spheres, however, are still rare. Everything happens as if the participants lived in parallel worlds, thereby reproducing a colonial and European classification of forms of knowledge and various disciplines, separating thought from the arts and reason and from emotion. Integrating artistic practices into the field of reflection is also to sketch out a new poetics, a "decolonial aesthesis" (Walter Mignolo), to express the plurality of modes of being in the world and experiences, to perceive other paths of knowledge that no longer turn their back on the body, but, on the contrary, inhabit the senses. To dare to promote such an approach comes from a lack of discipline, as an unruly and transdisciplinary approach. Since I know that I make sense, I allow myself to walk in step with others, to draw from the depths of a vast cultural heritage something with which to quench my thirst because I know that I am the co-producer of this heritage, wherever I find myself. Self-esteem therefore allows one to cultivate one's own form of perceptions, to liberate the senses and ways of perceiving the world in face of a dominant system of regulation, and to develop modalities of one's being in the world, of one's sensorial relation with the world, of one's sensibility. And to engage in an aesthetic rupture that "denounces and resists domination that seeks to reproduce the canon of modern aesthetics and to homogenize the perception of the world" (Rolando Vázquez).

Therefore, through the resilience and audacity that it allows, through the epistemic and aesthetic ruptures to which it can lend a helping hand, self-esteem participates in the development of other concepts, giving rise to new social forms that make sense. For if there must be some kind of rupture, it should also necessarily be emancipatory and in such a way that public space, for example, will not be experienced in the mode of exclusion but, rather, as a space for everyone. Self-esteem is also political in that it inscribes us in the life of the city and allows for a successful socialization when two conditions are met. I must know that I am respected as a citizen (that I have rights) and that I am recognized as such. And I must know that I am recognized as a producer of sense and meaning, that is, as someone who can contribute to shaping the society that grants me rights and duties; which supposes that the culture that already resides within me, and with me, is recognized, and that I am recognized in my individuality as being the bearer of a project and an agent of meaning: meaning is constructed collectively and I take part in it; which supposes that each and every one of us can partake in the development, establishment, and implementation of social norms that generate meaning, that integrate symbols which grant signification to human existence. Which is far from the case for so-called "visible" minorities that nevertheless systematically experience their invisibility (and their subsequent lack of recognition) at the heart of public space. Their re-presentation is erased and wiped clean. Their existence is completely effaced. Through acquiring rights and a correlative recognition as a member of a community, we acquire a certain dignity. Reading Joel Feinberg, Axel Honneth reiterates and places emphasis on the fact that:

> For the individual member of society, to live without any individual rights means to have no chance of developing self-respect: "Having rights enables us to 'stand up like men,' to look others in the eye, and to feel in some fundamental way the equal of anyone. To think of oneself as the holder of rights is not to be unduly but properly proud, to have that minimum self-respect that is necessary to be worthy of the love and esteem of others. Indeed, respect for persons ... may simply be to respect their rights, so that there cannot be the one without the other. And what is called 'human dignity' may simply be the recognizable capacity to assert claims."

It's in the preservation of one's self-esteem that a just society is constructed. And yet, it would appear that coloniality/modernity was constructed around a model of exclusion and contempt. A denial of recognition. To feel humiliated is to be wounded by the positive idea that I might have of myself to such an extent that I might become incapable of perceiving myself as a "legally equal interaction partner with all fellow humans" (Axel Honneth). My social value is judged negatively; my culture becomes depreciated.

How can I myself assign a positive meaning to my own existence in the heart of the community? In not being accepted by society, I can end up excluding myself from public life and refuse to participate in the production of meaning. Herein resides the vicious circle of humiliation and discrimination. Such a lived experience endured on a daily basis can severely affect one's self-esteem and make us dispossessed, alienated, and broken. One ends up endorsing the values of those who dominate you and by anticipating and integrating what they expect from you. Scientific studies have shown that "being chosen can only ... reassure, whereas being excluded is profoundly destabilizing" (Christophe André). Low self-esteem often leads one to question oneself, even leading to severe and excessive self-criticism and depression.

> The forms of practical maltreatment in which a person is forcibly deprived of any opportunity freely to dispose of his or her own body represent the most fundamental sort of personal degradation. This is because every attempt to gain control of a person's body against his or her will – irrespective of the intention behind it – causes a degree of humiliation that impacts more destructively than other forms of respect on a person's practical relation-to-self. For what is specific to these kinds of physical injury, as exemplified by torture and rape, is not purely physical pain but rather the combination of this pain with the feeling of being defenselessly at the mercy of another subject, to the point of feeling that one has been deprived of reality. Physical abuse represents a type of disrespect that does lasting damage to one's basic confidence (learned through love) that one can autonomously coordinate one's own body. Hence the further consequence, coupled with a type of social shame, is the loss of trust of oneself and the world. (Axel Honneth)

Slavery and colonization consisted of a series of rapes and tortures: mass murder, total dispossession of self, and commodification of the Black body, expelled from Reason. A crime against humanity. An experience of ultimate humiliation. One that continues to be written in the twenty-first century. A nameless suffering starting from which one must recover. One must fight. A suffering that we must refuse to submit to, since, deep down, we know very well that our lives have value. We know that the other lies. In the midst of the rubble, the embers of self-esteem can still be granted life, stoking the flames of resilience that will give us the confidence we need to confront injustice. One doesn't head out to battle if one doesn't think that one has a chance of winning, however infinitesimal that may be.

The consciousness of my own aptitudes, of my capabilities, will help me to react and to set limits on my adversary's behavior or on the one with whom I must seek to compose a world in common. It is refusal to engage in voluntary servitude, to correspond to the expectation of others, of the dominator, it is the rejection of assimilation that keeps me in a position of inferiority. Recognition alone is not enough. The other may very well recognize me without accepting me, so as to better control me, to take possession of me. I remain the other, the one who is different, the stranger. This is precisely what the first ethnological works demonstrated: it was a question of understanding African populations in order to better dominate and exploit them. We should recall that the first ethnologists were also members of the corps of the colonial administration, and even officers of the colonial infantry.

> The grammar of decoloniality begins at the moment when social actors, who have been stripped of their humanity, their languages and their subjectivities and who have been racialized, become aware of these effects of the coloniality of being and knowledge. One must recognize that the colonization of being and knowledge was achieved through a repressive use of knowledge, beginning with the experience of marginalization and humiliation. (Walter Mignolo)

To have self-esteem and to be faithful to oneself is to posit that an *I can* is possible. *I can* be a producer of meaning. *I can* make sense, *I can* therefore express myself. *I can* participate in the movement of the world and make it so that my values, my poetics, are also those of the other without imposing them on the other. *I can* actively participate in the world and the development of fair and just institutions. But with such momentum, for self-esteem to be decolonial, it must be accompanied by a liberating modesty. It must be accompanied by a well-meaning gaze. Without such a temperate position, it can end up resembling colonial self-esteem, which would end up transforming into some form of self-satisfaction, into a will to power, and arrogance.

Fidelity to oneself is not something one shapes alone but rather with the other. We cannot fully construct ourselves, raise ourselves up to the heights of our humanity, by taking away from the other a part of themselves. By denying the other the possibility of fully being themselves. Of being fully human. From a historical viewpoint, this means that the conquering European nations that compromised themselves in the transatlantic slave trade, through slavery and the colonial enterprise, and that have not tried to seek repentance for their actions, have amputated their own humanity. These nations were not capable of truly and fully realizing themselves. These European cultures remained incomplete, unfinished. They failed. They were not capable of reaching the height of their own humanity. Their completion could only be possible through a traversal of recognition. For that's what repentance is: it's about participating in an act of recognition. It's both to recognize the crime that I have committed, and also to recognize the humanity of the men, women, and children that I commodified. As long as these nations refuse this approach, as long as they have not provided reparations for their actions, they will continue to impose their values and norms. The decolonial rupture cannot only be epistemic. If we truly want to create a humanity for everyone, it must be accompanied by a complete overhaul of the ethical order. This other humanism is an ethics of self that privileges the relationship and reintegrates us into our dislocated humanity of Black/White, Catholic/Muslim, men/women, heterosexual/homosexual, African/Westerner ... . The principal motor of the decolonial process – self-esteem – leads me either to refuse to accept being invisible and being outside-the-world, or to refuse de facto to belong to a coloniality/modernity that would somehow separate me from the rest of humanity. And it's because I have an enough self-esteem that I refuse – by my behavior, my aesthetic, ethical, and epistemic choices – to subscribe to a coloniality that is not up to what I know myself to be. Not at the height of my dignity. To be complacent in a society that humiliates a significant portion of its people simply because they do not have white skin is to be an accomplice to the executioner and, therefore, to be the executioner oneself. It's because we lack confidence and self-assurance that we are not prepared to call into question "white privilege." In both cases, self-esteem leads us to construct an ethics that goes beyond mere recognition and accepts that the foundational grounds for the production of sense are multiple. This is the only possibility in order for difference to be experienced and lived as a mode of exclusion or in a negative manner (of non-belonging). This ethics explores meeting places, displaces the lines that have already been drawn, creates new demarcations in the margins, occupies the boundaries, and, above all, calls for movement to be inhabited in the way the nomad inhabits the world by continuously being on the move. Such a practice explicitly shows us the possibilities that make up our common world and rejects the universal in the plural.

The self-esteem that drives us to decolonial action ensures a self that is solid enough to go out and encounter the other and endow them with a courage animated by a life force. Life for oneself as much as for others. It is no longer a matter of asserting oneself in order to destroy the other, but of asserting oneself without denying the other. Only under these conditions can recognition be mutual. The refusal of the destruction of the other is also the refusal of one's own destruction. When one's self-esteem begins to crumble due to a lack of love, what keeps us alive is nevertheless still there. When an entire portion of the population has been abandoned or held in contempt by their own people, a nihilistic temptation can certainly resonate like the sweet sound of the sirens' call. And can lead to the trap of fanatical terrorism or clandestine exile closing in on us. When we arrive at a point where our death far out at sea, or that of others during a terrorist bombing, no longer holds any feelings of horror, something terrible has occurred. Such instances of nihilistic death perhaps do offer a certain social recognition. As long as our societies, in the West as well as in Africa, do not do everything they can to nourish the self-esteem of all members of their various societies by granting them the recognition they deserve, at the height of what they are, and by granting them the opportunities and means to reach the heights of their possible achievements, they will instead continue to feed the ranks of the Daesh or Boko Haram. And in so doing, these societies will contribute to their own death.

Bibliography

Jean Amrouche, *Un Algérien s'adresse aux français* (Paris: L'Harmattan, 2000.)

Christophe André, "L'estime de soi," *Recherches en soins infirmiers*, 3/82 (2005), pp. 26–30.

Rajeev Bhargava, "Pour en finir avec l'injustice épistémique du colonialism," trans. Aurélien Blanchard, *Socio*, 1 (2013). http://socio.revues.org/203.

Jean Godefroy Bidima, "De l'esprit managerial à 'l'économie de l'attention': vers une violence du 'psychopouvoir' en postcolonie," in Jean Godefroy Bidima and Victorien Lavou Zoungbo (eds.), *Réalités et représentations de la violence en postcolonies* (Perpignan: Presses Universitaires de France, 2015).

Nathalie Etoke and Melancholia Africana, *L'Indispensable*

dépassement de la condition noire (Paris: Éditions du cygne, 2010).

Axel Honneth, *The Struggle for Recognition: The Moral Grammar of Social Conflicts*, trans. Joel Anderson (Cambridge: Polity, 1995).

Walter D. Mignolo, *La Désobéissance épistemique. Rhétorique de la modernité, logique de la colonialité et grammaire de la décolonialité*, trans. Yasmine Jouhari and Marc Maesschalck (Brussels: Peter Lang, 2015).

Davide Sparti, "La reconnaissance distribuée. Estime, respect et autres biens d'identité," *Terrains/Théories*, 4 (2016). http://teth.revues.org/664.

Ngugi wa Thiong'o, *Decolonizing the Mind: The Politics of Language in African Literature* (London: James Currey, 2011).

Rolando Vázquez, "Entretien avec Rolando Vasquez, Aesthesis décoloniales et temps relationnels, by Miriam Barrera," in Walter D. Mignolo, *La Désobéissance épistemique. Rhétorique de la modernité, logique de la colonialité et grammaire de la décolonialité*, trans. Yasmine Jouhari and Marc Maesschalck (Brussels: Peter Lang, 2015), pp. 175–185.

Dictionary for Lovers of the African Continent: Two Entries

Alain Mabanckou and Abdourahman Waberi

Alain Mabanckou is a poet and novelist. A former professor at the Collège de France, he is the author of several well-known works, including Black Moses, Verre-cassé, Mémoires de porc-épic – *which won the Prix Renaudot – and* Le Monde est mon langage. *He currently teaches literature at UCLA.*

Abdourahman A. Waberi was born in 1965 in Djibouti. He lives between Paris and the United States, where he has taught francophone literature at Claremont College, California. Currently, he is Professor of French and Francophone Literature and Creative Writing at George Washington University in Washington, DC. Poet, critic, novelist, and short-story writer, this tireless chameleon is the author of, among others, the pan-African novel The United States of Africa *(Bison Books, 2009), and of a reflection on the genocide of the Tutsis –* Harvest of Skulls, *trans. Dominic Thomas (Indiana University Press, 2017). In 2015, he published* La Divine Chanson, *translated as* The Divine Song *(Seagull Books, 2020), a labor of love in homage to the great African American artist Gil Scott-Heron. Former resident at the Villa Médicis in Rome, Waberi was a columnist for* Le Monde *and is Assistant Professor of French at George Washington University.*

By way of an introduction

The following texts are two short groundwork entries for a dictionary for lovers of African cultures concocted by Alain Mabanckou and Abdourahman Waberi. The work will not be an essay, but a dictionary. An A to Z that will be at once informative, subjective, and playful. A love song cast out over the continent, to its diasporic extensions, its inhabitants of yesteryear and today, to its exceptional resources, and its speculative planetarization. A journey comprising sketches, reflections, memories, legends, stories, portraits, monuments, friendly complicity, and intuitions ...

The echoes of the various questions of our time are numerous. Far from being an obstacle, the fragmented aspect of a dictionary and its assumed taste for the unfinished offer, on the contrary, the freedom to follow up in areas where the authors had hitherto been unable, or perhaps wanted to hold back from attempting, to create. This dictionary, then, is an invitation to create other dictionaries, other works of fiction, images, dreams, and reflections ...

Arlit

These two tightly knit syllables will stick to your palate and not ever want to leave it. No, Arlit is not some new hip spot dedicated to the visual arts and creative writing, nor is it the literary twin of the Fespaco (the pan-African film festival of Ouagadougou). Arlit was just a tiny village before becoming an important urban commune in the Agadez region of Niger. The administrative center of the eponymous regional department, Arlit is located 800 kilometers from Niamey, the capital of Niger, and 200 kilometers from Agadez, the pearl of the desert, and just 160 kilometers from the Algerian border. A landlocked country in the Sahel region, it is surrounded by the following countries: Algeria, Mali, Burkina Faso, Benin, Chad, Libya, and Nigeria. Let us repeat: Africa is a vast continent, and, contrary to appearances, it is a fairly underpopulated continent. The discourse surrounding the claim that Africa is a demographic bomb is the result, in part, of pure fantasy.

First, it should be noted that Arlit is the daughter of the Aïr, the mountainous massif that straddles the north of Niger and strongly calls to mind the Algerian Hoggar Mountains. The region's arid and rugged terrain in no way discouraged the Tuareg people from building a life there and being at one with the region since the beginning of time. In 1969, the discovery of uranium deposits by French nuclear power companies sealed the fate of the city of Arlit. First, there was the construction of two uranium mines, then ten, catapulting Arlit into the national, French, and international consciousness. And very quickly, Arlit became synonymous with Areva: a French multinational company specializing in nuclear energy and extraction procedures. And to this very day, the mines of Niger still provide most of the uranium used in France as fuel in their nuclear power plants, serving as their principal sources for the production of electricity, and for the creation of nuclear weapons. In the 1980s, it was estimated that, on the one hand, approximately 40 percent of world production came from the Arlit region, and that, on the other, uranium represented 90 percent of Niger's total exportation revenue. Today, the decrease in the amount of uranium still to be mined and the absence of other economic alternatives have led to a significant ongoing paralysis of Niger's population.

Often identified for his Nobel Prize in Literature, the author, essayist, and Kenyan activist Ngugi wa Thiong'o began a new project to draw global attention to the mining of Niger uranium. In his essay *Secure the Base*,[1] the Kenyan thinker invites us to consider questions relating to the proliferation of nuclear weapons, reminding us of the fact that these global questions are also African questions. Africa is in the world, and the world is in Africa. The same can be said for all the other continents given that our destinies are inextricably tied together for better or for worse.

Ngugi wa Thiong'o forces each of us to confront the reality in these times of generalized disorder. His questioning should not leave any of us indifferent: why is Africa absent in the debate regarding the proliferation of nuclear arms? Ngugi wa Thiong'o is not content with simply asking such a question; he also provides us with some answers. Africa must rise to the occasion to plead not only for a non-proliferation pact concerning nuclear weapons, but also for the progressive dismantling of such arsenals of destruction. And Ngugi wa Thiong'o hammers home his proclamation by emphasizing that Africa is the only continent that has at its disposal the necessary moral credit, and rightfully so, he adds: two nations (Libya and South Africa) have voluntarily done away with their nuclear programs. To cite one example, the author of *Decolonize the Mind* shares with us that the Libyan government relinquished the remains of its nuclear arsenal to the United States. What did the country gain in terms of goodwill for handing over its weapons?

An invasion of Tripoli by military forces, themselves endowed with nuclear weapons, under the auspices of NATO, transforming the entire territory into ruins. The African Union must awake from its slumber and make its voice heard in a debate that concerns the entire planet.

In the past, two superpowers have conducted nuclear weapons tests on the African continent: France undertook its first test in the Algerian Sahara between 1960 and 1966, and Israel conducted its tests during the era of apartheid, on the Prince Edward archipelago, a chain of islands located in the Indian Ocean that belonged to Pretoria. So, we can see that Africa has already suffered and endured the use of nuclear weapons on its own soil, without even being the beneficiary of the technology, just one more reason to advocate for the prohibition of all nuclear armament. Ngugi wa Thiong'o, as an ardent defender of African languages, doesn't hesitate to make a reference to Arlit, which only reinforces his argument: namely, an area with an abundance of uranium, a mineral capital for the fabrication of nuclear weapons, beneath one's very feet under the African soil. During the most recent war with Iraq, the United States long suspected Niger, one of the principal producers of uranium, of ignoring the trade embargo and furnishing Saddam Hussein with ore, in an ongoing arms race for weapons of mass destruction. We all know the rest of the story.

Ngugi wa Thiong'o continues his argument with an ongoing litany of claims calling into account the ongoing exploitation of Africa by Western colonial powers. The great superpowers – France, Great Britain, and the United States – have all had privileged links with Africa by way of colonial interventions on the continent, including the slave trade. The slave trade, colonization, and the nuclear arms race all arose from a single source: a contempt for the life of the other – and an even more flagrant contempt when the other had Black skin! And we shouldn't forget the two world wars, in which European countries were primarily involved but which were, in the end, rather costly for Africans. Is it really reasonable to simply sit back, with one's arms crossed, in the hope that African peoples will not in some way or another in the future be persuaded to take part in another devastating war hatched elsewhere and against their best interests? In order to prevent such an eventuality, is it not preferable for Africa to place itself at the head of a large coalition calling for the abandonment and cessation of all military programs using nuclear weapons? In this case, Arlit would recover a more appealing and green-friendly appearance. The continent of Africa can and must move forward in calling on the rest of the world to withdraw from the deadly embrace of nuclear power – it has morality on its side!

The urban adventure

There is no doubt about it: for anyone who seeks to understand or observe the ongoing developments of contemporary globalization, Africa is one of its finest laboratories. And from now on, this "globalization" will overlay the continent's traditions and cultures, so that Africans must be capable of dealing with this new "three-headed culture": that of their ancestors, that imposed on them by colonization, and, finally, that born of their experience as migrants, often displaced in the inner regions of their own country or continent. For the Dark Continent, this coexistence of mindsets often comes with consequences: when one of the three heads/mindsets takes control over the others – generally, globalization – we end up reading in the newspapers about tragedies arising on the high seas off the coast of Europe, as Africans attempt to relocate to the North in order to escape the economic austerity of this or that African country, or a political regime that has been in power for decades.

Migration, however, is nothing new. Without needing to resort to a biblical reference of the Great Flood, all one needs to do is think about the migrations that took place during the colonial era when they generally involved nothing more than movement from the village to the city. And there were consequences for those "adventurous individuals" who sought out such voyages, leaving behind their peaceful life in the countryside, seeking out a mirage of European cities somewhere on the African continent. There was always a worry that these mass departures would result in small villages, whose sources of vitality lay in agriculture, which was the economic driving force of many countries, being abandoned. Following the logic of earlier times, the city was perceived as the site of "civilization" – as is still the case today with European cities for African city-dwellers – and even as part of an evolution, to use one of the terms popular in the Congo-Brazzaville. There are a great number of African novels that clearly highlight this division, for example *Cruel City* by Eza Boto (pseudonym of the celebrated author Mongo Beti). In this classic of African literature, the city of Tanga, an administrative and commercial hub of the country, indirectly shows us that "white civilization," according to an omniscient narrator, will have brought to the citizens nothing but "clever calculating," "neuroses," "alcoholism," and, above all, a "contempt for human life – as in all countries where various interests in a large number of materials are disputed." And this same narrator emphasizes, with regard to the Westernized part of the capital city: "The city held the record number of murders ... and suicides! One killed or killed oneself over everything, over anything, sometimes even over a woman."[2] In a certain way, the southside of this city was a reflection of the decadence of African values, since it was a mirror of the West in terms of what one could retain from it that was negative and constricting. Our narrator, evoking the impressions of the hero Banda, will emphasize: "He [Banda] had often felt how cruel and hard the city was with its white officers, its regional guards, its territorial guards with bayonets fixed to their barrels, its one-way streets, and its 'no natives allowed' policy. But this time, he had been its victim: he realized everything that was inhuman about it."[3] This northside neighborhood was the area where the natives lived, a place that was "a true child of Africa," that quickly grew and developed and often "found itself alone in the wilderness," like "children abandoned to their own devices." From this vantage point in the city, "no one could say what the city would become, not geographers nor journalists, and even less the explorers."[4] And yet, residing in a so-called "evolved" zone of a city already created a separation between different populations. The White folk lived there, and only a few Black folk could become their neighbors, unless they were there to sell their labor force as gardeners, servants, etc.[5]

Such would be the "physiognomy" of African cities: the city center inhabited by White folk, and the indigenous neighborhoods, where misery and deprivation were easy to discern just by looking at the buildings, the pothole-laden streets, and the absence of electricity, potable water, etc.

In spite of its cruelty, the city would represent the space of encounters for various peoples. And it would be there, in the city, that a large number of Africans would come into contact with White folk for the first time – not counting the priest, who would make his way through the village to "officially" bring them the Word of God. It was always in the city that one would meet other Africans – in particular from West Africa – owners of the general neighborhood grocery stores or of the shops along the main boulevards that served as arteries cutting the city into two separate areas. These merchants were "promoters" of an intra-African economic migration. In Congo-Brazzaville, one encountered Senegalese and folks from Benin – who took care of the fishing on the port Pointe-Noire – as well as Mauritanians, and later the Lebanese who would end up "completely destroying" African merchants' way of life before later (but much later) having themselves to deal with other economic competitors from Asia and, more specifically, China. Perhaps the reason for this could be summarized by an alarm sounded by the former Gaullist minister Alain Peyrefitte: when China awakens, the world will tremble …

In conclusion, it's rather curious to discern that even today the pattern of migration hasn't changed: our nations have become villages, and Europe has become the city. We find ourselves deserting our towns for the vast cityscape, with its temptations and its lakes.

Emancipatory Utopias

Françoise Vergès

***Françoise Vergès** is Professor of Cultural Studies at the Africa Institute, UAE. A filmmaker and independent curator, she has published in both English and French on topics that include republican coloniality, memories of slavery and colonialism, the circulations of ideas and objects across the Global South, decolonial feminism, Aimé Césaire, and Frantz Fanon. Her most recent works, A Feminist Theory of Violence: A Decolonial Perspective (Pluto Press, 2022) and A Decolonial Feminism, trans. Ashley J. Bohrer (Pluto Press, 2021), explore the representation of decolonialism as a debasement and reconnect with feminism's utopian force.*

Utopia is what tears apart the web of time that wants to remain unchanging and immutable; it is a narrative that speaks of hope and expectations, bearing a vision for the future. It hints at something that does not yet exist, and in this manner it prefigures *that which is not yet*. It speaks of terrestrial and planetary space that is open and free, something immaterial that will become concretely translated. Utopia is one of the counternarratives that contribute to the production of a regime of historicity seeking to escape the deadly and paralyzing clutches of melancholy and, in so doing, carry within them a *historical future*. Such a time casts itself forward. And yet, utopia always gets a bad press. Too many utopias, which made a name for themselves throughout the history of humanity, eventually gave way to totalitarian regimes, and dreams became nightmares.

And yet, throughout history, there have been utopias that break so radically with the powers and orders in place that they end up continuing to carry with them the idea of a possible – marronage [escape from slavery], cities of refuge, communities of hackers, autonomous communities, cooperatives – not to forget utopian literature. The "lower" utopias, forged by all those anonymous figures of history, who attempted to place equality at the core of their projects, by all those who attempted to shake up the unjust order, but who rarely sought to leave behind their names or their writings. They have nevertheless survived in the form of memories, not nostalgic memories, but memories oriented toward the future. Today, Africa has all the elements at its disposal for becoming a solid terrain from which to launch a new utopia, where future counternarratives will be written. These emancipatory utopias constitute an urgency in an era when a deadly form of politics seems to pass for a future politics, claiming to ensure peace and security when, in reality, they propagate nothing but war and ravage the planet. Imagining new utopias in a world that excludes all practical and concrete possibilities of realizing this utopia is a gesture that aligns thought and practice, that demands traversing a multiplicity of levels, and radically shifting one's field of vision. It is part of what is, of what we have, and not of what we should have had. This doesn't mean we should abandon struggles for equality, the effort to express through our words and actions what *we should* all possess as inalienable rights – that is, take into account wealth that is not measured in terms of the profit we might gain from it, by the extension of our power, but in terms of the creation and production of a common space.

Whereas the second decade of the twenty-first century has not yet ended, clouds continue to gather on the horizon announcing the arrival of greater storms to come. Inequalities continue to grow, the wealth produced in the world is concentrated in a small number of hands. Gaza remains a prison under an open sky, Europe continues to plunge ever deeper into an even greater sense of authoritarian nationalism, and in the United States we see a continued increase in the militarization of the police where it would appear that prison is the only horizon for hundreds of thousands of Blacks, Latinos, and Asians. And as far as the eye can see, it would seem that rivers, forests, oceans, lakes, and forests, the skies overhead, as well as the ground and earth beneath our feet, all continue to become nothing more than merchandise for exploitation. "War against terror" has become its own sort of politics, a disciplinary technique. In the

West, capital has increasingly freed itself from labor by displacing it to the Global South and by developing technologies that allow it to be free from the human workforce. The gap between the speed and the scale of technological discoveries, created in large part by young Whites for young Whites,[1] *and* an increase in ongoing social development and progress – access to clean drinking water, employment, a decent life, and clean air – is also increasing. The same is true of science. The humanism extolled by the emancipatory movements in the aftermath of World War II – which translated into policies of social progress, decolonization, and struggles against totalitarianism and military dictators – is in crisis. This crisis is profound and irremediable. And yet the responses presented by the decolonial movements during the second half of the twentieth century are no longer pertinent. Such movements carried with them a strong sense of hope, a striking creative energy, as well as yearning for solidarity and empathy. They opened doors to the future. But attempting to resuscitate old utopias in our current landscape would be nothing more than a deception. One must instead imagine new forms of dreaming, new forms of hope in a world where capital finance has already established its hegemony, with its worship of commercial products and instant gratification. Such financial capitalism proposes that we seek out new ways of being human, which would recognize no limits, where one could, at any given moment, change one's skin, one's identity, or one's opinion. Hubris and excess.

If utopia is what allows us to glimpse something else when everything that surrounds us tells us endlessly that there is no alternative, that inequalities are natural, that war is necessary, then one of the concerns of the African Workshops of Thought would be to contribute to a development of new utopias. Utopia tears down the veil of a reality on which a factitious, everyday reality is projected, where happiness is acquired simply by purchasing more consumer products, by accumulating privileges and material wealth. Utopia dares to question all that has become naturalized: exploitation, violence, racism, linear time, injustice. It proposes instead a conception of emancipation turned toward the future. Utopia speaks of daring, that is, of having the audacity to imagine a future when powerful masters claim to be the only beings who know what the future must hold. It goes directly against what is set up by powerful masters as truth, but which, in reality, is nothing more than lies, artificiality, and a perversion of language.

There are several reasons why Africa is a propitious space for the development of new utopias, not the least of which is that the continent has all the elements at its disposal for calling into question the ideology of lack and an economy of absence on which the ideology of development was founded – namely, the notion of humankind's absolute mastery of the world, the fantasy of a robust economy, of a plenitude that would be capable of satiating human life. As a victim of such ideologies, Africa occupies a paradoxical place for having been, in the eyes of Europe, at once the site of lack, of absence, and also that of abundance, of unlimited wealth whereby one could extract all that was necessary for the construction of the West. That is, Africa was considered as an absence of a presence in the world as human beings but simultaneously as an unparalleled source of abundance. As far as the notion of absence is concerned, the writings of the philosopher Friedrich Hegel still resonate when he designates the continent of Africa as the site of an ontological absence:

> Africa proper, as far as History goes back, has remained – for all purposes of connection with the rest of the World – shut up; it is the Gold-land compressed within itself – the land of childhood, which lying beyond the day of self-conscious history, is enveloped in the dark mantel of Night. Its isolated character originates, not merely in its tropical nature, but essentially in its geographical condition. [Still today, the continent remains unknown and without any relation with Europe.][2]

But this land of childhood was also a land of gold. If civilization was absent, wealth was not lacking, the first being human capital. In effect, one of the most indispensable sources for generating the wealth of Europe and the Americas was the human capital that Europe purchased in Africa in order to redirect it and invest it in the form of slavery in the colonies. Without such a relation, there would be no birth of capitalism or accumulation of wealth in Europe and the Americas. Africa was forced to "pour" into the dark waters of the Atlantic human beings whose births it had borne witness to. "Without slavery, you don't have cotton; without cotton, you don't have modern industry," and for that to happen, a way of "turning Africa into a warren for the commercial hunting of Black skins"[3] became indispensable. The continent, to which Europe attributed an absence, was the very same one that assured Europe's presence in the world, providing it a way to establish its power over the world.

European colonial expansion in the sixteenth century rested on the idea that labor and nature were infinite resources that could be exploited. "Nature" was perceived as an extra-economic process since it ensured its own reproduction. The conception of a *cheap nature* that was renewable *ad infinitum*, without any costs, became an essential component in justifying colonization. Nature "worked" for the European, but it was unpaid labor.[4] The notion of *cheap nature* became inseparable from *cheap labor*, thereby producing a utilitarian and mercantile approach to the world at large. In such an optics, nature and the African peoples were offered up by the heavens and placed at the disposal of the colonizers. Africa offered a space for *cheap nature* and *cheap labor*, both central to the development of the West, but all this had to remain hidden, and therefore veiled by a rhetoric of absence.

The African continent was considered as simultaneously replete with wealth as well as "lacking," as opulent *and* "poor." Rich in gold that the Europeans coveted, rich in a labor force where bodies were collected and deported, subjugated and enslaved for centuries; rich in natural resources – rubber, precious woods … – sources of energy – water, oil, gas, etc. – and minerals. In other words, the continent was a vast space offering up an infinite source of *cheap labor* and *cheap nature* – a "priceless" labor force and a "priceless" nature were in fact the two crucial elements that constituted capitalism. A continent-source comprising bodies and natural goods, objects ripe for exploitation, for trafficking, for putting into circulation to meet an inexhaustible thirst. These sources of wealth accumulation made the African continent a *planetary necessity*. And it's in large part due to trade and slavery that the wealth uncovered in the Americas and the Caribbean – silver, sugar, coffee, tobacco, cotton, gold – shifted the axis of wealth, thereby instituting a North–South axis and weakening the South–South relations and ties that had been held for thousands of years, that is, between the continent and the Persian Gulf and Asia. In other words, Africa was too poor *and* too opulent. Too poor because it didn't have a civilization and opulent because it possessed a vast wealth of resources. The discourse around Africa's absence has been so hegemonic that it ended up masking the continent's other side – that of an Africa that was too wealthy for its own good, and that one therefore had to plunder for its own good. Such a dual rhetoric of both absence and plenitude explains the greed of the Europeans. If we wanted to delve into the psychology of it, we could say that the ideology of absence and lack is based on jealousy and envy, two emotions that are fairly close to each other, but which differ in their affects. Whereas jealousy always contains some element of love, envy excludes it. Envy contains some element of ill-will, an evil eye, cruel intentions. Envy aligns itself with hatred and these two emotions fortify each other in the same person. Not only is envy the desire to possess, it is also the compelling need to destroy what the other possesses. In Europe's desire to possess Africa – while simultaneously denying the continent's presence in the world – is the fact that it is *inhabited*, and, as such, is a site of culture and social ties; desire that bears witness to the intensity of evil, of naked rivalry, found in what is the most archaic and fundamentally murderous envy. As for jealousy, it is always subject to the mediation of a third party, since the one who is jealous, even murderous, always refers to statutory rights. The envious person seeks extermination, staking a claim to a right of possession and absolute supremacy by granting themselves all the rights. In Africa one finds reflection on the consequences of envy and jealousy, in African tales that serve as a philosophy of the world. In referring back and making use of this critical literature, Africans can develop a counter-discourse that, in recognizing that these emotions are inherent to the human condition, demonstrates the deadly and depressing consequences of envy and jealousy, which end up weakening self-esteem. A concise reading of the ideology of lack and the rhetoric of Africa's ontological absence reveals Europe's avarice and cruelty disguised as a civilizing mission. It demonstrates that the accumulation of profit at the expense of the destruction of peoples, lands, and policies of dispossession have been reconfigured into a conception of aid and "development." Such tactics merely shed light on the same colonial narrative that African civilizations, cultures, and technologies don't exist and that it's therefore proper and just for Europe to intervene.

This envy for a certain energy that Africa already had in its possession but didn't know how to transform, an energy that was simultaneously at the continent's disposal and yet denied to it, nourished – in nineteenth-century Europe and later in the interwar period – a discourse on an emasculated, exhausted Europe that, lacking vital energy, would be revived on the Africa continent. The metaphors during this period were very masculine: lack of vigor and vitality. Victor Hugo ended up getting lost in such images and representations so as to justify the colonization of the continent:

> Remake a new Africa, render the old Africa malleable to civilization, that's the problem. Europe can solve the problem. Come on people, take this land, get it. To whom does it belong? To no one. Take this land for the sake of the Lord, it is he who gives the land to the people, and

the Lord has given Africa to Europe. Take it ... Pour your overflowing abundance into this Africa, and at the same time resolve your social questions, transform your proletariat into property owners.[5]

Young European men would rediscover in Africa what they had lost in Europe: the sap of virility. This speech will provide themes for both literature and cinema: if Africa is the site of barbarism, it can also be that of redemption and the return of a masculinity weakened by a Europe where military glory and masculine power seem to have lost some of their shine. Today, we find a similar discourse with regard to the continent's vital energy coming from the mouths of Africans themselves: its capacity to regenerate the world, the wealth it contains underground in the form of minerals, as well as the capacities of its youth. Of course, it becomes a question of reacting to a discourse that locked the continent and its peoples in a degenerate state, but the words used are still important. The term "regeneration," either referring to an earlier state judged to be superior, such as in the statement "regenerate society," or "returning to a substance its initial properties, altered, or modified during the course of its treatment," is strongly marked by the thought of some sort of lost *before* that must now be found. Regeneration will be the way to recover what will have been diminished and atrophied. Africa will, on the contrary, not be in a position of lack but, rather, it will be the source of a vital force that other continents will have exhausted. But do we not uncover here the paradox of plenitude and emptiness that fed the West's greed? Is there not a way for us to get past this philosophy of wholeness? Is there not some other way of contradicting the ideology of lack and absence? Should we not also seek to dispel and attack the desire to be all-powerful, the virility of a vital force, of an ejaculation that quickly sows itself, and instead rehabilitate a temporality of waiting, patience, and a process of slow gestation, a time for learning, knowledge that is not immediately acquired? We are not speaking here of returning to a mythic time where knowledge was transmitted while sitting around the baobab tree, but of distancing ourselves from the ideology of lack and absence, of accepting lack and absence as being a part of our existence. Understanding that we will never be able to grasp *everything*, that the world cannot be reduced to a perception by applications that would render it immediately accessible to us. To admit a certain opacity, not demanding transparency, so as to develop an "archipelagic thought,"[6] in other words "a more intuitive, more fragile, threatened in tune with the chaos – world and its unpredictability ... a non-systematic, inductive thought form that explores the unexpected in the world-totality and reconciles writing with orality and orality with writing."[7]

In the twenty-first-century global economy, Africa is still an economic planetary resource. It continues to provide *cheap labor* and *cheap nature*. Containing up to 90 percent of the world's chromium and platinum reserves, 80 percent of coltan, 50 percent of cobalt, 57 percent of gold, 20 percent of iron and copper, 23 percent of uranium and phosphates, 32 percent of magnesium, 41 percent of vanadium, 49 percent of platinum, 60 percent of diamonds, 14 percent of oil, Africa also has a population of 200 million youth between the ages of 15 and 24 – namely, 20 percent of its total population. This youth comprise 36.9 percent of the active population but represent 59.5 percent of the total unemployed – a percentage that is far superior to the rest of the world. According to Ibrahim Thiaw, revenue losses due to the global black market of natural resources have cost the continent $213 billion a year.[8] Africa's share regarding the production of natural energy resources in relation to the rest of the world is of the order of 10 percent, even though it only assumes 0.5 percent of the global production of the manufacturing of goods. The continent also contains more than 10 percent of the world's raw materials – both energy and non-energy – because these reserves have been underexploited. South Africa alone produces almost half of the revenue from mineral deposits, and almost three-quarters of the world's gold. Zimbabwe is next on the list, followed by the Democratic Republic of the Congo and Ghana. Nigeria, Libya, Algeria, and Angola are among the top global producers of oil. Coal is mined in Zimbabwe as well as in South Africa. Africans provide more than half of the world's demand for coffee, cocoa, and peanuts. But Africa still doesn't draw a profit from what it produces. As such, the consortium Desertec, composed of twelve companies based in Europe, the Middle East, and North Africa, are seeking the construction of a network of solar energy stations that would be fed by generators installed throughout the Sahara Desert. They envision covering 5 percent of the desert with solar panels that would generate enough electricity to supply the entire planet – that is, a rate of global energy consumption of around 18,000 TWh (terawatt hours) per year. But all this energy produced by Desertec will be redirected toward Europe via underwater cables. What we are witnessing here is a similar rush to acquire resources from Africa that calls to mind the era of the industrial revolution and the birth of capitalism. Africa was the name given to a crucial step in both capitalism and coloniality and power at a global level. And the continent remains vital to a planetary system of development that is based on the exploitation of *cheap labor* and *cheap nature*.

Characterized by genocides, wars, and large-scale massacres of entire civil populations throughout a world that professed the hegemony of progress, the twentieth century was conducive to the development of a productivist economic model, adopted by all nation-states and leading to vast human and ecological catastrophes that haunt the present. It was a century that witnessed exceptional changes in the environment. The forms generated by development in its strictly productivist dimension, as well as progress, have organized the life of societies. The unprecedented intensity of such a colossal reshaping of the world was such that the ecological imprint that it left on the environment during the last century was more profound than all the previous generations combined. This intensity was largely the result of a social, economic, and intellectual order, that is, a *cultural form* that can be summarized in a belief in infinite progress and in an absolute mastery of the environment by mankind, a belief shared by all political and economic systems. From this strictly economist perspective, culture becomes nothing more than one of the fields of consumption, a tool for gratification: a leisure activity. If the customer seeks out the "dream," the "authentic" in a world where such notions have been lost, then any travel agency can help them to find it. If the customer wants to "do humanitarian work," no problem. If they want to party, no problem. Both the true and the fake are accessible and the boundary between the two becomes blurred. The human being is a "customer" or a "client," with either a "weak" or a "strong" "potential rate of consumption," "free" to make his or her own choices, but who is above all an economic animal seeking wealth and whose egotistical interests are comprehensible. Even if the notion of infinite economic progress is called into question, if the planet no longer has the necessary resources to respond to our insatiable need to control and to consume, belief in the unlimited capacity of human beings to master reality, nature, and the elements nevertheless continues to hold sway over humanity.

It is impossible to maintain our reliance on a productivist model, not only because it destroys the habitat and the environment, but because it is now accompanied by an inexorable separation between capital and labor. Blondin Cissé, a young African economist present at the African Workshops of Thought in Dakar (October 2016), emphatically noted that it was utterly absurd to think of offering jobs to millions of Africans as long as work is still conceived of in the hegemonic form it took on during the Fordist and industrial revolution, along with programs of development and structural adjustment. The entire effort of capital now resides in an ongoing separation between labor and capital; no longer dependent on human beings, but on robots and the mechanization of labor. No more strikes, no more protests. No more uprisings. We must therefore attempt to rethink what work and employment might be. Of course, this separation is already being felt in the Global North and sociologists and other commentators have declared the end of the working class, forgetting that capitalism has largely displaced this class into the Global South, where it can seek out complaisant regimes, and absence of worker's rights, and wages that are significantly inferior to those in the Global North. A global working class will always exist, but it now resides in the Global South, in the maquiladoras, the free trade zones, the clothing sweatshops, agribusiness, the factories functioning with new technologies and robots, the camps, the port cities, and the megacities of the Global South that offer up a new cartography where work brings together bankers and the wretched of the earth. That being said, the remark concerning the separation of labor/capital and its consequences for Africa cannot be more pertinent. Alongside this new social structure that we must imagine, there is the additional need to overcome and move beyond the disastrous effects that dictators have created in Africa, the abduction of power by the old and a myriad of vampiric despots. The rehabilitation of the Black continent will be achieved through a reappropriation of its dignity. And utopian thought can help one to glimpse possibles other than emigration, misery, dictatorships, and hunger.

We are living in the era of the Anthropocene where, from now on, human actions have a direct impact on nature, and the latter will no longer be something that humans can control. One response to this involves green capitalism, which would seek to create technological and environmental solutions. A kind of Promethean thought continues to dominate – humankind is capable of conquering everything through its will. And yet, it's precisely this way of thinking that led to industrial practices that are so devastating for the environment and societies. And we should recall that destruction of the environment was a reality and continues to be a reality, for the great majority of people on the planet. Slavery was a turning point in the destruction of the environment, which has largely been underestimated in most historical narratives; colonialism and imperialism have continued their destructive policies – the imposition of monocultures that have been devastating for crops, agricultural knowledge, and techniques; the pollution of rivers and lakes; the pillaging of vernacular knowledge-forms, mining resources; and a utilitarian and commercial approach to nature... What follows will be even more destructive.

One of the responses to such narratives of lack and absence initially tied to the ideology of catching up with the Western productivist model – the only model that could assure happiness and abundance – has been Afrofuturism, which began to emerge in the 1960s–70s. This proposes a way to reverse this notion of catching by creating "temporal complications and anachronic episodes that disrupt linear progress," as Kodwo Eshun wrote in his *Further Considerations on Afrofuturism* (1993), since progress, as it has been defined in the West, condemns Black subjects to prehistory. The artists of Afrofuturism rid themselves of this problematic by imagining utopias and dystopias. We get the following definition of Afrofuturism from the literary critic Lauri Ramey, reflecting on the work of the British-Trinidadian poet, writer, and musician Anthony Joseph, author of *The African Origins of UFOs* (2006): "Philosophically, it's a current that attempts to turn itself toward the future in order to correct the errors of the past."[9] Afrofuturism "rests on the overflowing of its own limits, thereby escaping anything that would box it in that it hadn't chosen for itself. But it's also because its very nature resides in being in a network that is 'adaptive' for ideas, inspirations, and a variety of propositions that it endlessly calls itself into question and therefore endlessly transforms itself."[10] For Mantse Aryeequaye, "Afrofuturism is founded upon the transformation of perceptions that people have of themselves and their awareness of their own power."[11] The filmmaker Cédric Ido from Burkina Faso has imagined a future without a future. The scenario of his film, *Hasaki ya suda* (*Hasaki* in Japanese means *swords* and *ya suda* in Lingala creole means *the south*, so the English title is, literally, *Swords of the South*; in French, it is *Les Sabres,* 2011) mixes the Japanese culture of the samurai and the African culture in relation to earth. We are in the year 2100. Climate change has led to terrible droughts resulting in war and famine. The first victims are those residing in the Global South, forced to leave their homes and emigrate to the Global North – a mass exodus that creates chaos and destroys the ruling global order. We follow three men – Warubema, Shandaru, and Kankaru – survivors who live as samurai and who attempt, with swords as their one and only weapon, to conquer the last remnants of the natural and fertile regions on the planet. With this circulation of languages, ideas, images, representations, and where there are no women, Cédric Ido's work suggests a dystopian future. Afrofuturism is one of the sources of inspiration for utopias. It would be needed to identify African utopian experiences and practices in order to better understand the extent of their diversity: religious, artistic, social, and political utopias so as to mix these utopian practices and experiences with African thoughts of the possible.

Can culture still be a site of resistance? Can a cultural center or a museum still be a site where citizenship and solidarity, a sense of the common good, can be constructed? What sort of utopias are being constructed today? Does the present not call for a Copernican revolution in mentalities, as suggested by Aimé Césaire in 1956, which requires us to rid ourselves of a certain "habit of doing for us, arranging for us, thinking for us – in short, the habit of challenging our possession of this right to initiative of which I have just spoken, which is, at the end of the day, the right to personality"?[12] It should not be surprising, then, that utopia finds its place in this Copernican revolution of mentalities. When everything around you tells you that there is no alternative, that the reigning system in place is as natural as night and day, that you must remain in a specific assigned place, remain in a specific role, that you are disposable, an object, and that you are breaking through this order, tearing down the veil that masks the possible, and marking this rupture in such a manner that you end up literally disturbing order, upsetting its very structure, its certainty, its symbolic order. Here, I want to turn my attention to some utopian and mythic tales of the African diaspora: the pledge made at Alligator Forest that unleashed the Haitian revolution and other Maroon communities in the slave colonies of the Caribbean, the Americas, and the Indian Ocean. At the heart of these, the epic tales of Maroons shatter the pre-existing slave narrative. They trace the routes and paths of resistance. Their existence and harsh struggle for freedom will cut a path right through the very site of the real. Small marronage (escape for a day, flee for a brief moment), or grand marronage (head off into the mountains), it doesn't matter either way. Each gesture, each tale told by the Maroons will serve as a way to punch holes in the narrative fabric of history. The first gesture that must be performed by the Maroons is to name themselves, to choose their own name. They will reject the names given to them by their masters, they will forgo the names tied to a past of enslavement and servitude that they will henceforth reject. In a single sovereign gesture, they will name themselves and grant themselves their own site for a sovereign freedom. On one side are the subjects of the king – the settlers – and the "accoutrements" – the slaves. The Maroons alone are free. A hard-fought freedom that is always threatened, always fragile, but which is freedom nevertheless. As such, the Maroons carry with them a series of ruptures and fragmentation in the history of slavery. The event is rendered at its harshest and unpredictable dimension. Fragmentary speech sketched out in police reports expresses the forgotten history of a thousand tiny gestures of refusal and disobedience. We must acknowledge these "presences," these forgotten names, these erased destinies, these dusty words, so as to trace a community of presence. This attention to disorder, to suffering, to the singular does not reject history and its narrative, but, rather, wants to make legible the cries of suffering. They announce sorrow, pain, anger, tears, and the unspeakable aspiration for freedom. To be, if only for a few hours, this man or woman who dreams and listens to birdsong. And yet, many of these communities have been defeated. Will they be bearers of narratives that open up future horizons or of narratives that close them, locking their audiences in nostalgia? But do not the vanquished, those who've been defeated, rethink the past with a penetrating and critical gaze? Does not a victory that is all too easily won lead to complaisance and arrogance? The historian Reinhart Koselleck writes that "[t]he experience of being vanquished contains an epistemological potential that transcends its cause, especially when the vanquished are to rewrite general history in conjunction with their own."[13] In the Global South, the defeat of possible futures – decolonization, independences, revolutionary struggles – could easily lead to melancholy, to a rejection of the dreams of the older generation. But it is a melancholy that finds a force of inspiration in the defeat of the ancestors, a defeat that becomes a lively source of inspiration.[14]

The construction of new utopias arises from these diffuse elements – a critique of the temporality of lack, of absence that leads to a catch-up economy; a critique of defeat interpreted as the sign of a lack (of thought, knowledge); a critique of productivism. No longer, then, is it a question of catching up with or regaining "time," a hegemonic model, the norms of a globality constructed around the idea of *cheap labor* and *cheap nature* whose colonization is a principle, but rather it is about constructing a *heterochronia*, reinventing the notion of progress.

The path is wide open for a reinvention of utopia. While editing my presentation for the African Workshops of Thought, I read Felwine Sarr's *Afrotopia*. His project of an *Afrotopos* is in line with my own ideas – and it has nothing at all to do with withdrawing the singularity of one's identity. To take Africa as a point of departure, to rethink its presence in the world, to rehabilitate the itineraries and contact zones of its thought, revealing the thousand-year-old routes of South–South migration, trade, exchange, and encounters, in order to overcome the deadly ideology of lack and absence.

Part IV

Martiality and Death in Sexual Relations in Cameroon
Sociology for a Lexicon of Copulation

Parfait D. Akana

Parfait D. Akana is an anthropologist and sociologist. He holds two Master's degrees, in anthropology (University of Yaounde I) and in information and communication Sciences (University of Yaounde II-Soa, Advanced School of Mass Communication). He obtained his PhD in sociology at the École des hautes études en sciences, Paris (2013) and a degree in transcultural psychiatry (2012) at the University of Paris 13. His main areas of research are mental health, Covid-19, sexual and gender-based violence, digital cultures, media, and politics. He has been the coordinator of PhD and Master's programs at the Advanced School of Mass Communication (2019–22). He is the founder and executive director of the Muntu Institute (African Humanities and Social Sciences), editor of Social Scientists Initiative against Covid-19 in Cameroon, and an advisory member of Coronatimes. He has published several articles. Recent edited books include L'Afrique à l'épreuve de la Covid-19 *(Muntu Institute Press, 2022) and* Réflexivités africaines *(Muntu Institute Press, 2021).*

> I was incapable of the proper machismo that is well known in our country, that constantly obliges you to strut in front of the girls, to seduce them by insulting them, or, to "corrupt" them by all kinds of gifts.
>
> Achille Mbembe (2008: 183)

The forms of ordinary expression in the social world free up a mental space. Further analysis of this space grants us the possibility to specify the categories that reveal the organization of social exchanges and the production of the symbolic order that place the regimes of sexual interaction under the banner of usury. In this case, I'm attributing two meanings to the term "usury." The first sense is derived from the translation of an entire group of operations that the lexicon of usury expresses in Cameroon: exhaustion, dispossession, struggle, death, etc. The second sense refers to the dissipation of an original signification (Derrida, Merleau-Ponty) and to a work of alternative resignation on account of place.

We must absolutely forgo being seduced by striking, and often very clever, formulas, if we are to attempt, in the characterizations I will present here, to derive a critique arising from a crisis; namely, that of an analogical grasping of the other that is expressed in the mode of predation, in a context of "endemic violence." This is why it seems to me that one of the things that's most important in this work, beyond merely presenting and studying the fecundity of language in the realm of sexuality, is to show in what way the lexicon of copulation constitutes an artifact that is the version, always renewed, of what Françoise Héritier refers to as the "the differential valence of the sexes," which is also a sort of cognitive device ...

The description I want to propose elucidates the work of designation and signification of operations deployed by individuals, the various *members*, that is to say all those who, according to the language of ethnomethodology, in a given place, have mastered a *natural language*. Here, such work principally concerns the realm of sexuality. I will begin with a brief theoretical analysis regarding the relationship between place and signification as a means of understanding things, objects, and events in the social world. Next, I will sketch a description, taking into account place, of what the title of this reflection has focused on: namely the symbolization – through language – of the martial nature of sexual relations in Cameroon. For the purposes of this essay, I am willing to set aside other resources that ordinary language allows us to settle into and that belong to the realm of "agriculture." They allow us to understand sexual relations not only as a feast, but also as the manducation of women. In the third part of this essay, I will analyze the violent nature of these terms by placing them in a local sociological and anthropological context. And finally, I will end by proposing a critical questioning of what I consider to be one of the paradoxes of a recovery in which we see women integrating and often justifying an entire grammar that is both derogatory and violent and which is generally directed negatively toward them. I will postulate that such a recovery is only possible, in large part, because of a phenomenon of influence that draws its source from tyrannical and concentration camp-like spaces such as can be found in Cameroon. In such spaces, the liberation of women and the production of a healthy and hospitable mental space, with one's sights set on living well and with equal respect and dignity for everyone, corresponds to the liberation of everyone! Indeed, "the lone politics that calls for a transformative irruption of the woman is that which must be conceived as a continuous war taken up again and again in various forms against an enemy that bears the mask of famine, pandemics, decadent, stupid, and suicidal venality [and I would add to this sexism, self-contempt, and many others]" (Eboussi Boulaga, 2009: 43).

Signification and place

Merleau-Ponty says that what creates the "availability" of a signification is that it "has been instituted as signification to which users can have recourse through expressive operations of the same kind" (1964: 90). It should be added that place constitutes the flesh of every signification. I want to link the notion of place to that which resonates throughout the entire oeuvre of Fabien Eboussi Boulaga as a constant recourse to what he calls "topical art," which teaches us, "starting from sites of commonality and available resources, to philosophize, that is, to discover, by, in and through interaction and discussion with others, the problems and aporias that arise for every person and throughout a person's life" (2011: 231) My interest in these details, on the one hand on the availability of significations and on the other on topical art, aims to show two things.

The first, found in the theme that catches my attention, is the process of a definite description of the lexicon of copulation in Cameroon. New meanings that we find in the field of sexual relations reveal the experience of language in us and the fortunes of the utterances grasped, as Eboussi would say, in the dynamics of an "alternative alteration." What we are dealing with here are operations that lead us "to dwell in a speech apparatus" of the invested elements beginning by way of another significant intentionality; both in arranging them, according to Merleau-Ponty, "in a new sense," while taking into account "not only the hearers, *but the speaking subject as well* through a decisive step" (1964: 91).

Second, what Eboussi refers to as "topical art" is first of all the need to anchor the objects that preoccupy us in a place of life, thought, and action; indeed, it's this practice that allows for the "constitution of a milieu that will give rise to a flourishing, metamorphoses, and an epidemiological transmission of speech" (2011: 208). The foregoing therefore always obliges us to set out from common sites and the resources deployed there so as to think of the arts of creating and expressing, of being, etc. Without a topical posture that makes it possible to connect the speech event to the place as "an operator of selection and preferential organization according to criteria of participation and solidarity, pertinence, and transmissibility" (Eboussi Boulaga, 2011: 56), it is difficult to understand praxiologically, for example, these words that inundate the official propaganda of political and economic discourse: "emergence," "milestone," "great ambitions," "great achievement," "home base," etc. They are a product of a "localization" in the Husserlian sense of the term, that disperses the project for a "recuperation of the world" borne by the language of leaders and their networks. In the end, beyond these "coherent deformations" that render new meanings possible, what seems to me to require our utmost attention is the ethos of violence that constitutes the foundational web, sometimes in the form of jokes ... The realm of sexual relations that I'd like to describe by way of a lexicon of copulation provides an inexhaustible repertoire of this ethos whose incarnation resides in speech. One particular theme will play an important role here: war.

War

First, there is the scene that here, depending on the context, is the object that could be qualified as not being very reassuring in terms of the outcome. In Cameroon, one can, for instance, occasionally speak of the *slaughterhouse* as the site where the sexual act takes place, a site that is always the man's home and where his *victims* will end up. We should note, however, that the status of "victims" exactly corresponds to the lexical field of hunting and therefore to a violent and deadly (at least symbolically) confrontation that constitutes the foundational web of sexual relations. From the very first preparatory acts that will lead to its consummation, each step is a question of war. The attack begins. One speaks of *attacking* a potential conquest to court her, *trapping* her, or even *trapping the turkey*. One can even speak of surrounding her so she has no means of escape. The loop around her provides her with no other choice but to be *gathered up*. Like the spoils of war, or trophy, we get her. This animalization, which reveals the seizure of the other by means of violence and predation, culminates in those who represent an extreme state of anthropological regression and which we refer to locally in Cameroon as *coyotes*, that is, as prostitutes. Then come the instruments, the arms needed for killing. Percussion is the word that best represents the uses of terms here.

In the anthropology of André Leroi-Gourhan (1943, 1945), there is a very meticulous analysis and description that I will risk attempting to transpose here. He speaks of a "percussion posed with a firing pin" to signify the act that allows force to act with precision, decoupling it, in the desired direction. This percussion is the combination of what he had previously defined as a posed percussion, which is the process of applying the tool to the matter by the exertion of force; whereas a launched percussion corresponds to a projection on the material to be shaped. We should quickly remind the reader that, in the lexicon of copulation, *material* refers to an abundance of flesh, to advantageous forms. It is said of woman that she has *material*, that is to say, more specifically, a big ass and large breasts. Moreover, metonymically, she is often, in a performative way in language, a "real" woman because she possesses "*material*." This obsession with the flesh, with the "material," is also present in urban music and the verb "to have" always implies an excess, which directs the gaze and often plays a compensatory role. In a similar vein, the rapper Tenor, in his smash hit "La fille-là est laide,"[1] after having drawn a not so flattering portrait of a girl, tells us that "she is so ugly that, out of pity, her ugliness could actually stop the war with Boko Haram … and [that] she has pimples and spots on her face like a mushy plate of beans," and concludes with a supreme qualifier: "She doesn't have any ass whatsoever, she has no breasts, father, this girl is ugly!"

Flesh, then, becomes the support on which this musical percussion is exerted, and there is an entire taxonomy of martial and deadly techniques of which speech becomes the incarnation. The words used leave no doubt as to the violence, as well as the passivity, of the subjects at the mercy of a force in front of which submission is the only rule. At each turn, it is a question of torpedoing, crushing, hitting, spanking, whipping, banging, pinching, tanning, butchering, correcting bad behavior, pricking, climbing, destroying the animal, punching, hurting the young woman, in the intensive sense of the word – to put an end to her, to stop it all right here, *to kill her* – in other words, to have sex with her. The language presented here shows us to what extent the imaginary of copulation is not so very different from what we see presented in the most horrible and somber, the most marginal pornographic films known by the term *snuff movies*. Similar representations are presented here. An intentional aim of the choreography of the sexual act is symbolic murder: one must smash the young woman, one must kill her. This death necessarily involves excessive self-depletion, a debauchery of energy, a maximal use of force whose intensity must carry out the final death blow. Moreover, in this lexicon, to *give a blow* means to ejaculate, a terminal and deadly act that marks the donor's own wear and tear, but which also opens up a jubilant euphoria since it also can signify, for certain individuals: *to score a goal*.

The musician Petit-Pays was the first to begin using metaphors of the sexual act as death. In 1996, in a song called "Tue-moi ce soir" (Kill me tonight), he writes: "Alain Njocké, you always want to kill me. Everywhere you are, you want to kill me. No. Kill your wife … We don't kill men, we only kill women during this stuff." More recently, the rapper Maahlox, inscribing himself into the same tradition, describes sexual relations in an even cruder fashion in a song called "Tuer pour tuer" (Kill to kill). The artist is even moved by the possibility of any woman daring to refuse him! As if she should "naturally" and spontaneously consent, given the abundance of feminine offers he receives for sexual relations. Following this line of thinking, he asserts: "They tell you to give, you cringe while it's poured out" – obviously, in such a context, this doesn't connote a class of women, as subjects with rights, but female bodies, and much more: a profusion of available vaginas over which there is no censorship, not only because of the abundance that makes of the "body" chosen for the sexual act a vacant body, waiting, lacking, and therefore with a suffering that would make it accept the first assault as if by grace; but also because death will end up exhausting what remains of the flesh by delivering into verse: "You mimbas (you brag) with something that the maggots will eat when you die?" he says. The heresy of refusing the sexual act, whose condemnation draws comparisons with the inevitability of death, is a banal thing in Cameroon that this excerpt from Maahlox merely repeats in its own manner. The wear and tear of bodies, abandoned to tyrannical and diverse enjoyment (in the interactions of daily life and in a certain song, we often hear people say, "You drink, you die, you don't drink, you die – might as well drink!") bears, by way of this very fact, a certain morbid stoic hedonism. We can bear witness to this through these passages, where feminine will is apprehended as some sort of hindrance and heresy: the body must be made available, one must be able to "split the wood," an expression that we hear reiterated in this song and which is derived from ordinary language that in this case signifies having sexual relations with a woman. It is interesting to note here that in this metaphor, the woman, and thus in a metonymic logic that still is still predominant here, her genitalia, is identified with wood, an inert material on which the activity of a man and his axe (his sexual organ) must be exerted to "cut," "kill" ...

Reasons for violence

Clinical phenomenology and the psychopathology of sex crimes do a good job of analyzing this phenomenon, which it describes as a "completed form of murder without a corpse" (Bessoles, 2011: 23). It is at once the result of a "breakdown in representations," an "impoverishment of sexual fantasy," and, in conclusion, an instance of "seduction avoidance," which, as we have already seen here, takes the form of a woman who has been abused and beaten. I would like to postulate two hypotheses regarding the development of this aggressive and degrading vocabulary.

The first hypothesis holds that such a lexicon is a kind of avatar acting as compensation for the primitive desire to seek sexual relations without the whole anthropological machinery that, through the domestication of violence, was able to establish persuasion and conviction as the basis of sexual encounters. Seduction therefore becomes the means of the possibility of such a trade, by the specular staging of an individual and their construction as a desired subject, containing something that is decisive and incentivizing. In effect:

> Seduction is constructed on an invention of the individual by him or herself in an image that he or she chooses to assume in order to create a link with the opposite sex. Being a specific mode of communication, seduction needs to pass through a stage of ritual, which constructs simultaneously the speech act and the gestural attitude taken in the sense of a particular positioning of the body. These codes must be shared by the two individuals in order to be perceived, read, and deciphered. As such,

laughter or the shared gaze establish a means of communication that appears as spontaneous and ludic. But the foundations of this interaction are more the result of a fictitious character. In reality, everything in this game is a construct: the clothing, the intonation, the voices, the posture chosen all reveal some kind of staging of a strategy in order to please. The individual seducer is an emitter to which the receiver will be more or less receptive. Seduction then should be understood as a verbal or nonverbal communication that is deliberate and intentional. Seduction mobilizes the human senses, notably the visual field, in order to capture the other, to interpret his or her verbal or gestural reactions in terms of the produced effects on the receiver by modifying and adapting itself to his or her own behaviors. Seduction overcomes a distance so as to establish a proximity, it allows the interaction to remain tense, by playing both with the real and the ludic. (Boetsch and Guilhem, 2005: 181)

There is a flaw in seduction, which is how we see the violence that language expresses. This flaw, among numerous other explanations, resonates with a massive psycho-sociological phenomenon that is principally found in the Cameroonian urban environment: namely, low self-esteem. Erero Njiengwe has concluded, in a magisterial piece of field work that we are still drawing beneficial lessons from, and which provides decisive insights into the understanding of a Cameroonian ethos developed by years of authoritarianism and moral devaluation, in general, that Cameroonians have a fairly low self-esteem and are an example of "a clinical indication of gloom." Using such tools as Coopersmith's Self-Esteem Inventory (SEI) in order to understand a large and varied palette of attitudes such as violence, bitterness, imposture syndrome, abuses of power, cheating, a "symbolic or real lynching of those who succeed," Njiengwe concludes:

> Let us look just for one moment at the general scale of Self Esteem Inventory to note that 51.4 percent of the 932 Cameroonians tested presented a general low sense of self-esteem, in contrast to only 9 percent who had a high sense of self-esteem ... What we have here is a clinical indication of gloom; we're not even talking about depression at this point, this one element is not enough to indicate depression. Whatever the case may be, a sense of low self-esteem is tied to an inner feeling of insecurity, and an erroneous perception in relation to others and, at the cognitive level, negative representations that negatively influence behavior. It is also a predictor of depression. (2009: 443)

My second hypothesis allows me to tie this "interior attitude of insecurity" more specifically to male subjects with regard to the increasing and hegemonic crises of masculinity that can be seen throughout the entire African continent, which largely corresponds to more women taking on important roles of power in the social and economic spheres. Such a shift in power has eroded certain "traditional" privileges once enjoyed by men in a societal framework that, with the help of the state, ensured a relative financial and economic security. The decay of a state that no longer functions properly, combined with a severe economic crisis and other structural and organizational impasses of an unproductive postcolonial regime, appears as a site for the expression and intensification of women's initiatives. Women's work, especially, rendered invisible or obscured by a tyranny of low wages, becomes, in an "economy of predation and dissipation" (Eboussi Boulaga, 1999: 137) like ours, a resource of the first order, a saving grace. This turn of events can be seen as decisive through the opportune castration that it makes possible. Here, I think castration reveals a violent and obscene gesture on the part of the deception of wage labor. In his analysis, Fabien Eboussi Boulaga argues that the decomposition of the civil service and wage labor "is equivalent to that of the whole [of our social system] and shines a vivid light on it. It can reveal the nature and magnitude of the changes needed" (1999: 136). A new world, hidden and oppressed, thus emerges from the ruins and rifts of an unjust system. Masks are falling off; we discover that our own impotence, returned to itself, to its raw truth, is an upheaval. At the same time, confronted with this state of things, ordinary conjugal violence becomes sophisticated and reveals its own constant: namely, "a certain masculine order is desperately tied to a polymorphic repression of the feminine" (Tsala Tsala, 2009: 172). In this new society of downgraded men, often living off the incomes of their partners in a configuration that reactivates "traditional" and ambiguous cultural questions of "conjugal roles" or "mothering," violence, as the analysis Jacques Philippe Tsala Tsala indicates, is often the way in which women are compensated for their success. Some men even refer to their wife as "Mommy" but, at the same time, don't hesitate in beating her or swearing at her. From 2004 to 2011, the main demographic health surveys in Cameroon clearly show that violence, in all its forms, is routine in conjugal relationships. The results of the inquiry published in 2011 are particularly eloquent and reveal that:

- By the age of 15, more than half of all women (55%) experienced physical violence, primarily carried out by their current spouse

or recent partner, but also at the hand of the mother/wife of the father, the father/husband of the mother or the sister/brother.
- Of the women who reported having had sex, 20% said it was their first time and they had been forced into it; this applied, in particular, to those who had sex before the age of 15 (30%).
- In total, 34% of women between the ages of 15 and 49 experienced only physical violence, while 8% experienced sexual violence, and 21% experienced both physical and sexual violence.
- 14% of women who were, or had been, pregnant experienced violence during their pregnancy.
- 60% of women who were, or had been, in a relationship had experienced sexual, physical, or emotional abuse by their current or recent husband.
- 43% of the women who had experienced violence from their partner in the previous 12 months had received some form of wound as a result of the violence. (Tchekanda and Niekou, 2012: 325)

So it is here, in sociological research, that the symbolization of violence is put into words. It feeds on an "objective" reality and its cynegetic images constitute an ideal way of being that incorporates hostile language, to the detriment of women. What the lexicon of copulation reveals, beyond its violence, is a general persistence of malevolent attitudes toward women, and unequal and unfair relationships, in spite of the slogans and other declarations that "place women in African culture." Following the National Institute of Statistics, we must grant more credence to interactions in daily life, popular songs, etc., and resolutely repudiate a certain fetishism for "African values," a sort of insidious naturalism that is silently at work in the most pernicious and hypocritical forms of violence, such as in "conjugal mothering." In our part of the world, there is confusion concerning the notion of value:

> [We use the term in an] indifferent manner to denote sources of an authenticity that we claim and honor and of negative atavisms that we hate and defend, in spite of everything, in the name of a solidarity or loyalty that is shielded from any ethical judgment, whether they be values nourished by one's mother, the earth, or the nation ... The first agreed upon proposition is that African values are values if, and only if, they are arrived at by way of discernment or judgment, of a preferential ... choice that is a risk taken over the absolute of the good to be done ... The second accepted proposition is that African values – as with all values incarnated in a society – are corruptible ... They are untenable

if their current conditions are eroded at the same time as the collapse of images, social organizations, and material systems of exchange that hold them together, in a single movement, organized to make sense and create symbolic goods or recognize human social ties. (Eboussi Boulaga, 2009: 27)

In the name of some kind of subtlety or nuance, as if to contradict, in the face of a massive discovery of enmity toward women, which makes a mockery of claims of congeniality in our societies and wound our honor, we often evoke outstanding female figures. Once again, it bears repeating this observation: we live in a society that is at war with women and our most definitive experiences teach us that woman is considered the weakness, the wound. Fabien Eboussi Boulaga is not mistaken when he asserts that, at the end of an analysis in which he paints a "clinical" picture of the condition of women struggling in a violent society: "It is ... is legitimate to focus on women, as predominant members of a group of those who experience radical negation, and who allow the mechanisms of the system of oppression that fall on them to be dismantled, placing such a burden on their shoulders" (2009: 43).

The paradoxes of a recovery

In light of the preceding analysis, one might think that the female subject is one whose existence appears as a truth since it declares itself largely as a form of weakness that makes it available to the most arbitrary of uses, which makes it a source of pleasure in the social framework of war. Conquest of the body, of female flesh, the uses that can be made of these, the deadly technologies that language describes, all of them placed under a percussion that seeks a joyous energetic release of energy, constitute, in a sociological and dominant fashion, access to sexual alterity, active verbs, what in German would be "strong verbs" (*starken Verben*), of a grammar of sexual acts where, in an athletic logic, the truth of effort, of expenditure, equates with joy. But we would do well to analyze this form of pleasure that I will connect back to what Philippe Bessoles calls the "whitening of thought spaces." In intersexual and inter-affective relations, he creates a cognitive apparatus that allows for an analogical grasping of the other in a world "saturated by the irrepresentable that inhibits cognitive efficiency. This saturation [therefore] engenders the whitening of thought considered as a space for the metabolization and inter-thought connections" (Bessoles, 2011: 105).

Indeed, the logic at work in the lexicon of copulation situates a world where everything happens as if, in the game of sexual relations and the choreography of foreplay, the female subject was the ultimate enemy. One of the most salient points of the logic of such relations is founded on the perception of the female subject as dangerous. At both the psychological and the anthropological level, Jacques-Philippe Tsala Tsala advances an explanation that merits being taken into account:

> We wanted to start from the mythical idea to understand part of what is at play in the common imagination of Cameroonian husbands desperately tied to positions of aversive control over their spouses ... The key idea behind this is that whoever grants life is also capable of taking it away or suppressing it. Fairytales for children of the Béti in Cameroon tell of a character (*emomodo*) similar to an ogre with a large (maternal) belly that swallows children whole, and even also their parents (who are themselves children of other children). This means that every mother is also the bearer of death, engulfing life. The ambivalence of this figure that grants both life and death is the source of many a masculine fantasy. Women are saved from such a fantasy by a maternity that is culturally and conventionally closer to them. As a result, to dominate or control a woman is to fantastically conjure one's own death. We are left to wonder then who is in a better position to speak in terms of a confrontation. Hence the idea that masculine violence can be the symptom of a certain narcissistic fragility. (Tsala Tsala, 2009: 175–6)

If the social construction of women's intrinsic evil is inscribed in the anthropological mechanisms of disqualification and domination, of exclusion from positions of power and "aversive control," as the previous excerpt suggests, what is to be said about women taking up and recovering the same codes and languages that reduce them to objects, covetable "things," that can be worked at will and that only understand the language of violence? How are we to understand the paradoxes of such a recovery, of such participation in one's own destruction? Once again, we must refer to local sociological and anthropological literature so as to situate the intussusception, by women, of social and organized gestures that marginalize the truth of the female subject.

In terms of what she calls the "pornographicization" of female singing in Cameroon, Flora Amabiamina shows that, if the resumption of a daring, aggressive language suggests a sort of revolution of the body and thought, there is objectively nothing:

> As a result, the eroticization and pornographicization of sung texts are the expressions of masculine virility celebrating masculine domination and power over woman according to a logic where verbs overdetermined by the Cameroonian imaginary (cut, tease, give, spank, punish, galop, ride, straddle, pounce, smash, screw, shag – to cite but a few) loom large. Female singers have done such a good job incorporating pejorative phraseology that they have relegated men to the background even if they have yet to escape from the ideological paths of male domination.
> The discourses articulating the women's songs we studied go well beyond a mere framework of fantasies. By framing these discourses in a pragmatic perspective, they become realities through their performative linguistic acts and through the non-verbal language associated with them, in particular the sensual or even sexual gestures, including the postures and facial expressions that accompany the speech during shows and performances and in music videos (what is understood here as scenography). As for the female enunciators in these performances, they come across as sex-crazed. The lexicon used has a profound impact on society at large and in particular the most vulnerable and influential societal subjects, namely adolescents and young women. It is undeniable that such a use of sexual images and performance in these songs raises concerns regarding a larger ethics in how sexual discourse is transmitted through song. How can we then explain this use of feminine speech for the perpetuation of male domination? (Amabiamina, 2015)

Furthermore, in a study on "the domestic economy of masculine domination" in Cameroon, we can read the following commentary:

> In south-central Cameroon, the Beti people make their women repeat the following hymn to violence: "I like it when my husband beats me, this is how I can feel that my lion still retains all his strength." The popular imagery goes as far as considering women as masochists, by emphasizing the message according to which Beti women identify a beating with love. The legitimization of conjugal violence equally takes its source from the commodification of woman. Staying with the Beti, and more specifically the sub-group ... bulu, a proverb says: "The woman is like dry corn; the one who has teeth will bite her." Such a saying implies that one can do what one wants with her. Moreover, popular songs are often hymns to violence. The *bikutsi* musical rhythm in Cameroon constitutes, in several different instances, the commodification of woman and the

normalization of marital violence. It is customary to hear melodies that distill a discourse of domination. When a female artist sings things like this: "My husband slaps me, and it feels good" – doesn't this constitute a call to violence? (Meye and Chantal, 2000: 171)

I'm of the opinion that, in a society organized in such a manner, for those of us who attempt not only to understand, in a broader context, such motivation toward violence, but who also seek to deconstruct it so as to work toward a more egalitarian and fair society, one of the greatest challenges is this incorporation by a large number of women of an apparatus that rationalizes and justifies their subjugation. According to the demographic inquiry into public health published by the National Institute of Statistics in 2011, "almost half of women (47%) think that, for one of the reasons cited, a man has the right to beat his wife/partner; only 38% of men share this same opinion" (Niekou and Dzossa, 2012: 309).

In commenting on the earlier report from 2004, Jacques-Philippe Tsala Tsala observes:

> The inquiry confirms the persistence of a certain conception of conjugal relations that admit violence as a means for the resolution of conflicts and education. Rural women who are less educated have more of a tendency to adhere to the idea that it's ok for their husband to beat them in order to "correct" them. So it is that we learn that 56% of Cameroonian women think that their husbands have the right to beat their wife when she is underperforming in her job of mothering (45%), or when she leaves home without permission (34%), or when she discusses her husband's opinion (27%), or when she burns the food (19%), or refuses to have sex with him (20%). (Tsala Tsala, 2009: 175)

Is it outlandish to propose here that such a recovery, this participation in self-denigration and the legitimization of abuse, betrays a phenomenon of control or influence whereby the subject assimilates and normalizes the violence experienced by sometimes even consecrating it as a form of tenderness or as an expression of love, as can be seen in its expression in popular songs? Both men and women adopt some of the fictions that organize the structure of social relations and make it possible to distinguish what a good woman is, namely, in a negative description that locally has the "value" of a normative essence – in this case, that conforms to a social order that freezes her in attributes of complete submission ... It will easily be objected, and with good reason, that there are women who resist,[2] resilient women, according to the new gospel of psychology and adherents to personal development, powerful women who seek to invent different lives that serve as a powerful denial of such submission. So be it. These women don't interest me. I'm concerned only with those who find themselves subjected on a daily basis to the most abrasive aversions and whose lexicon of copulation, with its "syncopations of civilization" (Bessoles, 2011: 116), reveals both this anthropological "Cameroonian decline" (Eboussi Boulaga, 1999) and also the dominant system that generates influence and this sort of pathogenic resignation in the face of what oppresses us. The Cameroonian language has a terrible way of confronting injustice and terror: "What are we going to do then?" Morality, let's submit, let's accept it! Precisely where one needs to dismantle dominance and disarticulate influence that has led to the learned notion that there are good reasons for the evil that happens, they instead seek to create an "adhesion to victimhood" (Boulaga, 2011: 37): women mimic the very codes that are dedicated to their relegation and contribute to the vitality of a grammar of denigration and violence.

Certainly, the ordinary Cameroonian man or woman, without differentiating between genders, is caught by influential phenomena that often have a political nature and are tied to the persistence of authoritarian and tyrannical political regimes. Alexandre Zinoviev provides us with a rather striking example during Stalin's regime:

> My mother, up until her death (1969), held on to a portrait of Stalin in her bible. She lived through all the horrors of collectivization, war, and the postwar period. If one had to describe in detail everything she had to endure, Western readers would not believe it. And in spite of everything, she held on to a portrait of Stalin. (Zinoviev, 1981: 8)

And yet, make no mistake, in a general regime of influence, it's the woman who is the subject and the most radical interpreter of the violence in an aggressive system such as our own, which is built on what Célestin Monga calls a work of "unsocialization." He observes:

> In Cameroon where those who clamor for leadership have neither a vision nor ethical concern, the socialization of the citizenry is a chaotic and unstable process of the legitimization of philosophies of oppression, an exchange of survival techniques, appropriation of instruments of power, and the symbolic validation of self-hatred – that is, hatred of others. (Monga, 2008: 10)

Conclusion: What is the takeaway?

Should we consider this language of violence to be a force that renders accessible and profane that which is forbidden in individual and social institutions? Subscribing to such a hypothesis would be the result of an error in judgment, perhaps even a moral flaw, since we would then presume that speaking doesn't really have any signification. Words would become, following Fabien Eboussi Boulaga, "'sounds' ... 'ideas' without any specific consistency" (1999: 18). What could be more natural than that power might at certain times abuse it. No! We know very well the significance of reference, of language, in our society. Eboussi makes the following observation: "The very facts of your most solid and palpable experiences are not what you believe. They are merely what the official press releases and speeches tell you they are. War is called peace, the dead are alive, and lies are true" (1999: 18). You can *pick up* or *take* a young woman to *kill* her; *surround the animal to shoot it*. It's nothing more than a way of speaking, you're not actually going to want to commit a murder.

Such rhetoric constitutes the site itself from which one must think about the accomplishment of the promise that exists in any desire for justice. This is the first stage in dismantling "pathological support structures" (Martucelli, 2002: 105) of our sociality and the beginning of an effort for a diagnostic clarification concerning the threat of this "atmospheric death" whose arrival approaches when, in the guise of jokes, a word becomes a wound, and the wound, an anthropology. Pure denial and blindness that makes the animalization and commodification of women the secret cipher of an endemic lie, about what we are and what Cameroon is. Make no mistake, as Eboussi's pertinent analyses make clear: "It's the feminine part of our society that will save our society from famine, the effects of cultural alienation and the pauperization of a postcolonial and neocolonial system of inefficiency. What we refer to as the informal sector is the empire of women, that which endlessly escapes from the stifling or derangement of foreign forces." And he continues:

> The hegemonic role and saving grace of women as sociological fact has been powerfully elucidated by Mongo Beti with regard to his notion of village society, but we can expand and generalize his observations with irrecusable accuracy ... What immediately strikes the author is

the radiant, animating, and inventive vitality of women confronted as they are with the morose decadence and platitudes of men ... More generally, it's the women who create and introduce new rites, unusual or exotic investment practices such as *tontine* with its complicated rituals. (2009: 40)

Bibliography

Flora Amabiamina, "Célébrer la sexualité permissive. Une socio-sémiotique de la chanson féminine camerounaise moderne," Codesria, *Créer l'Afrique de demain dans un contexte de transformations mondialisées: enjeux et perspectives*, June 2015.

Philippe Bessoles, *Le Viol du féminin. Trauma sexuel et figures de l'emprise* (Nîmes: Champ social Éditions, 2011.)

Gilles Boëtsch and Dorothée Guilhem, "Rituels de séduction," *Hermès*, 43 (2005), pp. 179–188.

Fabien Eboussi Boulaga, *Lignes de résistance* (Yaoundé: Éditions Clé, 1999).

Fabien Eboussi Boulaga, "Femmes et pouvoir politique: sociologie d'une élection," *Terroirs*, 1/2 (2009), pp. 9–44.

Fabien Eboussi Boulaga, *L'Affaire de la philosophie africaine. Au-delà des querelles* (Paris: Éditions Terroirs/Karthala, 2011).

André Leroi-Gourhan, *Évolution et techniques*, vol. I: *L'Homme et la matière* (Paris: Albin Michel, 1943).

André Leroi-Gourhan, *Évolution et techniques*, vol. II: *Milieu et techniques* (Paris: Albin Michel, 1945).

Danilo Martuccelli, *Grammaires de l'individu* (Paris: Gallimard, 2002).

Achille Mbembe, "Souvenirs d'enfance," in Joseph Fumtim, *Cameroun, mon pays* (Yaoundé: Éditions Ifrikiya, 2008), pp. 171–189.

Maurice Merleau-Ponty, 1964: *Signs: On the Phenomenology of Language* (Evanston: Northwestern University Press).

Ella Meye and Lydie Chantal, "L'Économie domestique de la domination masculine. Droit, violence conjugale et société patriarcale," in Luc Sindjoun, *La Biographie sociale du sexe. Genre, société et politique au Cameroun* (Paris: Codesria, 2000), pp. 157–174.

Célestin Monga, "Poétique de la douleur," in Joseph Fumtim, *Cameroun, mon pays* (Yaoundé: Éditions Ifrikiya, 2008), pp. 5–18.

Rosalie Niekou and Anaclet Désiré Dzossa, "Statut de la femme et participation au développement local," in *Cameroun. Enquête démographique de santé et à indicateurs multiples 2011* (Cameroon: Institut national de la statistique, 2012), pp. 309–324.

Erero Njiengwe, "État des mœurs: opinions, attitudes, espoirs," in Fabien Eboussi Boulaga, *L'État du Cameroun 2008* (Yaoundé: Éditions Terroirs, 2009), pp. 407–464.

Émilienne Tchekanda and Rosalie Niekou, "Violence domestique," in *Cameroun. Enquête démographique de santé et à indicateurs multiples 2011* (Cameroon: Institut national de la statistique, 2012), pp. 325–351.

Jacques-Philippe Tsala Tsala, "Violences faites aux épouses et angoisse masculine chez les époux camerounais," *Le Divan familial*, 2/23 (2009), pp. 169–181.

Alexandre Zinoviev, *Nous et L'occident* (Lausanne: L'Âge d'homme, 1981).

Discography

Petit Pays, "Tue-moi ce soir," in Class F/M, Sonodisc, 1996.

Maahlox Le Vibreur and Phil B., "Tuer pour tuer," https://www.youtube.com/watch?v=vrCtzU0KcFI.

Tenor, "La fille-là est laide," https://www.youtube.com/watch?v=o2txk2 RxxEQ.

Demographic Challenges and Technological Mutations

Does a Good-Paying Job Have a Future in Africa?

Ndongo Samba Sylla

Ndongo Samba Sylla is a Sengalese developmental economist. After working as a technical advisor to the presidency of the Republic of Senegal, he became responsible for programming and research at the West African office of the Rosa Luxemburg Foundation (Dakar). Author and editor of many works, he has published on fair trade, labor markets in developing countries, social movements, democratic theory, and economic and monetary sovereignty, among other topics. He is also the distinguished four-time world champion of Francophone Scrabble.

One of the outcomes from the various reflections that we engaged with in these African Workshops of Thought is the desire to contribute to significantly improving the well-being of our citizenry. How can this noble aspiration be put into practice? The response normally advanced is that an increase in the rate of economic growth would, in the long term, reduce or even eradicate poverty. The subtext to such a hypothesis is that economic growth will generate productive jobs that will distribute purchasing power to a growing number of workers. This focus on job creation is not accidental. In today's world, employment contains three principal functions: it's the main means for distributing purchasing power; it's also the principal way of accessing social citizenry; and, finally, it's one of the principal mechanisms of social integration.

In order to significantly improve the well-being of our citizens, governments place a lot of their hopes and emphasis on the massive creation of decent jobs that economic growth is expected to lead to. This mode of reasoning implicitly supposes that African countries can successfully reproduce the trajectory of development observed in the West.

By way of a prospective approach, I would like to defend the idea that the model for the redistribution of social wealth via decent jobs – let's call it the "Fordist paradigm" – is not what Africa needs in the twenty-first century. More specifically, my thesis is that regular employment has no future in Africa, and that it is anachronistic in the twenty-first century to expect the well-being of Africans to depend simply on economic growth capable, if not of generating *full-time* employment, at least of making *decent* employment the dominant norm. The creation of jobs in order to increase purchasing power was a problem of the second half of the twentieth century. Throughout the twenty-first century, the biggest problem will be how to redistribute social wealth through methods other than employment.

So as to avoid any future equivocations or misunderstandings, I'd like to emphasize that my approach should not in any way be considered as "pessimistic." I'm simply trying to begin from an observation of some major trends to deduce the implications regarding the possibilities that then may be available for the continent during this century. Nor will my approach be easily situated in what could be described as the neo-Malthusian register, or even as eco-fascism, namely, analyses according to which the demographic growth of Africa will be a planetary threat and, as a result, we should take all the necessary measures possible, including authoritarianism, to stop it.[1] I don't think population growth is a problem in absolute terms. Rather, the problem lies in its association with capitalism: a global system of production and distribution that functions through a mode of polarization by favoring a small minority to the detriment of a large majority. My belief is that the downward trend in the number of hours needed for the production of goods and services can be a source of human liberation, provided that the appropriate political choices are made.

The employment situation in Africa

By way of an introduction to the following discussion, it's perhaps beneficial to briefly recall several structural characteristics of the current employment situation in Africa.[2]

The first structural characteristic is the bad use of the labor force. The bad use, or waste, of human resources is a symptom of the underdevelopment of productive forces and dysfunctional economic organization. It manifests itself in the form of open-ended and involuntary unemployment – a reality whose effects can be seen more in the urban population, most notably among middle-class youth and college graduates. Nevertheless, given that the vast majority of these individuals cannot afford to be unemployed, above all in the absence of any kind of social or economic safety net, it follows that open-ended unemployment, although a significant reality, is not the main expression of the waste of human resources.

Underemployment, in its different manifestations (an inadequate number of work hours, an inadequate income) is the overwhelming reality for the vast majority of Africans who hold positions that are not very productive in the agricultural sector or the informal sector. A decent salaried job, one that leads to a good living wage and significant social protection, unfortunately constitutes the exception rather than the rule. Salaried positions are generally not the main form of employment. Such positions are generally held by "independent contractors," in rural as well as urban settings.

A second structural characteristic of employment is that, over the past four decades, the growth in employment has been driven primarily – often more than 90 percent – by informal jobs. The increase in economic growth that began in the early 2000s has not led to a massive increase in good jobs on the continent. This reality, typically referred to as "jobless growth," implies that economic growth largely creates informal kinds of employment (Economic Commission for Africa and the African Union, 2010).

Finally, the third important structural characteristic: due to its high population growth, Africa is currently the region where the labor force is growing faster than anywhere else. And this trend is only going to become more pronounced throughout the rest of the century.

A brief overview of demographic tendencies

The population of the African continent was estimated at 1.18 billion in 2015, projected to reach 1.68 billion in 2030 (according to a United Nations survey), 2.5 billion in 2050, and 4.4 billion in 2100. In other words, Africa will represent 20 percent of the global population by 2030, 25 percent in 2050, and 39 percent by 2100.

Between 2015 and 2050, the global population will increase by 2.4 billion. More than half, that is 1.3 billion, of these people will be in Africa. Between 2050 and 2100, Africa will be responsible for most of the world's population growth (128 percent). North America and Oceania will record only a small growth in population. The other regions – Asia, Europe, and Latin America – will see their populations decline in absolute terms.

In 2100, Nigeria will have the world's third largest population, with 752 million inhabitants, placing the country behind only India and China. In Africa, it will be followed by the Democratic Republic of the Congo (389 million, fifth in the world), Tanzania (299 million, eighth in the world), Ethiopia (243 million, ninth in the world), Niger (209 million, tenth in the world), and Uganda (203 million, eleventh in the world).

At the present time, the active population (15–64-year-olds) of sub-Saharan Africa increases each year by 17.5–18 million. In 2030, the number of new entrants into the job market will be around 27 million. More generally, the active population should double or even triple in size in forty-one sub-Saharan African countries between 2010 and 2050 to reach a figure of around 1.25 billion (see United Nations, 2015; FMI, 2015; Beaujeu et al., 2011).

Confronted with these demographic trends, the following question must be asked: will it be possible to incorporate this growing labor force into decent jobs? Or, to put it another way, is decent full-time employment a realistic aspiration?

To respond to this question, it is perhaps beneficial to reflect on the experience of China and India, two countries that have been – and continue to be – faced with significant population pressures and that have obtained impressive economic results over the past four decades. The goal of such an exercise is not to merely to compare these two countries with a continent of fifty-four countries made up of so many diverse and unique cultures. Rather, it concerns what can be learned from the two most powerful demographic powers in the world today in terms of how they absorb their labor force.

Learning from India and China

Between 1970 and 2014, the GDP per capita in India increased tenfold.[3] Did such economic growth lead to a large-scale creation of decent jobs? Or, rather, did it lead to a higher growth rate of decent jobs than that of the labor force?

Each year, 15 million Indians enter the job market (Center for Equity Studies, 2014: 11). Although this number is significant in absolute terms, it is relatively low because it corresponds to a rate of activity (56 percent) well below that seen in other developing countries. This largely has to do with women's low rate of activity,[4] which is in the order of 31 percent (Sharma, 2013: 3).

Throughout these four decades, the rate of job creation was relatively low in comparison with the growth of the labor forces. The dynamism in sectors that generally create jobs remained depressed. Agriculture is always the first line of employment. One worker out of every two finds a position in this sector at the national level. And in rural areas, two out of every three workers are in jobs to do with agriculture. The manufacturing and services sectors occupy, respectively, 13 percent and 27 percent of the job market (Sharma, 2013: 3).

The paradox to be found in this period between 1994 and 2010, where we witnessed an acceleration of economic growth, is that we also saw the lowest increase in job creation compared to the two preceding decades, when economic growth was much less significant. Much as in Africa, we find the same phenomenon in India of *jobless growth*. As such, the jobs that are created are mostly informal. The industrialization of India has not put an end to informal forms of employment. Rather, it has encouraged their increase. In the manufacturing sector, the informal sector contributes up to 20 percent of GDP and 80 percent of the jobs, while representing 99 percent of new businesses (Ghani et al., 2015).

The bad news is that the modern sector has not been saved from the informalization of work. More than half of current employment is of an informal nature. Including all economic sectors, one in two workers is self-employed. What's more, 92 percent of Indian workers – that is, 400 million people, more than the entire population of the United States – do not have significant access to social protections (Papola and Sahu, 2012; Center for Equity Studies, 2014; Sharma, 2013).

We should conclude by noting that youth unemployment remains worrisome, especially among graduates, who represent 30 percent of the overall unemployed (Sharma, 2013). Even if the overall unemployment figures are relatively low, it was estimated in 2012 that 17 million unemployed people were looking for work. If we add to this the working poor, the chronically unemployed, and new job-seekers, we arrive at a figure of 94 million (Papola and Sahu, 2012: 49).

To summarize: after forty years of supported economic growth and real progress in terms of industrialization, less than 10 percent of the Indian population holds a decent job.

As for China, it is a country whose experience of economic growth is even more unique, since it has functioned under the one-child policy since the late 1970s, which has prevented the birth of more than 400 million Chinese, if we trust in the figures provided by the Chinese authorities.[5] China has finally been forced to confront some of the ramifications created by an anti-natalist politics that was in place for more than four decades. Most notably, it must begin to deal with its aging population, a decline in its labor force, and the emergence of a "labor shortage" phenomenon in some sectors.

China's GDP grew at an annual average pace of 9 percent between 1970 and 2014. In other words, it multiplied by a factor of forty-four during this period. Such a remarkable economic performance stimulated a large increase in job creation. Urban job creation doubled during the past two decades to reach 393 million jobs in 2014, the year when urban employment overtook rural employment (Lam et al., 2015). As for how the employment figures were divided up into various job sectors, agriculture represented 34 percent of employment in 2012, in contrast to 30 percent for industrial jobs and 36 percent for service industry work (Majid, 2015: 46).

Unlike other developing countries, informal types of employment in urban areas remained relatively low in China until the early 2000s, largely due to the control of the free movement of workers from rural areas. According to certain estimates, which one must take with a grain of salt, given the scarcity and quality of the data provided, 60 percent of jobs in both the industrial and the service sectors in 2012–13 were informal (Schucher, 2014: 32; also see Liang et al., 2016; Zhou, 2013).

Youth unemployment is particularly problematic, most notably among graduates: 15 million of the 20 million young adults seeking employment are urban graduates (non-migratory workers). The Chinese government is fearful of the threat of a "Chinese spring" that would be fueled by the discontent of these young, educated, unemployed workers (Schucher, 2014: 20). Indeed, according to some estimates, which we should still consider with caution, the number of unemployed increased from 5.7 million to 21.6 million between 1990 and 2011 (Majid, 2015: 15).

What can we learn from these economic experiences in India and China? They are both powers that will continue to face lower population growth than that in Africa throughout the twenty-first century. Each country in its own way has attempted to lessen or slow down the increase in the size of their active population – the former via a withdrawal of women from the workforce and the second via a drastic anti-natalist policy. Even though both countries saw a significant rise in economic growth over the past four decades, they were not capable of absorbing the vast majority of their labor force into decent work.

The thing to remember regarding both India and China can be generalized: informal employment – or to be more specific, forms of so-called "atypical employment" – constitute the employment opportunities and contemporary living conditions for the vast majority of the world's workers, above all in countries of the Global South. After 500 years of capitalism, it is estimated that, on a global scale, 80 percent of people considered as active (and their families) have no access to social protection (ILO, 2010: 33). This means that the model of a regular, salaried, decent job is a historical exception. And, in the end, it's this form of employment that should be considered as "atypical."

Confronted with the specter of technological unemployment: where will the millions of decent jobs come from?

Faced with my thesis that claims it is highly improbable that full decent employment can be achieved, some people may, in spite of everything, argue that Africa, as a continent with a significant reservoir of natural resources, has the potential to create decent jobs at a pace consistent with the evolution of its workforce. Such an argument is defective for two reasons.

First, it rests on the idea that we can create an unlimited number of jobs, which is another way of simply reiterating the myth of unlimited economic growth – an absurd belief that political ecology has easily dispelled. If we reflect from the vantage point of a "rational" civilization – one that is not based on waste (which is the case with capitalism) – the goal should not simply be to create more jobs, but rather to respond to social needs in the most economical way possible. From this vantage point, certain forms of employment should not exist or should be discouraged due to their harmful or "irrational character." The important question in this case would not be "Are we capable of creating more jobs?" but "Are we capable of responding to all social needs with the minimum amount of waste?"

Second, the argument for the important potential of decent job creation does not take into account the disastrous impact that recent technological innovations will have on the workforce in terms of net job destruction. And it's this latter point that I'd like to discuss here.

Recent technological innovations have made it so that human work is becoming less necessary in the creation of social wealth, which will depend more and more on scientific and technical progress. The anthropologist Paul Jorion (2014) speaks of a "tendential decrease in the rate of work." The implications of such a formula are clear: the generalization at a global scale of the logic of "technological unemployment" that Keynes defined (1930) in the following way: "This means unemployment due to our discovery of means of economising the use of labour outrunning the pace at which we can find new uses for labour." Randall Collins (2013) provides the following definition: "Technological displacement is the mechanism by which innovations in equipment and organization save labor, thereby enabling fewer employed persons to produce more at lower cost."[6]

Current technological mutations follow two principal logics: (1) to obtain more flexibility – to constantly adjust the productive processes according to new needs and designs, and (2) to reduce the share of wages in added value. They don't just save on unskilled work, they also save on skilled work. The more specialized the job, the more it is predictable, the more susceptible it is to automation, robotization, and informatization. Employment as specialized as radiology is threatened by automation. Practically everything that is not truly creative is susceptible to being replaced by machines or algorithms. A study by two researchers at the University of Oxford (Frey and Osborne, 2013) estimated that in the United States, 47 percent of the US labor force occupies a job that will be replaced at some point by a computer – a figure that is considered conservative by some.

The negative impact in terms of creating new jobs from contemporary technological developments is not accepted by all economists. Based on a specific reading of the first industrial revolution, some researchers tend to think that new innovations in science and technology will create an equal number of jobs in relation to those it renders obsolete. But comparisons do not always align with reason. There are two fundamental differences between the industrial revolution of the eighteenth century and the current wave of technological innovations.

The first concerns context. The first industrial revolution was not capable in and of itself of stripping Europe of its surplus labor force of the period. The transformation in the productive process of the initial industrial revolution led to the unemployment of a substantial layer of important workers who concentrated on small forms of production. The mass migration to the Americas was the principal means by which Europe was able to significantly reduce its labor surplus induced by the industrial revolution. It's one point that we don't emphasize enough (Patnaik and Patnaik, 2017). However, one of the principal characteristics of contemporary globalization is that the mass movement of skilled work is very low, especially in the North–South axis. At the current rate of migration, it would take 200 years to relocate 10 percent of the poor population from the Global South to the Global North (Milanovic, 2012: 124). This difference in historical context also explains why countries of the Global South cannot successfully emulate the model of development used in Europe – the famous "catch-up by imitation." According to Samir Amin, if one were to follow that model of development, it would require five or six more Americas (2013: 142–3).

The second major difference is that the current impact of technological innovations is not "sectorial." It is transversal. No economic sector whatsoever is spared, not even the service industry. This implies a limited redistribution of skilled jobs fallen victim to automation, roboticization, and computerization. In such a context, one might begin to wonder where exactly the millions of good-paying jobs that young Africans will aspire to will come from.

They are certainly not going to come from agriculture, notwithstanding the need to defend the development of small-scale local farming in Africa. Indeed, throughout the process of economic development, agriculture's vocation is not one of creating jobs. Rather, thanks to technological innovation, its development in relation to technology actually tends to destroy a vast number of jobs. The surplus of labor in the agricultural sector should in principle be allocated to a secondary sector of employment and to the service industry. The difficulty today is that the manufacturing sector – a sector that was traditionally labor-intensive – no longer creates as many jobs as did in the past. This new reality, that some economists such as Dani Rodrik (2015) refer to as "premature deindustrialization" – "premature" because deindustrialization intervenes at a level of income much lower than the level at which deindustrialization began in wealthy countries – can already be observed in countries that have only very recently been industrialized.

If China ended up faring better than India economically, it's largely due to the fact that the former industrialized much faster. And in so doing, it was able to create millions of jobs in the manufacturing sector. But it now seems that these positive trends are beginning to unravel. China is in fact experiencing premature deindustrialization: 16 million jobs were destroyed in the Chinese manufacturing sector between 1995 and 2002, which represents 15 percent of its workforce. What is the reason for this? Answer: the automation and robotization of the manufacturing sector. Nowadays, international trade in robots is one of the most dynamic markets in the global economy, first and foremost in China (Ford, 2015: 3, 10).

One of the consequences of accelerated automation in the manufacturing sector is the process of *reshoring* – the opposite of offshoring. As robots are more "productive" than the world's lowest-paid workers, the need to offshore, which was once driven by differences in unit labor costs, has been less and less apparent. As such, with reshoring, countries such as the United States are gaining a competitive edge, but this increase in competitiveness will have only a small impact on increase. In such a context, the problem of industrialization in Africa as well as the rest of those countries still in the midst of development is now posed in relation to a new set of terms (UNCTAD, 2016). First, it's not certain that Africa will benefit in the same way as Southeast Asia from offshoring driven by differences in unit labor costs. Second, if Africa aspires to industrialize and to export goods at a competitive price, it must also make use of automation, roboticization, and computerization. All of this implies that an industrialized Africa will have far fewer industrial employment opportunities than hoped for.

If we suppose that the economic development of Africa will continue to accelerate, via a prodigious increase in productivity, very few decent jobs will be created in light of observed realities from the past and in relation to the projected labor force of the continent.

On that basis, the question arises whether or not we are in fact condemning a majority of Africans to jobs that would eventually be useless or superfluous in a better-organized society simply because we dare not imagine another model for the redistribution of productivity gains.

Conclusion

Not too long ago, André Gorz wrote: "Full employment of the Fordist type is not reproducible by digital post-Fordism" (2010: 132).[7] African leaders should carefully reflect on this proclamation replete with wisdom and draw their conclusions from it. There is no doubt that Africa possesses an enormous amount of economic potential and an important margin in terms of economic progress still to be achieved. Millions of good jobs could be created in the near future provided that the continent grant itself the means as well as the courage to create its own form of agriculture, of industry, by focusing in particular on the local transformation of natural resources and raw materials.

But reliable full-time work is an illusion. No African government can create enough decent jobs for its young people. Over time, in a context where a decent job will become *relatively* rare – an island in a digital ocean – the priority will be, beyond seeking a way to slow down population growth in a non-authoritarian manner (by investing in education and reinforcing gender equality in particular), to put in place policies that *disconnect* access to (1) a decent income, (2) significant social security, and (3) the possibilities of financing economic projects that offer formal salaried jobs. Establishing a new paradigm of distribution, such is the major challenge at the intersection of demographic evolution and contemporary technological mutations for Africa in the twenty-first century.

These two dynamics have the potential to contribute to the flourishing of a civilization of abundance, gratuity, sharing, and human liberation. For example, one often hears talk of encouraging political participation of the working classes. Such a legitimate aspiration will remain nothing more than a pious wish as long as the working classes are not significantly liberated from the dictatorship of employment. A reduction in the length of the working week combined with economic security are two prerequisites without which it is difficult to see any true political participation by ordinary people. But striving to think in this way is to already articulate logics that are incompatible with the maintenance of capitalism and the political and cultural institutions on which it relies. Hence the burning question: if capitalism has a future, will it be capable of creating a future we want for the younger generations of today and tomorrow? In my opinion, I don't think so. Whatever the responses may be to this question, we must at least keep the debate open.

Bibliography

Samir Amin, "Postface," in Gabriella Roffinelli, *Samir Amin. La théorie du système capitaliste, critique et alternatives*, trans. Florence Curt (Lyon: Parangon, 2013 [2005]).

Raphaël Beaujeu et al., *Transition démographique et emploi en Afrique sub-saharienne. Comment mettre l'emploi au cœur des politiques de développement*. Agence française de développement, April 2011. http://www.afd.fr/jahia/webdav/site/afd/shared/publications/ recherche/Scientifiques/A-savoir/05-A-Savoir.pdf.

Center for Equity Studies, *India Exclusion Report 2013–2014* (Bangalore: Books for Change, 2014).

Randall Collins, "The end of middle-class work: No more escapes," in Immanuel Wallerstein, Randall Collins, Michael Mann, Georgi Derlugian, and Craig Calhoun (eds.), *Does Capitalism Have a Future?* (Oxford: Oxford University Press, 2013), pp. 37–70.

Economic Commission for Africa and the African Union, *Economic Report on Africa 2010. Promoting High-level Sustainable Growth to Reduce Unemployment in Africa* (Addis Ababa: Economic Commission for Africa, 2010).

F. William Engdahl, *Full Spectrum Dominance. Totalitarian Democracy in the New World Order* (Chippenham: Third Millennium Press, 2009).

FMI, *Perspectives économiques régionales. Faire face aux vents contraires*, Fonds monétaire international, 2015. Chap. 2: "Comment l'Afrique sub-saharienne peut-elle tirer parti du dividende démographique?" pp. 27–48.

Martin Ford, *Rise of the Robots. Technology and the Threat of a Jobless Future* (New York: Basic Books, 2015).

Carl Benedikt Frey and Michael A. Osborne, "The future of employment: How susceptible are jobs to computerization," September 2013, University of Oxford: http://www.oxfordmartin.ox.ac.uk/downloads/academic/The_Future_of_Employment.pdf.

Ejaz Ghani, William Kerr, and Alex Segura, "Informal tradables and the employment growth of Indian manufacturing," June 2015: http://voxeu.org/ article/employment-growth-indian-manufacturing.

André Gorz, *Ecologica*, trans. Chris Turner (London: Seagull Books, 2010).

ILO, *World Social Security Report 2010–2011: Providing Coverage in Times of Crisis and Beyond* (Geneva: ILO, 2010).

Paul Jorion, "La grande transformation du travail," *Le Monde*, 21–22 April, 2014.

John Maynard Keynes, "Economic possibilities for our grandchildren," in *Essays in Persuasion* (New York, W. W. Norton & Co., 1963 [1930]), pp. 358–373.

W. Raphael Lam, Xiaoguang Liu and Alfred Schipke, "China's labour market in the 'new normal'," IMF Working paper 15/151. IMF, July 2015.

Zhe Liang, Simon Appleton and Lina Song, "Informal employment in China: Trends, patterns and determinants of entry," IZA DP no. 10139, 2016.

Nomaan Majid, "The great employment transformation in China," ILO Working paper 195, 2015.

Branko Milanovic, *The Haves and the Have-Nots: A Brief and Idiosyncratic History of Global Inequality* (New York: Basic Books, 2012).

T. S. Papola and Partha Pratim Sahu, "Growth and structure of employment in India. Long-term and post-reform performance and the emerging challenge," Institute for Studies in Industrial Development, New Delhi, March, 2012.

Utsa Patnaik and Prabhat Patnaik, *A Theory of Imperialism* (New York: Columbia University Press, 2017).

Dani Rodrik, "Premature Industrialization," NBER, Working paper #20935, February 2015.

Günter Schucher, "A ticking 'time bomb'? Youth unemployment in China," GIGA Research Unit: Institute of Asian Studies, 2014.

Alakh N. Sharma (ed.), *India Labour and Employment Report 2014. Workers in the Era of Globalization* (New Delhi: Institute for Human Development, 2013).

Ndongo Samba Sylla, "Mesurer les difficultés d'absorption de la force de travail dans les pays en développement: Les limites du concept du taux de chômage," *Revue international du travail*, 152/1 (2013), pp. 31–46.

UNCTAD, "Robots and industrialization in developing countries." Policy Brief #50, October 2016, United Nations Conference on Trade and Development. http://unctad.org/en/PublicationsLibrary/presspb2016d6_en.pdf.

United Nations, *World Population Prospects: Key Findings and Advance Tables* (New York: Department of Economic and Social Affairs, UN Population Division, 2015).

Martin K. Whyte, Wang Feng, and Yong Cai, "Challenging myths about China's one-child policy," *The China Journal*, 74 (2015), pp. 144–159.

Ying Zhou, "The state of precarious work in China," *American Behavioral Scientist*, 57/3 (2013), pp. 354–372.

Healing Commonality

Contribution to an Anthropology of Political Corruption in Senegal

Abdourahmane Seck

Dr. Abdourahmane Seck is an associate professor at the Université Gaston-Berger in Saint-Louis (Sénégal). After publishing La Question musulmane au Sénégal. Essais d'une nouvelle modernité *(Karthala, 2010), he coedited two books:* Figures et discours de migrants. Mémoires de routes et de corps *(Riveneuve, 2015) and* États, islam, et sociétés au Sénégal *(Karthala, 2015). He is a founding member of the Groupe d'action et d'étude critique – Africa (Gaec-africa).*

Introduction

Was it really possible to emerge unscathed from the Workshops of Thought?[1] We never really thought it was. An obvious fact that requires a certain amount of clarity on our part in the way in which our current era appeared to us that has become all the more evident. We live in a time of severe social, national, and international contradictions, and nothing we say or keep silent about can be done without our also being engaged, in one way or another, in the fray.[2] What can one write and reflect upon in such a context bearing on the condition of Africa and its countries, but also its diasporas around the world and the world within it? It may very well be that any response can only be found by way of a new question! Indeed, faced with such a situation, how can one not be condemned to rethink the relation between vocations, constraints, risks, and other various issues, I was going to say in our task as watchmen? Clarify and explain foundations, reveal the mechanisms at work, place certain dynamics into perspective – this is to expose oneself to them as much as to be exposed. So, here we find ourselves announcing the tragedy of the present in the brutal tensions between the giving of self and tearing oneself away, a possible or fatal horizon, but always on the edge of a traumatic experience that one either returns to or finally allows to come to an end.

It's that, from where we are speaking, the explosion has already taken place and we are now reasoning in its aftermath: the space between where the future anterior and the unfathomable depths of the past and present are woven together. From this place or time of impact that we neither can nor even seek to escape, what we will assume has more to do with the idea of thoughtfulness, that is to say a need to deal with a present concern that it is only possible to hear because it is signaled by silence. Jacques Derrida translated it in the following way: "The trauma remains traumatizing and incurable because it comes from the future. For the virtual can also traumatize. Trauma takes place when one is wounded by a wound that has not yet taken place, in an effective fashion, in a way other than by the sign of its announcement. Its temporalization proceeds from the to-come."[3] Here and there, the trauma for us is our awareness of the human condition as a gratuitous target. Living in this condition, and above all reflecting on the cost and nature of social and political transactions that guarantee our paltry survival, can lead one to have cold sweats. On an order of magnitude, the disaster merely seems indomitable, in that bloodletting, paradigmatic revolutions, and lessons in unlearning and languages for reinvention seem almost incommensurable.[4] But there are no other options on the table: get ready for the swell.

And up until now, it's true, all the ridiculous theories of an Africa "without" have been beaten to the ground, with a great deal of inspiration: the famous theory of a library of denigration from the nineteenth century, the adjacent theories of backwardness, and the subsequent need to catch up with the West – all of these have been beaten to a pulp. Yes, it is true. Nevertheless, have we not already put forth everything we need regarding the insidiously labile barbarism, of the failure that Cheikh Hamidou Kane reminds us of, by invoking Césaire in a preface:

At the brink of dawn, this flat town – staked out, stripped of its common sense. And in this inert town, this squabbling crowd so strangely swayed from its own cry as the town is swayed from its own movement and meaning, without concern, swayed from its only true cry, the only cry one would have liked to hear because one senses this cry alone is its own.[5]

It's not that we're not running, but the race that we're running in is not made of our history.[6] The order of multiple reasons that keeps us waiting for some kind of prophetic promises of a finish line (when we will have finally developed or emerged), in reality, has more to do with a *dispositif* in the Foucauldian sense of the term, in other words, with an order that buckles down on us from all sides.[7] If it's good to know, there's nothing to do about it, if, at each attempt at a rebuke, it integrates us all the more, then to stray from oneself amounts to saying: rip oneself away from it all. And to do that requires more than a good lawsuit brought against a "system"; rather, it requires a praxis of a renaissance into a new condition, under a dual condition of a pledge and irreversibility, as Fanon maintained.[8] An intellectual order that is unable to assume such a task is an *establishment*. Between such an order and "its" people resides a deaf discord that will surprise it in its tranquil sleep. One needn't beat oneself up about it. Rather, one must recognize that seeking out transformation without also desiring to be affected in one's potential, one's condition, one's status, and one's resources is a never-ending fiction.[9] And it's still this same question, in the fact that African elites – impostors and comfortably functional pilferers in several of its sectors – are also the very roots and cogs, the inexhaustible depths of personnel that bind the continent to that which tears it apart and afflicts so many misunderstandings under the pretty rubric of participation at an international order. An order, it's perhaps good to recall, that doesn't really decide anything.[10] Such is the weak link that, if it is not attended to in both its anchoring and trajectory, will be nothing more than an impoverished aid for constructing this Africa to come that Fanon described as "the Africa of everyday life ... not that which is slumbering, but the Africa that prevents one from sleeping, for the people are eager to do, play, and speak."[11]

This paper will seek to return to the foundation of waste: an exorcism of a *demoncratic* present. The different sections will attempt to discern the roots of political treachery and also what triggers such sentiments in the body and imaginary of the nation.

They also seek to explore the areas that serve as sutures, journeys of healing, as well as self-healing and that of the Other. The guiding light behind all of the sections is the idea that healing the commonality, re-establishing its urgency, is a path of reconciliation and redemption.

The two cases that will serve as material for reflection are, on the one hand, the presidential pardon granted to Karim Wade, condemned by the Senegalese legal system for the illicit accumulation of wealth, and, on the other hand, an ordinary story about a ride in a taxicab in Dakar.

Without a doubt, these two cases are far from the most significant in what we are attempting to reflect upon here. Indeed, there were a great many other occasions and events that could have served our purpose. And yet, neither case lacks interest. Each in its own way sheds a light on the foundations of waste: the site that endlessly nourishes the bottomless abyss. Each in its own way traverses postnational and decolonial troubles, allowing us a way to plumb the folds of history that make us vulnerable to death without a tribe, since our existences are endlessly "available" both for others and for our own kind.

Ordinary self-dispossession ... or when history can be read everywhere

This section was written following a lively conversation with a cab driver in Dakar in June 2014. The "bush anthropology" that we have practiced in the field for a number of years in Dakar has taught us that all paths of chance conversation tend to lead to politics or religion. From everything to nothing. From nothing to everything. Our conversation with our compatriot suddenly veered into a discussion about the heritage of the former president of the republic, Abdoulaye Wade. What had he completed or left behind in his wake (*Li mu fi def* – in Wolof)?

A man of a certain age, somewhere in his early 50s, the cab driver was a man with a strong and assured voice, attempting as best he could to explain to me why he could neither understand nor admit that we couldn't "recognize that the old man had done a lot of work" – in other words, that he was deserving of the respect of the nation. The idea that Wade had *achieved a lot of things* was one of the leitmotivs of this conversation. The new tollways occupied an important and enthusiastic place in his discussion, which it would be almost impossible to criticize. Was it possible, for example, to have a discussion with him beyond the factual achievements of Wade, to have an exchange about the cost, their relevance, the transparency of their execution, concerning those who would, in the end, benefit from such a project? This seemed impossible not so much because of a rupture in the art of his practice of palabra, but because of a more profound feeling that seemed to lead back to indignation and sadness.

The simple idea that I attempted to suggest concerning the rights and duties of citizens to seek to know whether or not their achievements were the most beneficial and in accordance with the interest of the whole nation or of a small group was systematically rejected as not being necessarily the *true* subject. The old man had *given* to Senegal that which, prior to him, no other person, sitting in his same chair, had wanted to do or could even achieve! That was enough, in the eyes of the cab driver, to claim, on the one hand, that the "old man" deserved to be honored and, on the other, to recognize that I was the one who was *ungrateful* or *bitter* and the one who belonged to a small group of privileged (university teachers) for whom, moreover, the old man had "done a lot."

Was this monsieur the umpteenth unconditional Wade supporter whose every discussion would conclude by such a statement? It seemed to us that at bottom our compatriot could not, perhaps, even suspect himself of being partisan, not to mention a fan of the president or even perhaps of being an uneducated naive person. His critical tone with regard to my profession indicated that he understood very well the idea of (undeserved?) privileged social categories. Moreover, the numerous examples that he cited, in passing, from the earlier days of the socialist party and from the new regime of President Macky Sall indicated that he understood very well the idea of a country being plundered by a predatory elite. It's this bias or committed stance concerning the former president, while perfectly aware of being indifferent to everything else, that we took up as the subject of our conversation. How was it that all these other aspects didn't seem to be of import in consideration of "the achievements" (amenities) that the old man had placed right before our very eyes?[12] What could we learn from our recent history, both individual and collective, as a result of this? Based on his stance, something recalled the blurred contours of a singular condition: an existence with a troubling quality. A hypothesis cannot be objected to by a simple wave of the back of a hand. Such amenities are more in the order of a fetish that produces a devastating fascination:

an exposed, shiny object, and, no doubt, more so than a practical instrument. What the era of "Big Projects" extracts from the earth takes flight into a world of wonders. A world in which all that matters is that which intoxicates and preserves one from beholding naked reality: that of a dispossessed consciousness. In this sense, the enchantment produced by "Big Projects" on the continent goes above and beyond any umpteenth magical formula with which the new regime seeks to cast a spell over society. Their use and efficiency arise more from a *cache-sexe*, from that which is hidden, and, in a certain logic, the illusion of desire evoked by Freud.

The permanence of this dispossessed consciousness, reinforced by the imbalances we find in international relations, goes hand in hand with any act, including the most miserable of them, as long as it is endowed with a coefficient of increasing one's trapped perceptions of psychological and social well-being. Such dispossession also constitutes the basis of political leadership in the sense of the innovation implied in the capacity to steal the models of others, based on a profound subterranean confusion between the production of public amenities and their well-understood cultural interests.

In a certain way, achievements that are performed without the need for inventions, for which our compatriot invented the wheel for our story, no doubt masks some kind of evil: that of a shameful nakedness. Or how else should we view such a situation? That is, the narcissistic wound of this unbearable nudity that has its roots deep in the colonial work of sapping our mentalities and placing our lives on hold, waiting for the conditions that will allow us one day to finally find liberation: as long as we work well and keep our nose to the grindstone, someday our chance will come!

Work and domestication therefore become the shared lot in a country worn down by its national and postnational history that can't stop scoffing at the modalities of its contemporary insertion into the world order. This ongoing suspension of our lives and our impulses is amplified just as it is absorbed in the social and partisan race for domestic material goods and other grandiose national edifices.[13] The logic of reparation and redress as a counterpoint to this race has been successful in redirecting a significant quantity of public funds, without ever truly reflecting on the misery of the guilty parties.

If the indignation and pride of our cab driver challenge us as a serious political issue and epistemological object, it's largely because this forces us to rethink and re-evaluate for how long, for far too long, care without listening and without looking, remedy without attention and concern for the patient, comprised the unquestioned prescription for our "decolonial troubles" and other bulimic crises. The conscience of the dispossessed that is the result of troubled forms of compensation as ostentatious as they are superficial overwhelm the rift between social classes. What revealed itself to us, in this cab ride, was indeed compliant with the image of our coastline, whose view has been taken away from the vast majority of the inhabitants for the benefit of a small barbaric minority who constructed between themselves and the rest of society supermarkets and sports stadiums with a view of the ocean. It is also the image that the younger generation on the continent covet – fascinated by management ideology and the model of neoliberal socio-professional success, and whose vain habits are from now on part of the urban landscape.

But all of this, as much symptomatic of the challenges that are impossible for us to ignore, in some way constitute good news. That is, we cannot continue much longer to hide ourselves under a coat woven of artificial and fetishistic compensations.

Yes, in a *democracy*, you can inherit the Republic ... because that is pardonable

The winds of dynastic temptation that blow like a projection in the democratic imagination that is becoming prominent across the continent have also swept across Senegal. This section will, first, seek to analyze what led to this misadventure, which we will refer to as the political abuse of power or, more specifically, political treachery, in this West African country that had for a long time been celebrated as an ideal or "democratic showcase" of the continent. Second, we will seek to analyze the feeling of indignation that was the result of such treachery and which appears to be flaring up again.

Let's set the stage. In 2000, Senegal entered the new millennium with a cheerful smile. A baobab had just been uprooted, or so we thought.[14] Four years later, cue the background music, the odyssey of Karim Wade began. The lowly elite could be heard exclaiming: "Onward to the summit!" We were not content, for the sake of convenience, just to procure a Senegalese national ID card for him, only a couple of months after his father took office. The new strongman of history needed roots, deep ones. So, in a manner much less discreet than the procuring of his ID card, we invented an extensive history for him as a militant in the shadows of the party of his hero, his father, and his long march toward the palace of the Republic.

An umpteenth son of a president, an umpteenth scandal, a couple of nicknames taken right out of the pages of wikileaks,[15] and several weak protests against the vague presumptions of the father as to what his son's intentions were in fact set on, were all quickly contained.

We know the rest: nothing was beautiful enough, dignified enough, worthy enough of his intelligence, in this Republic, which is not after all a banana republic, not to fall to him out of duty and in the name of the supreme interests of the nation. Everything that could pass high above our skies, everything that our seas can behold, and everything that can seduce an investor in this westernmost point of the continent was gathered together and placed in good hands. After all, a major nation, democratically uninhibited, but confronted with a serious problem of underdevelopment, can't afford to allow certain considerations to prevent it from taking advantage of these two "geniuses" bestowed on the country, offered from the heavens, and that an accident of history has made father and son.

And we know how the story ends: the fable turned into a nightmare, the streets of Dakar burned, and the elections did the rest. A new sentiment hovered over everything: never again. Majestic in spirit, the nation didn't want to hold a grudge, and did things in style by supporting, with the honors that were due to rank, the old man. There was talk of a strong social demand and the need for good governance, whereas inventories indicated there was material to be investigated and matters to be pursued. The fallen prince, too proud, refused to speak out in court. And yet, he sought out an impressive army of lawyers tasked with convincing the nation that their client was the victim of a witch hunt. When they were asked "But really?" the lawyers proclaimed with emphasis and repeatedly: "The truth is that we want to prevent him from being the next president of the Republic of Senegal!" As was always the case, the Senegalese people were divided and some of them bemoaned the evil intentions of the president's jealous political adversaries, while others only had eyes on the "return of [stolen] money" back to the continent.

Justice did its job and was swift. It condemned the accused in March 2015 of illicit accumulation of wealth, and sentenced them to six years in prison along with a fine of 210 million euros.

The intrigue of the history that led from the presidential palace to the penitentiary[16] will have a twist in decree number 2016-880, in the form of a (presidential) fall from grace, both literally and figuratively, in the middle of the night of June 24, 2016, during a disturbed night for the Senegalese people, in a brief press release from the palace of the Republic.[17]

In the symbolism of the facts, nothing happened by chance. On June 14, the Senegalese president held a tour of religious sites. Without attempting to deny it, the press reported that these visits were to announce the forthcoming news that Karim Wade would soon be freed from prison. Rumors began to swirl once again; in an interview granted to a foreign correspondent, the president indicated that the son would soon be freed. All of this took place during the release of the "Panama papers," filled with unequivocal citations from one of the principal co-accused (who was also pardoned) of Karim Wade.[18]

The principles of the Senegalese social contract have largely been emphasized by the communications specialists of the current regime so as to report on this sequence of events, which led to a public communication on their part showing a president who listens to the solicitations of socio-religious leadership. The latter, in fact, had constantly been asking for a larger role for the son of the former president.

But mixed with the joy of the faithful partisans of the former president, one could also hear the cries from the families of prisoners who otherwise were of little importance: "And for those of us who have no long arms, who will intervene in our favor?"[19]

The diverse receptions that accompanied the dramatization of this sociopolitical transaction suggested at least two types of registers.

The first is essentially backed by scholars of democracy![20] We speak of "felony" and above all we ask ourselves: "Monsieur le president, how are you still able to look your fellow citizens in the eye?"[21] What the author of this questions points out has something in common with the theme of our discussion. For as much as it is permissible to speak of an ontological horizon, political treachery is fed by the absence of the face of the other. In this sense, the gaze that Mody Niang speaks of can only be about absence and abolition. In this operation of erasure we see the perpetuation of a paradoxical murder, since the victim killed by the bullet is nonexistent insofar as his reality was previously annihilated in an absence of recognition. The only point from which the victim can draw a modicum of enjoyment is from reification of the non-connection, the non-place, non-being. This is the only way in which the author of treachery can, almost innocently, sleep peacefully after the pillaging. To some extent, he has done nothing, and is himself a victim of what "his" enemies seek, out of mere animosity, to burden him with. We despise him for what he "is" or what he "has." He cannot plead guilty and will always continue to request having his rights and legitimate belongings restored. As long as the law allows him to do so, he will pursue those who pursue him.

The second type, which we will pursue at greater length, concerns the observation of a protest organized by the youth citizen movement Y'en a marre (YEM) [We're fed up] on June 23, 2016, on the Ouakam highway in Dakar, celebrating the anniversary of June 23, 2011. This date represents a key moment in the popular rejection of the Wade dynasty. The National Assembly gathered together to vote in favor of a continuance but popular pressure led to a withdrawal of the proposal. The narratives that inspire our analyses here are derived from the occasion of this commemoration, which coincided with the launch, by the very same youth movement, of a sociopolitical campaign around the slogan "La justice tangue" [Justice is floundering].

Among the large number of witnesses attentively listened to, we held on to two principles emphasized by women: mothers, sisters, and wives of prisoners. Among these voices, we saw the relatives of two young men from the Colobane neighborhood who were sentenced to twenty years in prison, as well as those of a young man harshly imprisoned for the consumption of Indian cannabis.[22]

An analysis of their interventions allows us, first, to take the voices of these women out of their classic confined space: that of domesticity and non-public value. These women who spoke that day did not do so just wearing their domestic hat; they expressed an objective situation that was concretely situated in a collective adventure: that of a national community with its laws, its powers, its imaginaries, and its quarreling forces. They demanded recognition of their situation by asking the community about their rights, that they not be deprived of the fundamental dimension, or to be revealed as such, which had been stolen in their name: namely, living with relatives and partaking in the happiness and joy of being with them. What is at stake in these testimonies or protests is the very balance of justice, the order of its responsibility for each life that it impacts. And this was what continued to endlessly resonate with this audience. The pardon that was about to be bestowed upon Karim Wade haunted every utterance. The author of this pardon was invited to carry the attitude of a good family man and father, capable of taking care and alleviating the suffering of the latter and, above all, of doing so with the same level of solicitude. Those who spoke made reference to the generosity of the head of state, referencing his grace and his duty as the head of a great Senegalese family which he must also take care of in an equitable manner. In this way, the podium was also a pretext to question a central figure – the "president of the Republic – in a language that constitutes a dense matter worth reflecting on. In other words, the president was asked to raise his eyes toward people who *also exist* and who know that their only way for survival is to seek a lifeline to carry them away and to escape being dismissed and ignored. It's as if, for want of being able to hope for a balance or equity in modern law that does not grant them any visibility, this people therefore sought justice for the family: that of parents, a familial justice in which the people had traditionally learned to represent themselves. The familial and patriarchal protections and care owed by the father to the offspring constituted a powerful moment in the reclamation of speech. And yet, not even this justice of the father is warranted. Hovering above it, in fact, is cultivated an attitude of refuge in God as Master, ultimately, of the last judgment. Such an attitude thus means an uncertain and relative justice in regard to the father: "You no doubt have the power to undo or fulfil our destiny, at this hour, but watch out for there is something more powerful than you that is capable of rendering justice between us and you."

In these different displacements and localizations of the law, ranging from its modern virtues to those of traditional or even populo-theological imaginaries, a conflicting relationship is played out with regard to the question of justice in contemporary Africa.[23] In the reception of the presidential pardon granted to Karim Wade, the registers have their own nuances and differences, but they all align around one point: the Senegalese social contract would only be a social contract for a small few and not for everyone, and its ongoing experiment seems to be that of a space–time of ill-feeling and an absence of recognition of the vast majority.

This sense of not being a part of it all could be as strong as the reasons and conditions of this pardon granted by Macky Sall, criticized as inappropriate by a certain faction of his own political coalition, and yet which still seems not to have revealed all its mystery. A mystery in which a great number of speculations still reverberate. The former prime minister, Idrissa Seck, has spoken about an "international deal" with Qatar and suggested that Karim Wade would be under house arrest. Abdoulaye Wade himself indicated in December 2016 that his son would be forced into exile by Macky Sall and forbidden to return to Senegal. As far as the partisans are concerned, such a pardon is nothing other than a simple humanitarian gesture. What was then recorded daily and presented as the consecration of what could be considered as healthy for our democratic showcase and its republican tradition, made up of more than cordial agreements at the top between the holders of temporal and spiritual powers, seems to have split itself at another level of dispossession. A level in which the perimeters of sovereignty seem to be at stake.

The Karim Wade adventure has a genealogy: it did not arise from a madness without memory

Until 2000, Senegal lived under an unchanging democracy that favored the Socialist Party (PS). In the clientist democracy that made it possible for the Senegalese people to be held hostage for so long, Abdoulaye Wade's Senegalese Democratic Party (PDS) – which in its genesis and logical organization was close to the Socialist Party – never stopped getting "its hands dirty" in the political situation, often resulting in criminal activity.[24] And it's thanks to this irregular and often violent nature of the political protest, and not to some *aggiornamento* of Abdou Diouf, that Senegal also has the "best electoral code in the world."[25] When the PDS took power in 2000, it had already forged an experience in the art of shafting and conning pretty much anyone, including its own partners. From this perspective, we can begin to understand a bit better how the political dialectics of ending the political game instituted by the PS led to a number of aftershocks that didn't prevent anyone from wanting it to break its political hold over the country. For starters, not only had the nature of the problems that the PS had represented for a long time outlived it, but it had also somehow regained its health in the very solution that the nation had seen as its destiny, and at the very moment when it thought it had rid itself of the party after 40 years of governance.

At this point, there is a useful hypothesis for what will follow, which merits being defended. It rests on the idea that the Senegalese Democratic Party first and foremost represented a singular prototype for the political parties that would gain ground starting in the year

2000: *political/corporate parties*. These types of political parties are the result of international interventions from institutions from the Bretton Woods accord concerning the body and imaginaries of the nation whose possible political signification had been parasitized and scrambled. We have yet to understand the extent to which these political parties that emerged from independent political mobilizations will become consolidated before our eyes in favor of *political/corporate parties* or entities in the private sector. How can one deny that this spin-off of private parties has led to a significant political crisis? We can uncover two symptomatic characteristics: that of a crisis of personalities, on the one hand, and, on the other, a failure of language. The appearance of warriors and other cowboys, of onomatopoeia and other insults and cries as the only horizon of political discourse, finds its terrain in this short but dense sequence of decomposition and reduction of the meaning of things.[26]

Taking everything into consideration here, from the point of view of what we have been allowed to become in this time of political treachery, then it's not enough to simply note that Abdoulaye Wade's PDS, which triumphantly took over the destiny of the country in 2000, could only give birth to what it was also the product of and of which forty years of PS rule had already taught us so well.

As such, nothing in fact was really that new in the toolbox that the political strongman made use of in the year 2000. A panoply of clientelism, nepotism, judicial harassment to provide a legal framework, the practice of punishing or co-opting administrative bureaucracies, the various socio-religious networks along with the mix of business and other associations all remained the same. Certainly, the PDS adds to all this its own cultural nuance, whereby most of the party's political personnel come from the streets. And this class will end up being criticized, in a very instructive way, by the relatively educated middle class for "devaluing" the "prestige" of certain high-level ministerial positions as well as that of career governmental posts. These career politicians who had invested in the long waiting line toward the political summit, in meticulously cultivating their political or administrative careers, quickly found themselves submerged by a wave of Wade's political personnel. Nostalgia for a fantasy of a golden age of the Republic – of founding fathers and geniuses, of those with a sense of measure of the personnel of such a governmental profession – will suddenly abound on the basis of this narcissistic wound.

And we can then draw the conclusion that the hegemonic construction of Abdoulaye Wade's power rested on the experience that his party drew from its confrontation with the PS and its two long-term ruling leaders, Senghor and Diouf. In the aftermath of the change in governments in 2000, the profusion of *fictional discourses*, hints at redemption, obstructed the possibility of taking into account this element of analysis, notwithstanding the declarations that multiplied on the part of the most influential members of the PS concerning their intentions "of assuring the continuity of the nation-state" or even "to continue governing for 50 years." Here, it's not only a question of what politics can emancipate or render subservient, but also above all its potential for floundering in decay in the completion of a model of governance that consists in favoring the clash of "variables" around a head of state considered as "the only constant."[27]

Deregulation and hyperinformalization[28] will constitute, in the vein of their declared ambitions, two powerful modalities for the reconfiguration of the perimeters of possibility of the political. We should also mention another function of this deregulation – namely, the act of maintaining a volatile memory overcoming emotions and feelings by exhausting them in an ambient morality in which everything succeeds, and everything has a value. Wade was the only red line. Outside this line, all blunders were permitted. To identify in an exaggerated manner with this red line, to shape one's will and reason with it became the most assured protection one had in these uncertain times.

What's more, it's rather remarkable to note that the men who surrounded Wade self-identified not only as his "sons," but even as his disciples and better still as his *baay-fall*,[29] that is, his unconditional followers. The abandonment of anything like a political spatialization and its criteria of possibility become therefore the rule of thumb and demonstrate the zeal for a single constant as the virtue of the times. In this way, the context in this same era wherein the media began to greatly enlarge its presence and become more open, combined with an explosion of the internet, has contributed to the emergence of an economy of self-publicity, an entirely new society in which any sense of measure is immediately undesired. *Criers*, seeking good fortune, suddenly appeared on every public stage and seemed to be aware of current events or situations. We began to bear witness to a significant transformation in the boundaries of the political imagination. In effect, what had once been unthinkable now became realistic so long as the single constant was whispered into the ears of his diverse band of listeners: the most zealous of the "gardeners of dreams" would decipher such wishes like someone looking to pick out the proper "horse" to bet on. An entire political, social, and cultural machinery of excess became consolidated in this race to be consecrated by the master as a VIP. Resources so as to shine more brightly than all the rest led to all sorts of flames and fervor. The specter of disaster went from aligning itself with the most blatant chauvinism to that of the most disturbing religious conservatism, and in so doing, crossed paths with the most idiotic political *warriorism*.

Against the backdrop of passions and performing arts in the service of careers in public visibility, the depoliticizing machine was running full steam ahead, boosted by an outlandish logic of familial morality of political and social contradictions. In this light, the chaos that was unleashed in public affairs during the tenure of the Wades was not a simple accident or a mere example of incompetence. It made it possible to call for breath to be drawn which allowed for the reconfiguration of the perimeters, idioms, and repertoires of the political. In such an order of ideas, two powerful logics were expressed.

The first logic was a necessary condition for shoring up the privatization of the affairs of the nation-state by way of reinforcing, on the one hand, the intervention of socio-religious leadership, and, on the other, the ongoing promotion of the dynastic project of the Wades. These actions go hand in hand, suggesting a tightening up of elites against a backdrop of traditionalism. In such a context, the affairs of the nation are resolved much more decisively in the arcana of familial ceremonies, during times of bereavement, marriages, or baptisms, on the one hand, and, on the other, upon the occasion of the umpteenth memorial ceremonies that, moreover, feverishly clog up the republican and national calendar.

In the second logic, another dynamic presents itself in the light of day, which, in several ways, is in contradiction with the first logic. Namely, the creaking joints of a golden rule that we can identify as a weakness in the separation of powers. Indeed, for a long time a solidarity existed between the various entities that executed, legitimized, and oversaw justice, at least in terms of a kind of clan whereby they sought to preserve the power they shared among themselves. Everyone, at their own level, played their role so as to ensure the sustainability of the system without necessarily the need for prior consultation. In such a system, the institutions of the Republic certainly function, but only to empty out the very substance of the political profession of public space. The golden rule that served as the foundation for this gap between the juridical formalism of the country's institutions and their real institutional practices began to crack from the multiple axes referring both to the fractions and struggles in the presidential party and to the effects induced by the arrival and departure of certain forces from the opposing party in the state governmental apparatus. The mechanisms of adjustment that the Socialist Party had been beholden to mostly constituted growing the political base of the governing state apparatus. And this activity led to a rupture in the capacity for partisan reproduction of such a state, henceforth lined in various corners by a parsimonious loyalty. Such a sentiment only increased under Wade. A number of his ministers or former ministers found themselves subsequently leading other political parties in opposition to him, while also retaining significant bases in other arteries of the state.

Such contradictory realties combined to create immense uncertainty and added to the confusion of the time. As if trapped and forsaken, men become vulnerable. Too vulnerable.

The man who gave us Karim Wade is probably not without some merit, if only unwitting. And since in the end we're all dealing with him, then we should attempt to answer the question concerning who squandered his fortune, got himself arrested for making the slightest noise, saw all the young people who surrounded him being fired from their jobs, from their high schools, their universities, and tossed out onto the streets like common criminals. We must provide an answer to the following question: for whom were these secret funds (the famous K2 account) withdrawn in order to corrupt Wade's lieutenants?[30]

Political corruption is dehumanizing. That's the point. It strikes at the confidence of a bond and drains the foundations of recognition of the other, that is, everything that makes a space for the political and everything that makes a person equal to such a space.

The unbelievable wisdom that there is no "Senegalese who doesn't have a price" that we bestowed upon the man who would proceed to murder his own son in the public arena says quite a bit about the way in which he himself was murdered by the very history in which he had believed himself to be the winner, to the point of thinking that he could, without any additional costs, hand over Karim in exchange for prolonging his stay in power. In this sense, the history in which Wade was the loser (and us as well) is not simply the history of the Socialist Party behind closed doors, it's also the history of the incapacity of the Senegalese people to prevent the annihilation of Wade as political challenger, our inability to contest the murder of a member of our community. In a variety of different ways, the fiction of the long march conceals a path of demonization comprising undeniable subterranean mechanisms by which the wings of history are pumped full of lead. Way before his test of power, perhaps it was the case that, for quite some time, this man had already been everything that we had accused him of becoming during that time in the early 2000s when the (often innocent) hopes of the Senegalese people were placed on his shoulders.

This is why simply being content with handing over the dynastic desires of the Wades to the court of history will in no way allow for either a reconstruction of the political or the healing of the wound of political ties. Moreover, it's precisely such a predicament that the aforementioned authors pardoned us for without any problem whatsoever. Breaking the countercurrent requires tracing its roots. And yet, there are many signs that indicate a continuity of times. All wishful thinking about not having to join the consecrated circle is indexed, denounced, threatened, and forced on a march of penitence. The state will dispute the second stone cast with devastating popular fury, by faceless men without language who held the meaning of our traditions hostage by reinventing them exclusively in their favor.

Political corruption is born from our entrails and proliferates where critical thought has been defeated by mafias dressed in the cloaks of honor, under the public clamor and vociferations of the cliques.

From names for the production of poverty … to signs still worth believing in … So as not to conclude

To break with the production of poverty and with the self-centered dreams to the very core that supports and endlessly renews them: such is the major challenge. And yet, such a task is not presented by way of a fixed formula, but rather under considerable pressure from signs that go every which way and trends that constantly contradict each other by favoring facts, sedimentations, and condensation effects that generate consistencies and diverse territories. This polyphony of possibles should not suspend the momentum and install an impression of endless purgatory. What this means is that this Africa we speak about is already here – here and now – in its joys and pains, its failures and genius, its ghosts and majesty, its modesty and exuberance, its compromises and forms of resistance, in a world full of emboldened imperialisms and as crazy as ever. The entrance into a multipolar world under control of the powers of the Global South changes nothing. The latter are no less ferocious nor any less expeditious than the others. They are just as much engaged in the continuity of a neo-patrimonial order of families and in their support of presidential power and the economic and political dependence of the continent. Even if we can see its spirit reactivated here and there, the spirit of the Bandung conference for the moment provides no additional help.[31]

Propaganda for democratization and international security doesn't change anything either.[32] Certainly, in terms of the military, the promotion of an agenda for global security that also functions as a tool for strategic political influence by imperialist powers has become a godsend for the forsaken political regimes in Africa that have never had so many dangerous weapons at their disposal to monitor their political adversaries, but also their friends.[33] At a cultural level, the phenomenon is just as remarkable. Turkey, China, and Iran, in a very discreet and sumptuous manner, are generously providing institutes and schools, books, and tourist trips following the Arab Gulf countries. Saudia Arabia and Israel have distinguished themselves somewhat in recent years by offering pilgrimages not only to presidents and elite political and religious figures, but also to academics, journalists, and cultural figures in civil society. The reinforcement of bureaucratic, financial, and political methods both by the Francophonie and the Commonwealth is the other counterpart of this feverish push toward a collective unifying embrace. At the economic level, one can read in a report from the French development agency the following: "Beyond the academic spheres, the African market seems to have become a prioritized horizon for a number of investors and companies" (McKinsey and Company, 2010).[34] This trajectory, emphasized repeatedly, of its economies, can be seen, since the end of the 1990s, in a number of economic reports and inquiries, making the continent the place where direct foreign investments were the most lucrative, with returns on investments that defied all understanding. In this brief but instructive period, what is eventually understood is that the favorable circumstances were thanks to a war of influence that has been referred to "carnage."[35] At an international level, the development of so-called "house diplomacy" sanctions, in plain view, a new capacity for global powers, be they old or emergent, to exercise power and operate without having to deal with the state or modern civil society as interlocutors, but in a space of our "informalization of the political."[36] We have not yet understood the explosive extent of such an intrusion, which is as rich in uncertainties and spares no expense in its ties to international criminality, which concerns secondary social players as well as investment banks and diverse mafias.[37]

Neoliberal politics, applied to African populations, with the quiet and assumed complicity of African kings in waiting,[38] strikes quickly and indiscriminately kills masses of people who have not asked to be threatened by industrial fishing enterprises or to have to depend on agricultural exportation networks to sell their cotton, peanuts, or cocoa. Such neoliberal politics transforms these local farmers and populations into homeless people in the cities, into vendors of plastic fallen from the vast global factory, or even into fanatical soldiers for mad generals. We are already in the rubble of such neoliberal economics. Under such a tumult, the impact is insidious. Neoliberal politics exhausts individual energies in tensions without quality, and gives way to the destructive logics of compensation evoked earlier, which feed off self-dispossession. Such an impact is no less profound at the national level. The sell-off and sacking of sovereignties is a necessary political dimension for the maintenance of the crisis of dispossession.[39] Of course, under such conditions, we can always dwell on the ambiguities and complexities at work. The fact is that all this reflects processes and procedures that are inherently violent and, as such, they compromise our chances of assuming the one voice that is our own. The voice of those who, potentially, could teach us how to create new ways forward to a neoliberal model measured by intellectual, mental, and moral impoverishment.

Documenting, over and over again, the failure and imposture of such political horizons of development and of the liberal and democratic model of the market is a great historical task that an intellectual elite on African soil can in no way circumvent. It's a process that involves bumps along the way, perhaps, but it is nevertheless a redemptive task. No doubt, it will cut away branches of legitimacy down to their extraverted roots. It will more than likely bring to an end regimes of problematic privilege and will perhaps – who knows? – reconfigure a perimeter of leadership for which this elite can no longer be the pole of wisdom. In following such an option, history lessons, along with anthropological observation, become valuable to us. They awaken us from our long demoncratic slumber.

Why is it, in fact, that we go from one deception and disillusionment to another, and why is it that, even when we make progress, we do so always retaining a sense of curiosity? In the image of a confiscated Dakar coastline,[40] the upturns in African growth, which have been so valuable regarding the liberal market, will be reluctant to make space for everyone. Furthermore, as with the question regarding the popular demand for a just justice system, to the extent that it takes care of ties and connections, there is yet another rupture and umpteenth rift that reveals itself to us and within us. It's blatantly clear: supported by capital gains that are tempered neither by faith or law, nor by a political logic of equity and responsibility, this economic growth that we benefit from – unless we are careful – will only contribute to a proliferation of protected zones in more vastly devastated spaces. Severe disconnections will pit wealthy and poor neighborhoods against each other, in the cities as well as in the towns and countryside, leading to an aggravation of rifts in social and symbolic ties and to a rise in violence of all against all.

What we must reflect upon, in a political space–time where we easily experience the fact of being nothing, of always being available, of being the sucker in the farce, is the very malign logic of an anthropophagic political heritage that we consider to be an insurmountable civilizational option: the postcolonial nation-state.[41] As a heritage of a certain history, this space–time of the political is therefore subject to history; in other words, it is something that we can change and recompose.

We could then decide to counter such a project with some kind of bandage for what the postcolonial neoliberal state has damaged: *the commonality*, what in Wolof is referred to as *mbokk*, or kinship, or the principle of community. Such commonality is not yet another folkloric object.

It arises first and foremost from the matrix. For *being* is already to be in the midst of sharing, of already participating in sharing. It's by the very fact of being that we have, each and every one of us, first some kind of sharing. The notion of *ties* or *connections*, then, is the first of the horizons and spaces, the site of self-realization and preservation against a regression or return to the dark night. In a variety of ways, this is already imprinted in language itself. In the

Songhai languages, it might be expressed as "he's my relative," that is, more generally speaking, "that's my people" (*Ay boraa no*).[42] In the Hausa language, the word *zumunci*, for example, not only implies kinship or someone who is a relative, but also serves as an expression of "that which is shared or commonly belongs to all relatives in the larger sense of the term."

The term also derives from the political. Being together is not to simply reside in a solitary crowd; it comes with a practical perimeter of sense that is the ability to sit down together, in other words, to be capable of cultivating sociality. This is why the Wolof people say that kinship is something one works at. In the Hausa language, the same idea is expressed in an even more obvious way, since the word that translates as sociality is *zamantakewe*, for which the root, *zama*, means literally to sit down, but which our translator explains to us should be understood as "being together," "to share a life with someone."

It will not be a panacea. It must constantly be won over in the local and intimate time of a recovery of speech. In other words: how can we transform everyday tools and forms of knowledge into legitimate and equitable political resources that express social ties and that are largely held by everyone? The tools, languages, and spaces that the weight of political reality inherited from colonial intrusions[43] never truly succeeded in obstructing the efficiency found in social interactions. In Senegal, the term *mbokk* expresses both kinship as well as sharing, but also inclusion. This term, which is used all the time in everyday life, has nevertheless been excluded from the words we use to express ourselves with regard to the political. This ends up being an alienating form of decentering us from symbolic resources that are most accessible to the greatest numbers to express their social links and, therefore, their political responsibilities. There is no doubt that, in seeking to relocalize a possible order of the political in an order of ordinary social transactions, we run the risk of multiple criticisms. But we must traverse such issues to the extent that, from our viewpoint, such an approach proceeds less from an extensive or unwarranted vision of the political (and if even if that were actually the case, all the better!) than a return to its original impulse.

To heal the *mbokk*, the *zumunici*, the *Ay boraa no*, or commonality is to prevent the possibility of political treachery, which is, in a way, the private capturing of the political that democracy generates and endorses. Here, the bandage would be a careful reminder of the essential: that which never entirely belongs to us, but which always necessarily guarantees not only the irreducibility of our share (or our *âqh*), but above all our fair share of *terranga* or our prerogative to give and receive.[44]

In the end, such a healing of commonality will construct itself in times of social confrontations and engagements in the globalized scenes of new utopias from the time of the Commons in fermentations from the peripheries all the way to great centers of the capitalist system.

Bibliography

AFD, Macroéconomie & Développment, "La croissance de l'Afrique sub-saharienne: diversité des trajectoires et des processus de transformation structurelle," May 2015. Report available online.

Giorgio Agamben, *What Is an Apparatus? And Other Essays*, trans. David Kishik and Stefan Pedatella (Stanford: Stanford University Press, 2009).

Jean-François Bayart, Stephen Ellis, and Béatrice Hibou, *La Criminialisation de l'État en Afrique* (Paris: Complexe, 1997).

Charles Becker, Saliou Mbaye, and Ibrahima Thioub (eds.), *AOF: Réalités et héritages. Sociétés ouest-africaines et ordre colonial, 1895–1960* (Dakar: Direction des archives du Sénégal, 1997).

Aimé Césaire, *Notebook of a Return to My Native Land*, trans. Mireille Rosello and Annie Pritchard (Northumberland: BloodAxe Books, 1995).

Patrick Chabal and Jean-Pascal Daloz, *L'Afrique est partie. Du désordre comme instrument politique* (Paris: Economica, 1999).

Frederick Cooper, *Africa since 1940*, 2nd ed. (Cambridge: Cambridge University Press, 2019).

Frederick Cooper, *Africa in the World: Captialism, Empire, Nation-State* (Cambridge, MA: Harvard University Press, 2014).

Abdou Latif Coulibay, *Wade, un opposant au pouvoir: L'alternance piégée?* (Dakar: Éditions Sentinelle, 2003).

Aminata Diaw, "La démocratie des lettres," in Momar-Coumba Diop (ed.), *Sénégal. Trajectoires d'un état* (Dakar: Codesria, 1992), pp. 299–329.

Momar-Coumba Diop, Mamadou Diouf, and Aminata Diaw, "Le baobab a été déraciné. L'alternance au Sénégal," *Politique africaine*, 2/78 (2000), pp. 157–179.

Stephen Ellis, *This Present Darkness. A History of Nigerian Organized Crime* (London: Hurst and Company, 2016).

Frantz Fanon, *The Wretched of the Earth*, trans. Richard Philcox (New York: Grove Press, 2005).
Guy Feuer, "Visages nouveaux du non-alignement," *Géopolitique africaine*, 31 (July 2008), pp. 165–181.
Paulin Hountondji (ed.), *Les Savoirs endogènes: Pistes pour une recherche* (Dakar: Codesria, 1994).
Jeune Afrique, "Fils de presidents: des portes du palais à celles du pénitencier," January 9, 2014. http://www.jeuneafrique.com/135065/politque/fils-de-pr-sidents-des-portes--du-palais-celles-du-p-nitencier/.
Svérine Kodjo-Grandvaux, *Philosophie africaine* (Paris: Présence africaine, 2014).
Marc Lamont Hill, *Nobody: Casualties of America's War on the Vulnerable, from Ferguson to Flint and Beyond* (New York: Attia Books, 2016).
Le Monde: http://www.lemonde.fr/documents-wikileaks/article/2010/12/09/wikileaks-corruption-et-divisions-a-dakar_1451532_1446239.html.
Abdoulaye Ly, *D'où sort l'état présidentialiste du Sénégal?* (Saint-Louis-du-Sénégal: Xamal, 1997).
Sophia Mappa (ed.), *Les Métamorphoses du politique au Nord et au Sud* (Paris: Karthala, 2004).
Achille Mbembe, *Politiques de l'inimitié* (Paris: La Découverte, 2016).
Marcel Mendy (ed.), *Wade et le Sopi: la longue marche* (Paris: M. Mendy editeur, 1995).
Aliou Kane Ndiaye, "Panama papers – Sénégal – Pape Mamadou Pouye: prête-nom ou victime collatérale? Ce proche de Karim Wade est cité parmi les clients de Mossack Fonseca, le cabinet dont les listings alimentent le dernier scandale des paradis fiscaux." *Le Point Afrique*, April 8, 2016: http://afrique.lepoint.fr/actualites/panama-papers-senegal-pape-mamadou-pouye-prete-nom-ou-victime-collaterale-08-04-2016-2030918_2365.php.
Mody Niang, "Monsieur le président de la République, où trouvez-vous la force de regarder encore vos compatriotes les yeux dans les yeux?" http://www.seneweb.com/news/Contribution/monsieur-le-president-de-la-republique-o_n_185274.html.
Pierre Péan, *Carnage. Les guerres secrètes des grandes puissances en Afrique* (Paris: Fayard, 2010).
Recherche & Technologie, Lettre d'information: "Le monde va-t-il si mal?" http://www.rtflash.fr/monde-va-t-il-si-mal/article.
Felwine Sarr, *Afrotopia* (Paris: Philippe Rey, 2016).

Abdourahmane Seck, "Après le développement: détours paradigmatiques et philosophie de l'histoire au Sénégal," *Pensée contemporaine et pratiques sociales en Afrique: penser le mouvement*, 2/192 (2015), pp. 13–32.

Lamine Senghor, *La Violation d'un pays et autres écrits anticolonialistes*, ed. David Murphy (Paris: L'Harmattan, 2012 [1927]).

Luc Sindjoun, *Sociologie des relations internationales africaines* (Paris: Karthala, 2002).

Aminata Traoré, *L'Afrique humiliée* (Paris: Fayard, 2008).

Aminata Dramane Traoré and Boubacar Boris Diop, *La Gloire des imposteurs. Lettres sur le Mali et l'Afrique* (Paris: Philippe Rey, 2014).

Mwayila Tshiyembe, *L'État postcolonial, facteur d'insécurité en Afrique* (Paris: Présence africaine, 1990).

Jean Ziegler, *Une Suisse au-dessus de tout soupçon* (Paris: Le Seuil, 1976).

Jean Ziegler, *Les Seigneurs du crime. Les nouvelles mafias contre la démocratie* (Paris: Le Seuil, 2007 [1998]).

Part V

Paths of the Universal

Sami Tchak

Sami Tchak was born in Togo in 1960. He holds a degree in philosophy as well as a doctorate in sociology and is the author of numerous novels, including Le Continent du tout et du presque rien *(J. C. Lattès, 2021) and* Place des fêtes *(Gallimard, 2001), and five monographs, including* La Couleur de l'écrivain *(Le Cheminante, 2014). He was awarded the Grand Prix littéraire d'Afrique for* La Fête des masques *(Gallimard, 2004), and the Prix Ahmadou-Kourama for* Le Paradis des chiots *(Mercure de France, 2006), the prix Ahmed-Baba for* L'Ethnologue et le Sage *(Éditions ODEM, 2013), and the William-Sassine prize for his novella "Vouz avez l'heure?"*

The universal is the only destination of literature, of any literature. By universal, I mean that which goes to the core of the human beyond any historical, geographical, political, or religious specificities ... A great many discussions concerning African writers lead me to recall this obvious statement. "Certain African writers of the new generation set their novels outside the African continent, in the vastness of the world, they want to touch the universal." At least two false ideas reside in such affirmations or reasoning: first, that the universal is the outside, or, better, the distant, above all the Western space (here there is clearly a confusion between the universal and themes found at the heart of globality, not to say globalization or Westernization); next, that Africa is the site of theatricalities so specific that they can only be understood by way of a comprehension of Africa (we are – they are – very different from them – from us.) However, in literature, the universal resides less in the themes than in how they are dealt with; it resides wherever a fragment of humanity exists so as to embody our common condition.

So, we can, we must, seek to attain the universal even from inside a bedroom, even from inside a water bottle, as we can only rest on the waves of this vast world, far from the characteristic interiorities of the human condition. The local, with or without walls, is enough for humankind. The outside, even when we grasp it from the most globalized end, is not in itself the universal, but the very site of its possibilities.

The truth is much simpler to explain: whether we're dealing with African literature or literature in general, great works are not the rule, and we must know, beyond the subjectivities of taste and judgment, how to extract them from the wave of ordinary, interchangeable books, which have found (on the African continent for example, but the phenomenon is global) new conditions that are favorable to self-publishing – a veritable current that confirms the notion that everything has value, and results in a multiplication of publishing houses content to publish manuscripts without truly reading or reviewing them as long as the author has received an important funding source (a vast forest where such elemental materials are rare). From a brief review of their texts or a short discussion of them, it seems that some self-published authors give the impression that there is a lack of general culture, of curiosity for books (so many today seem to have read so little, even those who are quick to brandish their diplomas and their teaching posts).

Of course, much larger, well-known publishing houses also publish ordinary works. And if my works still remain under the African label, they are often situated at the heart of some of the most striking dramas that lead fiction to take on a much larger holistic and sociological perspective, where the phenomena are understood as a whole with true characters, even those who occupy the place of the hero, but which lack singular depth, since they merely serve as ridiculous alibis for unoriginal discourses. However, in certain classical circuits of publication, the selections are objectively more rigorous.

In any case (and these are less my reflections than the hopes that matter to me), one has the impression that currently we are witnessing a "boom" in the publication of African literature. Such an impression is derived from the fact that there are more and more publications of African works of fiction, and yet such a boom shouldn't lead us astray from the exigencies at the heart of the work of any writer.

Exigencies relating to the poetry of specific theatricality. The space in which the theater of the novel and its specific constraints are situated may perhaps influence the aesthetics of the author, of every author, but what the author teaches us remains in us as an enduring echo thanks to the author's aesthetics, the author's poetry, if this latter is at the service of the depths of the work. For example, the *mise-en-scène*, the setting of a human tragedy in Dakar, can teach us many things about Dakar, about its cultural schemas that we are perhaps not that familiar with. But beyond this reflection on scenery and this enrichment from the fiction of a work, what allow us to better inhabit the singular universe of an author is their crafting of language, structure, style, and atmosphere.

Exigencies that touch on the specific interiorities of individuals but are also the site of profoundly philosophical questioning, that go beyond painting and setting, sometimes caricatural, even exotic (what plays out inside an individual, whatever their age, sex, social condition, place where they live, can be foreign to me, distant, quite exterior, but there is no essential question that a human can ask themselves that doesn't also touch on my own humanity. I don't necessarily have to identify with a character, but rather I must uncover within him or her the most intimate echo of humanity that the character shares with all humans).

Exigencies of depth, or density, to steer us clear of ridiculous characters singularly lacking in depth or psychological breadth so as to incarnate with an originality that which isn't original: the beauty and tragedy of the human starting from its most intimate conflicts and questions, starting from what the human bears within them that remains unchanging, that remains universal (beyond the extreme variability of external elements that act on our psychology and influence our living conditions, differentiating us from each other. Each human being carries within themselves the essential of humanity, in all its contrasts, and this is what the writer also seeks to attain. Which I already mentioned earlier on).

What is of interest here – and my own reflections and concerns are directed toward African literatures – is the aspiration for visions of the world that are not banal, but supported by an aesthetic that is sufficiently original as to resist the passage of time. A profound wish for the creation of even more great works of literature, bearers of a veritable vital breath, veritable imaginaries, and creations, beyond the circus and impact of book festivals.

I have already discussed such questions and hopes, in the form of critiques, in certain of my literary works, such as *Al Capone le Malien*, where I put into the mouth of one of the characters, Namane Kouyaté, the following words (after he had spoken about someone who had a fetish for collecting expensive cars, a character who was rather troubled and complex):

> African literatures rarely live up to our heroes. You will never see anyone in Mali dedicating a powerful, profound, and complex novel to a character as full of contradictions as Moustapha Diallo, a man anchored in our most profound values and just as much seduced by the brilliance of a bastardized, debased world. Our cultural wealth is so profound, our daily life is a veritable wonderland of enchantment, even in its most tragic of moments. But there are hardly any novels that attempt to express this cultural complexity. Many African authors produce caricatures of their country and Africa in general. They fail to live up to their own truth. Their writings lack a soul that only a work written and rooted in the culture can truly provide.

In *La Couleur de l'africain*, I also made a fictitious professor say:

> If many of your novels (I'm talking to you, so-called new generation of authors) bear witness to an apparent evolution in terms of both form and content, it is nevertheless quite easy to recognize that not much has changed, in most cases, at the aesthetic level. That's not to say you don't create works in a different way, you certainly do, but doing something differently doesn't necessarily imply innovation. Innovation is not a process of artifice like the way in which a peacock displays his feathers to attract a female. Innovation involves layers, levels. No mere artifice at the level of form is enough to mask the poverty of a work.

After I have expressed these thoughts, someone could counter with the following remarks, with good reason: "So write this work to which you aspire!" For why should a writer attempt to express what a writer should do instead of proving it in his or her own work? But the hopes and reflections that I'm formulating would be of no significance if they only concerned me – I, who, in this global concert, am still humbly attempting to make my own contribution. As such, by expressing such reflections, in contrast to what the fictional authors in my works say, I'm not trying to claim that

African novelists don't produce great works. Quite the contrary, it's because I'm the inheritor of a number of these great works that I can detect that there has been a decline or a need for innovation, which is another way of expressing my respect for the works that have already been written.

In the 1990s, when a group of young Mexican writers created the literary movement referred to as Crack, they were simply aspiring to carve out their own paths so as to attain the literary heights of their elders whose own experimental paths they deemed to have been exhausted. The most celebrated among them, Jorge Volpi, expressed the reasons for the movement very clearly in an interview he gave in March 2009 with the journalist Bruno Corty for the newspaper *Le Figaro*, when Mexican writers were honored at the Salon du livre in Paris:

> The Crack Literary Movement wasn't created in the 1990s to teach the literary process of Gabriel Garcìa Marquez and the rest of those writers that we refer to as part of the Boom Generation, but rather to refute the idea that "magic realism" is the lone expression of Latin American literature. Those of my generation have stated what they liked in the writers from the Boom Generation, and overwhelmingly, the one thing that they liked was the cosmopolitan dimension.

But, merely attempting to overcome magic realism (like asserting that negritude is an outmoded current) is not enough to grant meaning to this movement. What is also required is that its members, including Jorge Volpi himself, create works with the same level of density as those familiar works of their elders which had garnered so much respect. First and foremost, the Crack movement provided its representatives a possibility for collective reflection in order to promote the emergence and flourishing of several singularities. What these writers were most concerned with were what they defined as aesthetic lines, but they were also concerned with the very core of literary thought.

We can summarize their concerns with the following question:

> In relation to what already exists, to what has already been done, when one comes from a country such as Mexico with writers like Juan Rulfo, Octavio Paz, and Carlos Fuentes – and above all when one belongs to the South American subcontinent, which is home to a number of important writers – taking all this into consideration, what new questions should we be considering so that a new generation of writers can avoid literary decline and achieve similar results by way of different paths?

Here we can identify an expression of fear: that of becoming nothing more than mediocre writers, offering up to the world derivatives of classic literary productions on which they were nourished. What they really wanted to avoid was becoming the negative reference by which Mexican (Latin American) literature would lapse into a phase of devitalization. The members of the Crack movement were – *are* – inheritors of fairly imposing local literary references and wanted to be worthy of such a heritage.

I often refer to Latin American writers because their works have plumbed the same dramatic depths that our continent has also experienced. They have created dense, complex works starting from situations of extreme violence, and under the bloodiest of dictators. But also because, far off in Mexico, these writers are asking the same questions as we are: the lack of space for true literary criticism as well as sufficient local readership. For example, let us look at the question put by the journalist from *Le Figaro*, Bruno Corty, on March 12, 2009: "In a country (Mexico) with 100 million inhabitants, and where 22 million reside in the capital city, why is it that local writers are not read that much?" Jorge Volpi provides an answer that is familiar to African writers in relation to their readership in their own countries:

> For a very simple reason: the network of bookstores is very weak and there are not many publishing houses. While we represent almost a quarter of the population of the entire Latin America, the average print run for a novel in Mexico is only 2,000 ... Obviously this figure doesn't include the number of pirated copies that are distributed by various mafias, which represents 25 percent of books sold in Mexico!

And in response to the question concerning literary criticism in Mexico, Volpi replies: "The quality of literary criticism has completely disappeared. The writer today has never been as free and as alone!"

These questions – the lack of a local readership, the lack or nonexistence of publishing houses, and the lack of space for serious literary criticism – are all part of a sociology of literature, but they also have a negative impact on literary production itself in that they refer back, above all for authors published locally in our countries, to specific contexts that are not propitious to emulation, each author being focused on their own writings, mostly self-published, speaking with an almost laughable satisfaction about their own "oeuvres," which no reading public, or any other legitimate body, ever gets to see.

And yet, it's precisely because our literary creations are made under conditions that are hardly ideal that certain questions, which can appear redundant or useless, become important. The writer, in his or her solitude, claims to express the human. Whatever his or her objective or subjective constraints, their horizon must not be blurred. And this horizon, as I've stated before, is the universal. And when a painting doesn't aspire to or achieve what it is seeking, there is only caricature, exoticism. For me, exoticism is a specific form of superficial theatricality that at best can be amusing.

The rejection of exoticism is a requirement for a respectful reading, a more respectful reading, of a set of literatures, African ones, often reduced to an exterior theatricality, many authors themselves seeking to hold on to this superficial gaze, which is not lacking in sincerity, paradoxically, but it can also be a site of a not necessarily subtle condescendence.

The requirements or demands of universality that an author imposes on himself, seeking out the universal from an anchorage, are indispensable to the dialogue he engages in with other writers as well as the world. Beyond the more or less massive support of the reading public, such requirements are also necessary in the writer's quest for meaning and posterity.

Re-enchanting the World: Husserl in the Postcolony

Bado Ndoye

Bado Ndoye *is a specialist in phenomenology, epistemology, and the history of science. After teaching philosophy for a dozen years in a high school, he currently teaches at the University of Cheikh Anta Diop in Dakar. His works focus on Husserlian phenomenology, the history of science, and political philosophy.*

When Marcel Gauchet, borrowing the Weberian conception of a "disenchantment of the world,"[1] speaks of the event of modernity and defines it as "an exhausting of the reign of the invisible," what he has in mind is not only the end of the theological-political, but above all the birth of a new paradigm where any form of ideality as such is from now on revoked, or, at the very least, captured on the plane of immanence, according to the rules of a strict, objectivist rationality as the metaphor for capitalism expressed by Weber clearly suggests: capitalism's "iron cage."[2] Naturalism, which had proved its merit in the experimental sciences since Galileo by relieving natural phenomena of their secondary qualities, from now on serves as the framework for the comprehension of human and social reality, so that we are dealing here with only observable and manipulatable entities.

From then on, disenchantment is endowed with another signification: that of an irremediable loss of meaning, namely an ethical finality guiding human existence. If the crisis of capitalism is structural in the sense that, in a certain manner, it is consubstantial with the very essence of capitalism, then this is due to the methodological orientation that sees in each human being nothing other than a consumer, regardless of his affiliation or system of values, the challenge being to homogenize the market in such a way that no possible resistance at a cultural level is able to resist it or serve as an obstacle to it.

This process, then, explains how the unification of the global market under the banner of capitalism has been accompanied at a conceptual level by a metaphysics of a theologically inspired history, a metaphysics for which a plurality of cultural worlds becomes an aberration, that is, a loss of being, the universal only being capable of satisfying itself through a monist conception of the real. The disenchantment of the world is therefore a cultural expression of the crisis of capitalism; the two phenomena are perceived as an expression of a historical dynamics. In this essay, we would like to show that, if Edmund Husserl is often portrayed as the philosopher par excellence of "European humanity," the one who radicalizes and achieves this metaphysics of the One, it nevertheless remains the case that through some of his most profound intuitions – one of his more decisive ones being the notion of *Lebenswelt* (the lifeworld) that he established in the 1930s at the end of his life – he also contributed to the deconstruction of the classic conceptualization and unity of a world history that up until his time had always been considered as centered around the West. Under what conditions does the concept of the lifeworld bear the virtue of pluralizing the world and thereby giving back a certain new theoretical dignity to local cultures? Is it enough to recognize Husserl as a distant ancestor of postcolonial thought? Such is the question we will seek to explore in the following pages.

A postcolonial Husserl?

As is well known, Husserl is understood as a philosopher who wasn't much concerned with Africa. When he speaks of Africans or non-Western people in general, it's almost always in contrast to a certain idea that he constructs of "European humanity," whose essence he seeks to uncover as if it could only define itself and secure its foundations by opposing a radical exteriority. His comments are so scandalous that one wonders whether he ever thought that they would one day be read and commented on by Papuans, Indians, Romani, or Africans – all these figures of otherness.[3] And yet, by one of the greatest of paradoxes, he is among those who contributed to the deconstruction of the classical paradigm of the Enlightenment philosophers who attempted to unify world history under a single teleology, liberating the possibility of a pluralism for which the universal can no longer be thought of in the form of a Platonic idea, but rather as a demand to be constructed from our own particular roots in heterogeneous cultural worlds. The concept of *Lebenswelt* that he establishes, confronted with the urgency of thinking about history in view of the rise of fascism in Europe, inaugurated this new conceptuality that completely turned on its head the notion of reason that until then had oriented "Western metaphysics," but also the very foundations of classical philosophical anthropology. From then on, it becomes a question of aligning the ego with the cultural substructure that it carries without its knowledge, by way of a phenomenology of the "surrounding world" (*Umwelt*). In his famous letter to Lucien Lévy-Bruhl, he lays out a new understanding of the concept of relativism, which will serve as the touchstone for an open and polycentric world.[4]

In such a world, the universal is never a primary given but is, rather, that which is immediately lacking. And it's for this reason that it should be understood as a demand that calls precisely for the insufficiency of the given to support itself all by itself. In other words, the universal is conceived as an infinite task that renders all the more urgent the fragmenting of the world into a plurality of cultural universes centered around themselves and no longer having to justify themselves by way of an immanent teleology that would lead them to be reabsorbed in the wake of a European history, where they would cancel themselves out. With the figure of the subject and of reason, which emerges in the 1930s starting with the thematization of the *Lebenswelt*, Husserl's task will become that of recognizing that the concept of the ego without a world and without a past is a myth. The archaeology that he elaborates in *The Crisis of European Sciences* shows that logico-formal idealities are built in the last instance on a substructure of beliefs, practices, and opinions that confer on them form and unity, in contrast to the methodological exigencies present in his *Logical Investigations* from the second decade of the twentieth century, of a science that should presuppose nothing in advance but which was capable of solving anything.[5] Put simply, what the concept of *Lebenswelt* suggests is what we could refer to as the secondarity of the subject in relation to the prescientific data that constitute it as such in the lifeworld.

But what exactly is a lifeworld? In a first approximation, it designates the world as it is given in our daily experience, in contrast to the image of it provided by the experimental sciences and which is made up of abstractions and mathematical formulas. It designates that which is granted to us in the form of sensitive subjective appearances that vary from one individual to the next. Classical science (from Galileo to Newton) is built on the principle that this sensitive layer of the world – these "sensitive qualities" – is nothing more than a subjective appearance that must be disregarded if we want to accede to the true universe, that is, the mathematical structure that serves as its subterranean framework.[6] Via this method of reduction, doubtless necessary for any scientific practice, what science sets aside is this sensitive characteristic of the world in which we live, which nevertheless makes it a human world. Husserl shows that there are only two options at our disposal: either we consider that this Galilean reduction has a strictly methodological signification, which amounts to saying, on the one hand, that the demands of scientific knowledge are such that we cannot take subjective experience as a criterion and as a measure of the validation of the scientific method; on the other hand, that what lends itself to quantification is matter and its movements. We recall that Descartes was moved by the same intentions when he distinguished between the *res cogitans* and the *res extensa*.

Thus, Husserl in no way rejects this sort of *naturalistic method*, and in several places throughout his work he constantly repeats the need for it in one's engagement with natural phenomena, or we confer on the Galilean reduction an ontological meaning, which means that beyond its methodological significance it corresponds to the very reality of phenomena. What it then sets aside – namely, this subjective life and its host of modalities – we consider as not having much value, or rather, as a simple appearance, a sort of phenomenal double of reality. Here, by way of an imperceptible shift, science gives way to a scientistic ideology that it often provokes, but which it doesn't necessarily imply as an essential necessity. To truly take the measure of this Galilean reduction that is opened up by modernity is to take into account that, by setting aside the sensitive qualities of the universe, it does not only eliminate the inessential qualities of an object. First and foremost, this scientific reduction also eliminates subjective life, the phenomenological absolute life: that of the knowing subject. By erasing the subject from the process of knowledge, science not only ignores the subject but also places it on the plane of objects, since, as a result, the subject becomes an object like all the rest, which amounts to never being able to reflect on the question of mankind in any other mode besides that of naturalization, that is, a reifying objectivation consisting, in its most radical versions, of reducing humanity to an original animality of which it cannot rid itself.

In other words, by insisting on that which is beyond the grasp of the plane of physical reality, we cut ourselves off from all transcendence – this concept not being one we should understand in the strictly religious sense of the term, even if such an understanding shouldn't be excluded, that is, of the universe of values, ideals, and the meaning that we inscribe from then on, on the strict plane of the factuality of objects. The real can only be reduced to one of its determinations, namely matter and its elementary constituents. By therefore renouncing any thought of man as mind or spirit, which amounts to considering only his bodily dimension, the entire wealth of our spiritual life is reduced to being nothing more than the mere outgrowth of our brain, as the naturalist paradigm in neuroscience has attempted to establish.

This intellectual conjuncture has indirectly produced the field of study referred to as positivism, which, in turn, secretly nourished the anti-humanist philosophies of the 1970s based around the notion of the death of man. When Foucault states that man is a "contingent event" that will disappear the day when the conditions that have favored his appearance will have changed, he is aligning this fact with this positivist matrix. And yet, what then would a humanity be that considers itself, in its own eyes, as nothing more than a simple contingent fact? If we think of the destructive and sacrificial potentialities such a view can elicit in the context of the rise of fascism in Europe in the 1930s, for instance, we can begin to understand in what manner the demand for reorganizing or re-establishing the sciences in Husserl is above all an ethical requirement. Indeed, the disillusionment of the world produced by Newtonian-Galilean science, beyond the epistemological questions it poses, implies in particular ethical issues that can only be overcome by reconnecting the two poles of the process of knowledge: the subject and object.

Such a task corresponds to the *Lebenswelt* that Husserl rediscovers by way of a regressive approach that goes (1) from the sphere of the *cogito ego*, (2) to corporeality, and finally (3) to the world of the environment, where the subject discovers that the process of individuation by which he believed himself able to self-grasp as an autonomous subject was in fact a collective process, that of the group. Rather, it's to the transcendental subjectivity understood as an a priori original data that one should always turn, since it alone can give itself the infinite horizon of objectivity as a correlate, and therefore constitute the world. Husserl progressed rather far in this direction when he demonstrated that, if the transcendental subject is always caught in a network of social relations, then it's the social sciences, namely this intentional sociology that always appealed to his desires, that must take the baton of phenomenology. In 1935, after the publication of *Primitive Mentality* by Lucien Lévy-Bruhl,[7] Husserl provided a concrete phenomenological reading concerning the importance of historical sciences and the recognition of cultural relativism as a necessary moment. In a letter to Lévy-Bruhl, he writes:

> Naturally, we have long known that every human being has a "world-representation," that every nation, every supranational cultural grouping lives, so to speak, in a distinct world as its own environing world, and so again every historical time in its world. Yet, in contrast to this empty generalization, your work and your exceptional theme has made us sensitive to something overwhelmingly new: namely, that it is a possible and highly important and great task to "empathize" with a humanity living self-contained in living generative sociality and to understand this humanity as having, in and through its socially unified life, the world, which for it is not a "world-representation" but rather the world that actually exists for it. Thereby we learn to understand its [i.e. that humanity's] ways of apperceiving, identifying, [and] thinking, thus its logic and its ontology, that of its environing world with the respective categories.[8]

Pluralizing the world

This letter is crucial for our discussion since it lays the foundations for a new paradigm in which it becomes possible, in the framework of Husserlian phenomenology, to freshly posit the possibility of a thought of alterity and pluralism that up until then the classical ontology and metaphysics of the One had covered over. What we see here is that Husserl prescribes a methodological recommendation that seems to suggest he is no longer satisfied with a long eidetic procedure for ideally grasping alterity in its most foreign cultural forms. Henceforth, he puts forward the need for an effective encounter with historical cultures, the only way to understand from the inside what is happening in the surrounding world. In other words, one must learn how to remain in the element of the particular that constitutes each cultural formation so as to feel it from the inside, in what it can have, as Bergson would have said, that is unique and inexpressible.

And yet, only anthropology is capable of providing such knowledge, as explained by Merleau-Ponty, for whom not only is the moment of relativism necessary and perhaps also insurmountable, according to his understanding of Husserl's letter, but also that it would be necessary above all reverse the roles of ethnology and philosophy, which amounts to proscribing the pre-eminence of the latter over historical sciences.[9] There would thus be a first or early Husserl who was an idealist and therefore insensitive to historical reality, a Husserl for whom eidetic reduction, in its formal operativity, was sufficient for grasping the reality of foreign societies, and a second Husserl for whom heterogeneity comprised cultures that couldn't be overcome by a simple recourse to morphological essences: henceforth, one must begin by way of methods and resources that anthropology and the historical sciences provide us.

We immediately see that the rationality that emerges from this thematization of the *Lebenswelt* no longer has anything in common with that of a phenomenology of beginnings which was established in the second decade of the twentieth century. What we see clearly explained here is that science is built on a foundation of presuppositions, beliefs, values, and practices, basically, a universe of meaning that pre-exists it, a universe that it cannot take as a theme in turn unless it renounces its idealistic demands of a science centered around a transcendental ego that doesn't presuppose anything, and which, as a result, can explain everything. In other words, science must admit that its very principle is not immanent in it, but resides hidden in the very depths of a primordiality that escapes its grasp. What we are dealing with here is a question of an archaeological approach that meticulously uncovers, by way of a systematic sifting of sedimented layers, various grounds built one upon the other, so as to eventually arrive at the initial layer that constitutes the condition of possibility of philosophy as science "of first principles and first causes," as Aristotle understood it.[10]

What is the lesson that we can draw from this in terms of what is of interest to us here? First, thanks to this new type of conceptuality, it becomes possible to show that the ego always bears the mark of its inscription in a grounding of values and ideals, and that it's by way of this initial or originary inscription that it goes toward the ideal of the norm, whether this be ethical, aesthetic, or epistemological. What is first is not so much the norm – the norm not being factual – as it is the wordly, that is the cultural, conditions of its appearance. And yet, such conditions can only be heterogenous to each other because they translate the plurality and inescapable diversity of historical situations of humanity. And we can see straightaway then that, if the task of experimental science is to transcend this local anchor or rooting, so as to set its sights on the universal, it still remains the case that these sciences remain rooted in social praxis.[11] As for the historical sciences, they are subject to the necessity of providing a theoretical meaning to this local anchoring or rooting.

The second discernment – that stems from the first – is that this thematization's merit resides in its undoing of History with a capital H so as to give way to a plurality of singular histories, and, therefore, to reconsider universal history in the aftermath of the necessity of the Hegelian dialectic that attempted to reduce this universal history to a lone European history. There can no longer be a *Weltgeist*, a world Spirit in the sense that Hegel understood it, since each culture is a universe of meaning in and of itself, by the simple fact that it grants itself a world and justifies itself through this world, that is, by way of its own teleological point of view. Each culture can therefore be seen as the actualization of what the human spirit, in its infinite plasticity, can become. This plurality of human becomings must therefore be understood first and foremost for what it is: namely, a fragmentation of human experience into a plurality of experiences and journeys, each equivalent, since each of them reflects a figure of what human intelligence, placed in a given context, is capable of realizing.

This pluralization of the world can only be thought all the way through if we conceive of universal history as being polycentric, that is, as shattered and splintered history, and which is a priori non-totalizable. In other words, what I mean by historical polycentrism is the idea according to which world history is a polyphony of narratives, each recounting a singular tale of the fate of humankind, a becoming starting from a plurality of centers according to a random dynamic whose trajectory we cannot, a priori, determine with precision. And we can immediately see that this conception of History can only arise out of a paradigm of complexity, rather than from a determinist one, inherited from linear models of the Galilean-Newtonian dynamic. As a result, what we must seek out is a new approach whereby each center, in that it influences others, will also be influenced by them, following this logic of "confusion-conjugation," as the Senegalese historian Mamadou Diouf defined the ontology of paganism. A polycentric world is therefore a pluralized world, that is, a world in which people's human experiences are not only irreducible but first and foremost equivalent.

And yet, it seems to me that one of the principal themes of postcolonial studies precisely refers to this fragmentation of the world into independent entities, a fragmentation that one must indeed see as a consequence of critiques addressed to the humanism of the Enlightenment in whose name a great many people around the world were subjected or whose existence was simply denied. Paraphrasing Castoriadis, Achille Mbembe summarizes the main criticism of this humanism by the postcolonial: "Only I have value. But I can only have value as myself, if others, as themselves, do not have value."[12] Re-enchanting the world, then, means giving new meaning to these other voices and narratives, this non-totalizable totality by which humanity exists in its unshakeable diversity as a multitude of cultural entities, each expressing in its own manner the genius of humanity.[13]

But once we have established this pluralization of the world into so many different cultural worlds, we have only traveled halfway. It would be disrespectful to the spirit to believe that the historical realizations by which such a world manifested itself can be self-contained in all these different, foreign worlds, that one could be closed off in one's own separate world to such an extent that these worlds would be unable to communicate with each other. If each culture is a world, they all share in common their appearance against the background of a more encompassing world that constitutes them in the horizon of their deployment. This means that relativism, in the way in which it is expressed in his letter to Lévy-Bruhl, can't be Husserl's last word concerning scientific knowledge; he does not give up seeking to unpack the universal aprioric structures of sociality, which he finds largely in historicity that one must see as the principal characteristic of humanity, since no people is level with naturality but, rather, each is, in one way or another, historical.

What gives weight to an interpretation of Husserl's letter to Lévy-Bruhl such as that put forward by Maurice Merleau-Ponty is the possibility of an intercultural dialogue in which, by way of an iconoclastic reading of Husserl, he attempts to give it a coherent theoretical content. Merleau-Ponty's anti-Platonic position consists in claiming that this dialogue is not possible by some sort of metaphysical entity that is lodged somewhere in a hypostasized universe of essences, which we could refer to as the universal and which, looming over cultures from this position of exterritoriality, would judge them from the outside. In reality, there is nothing in the heavens above, and everything strictly plays out on the plane of immanence in a transversal manner. The "lateral universal" described by Souleymane Bachir Diagne responds to the necessity of thinking interculturality in the guise of a transaction by which meanings pass from one universe to another, from one language to another language, and this is how Diagne establishes his notion of a philosophy through translation.[14] There is nothing in the heavens above, which means that the universal is not a factual given that could be conflated with a specific culture, but rather it must be a construction, a patient development performed on the basis of particular historical data. A humanism carried by such a conception of the universal would therefore be rich in all particular historical determinations and would no longer be the theoretical expression of the imperial domination of the West.

During a period when Althusserian theoretical anti-humanism, of positivist inspiration, was all the rage, Senghor and Nyerere were defenders of this new kind of humanism. Senghor never shared in the Althusserian reading of an "epistemological break" that saw in the humanism of a "young Marx" an idealistic remnant that the achievements of *Capital* would overcome in the luminous clarity of thought that has reached scientific maturity.[15] Today, it is of the utmost importance for contemporary African thought to reactivate such a humanism with a view to reclaiming a new type of socialism, conceived from the viewpoint of African values of solidarity. The re-enchantment of the world depends on this.

Writing about the Humanities from the Vantage Point of Africa

Felwine Sarr

Felwine Sarr *is a Senegalese scholar and writer born on the island of Niodor, among the Saloum islands. He is Anne-Marie Bryan Distinguished Research Professor of French and Francophone Studies at Duke University. His scholarly work focuses on political economy, developmental economics, epistemology, and the history of religious ideas. He has published a number of works, including the novels* Dahij, 105 rue Carnot, Afrotopia, *and* Méditations africaines. *He is the co-founder of the publishing house Éditions Jimsaan, and editor of the* Journal of African Transformation *(Codesria-Uneca).*

The reflection that I would like to submit to your attention revolves around the question of *writing the humanities from the vantage point of Africa*. It begins through an understanding of a diversity of modes for approaching the real according to civilizations and eras, a plurality of modes of knowledge, as well as a gnoseological and epistemological relativity. This reflection proposes that we think about the plurality of the adventures of human thought starting from the idea of an equality of principle of traditions of thought, and by acknowledging their incommensurability.

This leads us to consider these different traditions of thought, starting from their horizons and configurations of the thinkable that they propose, as singular adventures of the spirit which have developed in parallel and adjacent ways, dependent on the cultures from which they emanate (François Julien).

Thinking about these questions in the African context calls for a necessary epistemic recentering for an improved and more fruitful engagement in the social sciences that takes Africa as its object. In order for these sciences to be operative, the realities they seek to elucidate must be better articulated. It is about integrating the complexity of African social formations and assuming them in their historical and cultural specificity. And this requires a subsequent shift in the very fields of constituted or reprised knowledge; an act of thought that is rooted in the present, and which focuses particular attention on its archeological milieu and on the real tendencies of the societies that it apprehends. But in a more fundamental manner, what such a recentering calls for is a way of gaining access to a deeper knowledge of African societies and cultures, since it would be founded on their own gnoseological criteria. In order for this to happen, we must take into account modes for the apprehension of reality other than scientific knowledge as it has been constituted until now. The exploration of relatively forgotten areas of research, such as African ontomythologies and epistemologies, provides a better account of the diverse forms of knowledge, having ensured the sustainability of African societies.

What would the prolegomena be for such a method?

This project of refounding requires a work of resumption in the social sciences that involves an epistemological interrogation of the objects, methods, and the status of knowledge produced by the human and social sciences, in the way they are practiced on African realities. The major obstacle of such an approach remains the determination of an epistemological field, that is, the specific objects to apprehend but also the singular methods for achieving this. A recurring critique addressed to the Western conception of knowledge is that it overestimates the prerogatives of the subject based on the illusion that the latter, by way of the means available to it alone (sense and/or reason), can produce a thought that reflects the complexity of the real. The European methodological trap consists in choosing a single criterion for explaining the real. Furthermore, its method is founded on a desire, in terms of knowledge, to produce a reality exclusively subjected to the discernment of experience and the debate of reason. The fecundity of a methodical approach based on the principle of the excluded middle[1] will be called into question. Such an approach, so as to apprehend the real, distinguishes the object from the subject. The punctualization of the object and the splitting up of reality into small bits, which we subsequently attempt to put back together (Issiaka Prosper Lalèye). This method has been used in the development of physics and the exact sciences, but reveals its flaws as a method once we enter into questions of the human and social sciences, since the objects being studied have a depth and the subject is not detached from the object. As is the case in quantum physics, the position of the observer modifies the thing being observed.

In African cultures and cosmologies, the project for an epistemic recentering can be found in their rich and inexhaustible resources. The depletion of technoscientific reason, as well as civilizational consequences of its impasses, calls for a renewal of the sources of imagination and thought. For Africans, these sources flow through a better integration of their own universes of reference in the quest for their societal balance.

So as to avoid the traps of the colonial library,[2] there must be a return to the resources of African cultures that can only be achieved through a knowledge that is founded on the gnoseological criteria of the very cultures themselves. Namely, through the various points of reference arising out of these specific cultures.[3] According to Valentin Mudimbe, "the singularity of historical experiences is its own evidence, and we can draw from each experience our own norms of intelligibility."

The philosophers who opened up the debate concerning the need for African social sciences have engaged very little in the notion of understanding African reality exclusively through science. Their project consisted mainly of an attempt to de-Westernize scientific knowledge and gain a better knowledge of Africa by a revision of epistemological positions. The legitimacy of the method that consists in attempting to grasp the African real(s) by way of this instrument we refer to as *science* was not itself called into question. And yet, a number of reasons lead us to question the ability of the scientific method *alone* to elucidate the real. There are many other ways to grasp the real and, furthermore, Western forms of knowledge do not exhaust all of these, and as far as the phenomenology of perception is concerned, the world exists only as an object of representation and as a discourse of subject situated in a given moment of an individual and collective history, as dependent on a way of seeing the world.

There is no doubt that a work of displacement in the interior of various fields of constituted knowledge still needs to be undertaken. But we must also explore the possibilities offered by other forms of knowledge and the apprehension of the real. These other ways constitute modes of knowledge that have demonstrated their functioning qualities over a long period of time, in diverse areas of human activity: therapeutic knowledge; environmental knowledge; technical know-how; and social, historical, psychological, economic, and agronomic forms of knowledge. These forms of knowledge have assured the growth and survival of African societies. In order to mobilize them, it is necessary to explore these cosmogonies, myths, and diverse cultural expressions, as well as African linguistic resources. In other words, we must seek to explore and understand African cultures through their own specific categories.

What will also be of crucial importance is to engage in a debate on a theory of knowledge limited by Western conceptions of what knowledge is, questioning the exclusivity of a logo-centric epistemology and the reasoning that can be undertaken by the mode of written thought alone. The path taken by Western reason is only one among many.

Enlarging the scope of and modes for conceiving a theory of knowledge will consist of reconnecting logocentric epistemologies with ontomythologies, that is, by taking into account their sources along with a critical reading of traditional myths and narratives; these are not exclusive to African cultures, but belong to all societies where the vehicle for the communication of thought is essentially oral (storytelling) and not that of the written word. Beyond a concern for a better understanding and apprehension of African social realities, by opening up other lines of access to knowledge, such an undertaking could constitute a necessary liberation and enlargement of a theory of knowledge.

This reflection takes up again at its root the question of knowledge. It is a question of rethinking the conditions of the possibility of knowledge. *What can I know?* This is what Kant asks in his *Critique of Pure Reason*. How is it possible to know something? Such questions were at the very heart of the metaphysics and physics that defined the eighteenth century.

This investigation of knowledge will be deepened through a reflection on the objects of the epistemological inquiry, but also by questioning its methods of apprehending reality. To explain, following Aristotle, would be to elucidate the causes that lead back to the first cause. Thinking that explanation is the only way to think about the world is a biased form of thought. Thought reliant on linear causality has its support structure: the first cause. Complexity (Morin) and dialogical thinking made it possible to relativize this mode of apprehending reality by pointing out its limits.

African cosmologies[4] in their turn also relativize the omnipotence of the subject, which is nothing more than a transient aggregate of psychological and biological elements subject to continuous transformation and passage in different orders of reality. Such cosmologies are skeptical about the ability of discourse to take into account the entirety of reality and to reflect the order of things. The ultimate nature of reality transcends our faculties of reflection and expression. The world is an enigma that is not perfectly capable of being read or deciphered, and it would therefore be illusory (according to these aforementioned cosmologies) to decipher all of reality's laws and establish our actions upon them. From this viewpoint, knowledge concerning the cosmos can certainly be acquired through properties of the mind, and also those of the real. And in this way, a confrontation with the real allows one to avoid an excess of subjectivity and objectivity.

European thought has mainly been driven by the search for truth. It's through this central notion that it was forged. However, in African or Asian practices of thought, the search for truth is not the primary concern. In the latter practices, vitality, vital force, the liveable, the viable … these seem to be the knots that this thought seeks to untangle. The idea of truth understood as an "adequacy of the thing to the mind" is not transcultural. Moreover, the thing must be (palpable, present, material) in order for there to be truth. What about, in this case, the future, the probable, the possible, the contingent, the objects of metaphysics?

In other discursive regimes (systems of thought), the horizon of configuration is not the notion of truth. In these instances, thoughts must be envisioned in their own horizons of meaning.

Human intelligence resides in the capacity to pass through different possibles of thought, to understand each one of them, and to place them in a dialogue. Which leads one to think of truth as the source of intelligibility. The opposite of truth would therefore not be the false, but that which is unthinkable, undiscovered, inaccessible, etc. What is true is that which produces the intelligible and serves to enlighten experience.

Nevertheless, the objective is not to resolve, by way of some unifying and convergent dialectic, the gap that exists between the various methods of approaching knowledge and the real. It is not a question of a systematic search for some ultimate truth or synthesis, but rather of making these possibilities communicate so as to produce the intelligible, starting from their own self-reflection, by establishing a tension and maintaining this exploratory gap

(François Julien). As such, we must see cultures as contingent resources, in order for the different configurations of the thinkable that they allow to furnish us with a glimpse of the unthinkable and to better elucidate the human experience in all its diversity. We must also include other non-discursive forms of knowledge in the field of the humanities, and, in particular, grant a place to artistic writings as foundational elements of cognitive human experience.

To enlarge the possibilities of thought, to examine the conditions of possibility of the diverse modes of knowledge, as well as their relation to experience, requires a necessary decompartmentalization of what we understand or conceive of as a theory of knowledge. In order for this to happen, we must think the unthinkable of philosophy and of the humanities and social sciences. Such an approach seems necessary in order for the expansion of all the possibilities of thought.

Thinking about the World from the Vantage Point of Africa

Questions for Today and Tomorrow

Achille Mbembe

Achille Mbembe *is Professor of History and Political Science at the University of the Witwatersrand in Johannesburg, South Africa, as well as a researcher at the Wits Institute for Social and Economic Research. He is the author of many works in French and in translation, including* Out of the Dark Night *(Columbia University Press, 2021),* Necropolitics *(Duke University Press, 2019),* La Naissance du maquis dans le Sud-Cameroun *(Karthala, 1996),* De la Postcolonie. Essai sur l'imagination politique dans l'Afrique contemporaine *(Karthala, 2000), and* Politiques de l'inimitié *(La Découverte, 2016).*

It would be preposterous to claim that we are speaking in the name of all Africans. This is not something they have asked of us. If they were to do so, it wouldn't make things any easier. We know that in Africa the answers given to the question of knowing "how to think about Africa in the world" – or, to put it in other terms, "how to think about the world from the vantage point of Africa" – are divergent and contradictory, even irreconcilable.

The concern that we all have for Africa – and that Africa causes for us – goes without saying. And in this regard, any authority that claims to draw its legitimacy from the principle of indigeneity would be quickly confronted with its own limits. Since, basically, to speak as an *African* guarantees very little, sometimes not even the slightest measure of authenticity.

1

And yet, there are many in Africa and the diaspora who believe not just that Africans alone have the right to study their societies and cultures, but also that Africans alone are up to the task of telling the truth about Africa. These same voices argue that all knowledge production is necessarily local; and that the universal is, in reality, a closed discourse that is ignored. Hence the quest for an "African" paradigm of the social sciences. Hence, too, the desire – manifested by a large number of Africans – to make use of their understanding (without any guidance from others) so as to escape being *governed by others*.

We are tempted to understand their reasoning. How else should one react when we know to what extent colonial or imperial knowledge served, for such a long time, as a weapon used for the material and symbolic subjugation of non-European worlds? Indeed, as we currently understand it, each time we pronounce the name "Africa," we not only convoke a physical, spatial, or geographical fact; we also set in motion, sometimes unconsciously, a series of images, a mass of prejudices, attributes that are supposed to typify those who inhabit this physical space, their customs and ways of living and being, and in particular their relationship to a life whose duration is never certain, since death, as many believe, is never far off.

In many modern regimes of discourse and knowledge, the term "Africa" almost automatically evokes a world apart; a world with which many of our contemporaries have a great deal of difficulty identifying; a reality they often only know how to speak of in terms of some distant and anecdotal form, like some sort of gray parenthesis.

Why is this? Because for them, *life in Africa is never simply an ordinary human life*. It often appears as the life of other distant people residing elsewhere. As such, at certain times, it elicits gestures of charity or pity – the politics of the Good Samaritan. And precisely because the name "Africa" always refers to some kind of arbitrary "primordial," that of designations to which nothing in particular really seems to respond except perhaps *an inaugural prejudice in its infinite regression*, one always assumes that, in a general way, some form of non-sense is already implied and understood in the name itself.

Under these conditions, in attempting to express Africa, one always runs the risk of entering into an infinite regression of the presupposed, of constructing certain figures (it doesn't matter which) above the void. As Raymond Roussel says,[1] all it takes is to choose words and images that are pretty much identical, and to add similar images and words but taken in a different context, and one eventually ends up uncovering the narrative of which, in any number of ways, we already had knowledge.

At the foundation of modern regimes of knowledge, therefore, we uncover the notion according to which humanity does not share a common world. Sharing hardly any common world, global politics (as well as the politics of knowledge on a global scale) can hardly be a *politics of similarity*. It can only be a politics of difference.

2

Today, many among us belong to so many universes of meaning that it is impossible for them to claim any kind of clear or transparent forms of belonging or immaculate filiations. In fact, whether they have physically left or remained in their birthplaces, many people will have spent the bulk of their adult lives traversing the globe, that is, endlessly making compromises with all sorts of conventional traditions, reconfiguring their sense of belonging that they want to take for granted.

Throughout such a journey – and often due to the force of events – they have learned much through contact with other worlds. At the same time, many people have also partaken in a quasi-mystical experience: becoming human implies exiting oneself and encountering – never guaranteed in advance – the foreign and the foreigner, the stranger. Every true thought emerges from the point of contact with that which is not oneself. At the point of contact with what cannot reduced to oneself, thinking, like nourishing one's life, inevitably becomes inhabiting the gap or interval, making this gap work.

Under these conditions, how can we articulate a reflection that honors the historical (even existential) relation with the place that bore witness to our birth (or which bears our ancestral ties), while also consciously separating ourselves from it, and using this gap, without which it would be difficult to escape some sort of atavism in one way or another? The answer to this question should be unequivocal – by taking risks, starting with the risk of pronouncing disputable views; by striving to think from a *third-place* at once geographical and theoretical; by voluntarily assuming the risk that our remarks will be considered as inauthentic.

There is no doubt that existing for oneself in the first person, acting for oneself, being present to oneself, being capable of saying "I think," being concerned for oneself, making rules for oneself, governing oneself, constitute the starting point for any politics of liberty, and, in so doing, of thought. But there is no self that is situated outside a world of which we are all inheritors, as Frantz Fanon was often quick to note. It's true that the matrices of historical human experience are not the same everywhere. But recognizing that every human experience is unique does not mean that a given experience is ineffable and untranslatable in other human languages.

3

For those who are concerned about Africa, the essential challenge from now on is, therefore, to work at the intersection of several exteriorities, convinced that there is no longer any sort of outside that could be opposed to an inside. Because, at bottom, everything has moved inside. There is no part of the world whose history doesn't contain some African dimension, in the same way that African history only exists as an integral part of world history. There hardly exists – either for Africans or for other peoples in the world – any totally hidden forms of knowledge that any one person or group considers as belonging only to themselves and not to others. It is therefore time to move on from the problematic of origins and borders. Indeed, we must seek out and explore other bifurcations and branches of thought. In order to do this, we must openly assume once and for all the composite character of our face and the heterogeneity of our heritages no longer understood as factors of inauthenticity, but as the privileged resources of our own surpassing.

4

The big question that remains for us, as much today as for tomorrow, is therefore that of *our belonging in the present and in the world.*

Michel Foucault put this question in the following manner: "What is my actuality? What is the meaning of this actuality? And what does the fact that I'm speaking about this actuality do?" So we cite Foucault. But in reality this is a much older question that African thought made its own, especially in the New World, in the first half of the nineteenth century, without necessarily using the same language as Foucault – or before him of Kant, since Foucault is really translating Kant.

This modern thought of African origin (which is the work of the first African American intellectuals, from the Blacks of the Caribbean) posits the question of our belonging in the present and the world in the language of life, and in what provokes dissipation, etiolation. This thought considers the question regarding *what it means to truly live* – the truth of life, the affirmative forms of the implementation of life. It's therefore not simply thinking of life in the abstract. Rather, it's a questioning of *the will to live, and the future of affirmation*, especially where the reign of negation dominates. And finally, it's a form of thought that seeks to move beyond the cruel alternative: "kill or be killed."

The central object of this thought is therefore not the ethnological quest for an "African" paradigm of the social sciences. Furthermore, in this thought, Africa is not a physical place among other nation-states and their territorial borders. It is a diasporic project and, as a result, it is transnational. How then can we make of the present and African life (this present in which I belong) *an event of thought* for those certainly of African origin, but also for our world? In what language should we articulate the conditions for exiting the circumstances in which people of African origins find themselves?

5

In the work of Frantz Fanon, for example, the problem of belonging in the present and in the world is conflated with the project of human autonomy or even the self-creation of humanity. "I am my own foundation," he declares at the end of *Black Skin, White Masks*.

The context that determines his thought is that of colonial and racial violence as well as the war of so-called liberation. The principal theme of racial and colonial violence is to seek to expel the humanity of its victims, or even to suspend it. It no longer goes without saying. Why? Quite simply because in looking at the colonized, Europe constantly asks itself: "Is this a human being? Is this some other kind of human being? Is this a copy of a human? Or is it something other than human?"

In this context, Fanon explains to us that humanity is not a given. The eruption of self is inseparable from the eruption of the world. These two movements pass through the enlightenment of the colonized to consciousness itself – the process by which the colonized are capable of subjectively appropriating themselves, dismantling the very enclosure (notably that of race), and allowing themselves to speak in the first person.

In return, this appropriation of self seeks not only the realization of self, but, in a more significant manner, the very elevation of humanity: a new departure for creation, and as we will quickly emphasize as well: the *liberation of the world*.

6

Also in the work of Fanon, we find that this rise in humanity can only be the result of a struggle – a struggle for life. The struggle for life (which is the same as the struggle to nurture the world) has two dimensions.

On the one hand, it consists in the constitution of this capacity to be oneself and to act for oneself that Fanon compares to an upsurge – a surging forth from the depths of what he calls "an extraordinarily arid and sterile zone" of existence, this zone of "non-being" that is, in his eyes, that of race. "The Black man isn't. No more so than the White man," he says – which means that "the black man is a man similar to others, a man like the others," "a man among other men."

On the other hand, the rise in humanity is only possible if, at the outset, we postulate a fundamental similarity, of an originary human citizenship that we can formulate in the following manner: *all human beings are similar to others, all men and women are like all other men and women, humans among humans.*

And it's precisely this postulate that constitutes precisely, in Fanon's eyes, the key to the project of liberating the world, the project of human autonomy.

7

Let's take another example: that of Léopold Sédar Senghor. One of the paradoxes of Senghor is wanting to recognize an incalculable debt to the most racist, biological, and essentialist theories of his era. But Senghor made use of these theories in order to articulate an antiracist poetics of the world. What he refers to as *negritude* is obviously an attempt at a concern for self, a self-care, to reflect on that which belongs to oneself – a kind of racial narcissism.

But here as well, in this fraudulent terrain of essential difference, a concern for what belongs to oneself, and by which one can be defined, only has meaning to the extent that it is meant to be shared. Senghor gave a name to this project of *being in common*: *the rendezvous of giving and receiving*.

In his eyes, it's on this commonality of singularities that the rebirth of the world and the advent of a universal community depend – a *créole* community organized on the principle of shared differences, of what is unique. Only a community based on the pooling of one's own and sharing that which is unique to each of us is open to *everyone*.

We should also make clear that for Fanon as well as Senghor, we are the inheritors of the *whole world*. At the same time, both the world and this heritage are something we must create. The world is a creation, and we are creations within it. Outside this process of creation and self-creation, the world is silent and elusive. And it's through contributing to this process of creation and self-creation that we gain the *right to inherit this world in its entirety*.

8

In the work of other modern thinkers of African origin, we find this instance of the liberation of the world and belonging to it as a power that the subject grants itself in order to be whole. In the work of Édouard Glissant, for example, the liberation of the world consists precisely in engaging in an encounter with the world in knowing how to embrace the undeniable fabric of affiliations that form our identity and the entanglement of networks that make every identity necessarily function in relation to the Other – an Other that is always there, from the beginning.

The real liberation of the world is therefore the encounter with the whole world, what Glissant calls the *Tout-Monde* (Whole-World). In such an encounter, we see a politics of connecting and becoming – a becoming of affirmation.

This same theme of connection and the question of wholeness are also at work in the reflections of Paul Gilroy, for whom the liberation of the world takes on the contours of a new planetary consciousness.

Among all these thinkers, including those who begin from the premise of difference, the project is not one of partitioning the world and its division. They are all seeking a sphere of horizontality that grants a central place to an *ethics of mutuality* or, as Gilroy suggests, of conviviality: of *being-with-others*.

9

The call for an "African" paradigm of the social sciences could end up being dangerous if it is constructed on the basis of nationalist, nativist, or indigenist theses. These are based on the idea of a closure of worlds as opposed to their liberation and connection. Their ideological function is to encourage Africans to think of themselves as victims of history and to live their history as a form of witch trial. Such theses rest on the notion according to which there are different types of humanity and each one corresponds to a specific epistemic model. Veritable intellectual enclosures, they rise to the production, thanks to foreign funding, of works that no one reads or cites, and which serve for nothing more than appeasing the conscience of the ones performing such charity, and which cultivate in the recipients of such gifts a logic of resentment and a posture of irresponsibility.

10

The great preoccupation, as much for today as for tomorrow, is therefore to know what the African present is a sign of and what grants it this sign value. This preoccupation is to make Africa not only a site of intellectual provocation but *an event for thought*.

Since the middle of the twentieth century, the continent has experienced rapid and multifaceted changes, the result of which have been paradoxical. Whether it's a case of new forms of conflict, the life of new currencies, investments, or exchange, or even areas of cultural and artistic creativity, urban forms and cultural regimes, everything is being rebuilt in conditions of uncertainty that are often radical. Things that we were accustomed to end up dying. Other things that we had thought were forever dead and gone suddenly appear again under new names, with new masks, and often on the same stages as yesterday, but with new actors. In spite of appearances, the continent has become increasingly multicultural, multiracial, diasporic, and cosmopolitan. Here, phenomena of mobility sketch out the new maps of the world. How are we to imagine politically this new world with multiple maps? Mobilities and circulations help in the structuring of a new Africa, at once a site of destination and transition, a space of confluence at the crossroads of several cultures, races, and diasporas. What are the various flows at work within it?

We must describe and analyze the births of this new society without wasting our time by simply refuting, often rather clumsily, the sometimes erroneous interpretations of it produced elsewhere by others.

We must do this recognizing that our history, our present, and the extraordinary wealth of our realities are, more than we realize, objects and signs that, in the contemporary fields of knowledge, are likely to speak beyond our geographical and racial borders. In order to achieve this task we must decompartentalize, break down barriers, open up to international and cross-cutting questions, embrace the humanities and natural sciences, and deepen our philosophical and historical inquiries. We must also be prepared to go beyond established academic territories and the disciplinary and institutional formulas whose sole function is to reproduce preconceived ideas. We must accept a journey along paths that are as oblique as they are indirect in order to connect areas that we generally tend to keep separate.

11

To reiterate, it will not be so much a question of stating what Africa is *not*, less still what Africa is lacking. We will, rather, begin from the hypothesis that *it's on the African continent that the question of the world (where it is going and what it means) is henceforth posited in the newest, most complex, and most radical manner.* And it's also starting from this hypothesis that all the categories that have served to make sense of art, as well as politics, ethics, and language, are in crisis, even while new alternative forms of life continue to emerge.

Reflecting on this phenomenon of the emergent, these aesthetic and political forms, as well as the ethical problems they pose, requires another way of problematizing that which, in human experience in Africa, refers back to a series of global questions that the world in its entirety is confronting.

Human experience in Africa thus poses to contemporary intellectuals questions whose radical nature has hardly, up until now, been the object of substantial research. And yet, a *thought of the world* that would take seriously this radicality would not only gain a form of depth or density. In fact, the renewal of our imagination of culture, politics, and language, as well as our thought of the human in general – all this passes through this mirror of the world that Africa has become.

12

For the most part, the African archives are largely constituted around the Atlantic triangle (Africa, the Americas and the Caribbean, and Europe). But they extend far beyond this triangle and also include the Islamic worlds as well as those of Asia. It has been established that these archives denote *diverse figures of modernity*.

To render these figures legible requires that the questions of "originality" and "singularity" be posited in new terms and that the conditions are ripe for transition to a *post-anthropological gaze* on Africa. Without this, it will be difficult to overcome the aporia of the various discourses concerning "difference."

It should be understood that such a project reserves a special place for literary and artistic archives. The way in which the African postcolonial novel has dealt with the question of "writing" and "language" makes it possible to open up new perspectives concerning the themes of originality and singularity, of the "near" and the "distant"; of "distance" and "proximity," of the "self," and of "time" and "style." The same goes for the visual and plastic arts (painting, sculpture, cinema, fashion, photography), music, dance, and architecture.

Under what terms does African cultural creation pose the problem of Africa belonging in the world, the ways in which to inhabit it, to reclaim itself and its values from it? Starting from African experiences, can we consider that, in an era dominated by the theme of insecurity and terror, certain figures (the migrant, the refugee, the foreigner, the child, the enemy) are more emblematic of a "precarious life" than others? What can we say of the present and of the future of the state in the contemporary world, or even of the global order in its generality? Is the "time of the nation-state" really that different than that of the "market"? In the contemporary context, how can we rethink the – classic – problem of the relationship between force and law, security and vulnerability? In what terms can we once again re-examine the status of hope and the place of the future in the contemporary imaginations of time and life? What are the futures in question, and what are the resources that would not only allow us to think about them, but also to precipitate their arrival?

Notes

(European?) Universalism Put to the Test by Indigenous Histories

1 Claude McKay "Home to Harlem," in Rafia Zafar (ed.), "Home to Harlem," in *Harlem Renaissance: Five Novels of the 1920s* (New York: The Library of America, 2011), pp. 137–295; p. 251.
2 Cheikh Anta Diop, principally, in *Nations nègres et culture: de l'antiquité nègre égyptienne aux problems culturel de l'Afrique noire* (Paris: Présence africaine, 1954). *The African Origin of Civilization: Myth or Reality*, trans. Mercer Cook (Chicago: Lawrence Hill Books, 1974); *Civilization or Barbarism*, trans. Yaa-Lengi Meema Ngemi (Chicago: Lawrence Hill Books, 1981).
3 Aimé Césaire, *Discours sur le colonialism* (Paris: Présence africaine, 1955).
4 See the series by Léopold Sédar Senghor, "Liberté," specifically, *Liberté 1: Négritude et humanisme* (Paris: Seuil, 1964) and *Liberté III: Négritude et humanisme* (Paris: Seuil, 1977).
5 Ranajit Guha, *History at the Limit of World History* (New York: Columbia University Press, 2002).
6 Karl Marx, *Capital: A Critique of Political Economy*, vol. 1. Max Weber, *The Protestant Ethic and the Spirit of Capitalism*, trans. Peter Baeher and Gordon C. Wells (New York: Penguin, 2002). Max Weber, *Economy and Society*, trans. Keith Tribe (Cambridge, MA: Harvard University Press, 2019).
7 Chapter 5 of Guha's *History at the Limit of World History*, "Epilogue: The Poverty of Historiography – A Poet's Reproach," analyzes the

critique of historiography and the appeal for a return to the historicality of Tagore. Tagore denounces the obsession with an academic historiography of the state and public affairs, and its inability to question creativity and envision history as a narrative concerned with the everyday world (p. 75).

8 Concerning such Tocquevillian theses and their implementation within an Indian context, see Sudipata Kaviraj, "The Empire of Democracy: Reading Indian Politics through Tocqueville," in Partha Chatterjee and Ira Katznelson (eds.), *Anxieties of Democracy: Tocquevillian Reflections on India and the United States* (Oxford: Oxford University Press, 2012). He notes that, when de Tocqueville uses the notion of "democratic transition," he is in fact referring to two entirely different processes: "the first referring to the transition from totalitarian systems of governance toward democratic systems. And such transitions could also refer to much slower processes of historical transition that are more problematical regarding pre-modern forms of social organization toward a society totally or partially defined by a democratic social imaginary" (p. 21). This distinction forms the basis for a distinction between "democratic institutions" put in place by regimes resulting from democratic transitions in the 1990s, and the impossible democratization of African societies that fed multiple crises that called into question the validity and survival of such democratic institutions, and a total loss of confidence in their future functioning on the continent by a large majority of young Africans. Rather than remaining on the continent, are they not risking their lives at sea and in the desert?

9 Weber, *Economy and Society*.

10 Édouard Delruelle sketches out a very precise genealogy of what he refers to as the "quarrel of humanism" in his essay "Humanisme pratique et antihumanisme théorique," *Espace de liberté*, April 2012, citing in turn: Louis Althusser, "Theoretical anti-humanism was the lone theory to truly authorize a real practical humanism," in *L'Avenir dure longtemps* (Paris: Imec, 1992), p. 209; Martin Heidegger, "This being [Seiende], which we ourselves in each case are and which includes inquiry among the possibilities of its being, we formulate terminologically as Dasein," *Being and Time*, trans. Joan Stambaugh (Albany: State University of New York Press, 1996), p. 7; Roquentin, the protagonist of Jean-Paul Sartre's novel *Nausea*, who confides, "I will not be fool enough to call myself 'anti-humanist.' I *am not* a humanist. That's all there is to it," *Nausea*, trans. Lloyd Alexander (New York: New Directions, 1969), p. 169; and, finally, Michel Foucault, who notes: "In our current times, we can only think within the void of the disappeared man. For this void no longer carves out a lack; it does not prescribe any gap one must fill in, it is nothing more or nothing less than the refolding of space in which it is once again possible to think," "Qu'est-ce que les Lumières?" in *Dits et Écrits*, 2/339 (Paris: Gallimard, 2001), p. 1334.

11 Richard Wright, "Tradition and Industrialization," in *Black Power. Three Books from Exile: Black Power; The Color Curtain; and White Man, Listen!* (New York: Harper Perennial, 2008), p. 722.
12 Henry L. Gates, "A Third World Theory: Enlightenment's Esau," *Critical Inquiry*, 34/S2 (Winter 2008).
13 Gates accuses Wright of not only being fully aware of the epistemic violence of colonization (as Gayatri Spivak has also noted), but suggests that Wright also applauds this violence.
14 Manthia Diawara, *In Search of Africa* (Cambridge, MA: Harvard University Press, 1998).
15 Eric Havelock, *Preface to Plato* (Cambridge, MA: Belknap Press of Harvard University Press, 1963). According to Havelock, the principal characteristics of poetry, which is the language of the "tribal encyclopedia" ("the fountainhead of all social convention": p. 244) as well as "the 'library' of traditions, of habits and customs and professions," are "the rhythmic and visual apparatus (imagistic)" at the poet's disposal (p. 20) and the "style of composition and the effects he may achieve" (ibid.). Counter to these characteristics, Plato opposes the descriptive language of philosophical reason, in order to put his finger on the "gap between truth understood through reason and the illusions produced by poetry" (p. 30). See also Marcel Détienne, *L'Invention de la mythologie* (Paris: Gallimard, 1981).
16 A beautiful lesson that Senegalese politicians, always prepared to create coalitions so as to partake all the more in the pleasure of their power and privileges, should reflect upon.
17 Marc Augé, *Génie du paganisme* (Paris: Gallimard, 2008 [1982]), pp. 19–20. The same misunderstanding can be seen at work in other Islamic formulas when reciprocal comprise or accommodation has been called into question.
18 The initial sphere is the space in which the first communities, their social ties, and the feelings that unite their members have a strong influence over the individual, and determine its public interventions. The second sphere is historically associated with colonial administration; it has become the space of political activities in a postcolonial Africa by way of its army, administration, police, etc. Ekeh establishes a rigid separation between, in his words: "*The primordial public is moral and operates on the same moral imperatives as the private realm*" and "*The civic public in Africa is amoral and lacks the generalized moral imperatives operative in the private realm and in the primordial public.*" "Colonialism and Two Publics in Africa: A Theoretical Statement," *Comparative Studies in Society and History*, 17 (January 1975), p. 92; Ekeh's italics.
19 Catherine Coquery-Vidrovitch, "A propos des racines historiques du pouvoir: 'Chefferie' et 'Tribalisme'," *Pouvoirs*, 25 (1983), p. 51. We find the same historical, anthropological, and theoretical analysis of

a political historicity specific to African societies in the work of the English historian John Lonsdale. See in particular his two articles that have become classics: "Moral Ethnicity and Political Tribalism," Occasional Paper series by International Development Studies (IDS) at Roskilde University; and "The Moral Economy of Mau Mau: Wealth, Poverty, and Civic Virtue in Kikuyu Political Thought," in Bruce Berman and John Lonsdale (eds.), *Unhappy Valley: Conflict in Kenya and Africa*, vol. II (London: James Curry, 1992).

20 Al Schwartz, *Le Tiers-Monde et sa modernité de second main* (Natal, Brazil: Fundação Jose Augusto, 1992).

21 Jean-Pierre Chrétien and Gérard Prunier (eds.), *Les Ethnies ont une histoire* (Paris: Karthala, 1989). See also Jean-Loup Amselle and Elikia Mbokolo (eds.), *Au Coeur de l'ethnie. Ethnies, tribalisme, et l'état en Afrique* (Paris: La Découverte/Maspero, 1985).

22 Aristide R. Zolberg, *Creating Political Order: The Party-States of West Africa* (Chicago: Rand McNally Company, 1966), p. 1.

23 Ibid., p. 3.

24 David Apter, "Ghana is, for all intents and purposes, a one-party democracy," quoted in ibid., p. 5. The democracy of a one-party system refers, according to Zolberg, to the distinction made between variants that attempt to impose total control over society and others where the dominant party restricts its field of intervention, thus ensuring compliance with the law and with certain forms of opposition and associative activities.

25 Ibid., p. 4.

26 *Loi-Cadre* refers to the Universal Suffrage Act, created in 1957 by France, establishing universal suffrage for its overseas colonies and eventually leading the way to open elections and the ending of the colonial period. [Translator's note]

27 Edward Said, *Orientalism* (New York: Pantheon Books, 1978); *Culture and Imperialism* (London: Chatto and Windus, 1993). Terence Ranger, "The Invention of Tradition in Colonial Africa," in Eric Hobsbawm and Terrence Ranger, *The Invention of Tradition* (Cambridge: Cambridge University Press, 1981). Valentin-Yves Mudimbe, *The Invention of Africa. Gnosis, Philosophy, and the Order of Things* (Bloomington: Indiana University Press, 1981).

28 Rajat Kanta Ray, "Asian Capital in the Age of European Expansion: The Rise of the Bazaar, 1800–1914," *Modern Asian Studies*, 29/1 (1995). Ray is particularly interested in showing the resistance of the economy and the world system of the Indian Ocean, whereas Sugata Bose, in *A Hundred Horizons. The Indian Ocean in the Age of Global Empire* (Cambridge, MA: Harvard University Press, 2006), proposes a history that places an accent on a conception and projection of alternative forms of empire, modernity, and universalism to those already set in place in the Atlantic world. Concerning the singularity of the

system of the Indian Ocean, its plural and universalist "conviviality" that is in stark contrast to the violence deployed by the universality presented by the Enlightenment, we can also gladly refer the reader to the superb novels of Amitav Ghosh, *In an Antique Land* (New Delhi: Ravi Dayal, 1992) and the trilogy *Sea of Poppies* (London: John Murray, 2009), *River of Smoke* (London: John Murray, 2011), and *Flood of Fire* (London: John Murray, 2015).
29 Ray, "Asian Capital in the Age of European Expansion," pp. 553–554.
30 James de Vere Allen, "A Proposal for Indian Ocean Studies," in *Historical Relations across the Indian Ocean* (Paris: UNESCO, 1980), pp. 137–151.
31 Fernand Braudel, *The Mediterranean and the Mediterranean World in the Age of Phillip II* (Berkeley: University of California Press, 1995), in particular volume 1.
32 Kirti N. Chaudhuri, *Asia before Europe: Economy and Civilization of the Indian Ocean from the Rise of Islam to 1750* (Cambridge: Cambridge University Press, 1990), p. 36. See, in particular, Chapter 5.
33 Sheldon Pollock, "Empire and Imagination," presentation at the conference "Lessons of Empire" (New York: Social Science Research Council, September 2003).
34 Sheldon Pollock, *The Ends of Man at the End of Premodernity* (Amsterdam: Royal Netherlands Academy of Arts and Sciences, 2005), p. 78.
35 Ibid., p. 84.
36 Akeel Bilgrami, "Occidentalism, The Very Idea: An Essay on Enlightenment and Enchantment," *Critical Inquiry*, 32/3 (Spring 2006), pp. 381–404; Margaret Jacob, *The Radical Enlightenment: Pantheists, Freemasons, and Republicans* (London: George Allen & Unwin, 1981). See also Ian Buruma and Avishai Margalit, *Occidentalism: The West in the Eyes of the Enemies* (New York: Penguin, 2004).
37 Benjamin Schwartz, *China and Other Matters* (Cambridge, MA: Harvard University Press, 1996), p. 15.
38 Ibid., p. 54.
39 Pollock, *The Ends of Man at the End of Premodernity*, pp. 6–7.
40 Ibid., p. 7.
41 Ibid., p. 8.
42 Bernard Dadié, *Un Nègre à Paris* (Paris: Présence africaine, 1959), p. 12.
43 Bernard Dadié, *Légendes et poèmes: Afrique debout; Légendes africaines; Climbié; La ronde des jours* (Paris: Seghers, 1966), p. 217.
44 Bernard Cohn, *Colonialism and Its Forms of Knowledge: The British in India* (Princeton: Princeton University Press, 1996); Gyan Prakash, *Another Reason: Science and the Imagination of Modern India* (Princeton: Princeton University Press, 1999); Nicholas Dirks, *Castes of Mind: Colonialism and the Making of Modern India* (Princeton:

Princeton University Press, 2001); Dipesh Chakrabarty, *Habitations of Modernity: Essays in the Wake of Subaltern Studies* (Chicago: University of Chicago Press, 2002).

45 Edward Said, *Orientalism* and *Culture and Imperialism*; Mudimbe, *The Invention of Africa*; Hobsbawm and Ranger, *The Invention of Tradition*.
46 Sheldon Pollock, *The Language of the Gods in the World of Men: Sanskrit, Culture, and Power in Premodern India* (Berkeley: University of California Press, 2006); "The New Intellectuals in Seventeenth-Century India," *Indian Economic and Social History Review*, 38/1 (2001), pp. 3–31; (ed.), *Literary Cultures in History: Reconstructions from South Asia* (Berkeley: University of California Press, 2003).
47 Pollock, *The Ends of Man at the End of Premodernity*, p. 7.
48 Ibid., pp. 86–87.
49 Mahmood Mamdani, *Citizen and Subject: Contemporary Africa and the Legacy of Late Colonialism* (Princeton: Princeton University Press, 1996). See also Partha Chatterjee, *The Nation and Its Fragments: Colonial and Postcolonial Histories* (Princeton: Princeton University Press, 1993) and Jane Burbank and Frederick Cooper, *Empires in World History. Power and the Politics of Difference* (Princeton: Princeton University Press, 2011).
50 Partha Chatterjee, *Our Modernity* (Dakar/Amsterdam: Codesria/Sephis, 1997), p. 13. See also Ranajit Guha, *Dominance without Hegemony: History and Power in Colonial India* (Cambridge, MA: Harvard University Press, 1997), and Chatterjee, *The Nation and Its Fragments*.
51 Bernard Dadié, *Légende et poèmes*, p. 135.
52 Ibid., p. 137.
53 Ibid., p. 152.
54 Ibid., pp. 170–171, 190.
55 Ibid., p. 170.
56 Ibid., p. 175.
57 Ibid., p. 175
58 Shula Marks, *The Ambiguities of Dependence in South Africa: Class, Nationalism, and the State in Twentieth-Century Natal* (Baltimore: Johns Hopkins University Press, 1986).
59 Aimé Césaire, *Lettre à Maurice Thorez* (Paris: Présence africaine, 1957). For the English-language translation, see "Letter to Maurice Thorez," trans. Chike Jeffers, *Social Text*, 28, 2/103 (Summer 2010), pp. 145–152.
60 Senghor, *Liberté I*, pp. 22–38. See also "Hommage à Teilhard de Chardin," *Liberté V. Le dialogue des cultures* (Paris: Le Seuil, 1993), pp. 13–14.
61 These two expressions that became widely popular were borrowed from the writings of Father Pierre Teilhard de Chardin; see, in particular, *Phenomenon of Man* (New York: Harper Perennial, 2008)

and *Activation of Energy: Enlightening Reflections on the Activation of Energy* (Boston: Mariner Books, 2002).
62 Souleymane Bachir Diagne, "L'Art africain comme philosophie," MS (2007), p. 14. Citation derived from the English-language manuscript of *African Art as Philosophy*, trans. Chike Jeffers (London: Seagull Books, 2013). [Translator's note]
63 Cornel West, *Race Matters* (Boston: Beacon Press, 1993); Paul Gilroy, *Against Race: Imagining Political Culture beyond the Color Line* (Cambridge, MA: Harvard University Press, 2000).
64 C. L. R. James, *Black Jacobins: Toussaint Louverture and the San Domingo Revolution* (London: Vintage, 1989 [1938]); Michel-Rolph Trouillot, *Silencing the Past: Power and the Production of History* (Boston: Beacon Press, 1995); Susan Buck-Morss, "Hegel and Haiti (Critical Essay)," *Critical Inquiry*, 26/4 (2000); J. Michael Dash, "The Theater Revolution/The Revolution as a Theater," *Small Axe*, 9/2 (September 2005).
65 Aimé Césaire, *Toussaint Louverture: La révolution française et le problème coloniale*, repr. (Paris: Présence africaine, 2000).
66 Aimé Césaire, *Notebook of a Return to My Native Land*, trans. Mireille Rosello and Annie Pritchard (Northumberland: BloodAxe Books, 1995).
67 Dash, "The Theater Revolution/The Revolution as Theater," p. 17.
68 Ibid., p. 19.
69 Cheikh Hamadou Kane, *Ambiguous Adventure*, trans. Katherine Woods, Afterword by Wole Soyinka (Brooklyn: Melville House, 2012).
70 Simon Gikandi, *Uganda's Katikiro in England by Ham Musaka* (Manchester: Manchester University Press, 1998); *Maps of Englishness: Writing Identity in the Culture of Culturalism* (New York: Columbia University Press, 1996).
71 Ibid., p. 5
72 Ibid., pp. 23–41.
73 Donald Anthony Low (ed.), *The Mind of Burganda: Documents of the Modern History of an African Kingdom* (London: Heinneman, 1971).
74 David Boillat, *Les Esquisses sénégalaises* (Paris: Karthala, 1984 [1853]).
75 See Mamadou Diouf, "The French Colonial Policy of Assimilation and the Civility of Originaires of the Four Communes (Senegal). A Nineteenth-Century Globalization Project," in B. Meyer and P. Geschiere (eds.), *Globalization and Identity: Dialectics of Flow and Closure* (London: Blackwell), pp. 71–96.
76 He died in 2007.
77 Gikandi, *Uganda's Katikiro*, p. 21.
78 Kane, *Ambiguous Adventure*. See also, in a similar vein, Camara Laye, *L'Enfant noir* (Paris: Plon, 1953) and *Dramouss* (Paris: Plon, 1966).
79 Kane, *Ambiguous Adventure*.
80 Cheikh Hamadou Kane, "As If We Granted to Each Other a

Rendezvous," presentation for the colloquium organized by *Esprit*, published in *Unité africaine* (journal of the Union progressiste sénégalaise), December 1961.
81 According to Simon Gikandi, "If the superiority of Englishness depended on its mastery of the written word, as colonial subjects were often made to believe, then the colonized had, by infiltrating this form, claimed its authority," *Maps of Englishness*, p. 21.
82 Léopold Sédar Senghor, "La voie africaine du socialism. Nouvel essai de définition," in *Négritude et voie africaine du socialism* (Paris: Le Seuil, 1971).
83 See his famous article, "Colonialism in Africa," in P. Duignan and L. H. Gann (eds.), *Colonialism in Africa* (Cambridge: Cambridge University Press, 1969), republished in T. Falola (ed.), *Tradition and Change in Africa: The Essays of J. F. A. Ajayi* (Trenton: Africa World Press, 2000).
84 Joseph Ki-Zerbo, *La Natte des autres. Pour un développement endogène en Afrique* (Dakar: Codeseria, 1992).
85 Jacob Festus Adeniyi Ajayi, "Colonialism: An Episode in African History," in T. Falola (ed.), *Tradition and Change in Africa: The Essays of J. F. A. Ajayi* (Trenton: Africa World Press, 2000), p. 67.
86 Ibid., p. 171–172
87 Dadié, *Légende et poèmes*.
88 Jürgen Habermas, *Le Discours philosophique de la modernité. Douze conferences*, trans. Christian Bouchindhomme and Rainer Rochlitz (Paris: Gallimard, 1988 [1985]). In order to define modernity, he refers back to Hegel. Modernity finds within itself its own guarantees and normativity. Habermas conceives reason as an absolute auto-reference of the spirit.
89 Jean and John Comaroff, *Theory from the South: Or, How Euro-America is Evolving toward Africa* (New York: Routledge, 2016 [2013]).
90 Clapperton Chakanetsa Mavhung, *Transient Workspaces: Technologies of Everyday Innovation in Zimbabwe* (Boston: MIT Press, 2014), and *What Do Science, Technology, and Innovation Mean from Africa?* (Boston: MIT Press). Taking up the counterpoint of Jean and John Comaroff, he introduces his second work in the following manner: "For this book, the only requirement is that all these many pairs of eyes should concentrate on African ways of looking, meaning making, and creating and should take Africans as intellectual agents whose perspectives constitute authoritative knowledge and whose actions constitute strategic deployment of endogenous and inbound things" (p. ix).
91 The precisions placed in square brackets are those of the president-poet.
92 Léopold Sédar Senghor, *Oeuvre poétique* (*Chants d'ombre, Hosties noires, éthiopiques, Nocturnes, Lettres d'hivernage, élégies majeures*) (Paris: Le Seuil, 1990).
93 Birago Diop, *Leurres et Lueurs* (Paris: Présence africaine, 1960) and "Souffles," in Léopold Sédar Senghor, *Anthologie de la nouvelle poésie nègre et malgache* (Paris: PUF, 1948).

Laetitia Africana: Philosophy, Decolonization, and Melancholy

1 Lucious Outlaw, *Race and Philosophy* (New York: Routledge, 1996).
2 Fabien Eboussi Boulaga, *Muntu in Crisis: African Authenticity and Philosophy* (Trenton: Africa World Press, 2014). "Philosophy is included in the definition of being human, considered as a speaking animal capable of reason ... If such is the case, any person can philosophize as soon as one opens her mouth ... To claim philosophy is therefore to reclaim one's due property, to exercise one's humanity and demand that it be recognized" (pp. 5–6).
3 bell hooks, *Teaching Critical Theory* (New York: Routledge, 2010). Specifically, we would be wise to recall the chapter "Black, Female, and Academic" (pp. 95–102).
4 Lewis R. Gordon, *Existentia Africana* (New York: Routledge, 2000). Frantz Fanon, *Black Skin, White Masks* (New York: Grove Press, 2008).
5 Jacques Derrida, *Who's Afraid of Philosophy? Right to Philosophy 1*. Meridian: Crossing Aesthetics (Stanford: Stanford University Press, 2002).
6 hooks, *Teaching Critical Theory*, pp. 24–25. hooks evokes the work of Freire, Fanon, Memmi, Cabral, and Senghor.
7 Ibid., pp. 106–109.
8 Ibid., p. 108: "When we have two favorite writers and thinkers whose work we love and learn from, but who are still wedded to dominator thinking in any form, however relative, it disappoints."
9 Lewis R. Gordon, *Introduction to African Philosophy* (Cambridge: Cambridge University Press, 2008), p. 1.
10 Cf. Walter Mignolo, *La Désobéissance épistémique*, trans. Yasmine Jouhari and Marc Maesschalck (Brussels: Peter Lang, 2015); for more, see his *On Decoloniality: Concepts, Analytics, and Praxis*, with Catherine Walsh (Durham: Duke University Press, 2018).
11 Léopold Sédar Senghor, *Liberté 1. Négritude et humanisme* (Paris: Le Seuil, 1964), "L'esclavage et le colonialisme ont vidé le nègre de ses virtus, de sa substance, pour faire de lui un assimilé, ce négatif du Blanc où le paraître s'est substitué à l'être: un néant" (p. 137). Aimé Césaire, *Tousaint Louverture* (Paris: Présence africaine, 1981), "Telle était la société coloniale: mieux qu'une hiérarchie, une ontologie: au sommet l'homme blanc – l'être au sens plein du terme – en bas, l'homme noir ... la chose, autant dire rien" (p. 33).
12 Jacques Derrida, "The Future of the Profession, or the University without Condition (thanks to the Humanities, what could take place tomorrow)," in Tom Cohen (ed.), *Jacques Derrida and the Humanities: A Critical Reader* (Cambridge: Cambridge University Press, 2001).

13 The act of epistemic decolonization can be deployed around three critical gestures: (1) "to configure other epistemic spaces – non-European – of the production of knowledge" (Grosfoguel); (2) to determine the relations that the development of non-European forms of knowledge can engage in with those productions of knowledge that are essentially Eurocentric; (3) to question the institutionalization of the production of knowledge, through a process of an analysis of the legitimization of this production and the subsequent cultural inequalities or asymmetries that guide it.
14 Achille Mbembe, "A propos des écritures africaines de soi," *Politique africaine*, 77/1 (2000), p. 17.
15 Here will refer to the proceedings from the international conference "Mort de l'enseignement philosophique ou épuisement du paradigme cousinien," organized by Université Paris 8, the Collège international de la philosophie, the ENS of Paris, the ENS of Lyon, the Archives nationales de France, under the patronage of the Inspection générale de la philosophie, on January 13–17 in Cannes and Paris.
16 An expression that directly echoes the work of historian Jean-François Sirinelli. See his *Intellectuels et passions françaises* (Paris: Gallimard, 1999).
17 Jean-Louis Fabiani, *Qu'est qu'un philosophe français?* (Paris: Éditions de l'EHESS, 2010), "The interest of the French case resides specifically within the inseparable character of the legitimization of the process of philosophical legitimization of the Republic along with the republican institutionalization of philosophy as a central discipline of the organization of knowledge. There exists an actual demand for what we could call a republican philosophy: Gambetta in 1871, in this manner, orders the Kantian philosopher Jules Barni to provide him with a *manuel républicain* and calls on other philosophers to aid in the creation of the administrative apparatus of the 3rd Republic" (p. 40).
18 Boulaga, *Muntu in Crisis*, "Conventional wisdom reveals itself in dosages, blends, hybridizations and crossbreeding. It is the synthesis of the poor and the alienated. It is the way 'civilizations' and 'philosophies' go, through felicitous blending of bloods, humors and values while heading toward universal concord" (p. 30).
19 We have chosen to follow the French version of Boulaga's book where the term used is *"métissage,"* and have chosen to translate this as "creolization" as opposed to "crossbreeding," which is the term used in the English version of the book. [Translator's note]
20 We've chosen to stick with the French term employed by the author; the English translation refers not to a *universal rendezvous*, but to a "universal concord." Boulaga, *Muntu in Crisis*, p. 35. [Translator's note]
21 Aimé Césaire, *Notebook of a Return to My Native Land*, trans. Mireille Rosello and Annie Pritchard (Northumberland: BloodAxe Books, 1995), p. 133.

22 Jacques Rancière, in an interview with Bertrand Ogilvie and Julia Christ, evokes the "cannibalism of the dominant culture" – in *Saint Denis à Vincennes*, Les Cahiers philosophiques (Paris: Hermann, 2017). I'd like to thank Stéphane Douaillier for having brought my attention to this interview.
23 Rajeev Barghava, "Pour en finir avec l'injustice épistémique du colonialisme," *Socio*, 1 (2013).
24 Nelson Maldonado-Torres, "Actualité de la décolonisation et tournant decolonial," in Claude Bourguignon Rougier et al. (eds.), *Penser l'envers obscur de la modernité* (Limoges: PULIM, 2014), pp. 48–49.
25 Mbembe, "À propos des écritures africaines de soi," pp. 17–18.
26 Valentin-Yves Mudimbe, *L'Odeur du père* (Paris: Présence africaine, 1982).
27 Valentin-Yves Mudimbe, *Les Corps glorieux des mots et des êtres* (Paris: Présence africaine, 1984).
28 This is the meaning at work in Valentin Mudimbe's literary writing, in particular his novels *L'Écart* and *Entre les eaux* (both published with Présence africaine). *Entre les eaux* has been translated as *Between the Tides*.
29 Such solidarity has no need of an institutional university site in order to legitimize and reconsolidate itself.
30 Dipesh Chakrabarty, *Provincializing Europe* (Princeton: Princeton University Press, 2007), p. 46.
31 Achille Mbembe, "A propos des écritures africaines de soi."
32 Achille Mbembe, *Critique of Black Reason* (Durham: Duke University Press, 2017).
33 Judith Butler and Athena Athanassiou, *Dispossession: The Performative in the Political* (Cambridge: Polity, 2013).
34 We would do well to also refer to the reflections made by bell hooks regarding a culture of love as a new politics of relations, in *All About Love* (New York: HarperCollins, 2000).
35 Annamaria Rivera, *Les Dérives de l'universalisme*, trans. Michael Gasperoni, with Laurent Lévy (Paris: Éditions de la découverte, 2010).
36 Nathalie Etoke, *Melancholia africana* (Paris: Éditions du Cygne, 2010), p. 30.
37 Ibid., "Diasporic consciousness is flexible and open. It integrates pain as a catalyzer of freedom and not as a factor of victimization" (p. 33).
38 Enzo Traverso, *Mélancolie de gauche. La force d'une tradition cachée* (XIXe–XXIe siècle) (Paris: Éditions de la découverte), p. 16.
39 Jean-Marc Ela, *Le Cri de l'homme africaine* (Paris: L'Harmattan, 1993), pp. 70–100.
40 Henri Bergson, "La conscience et la vie," in *L'Énergie spirituelle* (Paris: PUF, 1982), p. 23.

For a Truly Universal Universal

1. Barbara Cassin, *Éloge de la traduction. Compliquer l'universel* (Paris: Fayard, 2017).
2. It seems as if the least separationist of formulations of the demands from the students at SOAS was that it wasn't a question of simply removing the aforementioned philosophers from the curriculum so much as reading them from a critical perspective.
3. We should remember that the term *propre* in French retains the conception both of the "proper" but also of the notion of one's "own," which seems like a vital nuance that merits mentioning in the context both of "thinking for oneself" and of *propre* being "specific and the particular" with regard to the larger conception of the universal and African forms of thought. [Translator's note]
4. For more on the author's reflections on Merleau-Ponty's notion of a "lateral universal," see his article "On the Postcolonial and the Universal?" *Rue Descartes*, 78 (2013). [Translator's note]

Migrant Writers: Builders of a Balanced Globalization of Africa/Europe

1. Jacques Lacarrière, "Le Bernard-l'hermite ou le treizième voyage," in *Pour une littérature voyageuse* (Paris: Complexe, 1999), pp. 105–106.
2. Gilles Deleuze, "Les voyages d'immigrants sont des voyages sacrés." https://oeuvresouvertes.net/spip.php?article3155.
3. Homi Bhabha, *The Location of Culture* (London: Routledge, 1994), pp. 6–7.
4. Speaking about his exile in France, then Syria, the Emir Abdelkader has affirmed that such an exile made him "a dead man" – see "L'Émir Abdelkader à Pau," in *Studia Islamica* (2011), p. 149.
5. Olaudah Equiano, *The Interesting Narrative and Other Writings* (London: Penguin Books, 1995 [1789]), p. 50.
6. Cathy Caruth, *Trauma: Exploration in Memory* (Baltimore: Johns Hopkins University Press, 1995).
7. Helen Cooper, *The House at Sugar Beach: In Search of a Lost Childhood* (New York: Simon & Schuster, 2008).
8. In Benaouda Lebdai (ed.), *Écrivains africains, entretiens* (Beaucouzé: Éditions Ebena, 2015), p. 73.
9. Salman Rushdie, *Joseph Anton* (New York: Random House, 2012).
10. Abdourahman Waberi, in Lebdai, *Écrivains africains*, p. 140.
11. Alain Mabanckou, *Le Monde est mon langage* (Paris: Grasset, 2016).
12. Cooper, *The House at Sugar Beach*.

13 Ibid., p. 192.
14 J. Nozipo Maraire, *Zenzele* (New York: Delta, 1996), p. 18.
15 See Maïssa Bey, *L'Une et l'autre* (La Tour-d'Aigues: Éditions de l'Aube, 2009).
16 Bhabha, *The Location of Culture*, p. 56.
17 Ibid.
18 The citation has been translated following the author's reference to a French translation of the original English edition. The original English lines are slightly different, "I believe in such cartography – to be marked by nature, not just to label ourselves on a map like the names of rich men ... All I desired was to walk upon such an earth that had no maps." Michael Ondaatje, *The English Patient* (New York: Vintage Books, 1992), p. 260. [Translator's note]
19 Boualem Sansal, *Harraga* (Paris: Gallimard, 2005), pp. 219–220.
20 Éric Essono Tsimi, *Migrant Diaries* (Paris: Éditions Acoria, 2014), p. 11.
21 Hakan Günday, *Encore* (Paris: Galaade, 2015).
22 Fatou Diome, *Le Ventre de l'atlantique* (Paris: Éditions Anne Carrière, 2003), p. 217.
23 Amnesty International alerted the global authorities to the tragedy unfolding on the borders mentioned in this work, *Réfugiés, un scandale planétaire* (Paris: Autrement, 2012).
24 Salim Jay, *Tu ne traversera pas le détroit* (Paris: Mille et une nuits, 2000). Youssouf Amine Elalamy, *Les Clandestins* (Paris: Au diable vauvert, 2001). Sadek Aïssat, *Je fais comme fait dans la mer le nageur* (Alger: Bazarkh, 1999).
25 Essono Tsimi, *Migrant Diaries*, p. 11.
26 Fatou Diome, *Celles qui attendent* (Paris: Flammarion, 2010), p. 100.
27 Mahi Binebine, *Cannibales* (Paris: Fayard, 1999).
28 Hicham Tahir, *Jaabouq* (Casablanca: Casa Express Éditions, 2012), p. 24.
29 Aminata Traoré, *L'Afrique humiliée* (Alger: Casbah Éditions, 2008), p. 262.
30 Diomé, *Celles qui attendent*, p. 200
31 Achille Mbembe, *On the Postcolony* (Berkeley: University of California Press, 2001).
32 Ngugi wa Thiong'o, *Moving the Centre* (London: James Curry, 1993).
33 Henri Lopes, interview with Pascale Haubruge: "L'Afrique intérieure d'Henri Lopes. Retour à la case depart," *Le Soir*, February 27, 2002, p. 49.
34 Zoë Wicomb, *You Can't Get Lost in Cape Town* (New York: Feminist Press, 2000).
35 Alain Mabanckou, "Les mots de Proust pour clore les assises du roman," *Le Monde des livres*, June 2, 2011.

36 See Mabanckou's novel *Black Moses*, trans. Helen Stevenson (New York: The New Press, 2017).
37 Derek Wright, "Pre- and Post-modernity in Recent West African Fiction," *Commonwealth*, 21/2 (Spring 1999), p. 5.
38 Dany Laferrière, comments collected by Jean-Luc Douin in the newspaper *Le Monde*, February 3, 2006.
39 Felwin Sarr, *Afrotopia*, trans. Drew S. Burk and Sarah Jones-Boardman (Minneapolis: University of Minnesota Press, 2019).
40 Julia Kristeva, *Strangers to Ourselves*, trans. Leon Roudiez (New York: Columbia University Press, 1994).
41 Salman Rushdie, cited by Chinua Achebe in *Home and Exile* (New York: Anchor Books, 2000).

For What is Africa the Name?

1 Of course, it's not about shouting cultural appropriation every time a cultural aesthetic is borrowed from another culture. The wearing of African *pagnes* [dress] or of sub-Saharan hairstyles by people from outside the continent is not annoying in and of itself. But it can become annoying when such aesthetic choices are not fully assumed and embraced in all circumstances, and are made only incidentally, without any thought truly given to the weight or risk involved in such decisions. It becomes problematic when someone reduces another person's culture to nothing more than spectacle, when the people within those cultures imitated are simply living their lives.
2 Only strategies of commercialization have softened the use of this term through discursive practices, such as when the Moroccans come to do business in sub-Saharan Africa.
3 Toni Morrison, *Beloved* (New York: Vintage, 1997), p. 190.
4 Philippe Chanson, *La Blessure du nom. Une anthropologie d'une séquelle de l'ésclavage aux Antilles-Guyane* (Brussels: Academia-Bruylant, 2008), p. 93.
5 Nathalie Etoke, *Melancholia africana. L'indispensable dépassement de la condition noire* (Paris: Éditions du Cygne, 2010), p. 30.
6 Felwine Sarr, *Afrotopia*, trans. Drew S. Burk and Sarah Jones-Boardman (Minneapolis: University of Minnesota Press, 2019), p. 25.
7 In this case, I'm thinking about the culture I know the best – the *doulas* of Cameroon – even if, today, they are no longer in agreement with some of the ancestral traditions and have changed. Which leads to the question of how other cultural groups retain certain knowledge and relations to their cultural heritage and what within their heritage they seek to retain or find solace in …
8 Open only to sub-Saharans.
9 Etoke, *Melancholia africana*, p. 28.

Epistemological Impasses Concerning the Object Africa

1 Lucian Pye, *Aspects of Political Development* (Boston: Little, Brown, 1966). Edward Shils, *Political Development in the New States* (London: Mouton and Co., 1962). Samuel Huntington and Myron Weiner, *Understanding Political Development: An Analytic Study* (Boston: Little, Brown, 1987). Daniel Lerner, *The Passing of Traditional Society: Modernizing the Middle East* (Glencoe: The Free Press, 1958). David Apter, *The Politics of Modernization* (Chicago: University of Chicago Press, 1965). Gabriel Almond, *Political Development: Essays in Heuristic Theory* (Boston: Little, Brown, 1970). James Coleman, Dankwart Rustow, Gabriel Almond, et al., *The Politics of the Developing Areas* (Princeton: Princeton University Press, 1960).
2 The Rostow Model of economic growth is articulated in five stages: traditional society, pre-take-off conditions, take-off, drive to maturity, and the age of high mass consumption. Each corresponds to a progressively more important level of political development. The final stage coincides with the state of developing democracies to which third world countries aspire, generally situated at the second stage: namely, that of the pre-take-off conditions. Walt Whitman Rostow, *The Stages of Economic Growth* (Cambridge: Cambridge University Press, 1991)
3 The indicators used are: the level of GDP (Gross National Product) per capita, industrialization, urbanization, and education, all of which are higher in democratic countries (the UK, the US, Australia, and Canada) than in countries with an authoritarian tendency (Cuba, Haiti, Paraguay). Seymour Martin Lipset, "Some Social Requisites for Democracy: Economic Development and Political Legitimacy," *American Political Science Review*, 53 (1959).
4 Charles Tilly, *The Formation of National States in Western Europe* (Princeton: Princeton University Press, 1975). *Big Structures, Large Processes, Huge Comparison* (New York: Russel Sage Foundation, 1974). Barrington Moore, *Social Origins of Dictatorship and Democracy* (Boston: Beacon Press, 1966). Perry Anderson, *Lineages of the Absolutist State* (New York: Verso, 2013). Bertrand Badie and Pierre Birnbaum, *Sociologie de l'État* (Paris: Grasset, 1979). Reinhart Bendix, *Kings or People: Power and the Mandate to Rule* (Berkeley: University of California Press, 1978).
5 Samuel Huntington, *Political Order in Changing Societies* (New Haven: Yale University Press, 1968), pp. 7–8.
6 Mussia Kakama, "'Authenticité,' un système lexical dans le discours politique au Zaïre," *Mots*, 6/1 (1983); Comi Toulabour, *Le Togo sous Éyadéma* (Paris: Karhala, 1986).

7 Bernard Badie, *L'État importé. L'occidentalisation de l'ordre politique* (Paris: Fayard, 1992).
8 Raúl Prebisch, *Le Développement économique de l'Amérique latine et ses principaux problèmes* (United Nations, 1950).
9 Fernando Henrique Cardoso and Enzo Faletto, *Dépendance et développement en Amérique latine*, trans. Annie Morvan (Paris: PUF, 1978)
10 André Gunder Franck, *Capitalisme et sous-développement en Amérique latine* (Paris: Maspero, 1968). Samir Amin, *L'Impérialisme et le développement inégal* (Paris: Minuit, 1976); *L'Accumulation à l'échelle mondiale: Critique de la théorie du sous-dévelopment* (Paris: Anthropos, 1971). Immanuel Wallerstein, *Historical Capitalism* (New York: Verso, 2014); *The Capitalist World-Economy* (Cambridge: Cambridge University Press, 1979).
11 Georges Balandier, *Sens et puissance* (Paris: PUF, 1971).
12 Felwine Sarr, *Afrotopia*, trans. Drew S. Burk and Sarah Jones-Boardman (Minneapolis: University of Minnesota Press, 2016), p. 44.
13 Max Weber, *The Protestant Ethic and the "Spirit" of Capitalism and Other Writings*, ed. and trans. Peter Baehr and Gordon C. Wells (London: Penguin Books, 2002). Louis Dumont, *Homo aequalis. Genèse et épanouissement de l'idéologie économique* (Paris: Gallimard, 1977). Karl Polanyi, *The Great Transformation*, 2nd ed. (New York: Beacon Press, 2001 [1944]). Goran Hyden, *Beyond Ujamaa in Tanzania: Underdevelopment and Uncaptured Peasantry* (London: Heinemann Educational Books, 1980). Emmanuel Sevni Ndione, *L'Économie urbaine en Afrique: Le don et le recours* (Paris: Karhala, 1994).
14 Bernard Charles, "Le socialisme africain: mythes et realités," *Revue francaise de science politique*, 15/5 (1965).
15 Julius Nyerere, *Ujaama: Essays on Socialism* (London: Oxford University Press, 1977).
16 Léopold Sédar Senghor, *Liberté II. Nation et voie africaine du socialism* (Paris: Seuil, 1971), and *Liberté IV. Socialisme et planifcation* (Paris: Seuil, 1982).
17 Nim Casswell, "Autopsie de l'Oncad: la politique arachidière au Sénégal, 1966–1980," *Politique africaine*, 14 (1984). Gellar Sheldon, *Senegal: An African Nation between Islam and the West* (Boulder: Westview Press, 1986).
18 Momar-Coumba Diop and Mamadou Diouf, *Le Sénégal sous Abdou Diouf. État et société* (Paris: Karthala, 1990). Momar-Coumba Dioup (ed.), *Sénégal. Trajectoires d'un état* (Paris/Dakar: Karthala, 1992). Momar-Coumba Diop, *Gouverner le Sénégal. Entre ajustement structurel et développement durable* (Paris: Karthala, 2004).
19 Daniel Bourmaud, "Aux sources de l'autoritarisme en Afrique: des ideologies et des hommes," *Revue internationale de politique comparée*, 13/4 (2006).

20 Daniel Bourmaud, *La Politique en Afrique* (Paris: Montchrestien, 1997).
21 Gérard Chalian, *L'Enjeu africain. Géostrategies de puissances* (Bruxelles: Complexe, 1984). Antoine-Denis Ndimina-Mougala, "Les manfiestations de la guerre froide en Afrique centrale (1961–1989)," *Guerres mondiales et conflits contemporains*, 1/233 (2009). Jean Savoye, "Les guerres dissemblables d'Angola et du Mozambique," *Relations internationals et stratégiques*, 23 (1996).
22 William Loehr and John Powelson, *Les Pièges du nouvel ordre économique international*, trans. Bruno Baron-Renault (Paris: Economica, 1984).
23 Jeanne Lopis-Sylla, Charles Becker, and Amadou Mahtar Mbow, *Le Sourcier du future. Un combat pour l'Afrique, un destin pour l'humanité* (Paris: L'Harmattan, 2016), pp. 211–255.
24 Léopold Sédar Senghor, *Liberté 1. Négritude et humanisme* (Paris: Seuil, 1964); *Négritude et civilization de l'universel* (Paris: Seuil, 1977); *La Poésie de l'action. Conversation avec Mohamad Aziza* (Paris: Stock, 1980).
25 Jean-François Bayart, Achille Mbembe, and Comi Toulabour, *Le Politique par le bas en Afrique noir. Contributions à une problèmatique de la démocratie* (Paris: Karthala, 1992), p. 15.
26 Ibid., pp. 13–14.
27 Jean-François Bayart, "L'énonciation du politique," *Revue française de science politique*, 35/3 (1985), p. 342.
28 Jean-François Bayart, "Le politique par le bas. Questions de méthode," *Politique africaine*, 1 (1981), p. 57.
29 Denis Constant Martin, "À la quête des OPNI, comment traiter l'invention du politique?" *Revue française de science politique*, 39/6 (1989).
30 Comi Toulabour, "Jeux de mots, jeux de villains. Lexique de la derision politique au Togo," *Politique africaine*, 3 (1981); "La derision politique en liberté," *Politique africaine*, 43 (1991).
31 Christian Coulon, "La science politique et les mode populaires d'action politique: la descente aux Enfers comme voie de salut," Journée d'étude du groupe "Modes populaires d'action politique," Paris, March 25, 1982, p. 1.
32 Bayart, "L'énonciation du politique," p. 368.
33 Bourmaud, *La Politique en Afrique*, p. 137.
34 Bayart, "L'énonciation du politique," p. 359.
35 Ibid., p. 361.
36 The "Bébête-show" and the "Guignols de l'info" each deploy a functionialist point of view that also serves a cathartic function for the unspoken popular voice. Eric Darras, "Rire du pouvoir et pouvoir du rire. Remarques sur un succès politique, médiatique et mondain: les Guignols de l'info," in CURAPP (Centre universitaire de recherches

adminstrattives et politique de Picardie), *La Politique ailleurs* (Paris: PUF, 1998), pp. 151–174.
37 Peter Geshiere, "Le politique en Afrique: le haut, le bas, et le vertige," *Politique africaine*, 39, (1990), p. 157; Jean-François Médard, "Politics from Above, Politics from Below," paper presented at the NFU conference, State and Locality (Oslo, June 1994). Luc Sindjoun, *L'État ailleurs. Entre noyau dur et case vide* (Paris: Economica, 2002).
38 Vieux Savane and Baye Makébé Sarr, *Y'en a marre. Radioscopie d'une jeunesse insurgée au Sénégal* (Paris: L'Harmattan: 2012). Yoro Ba, Amath Dansokho et al., *M23. Chronique d'une revolution citoyenne* (Dakar: Les Éditiond de la Brousse, 2014). Alpha Amadou Sy, *Le 23 juin au Sénégal (ou la souveraineté reconquise)* (Paris: L'Harmattan, 2012).
39 Jean-François Bayart, *L'État en Afrique. La politique du ventre* (Paris: Fayard, 1989).
40 Fernand Braudel, "La longue durée," in *Écrits sur l'histoire* (Paris: Flammarion, 1985).
41 Jean-François Bayart, "L'historicité de l'État importé," in Jean-François Bayart (ed.), *La Greffe de l'État* (Paris: Karthala, 1996), p. 18.
42 Bayart, *L'État en Afrique*, p. 24.
43 Ibid., p. 272.
44 Ibid., p. 12.
45 Ibid., p. 41.
46 Jean-François Bayart, "L'Afrique dans le monde: une histoire d'extraversion," *Critique international*, 5 (Autumn 1999), p. 105.
47 Bayart, "L'historicité de l'État importé," p. 33.
48 Tidiane Diakite, *L'Afrique malade d'elle-même* (Paris: Karthlala, 1986). Axel Kabou, *Et si l'Afrique refusait le développement* (Paris: L'Harmattan, 1991).
49 Jean-Pascal Daloz and Patrick Chabal, *L'Afrique est partie! Du désordre comme instrument politique* (Paris: Karthala, 1999).
50 Ibid., p. 6.
51 Jean-François Médard admonishes them for reducing modernity to mere contemporaneity, which is aberrant. Since modernity is intimately tied to development. As result of this, one would have a hard time referring to a specific modernity that would be somehow outside a certain progress. Jean-François Médard, "L'État et le politique en Afrique," *Revue française de science politique*, 50/4–5 (2000), p. 853.
52 Daloz and Chabla, *L'Afrique est partie!*, pp. 182–187.
53 Jean-François Bayart, Stephen Ellis, and Béatrice Hibou, *La Criminalisation de l'État en Afrique* (Brussels: Complexe, 1977).
54 Hans Stark, *Les Balkans, le retour de la guerre en Europe* (Paris: Dunod, 1993). Gérard Baudson, *L'Europe des fous ou la destruction de la Yougoslavie* (Paris: Club privé des Communautés européennes, 1993). Claire Boulanger, Bernard Jacquemart, and Philippe Grandon, *L'Enfer yougoslav: les victims de la guerre témoignent* (Paris: Belfond,

1994). Jacques Biollet, *Un genocide en toute liberté: la Bosnie à feu et à sang: essai* (Fribourg: Méandre/Walada, 1993).
55 Béatrice Borghino, *Clientèle européenne pour marabouts d'Arique noire. Du magico-religieux dans une societé moderne* (Paris: L'Harmattan, 1994).
56 Bourmaud, *La Politique en Afrique*, p. 143.
57 Yves Mény and Donatella Della Porta (eds.), *Démocratie et corruption en Europe* (Paris: La Découverte, 1995). Yves Mény, *La Corruption de la République* (Paris: Fayard, 1992).
58 Alain Marie (ed.), *L'Afrique des individues. Itinéraires citadins dans l'Afrique contemporaine (Abidjan, Bamako, Dakar)* (Paris: Karthlala, 1997). Alain Marie and Francois Leimdorfer, *L'Afrique des citadins: societés civiles en chaniter (Abidjan, Dakar)* (Paris: Karthala, 2003).
59 Mohamadou Kane, "Négritude et littérature," paper presented a conference on negritude, Dakar (April 12–18, 1972), p. 62.
60 Aimé Césaire, *Notebook of a Return to My Native Land*, trans. Mireille Rosello and Annie Pritchard (Northumberland: BloodAxe Books, 1995), p. 105.
61 Cheikh Anta Diop, *L'Unité culturelle de l'Afrique noire* (Paris: Présence africaine, 1959), p. 198.
62 Cheikh Anta Diop, *Nations nègres et culture*, vol. 1 (Paris: Présence africaine, 1979), p. 204–287.
63 Ibid., p. 31.
64 Ibid., p. 28.
65 Cheikh Anta Diop, *Alerte sous les tropiques, Articles 1946–1960. Culture et développement en Afrique noire* (Paris: Présence africaine, 1990), p. 48.
66 Ibid., p. 47.
67 Ibid., p, 48.
68 Ibid., p, 48.
69 Ibid., p, 85..
70 Ibid., p, 83.
71 Aimé Césaire, *La Tragédie du Roi Christophe* (Paris: Présence africaine, 1963), p. 59.

Reinventing African Modernity

1 Mohammad Iqbal, *Les Secrets du Soi. Les mystères du Non-Moi*, trans. Djamchid Mortazavi and Eva de Vitray-Meyerovitch (Paris: Albin Michel, 1989), p. 181. The translation of this brief poetic passage by Iqbal is mine. [Translator's note]
2 *Philosophy is the Culture of the Soul.*
3 Fabien Eboussi Boulaga, *Christianisme sans fétiche. Révélation et domination* (Paris: Présence africaine, 1981), p. 162.

4 Cf. Mamoussé Diagne, "Contribution à une critique du principe des paradigmes dominants," in Joseph Ki-Zerbo (ed.), *La Natte des autres* (Dakar: Codesria, 1992), p. 109.
5 Cf. Marcien Towa, *Essai sur la problématique philosophique en Afrique* (Paris: Éditions Clé, 1979).
6 Jacques Rancière, *On the Shores of Politics*, trans. Liz Heron (London: Verso, 2007).
7 Regarding this modernity, Guy Debord, in *The Society of Spectacle*, expressed very well the wrongdoings and misfortunes of the being of the Western man of modernity with regard to his relation to alienation. We are not going to revisit the controversies regarding modernity here except to recall its ideological content and the warnings issued by Charles Saint-Prot in *La Tradition islamique de la réforme*: "If tradition is not to be equated with conservatism, let alone sclerosis, modernity shouldn't be confused with progress," p. 13.
8 Cheikh Anta Diop, *Civilization or Barbarism: An Authentic Anthropology*, trans. Yaa-Lengi Meema Ngemi (Chicago: Lawrence Hill Books, 1991), p. 212.
9 Ibid.
10 Léopold Sédar Senghor, "Negritude is a Humanism of the Twentieth Century," in *Colonial Discourse and Postcolonial Theory: A Reader* (New York: Columbia University Press, 1994).
11 Léopold Sédar Senghor, *Nation et voie africaine du socialisme* (Paris: Le Seuil, 1964), p. 107.
12 Karl Marx, *The Eighteenth Brumaire of Louis Napoleon Bonaparte*, trans. Daniel de Leon (Chicago: Charles H. Kerr & Company, 1907), p. 5. The author is referring to this citation in Léopold Sédar Senghor's article: "Pour une relecture africaine de Marx et d'Engels," in *Discours* (Tunis, 1975).
13 Senghor, "Pour une relecture africaine de Marx et d'Engels," p. 74.
14 Kwame Nkrumah, *Consciencism: Philosophy and Ideology for Decolonization*, rev. ed. (New York: Monthly Review Press, 2009 [1970]), p. 70.
15 Ibid., p. 70.
16 Ibid., p. 84.
17 Marcien Towa, *L'Idée d'une philosophie négro-africain* (Paris: Éditions Clé, 1979)
18 The desire of Africans to construct and build their own path of development goes all the way back to the early days of their independence in the aftermath of colonialism. In particular, one can look at the Bandung conference held in 1955, at which African intelligentsia were able to forgo the grips of both capitalism and communism and of the West in general: it was at Bandung that we saw the emergence of a doctrine of non-alignment.

19 Cf. Stansislas Spero Adotevi, *Négritude et négroloques* (Yaoundé: Union Générale dl'édition, 1972).
20 Cited by Senghor in *Liberté 1. Négritude et humanisme* (Paris: Le Seuil, 1964), pp. 95–96.
21 I refer you to the debates around ethnophilosophy – namely the idea that emphasizes a philosophy comprising African traditions and civilizations – and europhilosophy, which postulates a complementarity, in the work of Senghor, or an overcoming in the resemblance to the other – since it becomes a question of grasping what can be understood as miraculous in Western culture as well – as we find in the work of Marcien Towa.
22 Towa, *Essai sur la problematique philosophique en Afrique*.
23 Gaston Berger, *L'Homme modern et son education* (Paris: PUF, 1962), p. 125.
24 Peter Abrahams, *A Wreath for Udomo* (Nairobi: East African Publishers, 2002), pp. 261–262.
25 Diagne, "Contribution à une critique du principe des paradigmes dominants," p. 109.
26 Cited in ibid., p. 110.
27 Fabien Eboussi Boulaga, *Muntu in Crisis: African Authenticity and Philosophy* (Trenton, NJ: African World Press, 2014), pp. 75–76.
28 Ibid., p. 224.
29 Frantz Fanon, *The Wretched of the Earth*, trans. Richard Philcox (New York: Grove Press, 2005), p. 235.

What Is a Postcolonial Author?

1 Anthony Appiah, "Is the Post- in Postmodernism the Post- in Postcolonial?" *Critical Inquiry*, 17/2 (1991).
2 Claire Ducournau, "Qu'est-ce qu'un classique africain?" *Actes de la recherche en sciences sociales*, 1/206–207 (2015), p. 38.
3 Sylvie Ducas, *La Littérature à quel(s) prix(s)? Histoires des prix littéraires* (Paris: Découverte, 2013), p. 207.
4 Gilsèle Sapiro, "Translation and the Field of Publishing," *Translation Studies*, 1/2 (2008), pp. 154–166. See also Gilsèle Sapiro in *French Global*, ed. C. McDonald and S. Suleiman (New York: Columbia University Press), pp. 315–316.
5 Jim Cohen, "Une bibliothèque postcolonial en pleine expansion," *Mouvements*, 3/51 (2007), pp. 166–170.
6 Graham Huggan, *The Postcolonial Exotic: Marketing the Margins* (London: Routledge, 2001). See also Sarah Brouillette, *Postcolonial Writers and the Global Literary Marketplace* (London: Palgrave McMillan, 2007).

7 Ducas, *La littérature à quel(s) prix(s)? Histoires des prix littéraires*, p. 207.
8 Including, for continental Africa, such writers as Koffi Kwahulé, Tahar Ben Jelloun, Alain Mabanckou, Mimrod, Abourahman Waberi, Wilfrid N. Sondé, and Boualem Sansal, as well as the Malagasy writer Jean-Luc Rahimana.
9 Felwine Sarr, *Afrotopia*, trans. Drew S. Burk and Sarah Jones-Boardman (Minneapolis: University of Minnesota Press, 2019), pp. x–xi.
10 Edward Said, "Traveling Theory," in *The World, the Text and the Critic* (Cambridge, MA: Harvard University Press, 1983), pp. 226–228.
11 Anne Begenat-Neufschäfer and Catherine Mazauric, *La Question de l'auteur en littérature africaines* (Berne: Peter Lang, 2015), pp. 17–23.
12 Roland Barthes, *The Death of the Author in Image-Music-Text*, trans. Stephen Heath (New York: Hill and Wang, 1977), p. 147.
13 Michel Foucault, "What Is an Author?" https://www.open.edu /openlearn/pluginfile.php/624849/mod_resource/content/1/a840_1 _michel_foucault.pdf.
14 Aimé Césaire, *Notebook of a Return to My Native Land*, trans. Mireille Rosello and Annie Pritchard (Northumberland: Bloodaxe Books, 1995), p. 89.
15 George Ngal, *Création et rupture en littérature africaine* (Paris: L'Harmattan, 1995).
16 Souleymane Bachir Diagne, "1968: Crisis in African Letters," *The Romanic Review*, 101/1–2.
17 Concerning the divergences of the postmodern and the postcolonial, see Appiah's foundational essay, "Is the Post- in Postmodernism the Post- in Postcolonial?," pp. 336–357.
18 Examples of such a reflection can be found in works like that of Lilyan Kesteloot, *Les Écrivains noirs de la langue française* (Brussels: University of Brussels, 1963). See also the example given by Mateso of the collection "approaches" in *Présence africaine* (1962–1981), which also makes use of a subheading, "L'homme et l'oeuvre" ["The artist and his work"].
19 We could note that we often speak of the "African novel," but very seldom of "African fiction," unless we talking about fictional television series from the Ivory Coast or Nigeria, or about science fiction.
20 *The Dark Heart of the Night*, trans. Tamsin Black, preface by Terese Svoboda (Lincoln: University of Nebraska Press, 2010).
21 Foucault, "What Is an Author?"
22 Read the work of Anthony Mangeon, *Crimes d'auteurs. De l'influence, du plagiat et de l'assassinat en littérature* (Paris: Hermann, 2016).
23 Jérôme Meizoz, "'Écrire, c'est entrer en scène': la littérature en personne," *COnTEXTES* [Online]. http://contextes.revues.org/6003. See also Jérôme Meizoz, *Postures littéraires. Mises en scène modernes de l'auteur* (Genève: Slatkine, 2007).

24 See Anthony Mangeon (ed.), *Postures postcoloniales* (Paris: Karthala, 2012).
25 We could think, for example, of the case of Marie NDiaye. For a more detailed discussion about the her entrance into literature, see Lydie Moudileno, "Fame, Celebrity, and the Conditions of Visibility of the Postcolonial Writer," *Yale French Studies*, 120 (2011), pp. 62–74.
26 Nathalie Heinrich, *De la visibilité* (Paris: Gallimard, 2012).
27 This "worldliness" of the writer is one of the theses put forth by Edward Said in *The World, the Text, and the Critic*.
28 Ruth Amossy, "La double nature de l'image de l'auteur," *Argumentations et analyse du discours* [online], 3 (2009). http://aad.revues.org/662.

How Can One Be *African/e*?

1 I have chosen to retain the emphasis on "*African/e*" in the first instance in the translation of this essay, given that the author is in part reflecting on the feminine notion of "*africain.e*" – "Comment peut-on être africain.e?" The questions of identity and feminism merit retaining something of the emphasis in English so as to remind the reader of the author's exact wording in French. However, when it comes to the term "*noir.e*," I have translated this as "Black woman" in some instances and, in others, simply "Black." The author is referring to a similar attempt at neutralizing the masculine or including the feminine in the common reference to identity terms that are masculine words in the French language. [Translator's note]
2 See Felwine Sarr, *Afrotopia*, trans. Drew S. Burk and Sarah Jones-Boardman (Minneapolis: University of Minnesota Press, 2019).
3 Steve Biko, *I Write What I Like: A Selection of His Writings*, ed. Aelred Stubbs (London: Heinemann, 1987), p. 92.
4 Hannah Arendt, *The Life of the Mind* (New York: Harvest House), pp. 19–20.
5 See Audre Lorde, *Sister Outsider* (London: Penguin, 2019 [1984]): "As Paolo Freire shows so well in *The Pedagogy of The Oppressed*, the true focus of revolutionary change is never the oppressive situations which we seek to escape, but that piece of the oppressor that is planted deep within each of us, and which knows only the oppressor's tactics, the oppressor's relationship," p. 123
6 Jean-Paul Sartre, *Notebooks for an Ethics*, trans. David Pellauer (Chicago: University of Chicago Press, 1992), p. 327. [Since the reader may benefit from the entire paragraph from which the author of this essay draws her reflections, Pellauer's translation is provided here: "If we pretend that man is not free, the very idea of oppression loses all meaning. In the first place, the oppressor not being free is assimilable to natural forces whose efficacy against man is borrowed from freedom

itself. Next, the oppressed, not being free, can only change states. A stone does not oppress, one does not oppress a stone. Oppression can have just one signification: although it may have the same result as natural forces do, that is, to kill or mutilate, or, in a general way, to crush, it has a completely different meaning and a completely different goal: it strikes freedom at its heart. It impedes freedom, but it must be so if it is to be the project of doing so, that is, consciousness of the other's freedom as not yet suppressed. Therefore fundamentally it is freedom." Translator's note]

7 Concerning this point, see again Lorde, *Sister Outsider*, p. 116: "Somewhere, on the edge of consciousness, there is what I call a mythical norm which each one of us within our heart knows 'that is not me.' In America, the norm is usually defined as white, thin, male, young, heterosexual, Christian, and financially secure. It is within this mythical norm that the trappings of power reside within this society."

8 Lorde, *Sister Outsider*, p. 146

9 Stuart Hall, "The After-life of Frantz Fanon: Why Fanon? Why Now? Why Black Skin, White Masks?" in Alain Read (ed.), *The Fact of Blackness: Frantz Fanon and Visual Representation*, Institute of Contemporary Arts (Ann Arbor: University of Michigan, 1996), p. 17.

10 Lorde, "Poetry Is Not a Luxury," in *Sister Outsider*, p. 36

11 Michel Foucault, *Discipline and Punish: The Birth of the Prison*, trans, Alan Sheridan (London: Vintage Books, 1995), p. 30.

12 Lorde, *Sister Outsider*, p. 50: "Black Women have been taught to view each other as always suspect, heartless competitors of the scarce male, the all-important prize that could legitimize our existence." See also p. 49: "For so long, we have been encouraged to view each other with suspicion, as eternal competitors, or as the visible face of our own self-rejection."

13 Malcolm X, Speech at Ford Auditorium (1965), "Black Past." https://www.blackpast.org/african-american-history/speeches-african-american-history/1965-malcolm-x-speech-ford-auditorium/.

14 Lorde, *Sister Outsider*, p. 102.

15 Jean-Paul Sartre, *Notebooks for an Ethics*, trans. David Pellauer (Chicago: University of Chicago Press, 1992), pp. 328–329: "Let us be clear that oppression is not some ideal. It is always some direct or indirect action that acts on the *body*, it is a constraint by means of the body. Oppression usually results in poverty, unemployment, a system of ownership, forced labour, etc. But there is no situation so miserable where the oppressed are held down that cannot also be conceived as having been chosen by a society of free men. ... Oppression is an internal metamorphosis of my freedom, which is acted upon through the freedom of the other."

16 This is the interpretation of Foucault that we find in Judith Butler's work *The Psychic Life of Power* (Stanford: Stanford University Press, 1997).

17 Sartre, *Notebooks for an Ethics*, p. 332.
18 Lorde, *Sister Outsider*, pp. 114–115.
19 Biko, *I Write What I Like*, p. 29: "One writer makes the point that in an effort to destroy completely the structure that had been built up in the African Society and to impose their imperialism with an unnerving totality the colonialists were not satisfied merely with holding a people in their grip and emptying the Native's brain of all form and content, they turned to the past of the oppressed people and distorted, disfigured and destroyed it. No longer was reference made to African culture, it became barbarism. Africa was the 'dark continent.' Religious practices and customs were referred to as superstition. The history of African Society was reduced to tribal battles and internecine wars. There was no conscious migration by the people from one place of abode to another. No, it was always flight from one tyrant who wanted to defeat the tribe not for any positive reason but merely to wipe them off of the face of the Earth."
20 Ibid., p. 28.
21 Malcolm X, *Le Pouvoir noir*, trans. Guillaume Carle (Paris: La Découverte, 2008).
22 Complex of the seeker that we find developed and expressed in these terms in the work of Fanon, or, in Malcolm X's work, according to the formula of the "perpetual beggar."
23 The distinction made here is inspired by that which Malcolm X made between the "Black Revolution" and the "Negro Revolution." (Cf. *Le Pouvoir noir*, 39.)
24 Achille Mbembe, *Critique of Black Reason* (Durham: Duke University Press, 2017), p. 182.
25 Étienne Balibar, *Des universels. Essais et conférences* (Paris: Galilée, 2016), p. 24.
26 Ibid., p. 42.
27 Article 14 of the imperial constitution of Haiti, 1805.
28 See the work of Marcus Rediker, *The Slave Ship: A Human History* (London: Penguin Books, 2008).
29 Malcolm X, "Message to Grassroots" (1963). https://www.blackpast.org/african-american-history/speeches-african-american-history/1963-malcolm-x-message-grassroots/. See also https://www.blackpast.org/african-american-history/x-malcolm-1925-1965/.
30 Ibid.
31 See Malcolm X, "The Ballot or the Bullet," April 3, 1964: "We need to expand the civil rights struggle to a higher level – to the level of human rights." http://www.edchange.org/multicultural/speeches/malcolm_x_ballot.html.
32 Ibid.
33 The book in question was Stokely Carmichael's *Black Power*. For a more recent print version, see, for instance, Stokely Carmichael, *Stokely*

Speaks, from Black Power to Pan-Africanism (New York: Lawrence Hill Books, 2007). [Translator's note]
34 "Being black is not a matter of pigmentation – being black is a reflection of a mental attitude. ... Any man who calls a white man 'Baas' [master, boss, in Afrikaans], any man that serves in the police force or in Security Branch is *ipso facto*, a non-White." *I Write What I Like*, p. 48.
35 Ibid. p. 66.
36 Lorde, *Sister Outsider*, pp. 146–150
37 Ibid., p. 51.
38 Ibid., p. 61: "Why isn't that male rage turned upon those forces which limit his fulfillment, namely capitalism?"
39 Malcolm X, "Message to the Grassroots": "The only kind of revolution that is nonviolent is the Negro revolution. The only revolution based on loving your enemy is the Negro revolution."
40 Lorde, *Sister Outsider*.
41 See Manning Marable, *Malcolm X: A Life of Reinvention* (London: Penguin Books, 2011).
42 Malcolm X, *Le Pouvoir noir*, p. 199. The author is referencing a French translation of various reflections and letters written by Malcolm X, regarding his 1964 pilgrimage to Mecca. The reference refers to a letter he sent back to colleagues regarding his surprise at partaking in his pilgrimage with people of all nationalities and ethnicities, and in particular in this instance, with people whose "skin was the whitest of white and whose eyes were the bluest of blue" and who "didn't regard themselves as white." For more on this letter, see the *New York Times* archive: https://www.nytimes.com/1964/05/08/archives/malcolm-x-pleased-by-whites-attitude-on-trip-to-mecca.html. [Translator's note]
43 Lorde, *Sister Outsider*, p. 62.

Rediscovering Meaning

1 Seeking to rediscover meaning is not merely a pure intellectual game or undertaking, but primarily the consequence of a profound doubt, alarmed as we are by the various problems in Africa, by the drifting of the continent that moves from one deadend to the next, blind as to what constitutes its identity, its place in the world and its future.
2 For more on this subject, see *Le Lexis, le dictionnaire érudit de la langue française* (Paris: Larousse, 2009) pp. 1496, 1507, 806.
3 Claude Lévi-Strauss, *Tristes tropiques*, trans. John Weightman, Doreen Weigthman, intr. Patrick Wilcken (New York: Penguin Classics, 2012).
4 Pierre Maxime Schuhl, *Essai sur la formation de la pensée grecque* (Paris: Librairie Félix Alcan, 1934).

5 "The bookish, formalist, and magical character of the knowledge of a pseudo-intellectual is not accidental, it is structural, essential to an unproductive lifestyle, and his way of inserting himself into the world. The African intellectual has exhausted and rendered his intellectualness sterile and has faltered in establishing his legitimacy and his raison d'être within the mimetic enterprise of granting himself a history, a culture, a form of national thought, an ideology of national construction ... The pseudo-intellectual's project is not the search for truth; nor does he search for a means for resolving some theory and reasoned action regarding various problems that life imposes onto him along with his relations to others. The intellectual wants to become integrated within administrative networks, enter into the circuits where the rare resources are stored and redistributed, along with honors and pleasantries." Cf. *L'Intellectuel exotique*: http://www.politique-africaine.com/numeros/pdf/051026.pdf.
6 Paul Ricoeur, *Memory, History, and Forgetting*, trans. Kathleen Blamey and David Pellauer (Chicago: University of Chicago Press, 2006), p. 91.
7 Valentin Yves-Mudimbe, *The Invention of Africa: Gnosis, Philosophy, and the Order of Knowledge* (Bloomington: Indiana University Press, 1988).
8 Concerning this reflection, I refer to my analyses in "Le bonheur entre politique and poétique: ou comment apprendre à penser avec Pierre Akendengue et Hugues de Courson," in Bruno Cany and Jacques Poulain (eds.), *L'Art comme figure du bonheur. Traversées transculturelles* (Paris: Hermann, 2016), pp. 363–377.
9 Édouard Glissant, *Introduction to a Poetics of Diversity*, trans. Celia Britton (Liverpool: Liverpool University Press, 2020), p. 8
10 "L'amour est un pari, extravagant, sur la liberté. Non pas le mienne, celle de l'autre." Octavio Paz, *La Flamme double* (Paris: Gallimard, 1994), p. 58. We have chosen to refer to a slightly different translation in the English translation, *The Double Flame: Love and Eroticism*, trans. Helen Lane (Mariner Books, 1998), p. 151: "The eagerness of all those in love and the subject of our great poets and novelists has always been the same: the recognition of the beloved. Recognition in the sense of acknowledging, as the dictionary states, the subordinate position in which one finds oneself. The paradox lies in the fact that recognition is voluntary, freely given ... It is a wager no one is certain of winning because its outcome is dependent on the freedom of the Other." And Paz concludes the same book with the following (p. 275): "We are the theater of the embrace of opposites and their dissolution, resolved in a single note that is not affirmation or negation but acceptance. What does a couple see in the space of an instant, a blink of an eye? The equation of appearance and disappearance, the truth of the body and nonbody, the vision of presence that dissolves into splendor: pure vitality, a heartbeat of time." [Translator's note]

11 Liang Shuming, *Les Cultures d'Orient et d'Occident et leur philosophies* (Paris: PUF, 2000), p. 7. Moreover, he notes the following (p. 13): "Eastern culture and its philosophy appear unchanging since Antiquity. They have remained the same throughout centuries. This has not been the case at all in regards to Western culture: its currents of thought have not ceased evolving and its modes of expression have become renewed throughout the ages." [Translator's note]

12 Jean-François Malherbe, "De la séduction à la spiritualité," *La Chair et le Souffle*, 1 (2006), p. 22.

Esteem for Self: Creating One's Own Sense/Carving Out One's Own Path

1 The original French title, *S'Estimer, faire sens*, contains several connotations. The term "faire sens" merits a brief explanation to the English-language reader. *Sens* can imply in French both *meaning* and *sense*. But it can also imply the notion of *direction* or *path*. While I have chosen to translate it by "creating one's own sense, carving out one's own path," such a translation is only one way to understand the notion that the author will develop and reflect upon in a number of ways throughout her essay: "to make sense, to carve out one's own path, to re-establish a relation to one's senses," I would suggest, are all contained in the French phrase here, "faire sens." [Translator's note]

Dictionary for Lovers of the African Continent: Two Entries

1 Ngugi wa Thiong'o, *Secure the Base: Making Africa Visible in the Globe* (London: Seagull Books, 2016).
2 Eza Boto, *Cruel City* (Bloomington: University of Indiana Press, 2013), p. 12.
3 Ibid., pp. 122–123
4 Ibid., p. 15.
5 For another good example of such a situation, read the first-rate novel by Ferdinand Oyono, *Houseboy*, trans. John Reed (Long Grove, IL: Waveland Press, 2012).

Emancipatory Utopias

1 "White" in this instance is a color denoting social status, access to social, cultural, and economic privileges produced by the history of racial capitalism and colonial and postcolonial state politics.

2 Georg Wilhelm Friedrich Hegel, trans. J. Sibree, *Philosophy in History* (New York: Colonial Press, 2001), p. 109; emphasis in original. [The final sentence in square brackets is included in the French translation of Hegel's book, but is not included in the Sibree translation. Translator's note]
3 Cf. Karl Marx, *Capital*, Vol. 1, Chapter 31, *Genesis of the Industrial Capitalist*. https://www.marxists.org/archive/marx/works/1867-c1/ch31.htm. The literature concerning the connection between trade, slavery, and the rise of capitalism is abundant. I cite a classic example here: Eric William, *Capitalism and Slavery*, 3rd ed., with an intro. by Collin A. Palmer and foreword by William A. Darity (Chapel Hill: University of North Carolina Press, 2021).
4 For the notion of nature as source of endless wealth and endless need, see Jason Moore, "Endless Accumulation, Endless (Unpaid) Work?" April 25, 2015: http://theoccupiedtimes.org.
5 Speech given by Victor Hugo during a banquet held in 1879 commemorating the abolition of slavery. The French citation can be found at: https://www.nedormirajamais.org/hugo. [Translator's note]
6 Édouard Glissant, *A Poetics of Diversity*, trans. Celia Britton (Liverpool: Liverpool University Press), p. 25.
7 Ibid.
8 Ibrahim Thiaw, "L'Afrique malade de ses resources naturelles?" *Jeune Afrique*, June 15, 2015. Thiaw is sub-secretary of the United Nations and adjunct executive director of the United Nations Environment Program (UNEP).
9 Quote taken from https://www.lesinrocks.com/musique/lafro-futurisme-tendance-retro-branchee-ou-art-engage-111643-23-03-2014/. See also Lauri Ramey's introduction to Anthony Joseph's book *The African Origins of UFOS* (Cambridge: Salt Publishing, 2006). [Translator's note]
10 Mawena Yehouessi, "Afro-futurism: le chevauchement des temps": http://blackstothefuture.com/afrofuturism-le-chevauchement-des-temps.
11 Ibid.
12 Aimé Césaire, "Letter to Maurice Thorez," trans. Chike Jeffers, in *Social Text* (Durham: Duke University Press, 2010), p. 150. See also the French version from 1956: https://www.lmsi.net/Lettre-a-Maurice-Thorez.
13 Reinhart Koselleck, *Transformations of Experience in the Practice of Conceptual History: Timing History, Spacing Concepts*, trans. Todd Samuel Presner et al. (Stanford: Stanford University Press, 2002), p. 77.
14 Enzo Traverso, *Mélancolie de gauche. La force d'une tradition cachée (XIX–XXI siècle)* (Paris: La Découverte, 2016).

Martiality and Death in Sexual Relations in Cameroon

1 A remix of the hit rap song by Minks ("Le gars-là est laid" ["That guy's ugly"]).
2 In his research on women and political power in Cameroon, Fabien Eboussi Boulaga does a good job of examining what he calls a "hegemonic inversion" in favor of women, which is not socially debatable. I share with him the idea that "most women do not situate themselves as victims," but I nevertheless hold to my thesis: to describe and analyze, outside this reality, the ongoing operativity and its logic of disqualification that is just as violent.

Demographic Challenges and Technological Mutations

1 The demographic evolution under way across Africa has been carefully monitored by the Pentagon because of the tensions concerning the exhaustion of the continent's natural resources. According to some authors, the control of the population of African countries rich in natural resources is one of the reasons that led to the creation of Africom, one of its missions being to bar China's access to these countries' natural resources (Engdahl, 2009: 78–79).
2 From the point of view of statistical measurement, the concept of "employment" denotes any economic activity of at least one hour of exerted activity during any given time period referenced. Such an elastic definition allows for (i) encompassing various employment situations under the same concept no matter what their duration or frequency, (ii) granting priority to employment over unemployment, which is defined as the absence of employment (zero hours worked during a period referenced), and (iii) measuring the volume of work that enters into production as conformity with the national system of compatibility of the United Nations. The concept of employment, in its statistical meaning, therefore does not make a distinction between quality employment ("decent" work) and employment classified as "vulnerable" or "precarious," "atypical," etc. As we will see here, it is essential to integrate this latter qualification when we are talking about employment in developing countries. (See Sylla, 2013).
3 The statistics concerning the GDP per inhabitant in India and China comes from development indicators of the World Bank. www.data-bank.worldbank.org.

4 It is probable that the women's apparent weak rate of activity in India is the result of the fact that they are often involved in employment relations that are "invisible," that is, employment that generally escapes statistical measurement.
5 The figure is contested by certain demographers based on the fact that China began its demographic transition before the implementation of its one-child policy and that the country's economic development also contributed to a lower fertility rate – two elements that weren't taken into consideration in the projections that led to the figure of 400 million (Whyte et al., 2015).
6 Randall Collins predicts the exhaustion of capitalist logic in the middle of the twenty-first century due to the impasse that capitalism will face in its inability to resolve technologically induced generalized unemployment. Concerning the socioeconomic problems associated with technological unemployment is the increase in inequality, the destruction of the economic foundations of the middle class, and the difficulty of finding outlets for the products placed on the market by companies. See Ford, 2015.
7 André Gorz, *Ecologica*, trans. Chris Turner (London: Seagull Books, 2010), p. 132.

Healing Commonality

1 This is the place to thank the organizers of these workshops, in particular Felwine Sarr and Achille Mbembe, who wanted to bring all of us together for these three days of reflection.
2 In a symptomatic manner, throughout these three days of common tension, the arc that was sketched out collided with two strong symbolic systems. On the one hand, that of a discourse concerning a world, which we are told remains difficult to construct but which we will never be in a better position to begin creating today, and that it's up to us (Africans) to stop moaning about it, and roll up our sleeves and learn to draw forth our happiness from it. For a quick overview of this position, I direct the reader to an article that took the time to gather together everything that seems to speak in this direction: "Le monde va-t-il si mal?" (http//: www.rtflash.fr/monde-va-t-il-si-mal/article). The reader of the commentaries collected there will not be disappointed. On the other hand, there is the symbolic system of a man whose breath was taken from him seven times by six white police officers who decided to end the life of an African American, one among many on a long list that Marcus Lamont Hill recounts in the sad tale *Nobody: Casualties of America's War on the Vulnerable, from Ferguson to Flint and Beyond* (New York: Atria Books, 2016).

3 Jacques Derrida, *Rogues: Two Essays on Reason*, trans. Pascale Brault and Michael Naas (Stanford: Stanford University Press), pp. 104–105.
4 The problems concerning conversion that are evoked here also tie together with another issue raised by Paulin Houtoundji around the international division of scientific work that relegates African personnel and spaces into Flow Zones of products, raw informative materials to be refined elsewhere, and also of linguistic reserve and communication for certain languages that appear endangered. See Paulin J. Houtoundji (ed.), *Les Savoirs endogènes: pistes pour une recherche* (Dakar: Codesria, 1994).
5 Aimé Césaire, *Return to My Native Land*, trans. Mireille Rosello and Annie Pritchard (Northumberland: BloodAxe Books, 1995), p. 75.
6 The possibility of breaking with the feeling of inhabiting the earth while being confined to the simple condition of a conformist is without a doubt what Felwine Sarr's *Afrotopia* (Paris: Philippe Rey, 2016) was able to communicate to an enthusiastic public who welcomed his critique of the tyranny in playing catch-up with Western models of development. For the English translation, see *Afrotopia* (Minneapolis: Univocal, 2020).
7 See Giorgio Agamben's *What Is an Apparatus? And Other Essays*, trans. David Kishik and Stefan Pedatella (Stanford: Stanford University Press, 2009).
8 "The militant therefore is the one who works. The questions which the organization asks the militant bear the mark of this vision of things: 'Where have you worked? With whom? What have you accomplished?' The group requires each individual to have performed an irreversible act ... A new militant could be trusted only when he could no longer return to the colonial system." Frantz Fanon, *The Wretched of the Earth*, trans. Richard Philcox, with commentary by Homi K. Bhabha (New York: Grove Press, 2004), p. 44.
9 Throughout the course of these workshops, and in particular during the debates held at the University of Gaston Berger, this question provoked several reactions indicating that the intellectual class had not yet beaten itself up enough. In reality, no one had truly asked it to do so (again!). What was pointed out resided elsewhere, and we'll return to this later on.
10 Sophia Mappa (ed.), *Les Métamorphoses du politique au Nord et au Sud* (Paris: Karthala, 2004).
11 Fanon, *The Wretched of the Earth*.
12 One of the campaign's themes remains from the old man *weddi giss bokk ca* (in Wolof): the evidence cannot be denied.
13 It's not incidental that the infamous 4 x 4 automobiles, fawned over for their ostentatious panoply of signs of opulence and comfort, are referred to by the meaningful phrase "Looking down on one's enemy." Moreover, the art of *sabotage* (making fun of someone in a direct manner or by way

of an interposed object) often refers to the state of *underdevelopment* (at the material level) of one's territory, or even one's country.

14 Momar-Coumba Diop, Mamadou Diouf, and Aminata Diaw, "Le baobab a été déraciné. L'alternance au Sénégal," *Politique africaine*, 2/78 (2000), pp. 157–179.

15 See the note in *Le Monde*: http://www.lemonde.fr/documents-wikileaks/article/2010/12/09/wikileaks-corruption-et-divisions-a-dakar_1451532_1446239.html.

16 For more, see the daily African newspaper *Jeune Afrique*, which devoted an entire series of articles on the sons of African presidents, from which we borrow this expression.

17 In article no. 2, the decree specified that Karim Wade and his two co-detainees, with this pardon, would benefit only from the execution of the remainder of their prison sentences.

18 See Aliou Kane Ndiaye, "Panama Papers – Sénégal – Pape Mamadou Pouye: prête-nom ou victim collatérale? Ce proche de Karim Wade est cité parmi des clients de Mossack Fonseca, le cabinet dont les listings alimentent le dernier scandale des paradis fiscaux," *Le Point Afrique*, April 8, 2016. http://afrique.lepoint.fr/actualites/panama-papers-senegal-pape-mamadou-pouye-prete-nom-ou-victime-collaterale-08-04-2016-2030918_2365.php.

19 The mantra reiterated over and over again by the youth movement Y'en Marre, which we will speak about again a bit later on.

20 See the chapter by Animata Diaw, "La démocratie des letters," in Momar-Coumba Diop (ed.), *Sénégal. Trajectoires d'un état* (Dakar: Codesria, 1992), pp. 299–329.

21 Mody Niang is the author of this contribution, which one can find at http://www.seneweb.com/news/Contribution/monsieur-le-pres-ident-de-la-republique-o_n_185274.html.

22 The two youths from Colobane were arrested in the aftermath of a policeman's death during violent protests which followed the announcement of the constitutionality of the third candidature of Abdoulaye Wade.

23 Séverine Kodjo-Grandvaux discusses several of the more powerful lines from this report in *Philosophie africaine* (Paris: Présence africaine, 2014), What she brings to light and what is of import for us here is indeed this question concerning the healing of social ties as the vital matter which, in traditional African societies, serves as the guiding light of justice – an idea, moreover, that is still maintained today.

24 Here we can reference the work of Abdou Latif Coulibay, *Wade, un opposant au pouvoir: L'alternance piégée?* (Dakar: Éditions Sentinelle, 2003).

25 This code from 1992 was one of the counterparts for a return to normalcy and calm after violent post-electoral riots which took place in Senegal in 1988–9.

26 It was above all after his second presidential mandate that political debate in Senegal, under Wade, took a turn whereby physical confrontations seemed to become the preferred way of handling conflicts. Without a doubt, the most significant image of this is one where a politician is armed with a pistol in each hand firing on a band of thugs who sought to overthrow the city hall. These events date back to December 2011.

27 During his twelve years in power, Abdoulaye will have garnered a fair number of nicknames, but one in particular, which he received at the very beginning, still serves to indicate a certain reality of the rules of the political game: "the only constant." Abdoulaye Wade pushes the Senegalese presidential model to its climax, about which the historian and former leftist activist, Abdoulaye Ly, provides us with a critical study in *D'où sort l'état presidentieliste du Sénégal?* (Saint-Louis du Sénégal: Xamal, 1997).

28 Beginning in the 1990s, studies concerning the state of Africa began to highlight the logics, causes, and consequences of its informalization against a backdrop of criminalization. See Jean-François Bayart, Stephen Ellis, and Béatrice Hibou, *La Criminalization de l'État en Afrique* (Paris: Complexe, 1997).

29 This term designates a sub-branch of the Senegalese Mouride brotherhood. The *baay-fall* distinguish themselves by being a sub-group dedicated to the physical tasks of brotherhood and in the service of maintaining order.

30 Concerning the history of the PDS, we could reference the work done by Marcel Mendy, in particular *Wade et le Sopi: le longue marche* (Versailles: Les classiques africaines, 2001 [1995]).

31 The journal *Géopolitique africaine*, 31 (2008), featured an article concerning this return of non-alignment, written by Guy Feuer: "Visages nouveaux du non-alignement," pp. 165–181.

32 There are a great number of texts that demonstrate the impasse of various democratic liberalizations underway on the continent since the 1990s, in the framework of a reflection whose most common foundation was the idea that a postcolonial nation-state constituted a factor of insecurity in Africa, to paraphrase the title of work by Mwayila Tshieyembe (Paris: Présence africaine, 1990).

33 In Senegal, a traditionally democratic country, a minister of the Republic can muster such an incredible response to the political class as the following: "As far as listening in on telephone calls, I can neither confirm nor deny it, but what I'm certain of is that we try to watch over and make sure that the personal data of all our citizens is protected." Between bluff, confirmation, and a hardly veiled threat, this seems to be where we have arrived. Cited in *Les Échos*: http://www.seneweb.com/news/Politique/aida-mbodj-et-les-ecoutes-telephoniques_n_204476.html.

34 AFD, Macroéconomie & Développement, "La croissance de l'Afrique subsaharienne: diversité des trajectoires et des processus de transformation structurelle," May 2015. Report available online.
35 Pierre Péan wrote *Carnage. Les guerres secretes des grandes puissances en Afrique* (Paris: Fayard, 2010). This evocative title serves as a rather humorous reminder in the literature of the relativization and ambiguous denigration of the militant engagements concerning France Afrique, namely that even in its most ambiguous reasoning, it does nothing but confirm what Lamine Senghor, in 1927, already referred to as "the violation of a country."
36 It's also in this sense that we maintain that Western administrations have become great Islamic figures in Senegalese society. House diplomacy allows them to get a leg into formal spaces and to insert themselves into others they deem important for their agendas. Such practices are also what make it so that the informalization of politics becomes a deep resource for international figures who take every occasion to take advantage of it. Concerning the question of the informalization of politics in Africa, it could be useful to read Patrick Chabal and Jean-Pascal Daloz, *L'Afrique est partie. Du désordre comme instrument politique* (Paris: Economica, 1999).
37 Already by the middle of the 1970s, Jean Ziegler described the contours of this, which are still as pertinent today, in his book *Une Suisse au-dessus de tout soupçon* (Paris: Seuil, 1976). In *Les Seigneurs du crime. Les nouvelles mafias contre la démocratie* (Paris: Seuil, 2007 [1998]), he also demonstrates how, in the aftermath of the Eastern Bloc, we saw the rise of an incredible number of mafias who attempted to assault the principles of sovereignty and democracy everywhere, buying and twisting the arms of a large number of decision-makers throughout the world, subtly crossing the boundaries of national sovereignties. A variety of situations described on the continent in relation to this principle of globality clarify the connections between local and international actors involved in organized crime. From this perspective, Luc Sindjoun has shown in his work *Sociologie des relations internationales africaines* (Paris: Karthala, 2002) how secondary actors dispose of fiefdoms within the interiority of their given territorial sovereignties that have means at their disposal much greater than that of the nation-states that incarnate this sovereignty and which they have defeated. Of course, against a backdrop of these ruptures in sovereignty and territoriality, the exploitation of the ground and underground in the frameworks of international contracts is an important given. The examples provided by Laurent-Désiré Kabila or even Charles Taylor or other rebel groups (p. 70) are evoked throughout Sindjoun's work. But other forms of international connections exist around organized crime described by the field work of Stephen Ellis in his posthumous

book *This Present Darkness: A History of Nigerian Organized Crime* (London: Hurst and Company, 2016). In this inquiry, the connections of Nigerian drug barons are described as leading all the way into parts of Asia and Latin America.

38 Contemporary African political leadership functions in many ways like the kings in waiting described in the works of Frederick Cooper. See, for example, *Africa Since 1940: The Past of the Present* (Cambridge: Cambridge University Press, 2002) and *Africa in the World: Capitalism, Empire, Nation* (Cambridge, MA: Harvard University Press, 2014).

39 Two recent works help us to grasp this crisis of self-dispossession in all its nakedness and finesse. In *La Gloire des imposteurs. Lettres sur le Mali et l'Afrique* (Paris: Philippe Rey, 2014), Aminata Dramane Traoré and Boubacar Boris Diop are able to grasp the new, unheard-of brutality with which an imperial power can strike a victim and take everything away from them, all the way to the dispossession of their conscience. More than a simple question of emphasizing the military violence of wars undertaken by France in Africa, they also zero in on how such powers are capable of the very pillaging of that which gives the victim their sense of being a human, a sense of self. Achille Mbembe's *Politiques de l'inimitié* (Paris: La Découverte, 2016) describes to what extent this man, beaten down, isolated in the corner of a cell and constrained to silence, this man who is a product of a "society [relation] of enmity," this man who has become sick, reclaims care that is called being supported in a connection or social tie, in a relationship with the world, with others. This connection or social tie is what protects him from death.

40 Citizens who feel they have become dispossessed organize themselves and attempt to lead campaigns of awareness and action. http://www.unevieenafrique.com/defense-du-littoral-senegalais-un-etat-des-lieux-pessimiste-juin-2015.

41 Frederick Cooper explains to us that this historical heritage was fermented between the immediacy of World War II and the moment of the independence of the colonies. See the two references cited, *supra*.

42 My colleague Mohomodou Houssouba, who spent some time working on this project, provided us with the following comments: "*Ay boraa no. Ay* – I/mine; *boro* – person (the definite form of *boraa*); *no* – lack of existence/being." My colleague Abdoulaye Sounaye helped me to construct this paragraph by also being available for questions and by sharing his knowledge of the Hausa language. I'd like to thank both of them here with my most profound gratitude.

43 The importance of such heritages is far from negligible. See the two volumes devoted to them in West Africa: Charles Becker, Saliou Mbaye, and Ibrahima Thioub (eds.), *AOF: Réalités et héritages. Sociétés*

ouest-africaines et ordre colonial, 1895–1960 (Dakar: Direction des archives du Sénégal, 1997).
44 Abdourahmane Seck, "Après le développement: détours paradigmatiques et philosophie de l'histoire au Sénégal," *Pensée contemporaines et pratiques sociales en Afriques: penser le mouvement*, 2/192 (2015), pp. 13–32.

Re-enchanting the World: Husserl in the Postcolony

1 Marcel Gauchet, *Le Désenchantement du monde. Une histoire politique de la religion* (Paris: Gallimard, 1985).
2 In *The Protestant Ethic and the Spirit of Capitalism*, Max Weber evokes this notion of the "iron cage" of capitalism to give an account of the diagnosis that can be made of capitalist society. According to Weber, capitalism has become by necessity a kind of machine, in which human activities are subjected to formal constraints of efficiency and productivity that deprive the them of any human meaning. In other words, we live in a sort of machinery where we have become nothing more than functioning cogs operating a system over which we no longer have any firm hold.
3 At the moment when Husserl wrote that, if Europe truly understands the historical teleology that animates it, it will never "become Indian" – see *The Crisis of European Sciences*, trans. D. Carr (Evanston: Northwestern University Press, 1970) – India had already been a major philosophical influence in Europe, for philosophers as important as Nietzsche and Schopenhauer.
4 Edmund Husserl, "Letter to Lucien Lévy-Bruhl. March 11, 1935." trans. Luka Steinacher and Dermot Moran.https://www.researchgate.net/publication/269573542_Edmund_Husserl%27s_Letter_to_Lucien_Levy-Bruhl_11_March_1935_translation_from_German.
5 Edmund Husserl, *Logical Investigations*, trans. J. N. Findlay (New York: Routledge, 2001).
6 Husserl, *The Crisis of European Sciences*.
7 Lucien Lévy-Bruhl, *Primitive Mentality*, trans. Lilian A. Clare (Boston, MA: Beacon Press, 1966).
8 Husserl, "Letter to Lucien Lévy-Bruhl."
9 For Merleau-Ponty, "Judging by Husserl's later views, philosophy would gain autonomy after, not before, positive knowledge. This autonomy would not exempt the philosopher from gathering in everything anthropology has to offer us, which means, basically, testing our effective communication with other cultures. Nor could it withhold anything from the scientist's jurisdiction which was accessible to his methods of research ... Although, anthropology, like every positive science and all these sciences as a whole, may have the first word

concerning knowledge, it does not have the last." *Signs*, trans. Richard C. McCleary (Evanston: Northwestern University Press, 1964), p. 108.
10 Aristotle, *Metaphysics*, A, 982-b8.
11 For Husserl, "The idea of a nature abandoned to itself, which would not be transformed (and therefore generally changed) in an egoic fashion by egoic subjects, can therefore be understood as a fictive possibility, but as possibility: the world as nature, how would it unfold and continue if all egoic subjects in general suddenly refrained from any intervention within it at the same time?" *Autour des méditations cartésiennes* (Grenoble: Millon, 1998), p. 292. The notion of a "fictive possibility" clearly indicates that idea of an primordial nature that would be the ultimate foundation is an idea worth calling into question in the same way as the fiction of a state of nature conceived of by Rousseau, that is, merely a regulating idea in theory and not as reality of empirical effectivity.
12 Achille Mbembe, "Qu'est-ce que la pensée postcoloniale?," *Esprit*, December 2006.
13 It is the metaphor of the rhizome, as repeated by Édouard Glissant to Gilles Deleuze and Félix Guattari, that immediately comes to mind here as a theoretical model for describing this decentered world whose law is henceforth interaction. "When I focused on the question (of identity), I began by way of the distinction put forth by Gilles Deleuze and Félix Guattari, between the notion of a singular root and the notion of the rhizome. In one of their chapters of *Mille Plateaus* (which was first published as a small volume with the title *Rhizome*), Deleuze and Guattari emphasize this difference. They establish from the point of view of the functioning of thought, the thought of a root and the thought of a rhizome. The singular root is that which kills everything around it, whereas the rhizome is the root that reaches out to meet other roots. I applied this image to the principle of identity. And I did so also in terms with regard to 'categorization of cultures,' which is my own idea, to a division of cultures into the atavistic and the composite." Édouard Glissant, *Introduction into a Poetics of Diversity*, trans. Celia Britton (Liverpool: Liverpool University Press, 2020), p. 37.
14 "Une seule langue nous enferme dans une seule pensée": Roger Pol-Droit, "Rencontre avec un philosophe d'ailleurs." http://www.cles.com/enquetes/arrticle/use-seule-langue-nous-enferme-dans-une-seule-pensee--.
15 We should recall that the Althusserian critique of humanism rests on an analysis of a "rupture" that affects Marx's theoretical production starting in 1884–5, and which leads the dialectic and materialism to move into a properly scientific phase, the challenge here being to locate the decisive moment that leads Marx to go from "a radical critique of *theoretical* pretensions of every philosophical humanism"

to a "definition of humanism as ideology," *Écrits philosophiques et politiques*, vol. II (Paris: Stock-IMEC), p. 500. This passage sees, in what it is appropriate to call the writings of the "young Marx," the remains of an idealism, a thesis that Senghor will reject, since, for him, humanism that is depreciated here is precisely what makes Marxian philosophy its value.

Writing about the Humanities from the Vantage Point of Africa

1 Such a conception has also been called into question in the core of Western epistemology by advocates of quantum physics and by thinkers such as Nicholas Georgescu-Rogen, promoter of transdisciplinarity and the principle of the excluded middle.
2 Valentin-Yves Mudimbe.
3 This is what Wolé Soyinka refers to as self-apprehension. For Soyinka, an apprehension of self by self, without reference to another, determines the possibility of thought (and literature) that is specifically African.
4 Such as the Eastern cosmologies (Japan, China), and elsewhere.

Thinking about the World from the Vantage Point of Africa

1 Raymond Roussel, *Impression of Africa*, trans. Mark Pollizzotti (Champaign: Dalkey Archive Press, 2011).

Index

Abrahams, P. 100
absence and abundance, paradox of 171–9
Adotevi, S. 99
aesthetic rupture 154–5
The African Origins of UFOs (Joseph) 178
African presence 12–13, 17–18, 25, 29–30, 107
African values 96, 194–5, 259
Africanity 72, 73, 74
L'Afrique humilieé (Traoré) 57
Afro-American/Black women 122–3, 125, 127, 134, 135
afro-diasporic subjectivities 37–8, 39–41
  melancholic disposition 41–3
Afrofuturism 178–9
Afropolitan identity 54, 58
Afrotopia (Sarr) 72, 181
agency of author 116, 117
Akana, P. D. 185–202
Akendengue, P. and de Courson, H. 145
Al Capone le Malien (Tchak) 246
alienation, theory of 98–100
Amabiamina, F. 196–7

André, C. 150, 156
Angelou, M. 77
Anténor, F. 26
anti-humanism 12, 254, 258, 259
Appiah, A. 106
appropriation 66, 98
Apter, D. 15–16
Arendt, H. 123
Arlit, Niger 162–5
Armrouche, J. 151
arts/aesthetics 154–5
Aryeequaye, M. 178
assimilation 66–8
auctor, role and issues 114, 117
Augé, M. 13–14
author-function and agency 116–17
authoritarian regimes
  and democratization 85–6
  and gender relations 192, 199

Balibar, E. 131
Bandung conference 44–7, 48–9
Barthes, R. 112
Bayart, J.-F. 86–7
becoming-negro 129–35
belonging/being-with-others 270–1, 272, 273

Beloved (Morrison) 68
Bentouhami, H. 121–35
Berger, G. 100, 140
Bessoles, P. 191, 195–6
Beti, M. 165–6, 200–1
Bhabha, H. 54
Bhargaval, R. 153
Bidima, J. G. 153
Biko, S. 122, 123, 127, 129, 132, 133, 134, 135
Black African ideology as doctrine in crisis 101–2
Black/Afro-American women *see* Afro-American/Black women
Black consciousness *see* self-shame to consciousness of oppressed
Black Egypt 89–90
Boetsch, G. and Guilhem, D. 191–2
Boilat, D. 27
Boko Haram/"Forbidden Book" 143, 144
Boto, E. 165–6
Bretton, H. 16
Butler, J. and Athanassiou, A. 39–40

Cameroon *see* sexual relations, Cameroon
capitalism
  crisis of 170, 250–1
  Marxist theory of history 11
  neoliberal economics 234–5
  paradox of absence and abundance 171–9
Carmichael, S. 133
Caruth, C. 52
Cautoni, R. 99
Celles qui attendent (Diome) 56–7
Césaire, A. 24–6, 44, 47, 89, 112–13, 179
Césaire, S. 31
Chabal, P. 87, 88
Chanson, P. 68
Chaudhuri, K. 19

cheap labor and cheap nature 171–2, 175–6
China: economic growth and employment 208–9, 212
Christianity 27, 96–7
  and paganism, distinction 13–14
Cicero 93
Cissé, B. 92–105, 176–7
citizenship rights 155
civil rights 132–3
civilizations
  Black/African 89–91
  dialogue between 145–6
civilizing mission 10–11, 15, 20–1, 23–4, 29, 91, 173
Collins, R. 210
"colonial difference" 34–5, 36, 151
colonial violence 34–5, 38, 270–1
colonialism 171–7
  forms of control 151
  independence 18
  and nuclear power 164–5
  postcolonial vision as counter-discourse 74–5
  universalism and indigenous histories 9–30
  see also decolonization
coloniality 36, 37
commonality (*zumunci*) and kinship (*mbokk*) 235–7
complementarity, philosophy of 95–6
conceptual decolonization 149, 152–3
conscienciism 96–7
contact spaces 20
Cooper, H. 52, 53
Coquery-Vidrovitch, C. 14–15
corruption *see* political corruption, Senegal
Corty, B. 248
La Couleur de l'africain (Tchak) 246
Crack Literary Movement, Mexico 247–8

creative core of Africa 138–42
creolization *see* hybridity/duality/creolization
criminalization of politics 87–8
Cruel City (Boto) 165–6
culture
 concept of 93
 as site of resistance 179–80
cultures, encounter with other 144–7

Dadié, B. 18, 22, 23–5, 28, 29–30
Dagne, M. 138, 142
Daloz, J.-P. 87, 88
The Dark Heart of the Night (Miano) 115–16
decentralizing thought and humanities 3–5
decolonization
 Bandung conference 44–7
 "decolonization of philosophy" 35–7, 39
 "epistemic decolonization" 33–5, 38–9, 41, 42–3
 and self-esteem 148–59
deconstruction
 of borders 54–7
 of Enlightenment paradigm 251–2
Deleuze, G. 50
democracy 15–16, 23
 democratization 85–6
 Senegal 222–7
demographic and employment challenges 203–4
 brief overview of demographic tendencies 205–6
 learning from India and China 206–9
 structural characteristics of employment situation 204–5
 technological unemployment 209–14
dependentism, hegemonic ruses concerning 82–4

deregulation 229
Derrida, J. 33, 217
desire of author, denial of fiction, and literature in person 114–18
development
 hegemonic ruses concerning developmentalism 80–2
 neoliberal economics 234–5
 postwar model 144
 self- 95, 101–2
 see also modernity/modernization
Devoir de violence (Ouloguem) 113
Dia, M. 16
Diagne, S. B. 44–9, 113, 259
dialogues between civilizations 145–6
diaspora *see* afro-diasporic subjectivities; migrant writers; self-shame to consciousness of oppressed; slavery
Diawara, M. 13
Diome, F. 56–7
Dione, M. S. 79–91
Diop, A. 101
Diop, C. A. 89–91, 94
Diop, O. S. 26, 29
Diouf, M. 9–30, 257
disenchantment of the world 12, 250–1
dispossession
 forms of 39–41
 self- 219–22
"double consciousness" 124–5
duality *see* hybridity/duality/creolization
Du Bois, W. E. B. 18, 124–5
Ducas, S. 107–8
Ducournau, C. 107
Dzossa, A. D. and Niekou, R. 198

Eboussi Boulaga, F. 33, 36–7, 93, 102, 142, 187, 193, 194–5, 199, 200–1

economics *see* capitalism
Egypt, Black 89–90
Ekeh, P. 14
emancipatory utopias 168–81
emotions
  arts/aesthetics 154–5
  and cognition 148–9
  envy and jealousy 172–3
employment *see* demographic and employment challenges; labor
The English Patient (Ondaatje) 55
Enlightenment 12–13, 20–1, 22, 29
  Cartesian mind 149–50
  deconstruction of paradigm 251–2
  envy and jealousy 172–3
  "epistemic decolonization" 33–5, 38–9, 41, 42–3
epistemological impasses 79–80
  relativistic thought 84–91
  universalist thought 80–4
epistemological rupture 112, 113, 153
  and aesthetic rupture 154–5
epistemology
  of epistemologies 146–7
  and phenomenology of oppressed consciousness 124–9
  see also knowledge/knowledge production
Equiano, O. 51, 52
eroticization *see* sexuality/eroticization
Eshun, K. 178
Esprit (journal) 45
Etoke, N. 41, 77
Europe and Africa
  historical displacements 1
  see also colonialism; decolonization; slavery
exile *see* migrant writers

Fanon, F. 26, 102, 124, 126, 129, 130–1, 144, 151, 218, 270–1, 272

Farah, N. 53
Le Figaro 247, 248
Foucault, M. 112, 115, 116, 126, 127–8, 254, 269–70
France
  nuclear programme and uranium mining 163, 164
  see also postcolonial author, France
freedom *see* liberation
Freire, P. 123
Freudian psychoanalysis 124, 221
futures, defeat, and melancholy 37–43

Gates, H. L. 13
Gauchet, M. 250
Géographie du danger (Skif) 56
Ghana 15–16, 18
Gikandi, S. 26–7
Gilroy, P. 272–3
Glissand, É. 4, 47, 59, 146, 272
Global North/Global South
  "decolonization of philosophy" 35–6, 39
  develomentalism and dependentism 82
  labor 177
Guha, R. 10
"gut politics" 86–7

Haiti 17–18, 25, 131–2, 179
Hall, S. 126
Hasaki ya suda (Ido) 178–9
Hegel, F. 171, 257
Héritier, F. 186
history
  universalism and indigenous histories 9–30
  of utopias 168–9
  see also colonialism; slavery
Honneth, A. 153, 155
hooks, b. 33–4
The House on Sugar Beach (Cooper) 52, 53

Hugo, V. 173–4
human rights 132–3
humanities
　decentralizing thought and 3–5
　and philosophy 33
　and social science 29–30, 260–5, 267, 270, 273
Husserl, E.
　in the postcolony 250–9
　pluralizing the world 255–9
hybridity/duality/creolization 145, 146
　hybridization of politics 86–7
　migrant writers 52–4, 58–9

Ido, C. 178–9
illegal migrants 56–7
independence of European colonies 18
India
　economic growth and employment 206–8, 209
　and Indian Ocean: European colonialism/expansion 18–20, 21, 22–3
informal employment 205
　India and China 207, 208, 209
informalization of politics 87, 229
innovative role of migrant writers 57–9
L'Interieur de la nuit (Miano) 115–16
Islam 27, 96–7
　and Black consciousness movement 134–5
　Boko Haram/"Forbidden Book" 143, 144

Jaabouk (Tahir) 57
Jaurés, J. 94
jealousy and envy 172–3
Joseph, A. 178
justice, restorative 72–3
justice system, Senegal 223–4, 225–6

Kane, A. 89
Kane, C. H. 27–8, 217–18
Kane, O. 92–3
Keynes, J. M. 210
kinship (*mbokk*) and commonality (*zumunci*) 235–7
Kisukidi, N. Y. 31–43
knowledge/knowledge production 267–8
　cognition and emotions 148–9
　colonialism and academia 152–4
　contact spaces 20
　humanities and social science 29–30, 260–5, 267, 270, 273
　and ideology of absence 174–5
　indigenous and Western forms 22–4
　postcolonial library 106–10
　scientific method 251–5, 261–2
　subaltern forms of 37
　and ways of knowing 108–9
　see also entries beginning epistem
Kodjo-Grandvaux, S. 148–60
Koselleck, R. 180
Kourouma, A. 113
Kristeva, J. 59

labor
　and capital 176–7
　and gender relations 193
　and natural resources 171–2, 175–6
　see also demographic and employment challenges
Lacarrière, J. 50
language(s)
　kinship (*mbokk*) and commonality (*zumunci*) 235–7
　oral culture/tradition 28, 138–9
　and philosophy 153–4
　plurality of 49, 70
　see also names; sexual relations, Cameroon

"lateral universal" vs "verticality" 48–9
leadership 76–7
Lebdai, B. 50–61
Lebenswelt (lifeworld) 252, 254–5, 256
Lebret, P. 16
Leroi-Gourhan, A. 189
Levinas, E. 46–7, 48–9
Lévi-Strauss, C. 141
Lévy-Bruhl, L. 255, 258
liberation
  emancipatory utopias 168–81
  politics of 129–35
  of the world 271, 272–3
lifeworld *see Lebenswelt* (lifeworld)
Lopes, H. 53, 58
Lorde, A. 122–3, 125, 126, 127, 128, 132, 133, 134, 135
love
  maternal/parental 150–1
  self- 68, 135

Maahlox 190
Mabanckou, A. 53, 58
  and Waberi, A. 161–7
Malcolm X 123, 127, 129, 132–3, 134–5
Malherbe, J.-F. 146–7
Maljoub, J. 52–3
Maraire, J. N. 53–4
Maroons 179–80
Marx, K. 10, 11, 131, 259
Marxism 82–3, 95–6, 97, 98
masculinity
  colonialization 173–4
  crisis of 192–3
  see also sexual relations, Cameroon
maternal/parental love 150–1
Mateso, L. 114–15
Mazauric, C. 111
Mbembe, A. 39, 58, 131, 185, 258, 266–76
  and Sarr, F. 1–6

McKay, C. 10
McKinsey and Company 233
Melancholia Africana (Etoke) 41
melancholy 41–3, 77–8, 151–2, 180
memory 41–2
  reconstructive 51–4
Merleau-Ponty, M. 48–9, 187–8, 256, 258
Mexico: Crack Literary Movement 247–8
Meye, E. and Chantal, L. 197–8
Miano, L. 65–78, 115–16
Mignolo, W. 34, 151, 154
migrant writers 50–1
  deconstruction of borders 54–7
  innovative role of 57–9
  reconstructive memory 51–4
migration
  Global South to Global North 211
  urban 165–7
modernity/modernization 10–13, 20–1, 23
  hybridity and adaptation 26–7
  political 16
  and race 18
  second-hand 15
  see also development; reinventing African modernity
Le Monde 109
Monga, C. 199
Morrison, T. 68, 69–70
Moudileno, L. 106–18
Mudimbe, V.-Y. 144
music and songs 189, 190, 196–8
Muslims *see* Islam
Mve-Ondo, B. 136–47
mythology
  philosophy as 32
  see also spirituality

names 65–78
  changes 68–9, 179–80
  of philosophy 31–7
  for production of poverty to signs still worth believing in 232–7

natural resources
  and labor resources 171–2, 175–6
  uranium 163, 164
nature, destruction of 177–8
Ndoye, B. 250–9
negritude
  movement 18, 34, 89, 153
  theory 13, 95, 272
neoliberalism 234–5
Niekou, R.
  and Dzossa, A. D. 198
  Tchekanda, E. and 193–4
Njiengwe, E. 192
Nkrumah, K. 96–7
nuclear power/weapons 163–5

Ondaatje, M. 55
oppression *see* self-shame to consciousness of oppressed
oral culture/tradition 28, 138–9
Other
  oppression of 125
  resemblance and appropriation of 98
  self-as-Othered 126
Ouloguem, Y. 113

paganism 12, 13–14
"Panama Papers" 224
Paz, O. 146
people-smuggling 56
Petit-Pays 190
phenomenology
  and epistemology of oppressed consciousness 124–9
  see also Husserl, E.
philosophy
  of complementarity 95–6
  "decolonization of philosophy" 35–6, 39
  names of 31–7
  philosophical synthesis 96–7
pluralizing the world 255–9
poetry 10, 126

political corruption, Senegal 216–19
  democracy 222–7
  history of Wade dynasty and political system 227–32
  names for production of poverty to signs still worth believing in 232–7
  ordinary self-dispossession 219–22
political regimes 15–16
politics of liberation 129–35
Pollock, S. 19–20, 21, 22–3, 28
postcolonial author, France 106–10
  definition of 110–14
  desire, denial of fiction, and literature in person 114–18
production of poverty to signs still worth believing in 232–7
productivist economic model 176–7, 178

race 18, 25–6
racism *see* self-shame to consciousness of oppressed
Ramey, L. 178
rappers 189, 190
rationalism 12–13, 20–1, 23
re-traditionalization 88
reconstructive memory 51–4
reinventing Africa
  conditions for inventing and 142–4
  in encounter with other cultures 144–7
reinventing African modernity 92–5
  Black African ideology as doctrine in crisis 101–2
  Nkrumah or philosophical synthesis 96–7
  Senghor and philosophy of complementarity 95–6
  Towa and theory of alienation 98–100

Index

relativism 252, 255, 256, 258
relativistic thought 84–91
resemblance, theory of 98
resilience 67, 77–8
resistance, culture as site of 179–80
restorative justice 72–3
Rous, J. 45
Roussel, R. 268

Said, E. 111
Sall, M. 220, 226, 227
Sansal, B. 55
Sapiro, G. 108
Sarr, F. 72–3, 109, 181, 260–5
  Mbembe, A. and 1–6
Sartre, J.-P. 18, 125, 128
School of Oriental and African Studies (SOAS) 47–8
Schuhl, P.-M. 141
Schwartz, B. 21
scientific method 251–5, 261–2
Seck, A. 216–39
second-hand modernization 15
secret names 68–9
self-development 95, 101–2
self-dispossession 219–22
self-esteem 148–60
  and sexual violence 192–3
self-hate 125–7, 133–4
self-love 68, 135
self-shame to consciousness of oppressed 121–4
  epistemology and phenomenology of oppressed consciousness 124–9
  politics of liberation: becoming-negro 129–35
Senegal 16, 85–6
  see also political corruption, Senegal
Senegalese Democratic Party (PDS) 227–8
Senghor, A. D. 27, 28, 29–30, 84, 95–6, 108

Senghor, L. S. 229, 259, 271–2
sexual relations, Cameroon 185–7, 200
  analogy of war 188–91
  paradoxes of recovery 195–9
  reasons for violence 191–5
  signification and place 187–8
sexuality/eroticization
  of Black women 127
  of domination 130
Skif, H. 56
slavery
  and birth of capitalism 171–2
  "field negro" and "house negro" 129
  Haiti 17–18, 25, 131–2, 179
  Maroons 179–80
  narratives 52
  and post-slave society 124–5, 130
  secret names 68–9
  transatlantic trade 51, 72, 75, 144, 157–8
social science and humanities 29–30, 260–5, 267, 270, 273
Social Science Research Council (US) 80–1
socialism
  Africanized 83, 95–6
  Marxism 11–12, 82–3, 95–6, 97, 98
Socialist Party (PS), Senegal 227, 228, 229, 231
Soleils des indépendances (Kourouma) 113
songs *see* music and songs
soul as prisoner of body 126–7
South African apartheid system 122, 133
Sparti, D. 152
spirituality
  authentic and pseudo- 147
  paganism 12, 13–14
subaltern subjects 36–7
Sylla, N. S. 203–15

Tagore, R. 10
Tahir, H. 57
Tchak, S. 243–9
Tchekanda, E. and Niekou, R. 193–4
technological unemployment 209–14
Tenor 189
terrorism 159
  Boko Haram/"Forbidden Book" 143, 144
thinking
  from African vantage point 266–76
  for new century 1–6
Thiong'o, N. wa 49, 58, 163, 164
time, conceptions of 139–41, 147
topical art 187, 188
Tout-Monde 4, 59, 272–3
Towa, M. 94, 98–100
tradition, return/reconnection to 88, 94, 143–4
transcendental subjectivity 254–5
translation
  knowledge (*translatio studiorum*) 48
  languages 49
transversality 72
Traoré, A. 57
Tsala Tsala, J.-P. 193, 196, 198
Tsimi, É. E. 55, 56

unemployment
  in India and China 207–8
  technological 209–14
  and underemployment 205
universalism
  epistemological impasses 80–4
  and indigenous histories 9–30
  paths of 243–9
  universal 44–9
university system 152–3
uranium 163, 164
urban migration 165–7
utopias, emancipatory 168–81

Vázquez, R. 154
Vergès, F. 168–81
violence
  colonial 34–5, 38, 270–1
  ethnic conflicts 87–8
  material and political dispossession 39–41
  physical 156
  self-hate 125–7, 133–4
  self-love as escape from 135
  systemic 134
  see also sexual relations, Cameroon
Volpi, J. 247, 248

Waberi, A. 53
  Mabanckou, A. and 161–7
Wade, A. 16, 86, 219–20, 227–32
Wade, K. 222–32
Wallerstein, I. 45, 47
wealth accumulation *see* capitalism
Weber, M. 10, 12, 250
Westernization *see* development; modernity/modernization; universalism
Wicomb, Z. 58
women
  Afro-American/Black 122–3, 125, 127, 134, 135
  see also sexual relations, Cameroon
Workshops of Thought 1–2, 3, 6
The Wretched of the Earth (Fanon) 102, 123, 130–1
Wright, D. 58
Wright, R. 12–13, 14

youth citizen movement (YEM), Senegal 225

Zenzele (Maraire) 53–4
Zinoviev, A. 199
Zolberg, A. R. 15–16